Indian Mythology

INDIAN MYTHOLOGY

An Encyclopedia of Myth and Legend

Jan Knappert

Illustrated by Elizabeth Knappert

The Aquarian Press
An Imprint of HarperCollins*Publishers*

The Aquarian Press
An Imprint of HarperCollins*Publishers*
77–85 Fulham Palace Road,
Hammersmith, London W6 8JB

Published by The Aquarian Press 1991
1   3   5   7   9   10   8   6   4   2

A catalogue record for this book
is available from the British Library

ISBN 1 85538 040 4

Typeset by Burns & Smith Ltd, Derby
Printed in Great Britain by
Mackays of Chatham, Kent

CONTENTS

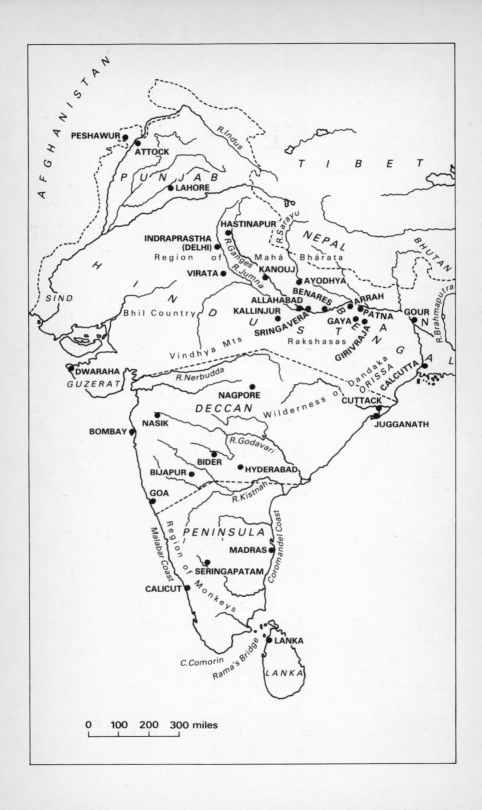

AFGHANISTAN

TIBET

R.Indus

PESHAWUR●
ATTOCK●

PUNJAB

●LAHORE

HINDUSTAN

SIND

HASTINAPUR●
INDRAPRASTHA
(DELHI)●
VIRATA●

R.Ganges
R.Jumna
R.Sarayu

NEPAL

Region of Mahá Bhárata

KANOUJ●
●AYODHYA

BHUTAN

BENARES●
ALLAHABAD●
KALLINJUR●
SRINGAVERA●
GAYA●
GIRIVRAJA●

ARRAH●
PATNA●
GOUR●

R.Brahmaputra

BENGAL

Rakshasas

Bhil Country

Vindhya Mts

R.Nerbudda

Wilderness of Dandaka

DWARAHA●
GUZERAT

ORISSA
CALCUTTA●

NAGPORE●

DECCAN

CUTTACK●

BOMBAY●
NASIK●

R.Godavari

JUGGANATH●

BIDER●
BIJAPUR●
GOA●

HYDERABAD●

R.Kistnah

Coromandel Coast

Malabar Coast

Region of Monkeys

PENINSULA

MADRAS●
SERINGAPATAM●
CALICUT●

C.Comorin
Rama's Bridge

●LANKA

LANKA

0   100   200   300 miles

PREFACE

Indian Mythology is such a vast subject that I would really need a dozen volumes to give it justice. It is a big subject both in time and in space: in time because our earliest texts, the Hymns of the Rig-Veda, are dated *c*.1500 BC; in space since India is a large country, much larger than all the EEC countries together. Finally, it is a large subject in terms of quantity: more religions commenced their history in India than in any other country.

Hinduism and Buddhism had to be compressed in this one volume although I had suggested two volumes, one for each of these rich religious, artistic and cultural traditions. In addition many adherents of religions from other countries have found refuge in India, such as the Parsis, so I have also dedicated a few pages to their beliefs.

Many readers will be disappointed that so little is said in this work about the incredibly rich living traditions of the many peoples in India with little or no written traditions, the so-(wrongly)-called natives or tribals. Perhaps a later volume could do them justice.

Of all the 745 languages of India, Sanskrit is best known to me, so naturally I have limited myself mainly, but not exclusively, to the vast Sanskrit literature which deals with both Hindu and Buddhist mythology. Sanskrit has by far the richest literature of all the Indian literary traditions (of which the best-known are Gujerati, Hindi, Bengali, Tamil, Pali, Panjabi and Urdu). It has also the longest tradition to which able writers from all the corners of India have contributed, including Tamils, Bengalis, Oriyas, Biharis, etc. The powerful (almost 100 million) Muslim population of India has a literary tradition entirely its own, including many legends of saints unknown outside India. We had to leave all that fine literature to — perhaps — a later publication. Only a few references to Islamic traditions have been included.

It should be stressed that this book is not about history. Although several of the persons mentioned in it are actually historical, such as Ashoka and Buddha, most of the events described in this book are mythological. For the history of India see the bibliography under Basham, Spear and Thapar, and the Introduction.

I wish to thank the publishers for giving me this opportunity to publish the results of many years of study.

INTRODUCTION

Mithuna, Gemini's heavenly couple

Though large compared to Europe, India is, with just over 3 million square kilometres, only one-fourteenth of Asia, less than half the size of Australia, a third of Brazil. However, India houses about 800 million people, more than a quarter of all Asians, the world's most populous country after China, which has three times more land, and so, only half as many people per square kilometre. The Indians speak 745 quite distinct languages between them, compared to 127 languages in the Soviet Union with seven times as much land. Of the population of India, 83% are given as belonging to the Hindu religion, 9% to Islam, 2% to Buddhism, 3% to Christianity, 2% are Sikhs, 1% are Jains, or approximately so.

In this alphabetical guide the main body of the mythology is composed of Hindu myths, whereas only a few references to Sikh mythology could be included. Christianity has been adequately described, and so has Islam, so that only a few mystic figures of the latter religion, in so far as they are typical for India, have been included.

What is mythology? The study of myths. But what is a myth? The origin of 'myth' is the Greek word *mythos*, which simply meant 'word', then 'tale', 'history', 'communication'. It is used by the oldest-known European poet when he refers to the communication he received from his Muse, the 'Daughter of Zeus', about the

heroes' deeds and the works of the Greek gods. In this Guide the
word myth will be used in exactly the same sense. In modern
English the phrase 'it is a myth' signifies that the speaker does not
believe a word of it. In this guide, however, the reality or otherwise
of the myths will not be discussed. That is a matter for historians
and theologians. However, this author did see it as his task to
discuss certain other aspects of Indian religions such as a few
religious practices, e.g. pious celebrations, as well as some Hindu
theology, Buddhist philosophy and Jain cosmology. Mythology is
part of the study of religion and every myth fits in the total structure
of the life of the society that believes in it. The myth in turn
motivates the people to perform certain special ceremonies, daily or
annually, as their lives move through the cycle of the seasons.

The Myths

Is there any historical truth in myths? The answer can be left to the
historians. The mythologist studies myths as colourful pieces that
form together the beautiful mosaic of a people's cosmology, which
is the totality of the world in which they live, their cosmos. Such a
cosmos is not the same as the world which *we* see. This does not
mean that they do not see the same rivers and hills that we see, but
they see those hills and rivers populated with their gods or other
spirits that we cannot see. The mythology of a people, that is the
structured collection of their myths, is a description of the world,
the past and the future as they see it. It may not be factually correct
but that is not the concern of the mythologist, who is a student of
religion as such. Religion is a subject in its own right. Mythology is
part of that subject. It tells us what people believe, and every
religion is based on beliefs, i.e. truths that can be neither proved
nor disproved. Myth is not a subject which a scientist could study,
since there is no palpable evidence for it. But if a sceptic regards as
'mere myth' which a believer presents as factual truth, then that
sceptic will place himself outside the world of the believer. He will
never understand other peoples. The student of religion must never
be so rash. He wants to be inside that world, that cosmos of the
believers in a certain religion. He does not have to share every belief
but he certainly has to reflect intensively about the mythology of
the religion he is studying. He or she will then realize that every
other aspect of that religion, the rites and ceremonies, the sermons
and prayers and much of the otherwise inexplicable sayings and
actions of the people's daily life is based and dependent on their
mythology. It is also, in its entirety, reflected in, and represented by
their language. Since we cannot hope to represent all the languages
of India, this Guide gives the majority of the terms and names in
their Sanskrit forms, using occasionally Pali, Hindi or Urdu.

The Languages

Of the 745 languages recorded in 1911 in British India, only 14 are official languages of education in India today. Among these are five Dravidian languages all spoken in the South: Kanarese or Kannada in North Kerala; Malayalam along what used to be called the Coast of Malabar. Tamil in the south-east corner of India by over 30 million people, Telugu in Andhra Pradesh by over 40 million people and Gondi in pockets further north by 3 million people. In the northern regions in the mountains all along the border Tibetan and closely related languages are spoken including Bara, Naga and Kachin. Tibetan is now widely spoken in North India and Nepal. Indo-European languages form the largest single group in India north of a line which runs with many bends from south of Goa on the west coast to south of Puri on the east coast.

The Hindi language is spoken most widely in India, by over a quarter of its population as a first language and by many millions more as a second language. With over 200 million speakers it is one of the world's chief languages, coming fourth after Chinese, English and Russian, if my figures are still correct. Hindi has an extensive literature including many volumes of poetry, from the beautiful Ramayana Epic by Tulsi Das (1543–1623), which is still recited and sung, to the famous modern film songs.

No less famous is Rabindranath Tagore, who used Bengali for his *Gita-anjali* 'a Liberation of Songs' celebrating his love for God. Bengali is spoken in West Bengal and Bangladesh by over 100 million people.

In the Punjab, on both sides of the border with Pakistan, Panjabi is spoken, another language sadly divided by religion, spoken by over 40 million people. Panjabi has been written in four different scripts: Devanagari (Sanskrit script), Roman (for the Christians), Persian (for the Muslims) and Gurmukhi (for the Sikhs). In this latter script it was used by the great Gurus of the Sikh religion for their beautiful poetry and wise sayings. There is much poetry in Gujerati and Marathi spoken in Gujerat and Maharashtra respectively. These two languages are also written in Devanagari, Roman and a script of their own. Newari or Nepali is spoken in Nepal, Bihari in Bihar and Oriya in Orissa.

Prehistory

India, having an attractive climate, invited early visitors to stay. The first human beings to wander along the banks of the Ganges found thick forest everywhere, through which herds of elephants pushed their way so that *Homo* and other animals made grateful use of the paths opened up through the jungle by the thickskins. Early Man was a hunter and great skill of archery was still highly honoured in the Epic period, though more for warfare than for killing game. The earliest arrows that have been found were tipped with chipped stones. Many such arrowheads and other 'flaked' stone tools have been found in India. They were made perhaps 200,000 years ago. There have been human beings in India ever since that time but we know very little about them except for their tools. At some period the hunter learned to train dogs as retrievers and perhaps to breed hounds to stay the game.

It has been argued that at this stage, more than 10,000 years BC, Dravidian languages were already being spoken in India, but there is no evidence for this. It has also been said that the people in those most primitive times worshipped a mother-goddess with fertility rites, but there is no evidence for that either. All we know about these primitive peoples is 'stones and bones', food for archaeologists.

The biggest step forward in human evolution was the so-called agricultural revolution which may have been accompanied by the invention of pottery, i.e. of baking clay to make cooking pots. From that time onwards only primitive tribes ate raw food. Cooked food, especially baked bread, became a symbol of civilization. Homer already spoke in the *Odyssey* of civilized people as 'bread-eating'. Whether agriculture preceded the domestication of the goat, the chicken, the pig, the sheep and especially the cow is another question we must leave to the specialists. The mythologist can only infer from his oldest myth-material that in mythical times there was already the Homeric division between savage tribes and civilized people with houses and without horrible habits. Whether distinct species of *homo* ever existed side by side or not we cannot know. The ancient story-tellers, however, often refer to hairy half-apes in the jungle who run naked, eat raw food, seduce human girls, steal cattle, and are as strong as buffaloes and equally stupid.

Another aspect of the most ancient world is that each kingdom had one city, the capital, which was surrounded by cultivated land, which in turn was surrounded by jungle. A person travelling from one town to another had to traverse considerable areas of forest. Those 'cities' were no more than small villages. Ancient Troy could never have accommodated more than a few hundred people. Every kingdom was thus inhabited by a few thousand people at most. In the next kingdom people spoke a different dialect if not a distinct language. Numerous languages once spoken in India have since died out. The situation was never stable; although some very ancient settlements survived for a long time, others were overrun by savage invaders, burnt, looted and the population decimated.

The reference to 'kingdoms' as the normal form of political organization is deliberate. Although some communities may have been ruled by councils of elders, these councils would normally accept or even appoint a monarch to lead the defence. If they did not, some usurper was bound to make use of the organizational weakness of such a community and, with a gang of raiders, set himself up as king, rightly or wrongly.

One thing seems certain: every kingdom had its own religion. Although gods and ceremonies can be borrowed from neighbouring peoples or even families, most gods belonged to the clans who worshipped them, often believing they were ancestors. Gods have to be kept alive by their worshippers; if the latter begin to worship newer gods the ancient deities are forgotten. Old gods are thirsty for the sacrificial blood, new gods only need prayers. No one knows how many Indian religions have died out; of some ancient gods only the names survive, or only the altars.

The famous Indus civilization, excavated in at least 25 sites along the Indus and Ghaghar rivers, with the two great centres in Harappa and Mohenjotaro, lasted from c.2500 to c.1500 BC. Apart from an advanced technology such as an intricate system of water supply and drainage of sewerage, this civilization seemed already to have worshipped Shiva and Devi. However, further details of this early Hinduism will have to wait until the system of writing is deciphered.

The Peoples

It is usually taken for granted that all the present-day peoples of India were living peacefully together in 1500 BC, when suddenly the merciless Aryans invaded from the north. No part of this statement should go unchallenged. It may be blamed on Adolf Hitler who called his pure Germans Aryans and pretended that they were a naturally aggressive and domineering race. French and English historians since 1871 have written books blaming all the adversities of their nations on the Germans, forgetting that they themselves, the Franks and the Saxons were also Germanic and therefore Indo-European.

Firstly, other races, too, invaded India at some stage of its history, one after another. If it is true as some Dravidologists maintain that the Dravidians once inhabited much of north-west India (before they were 'dislodged' by the Aryans) then they too may have invaded from the north. This is made even more probable by their possible relationship to the Altaic peoples. The Tibeto-Burmese peoples, too, migrated south at a certain stage from what is now north China, to occupy their present habitat. They were preceded by scattered groups of peoples called collectively Austro-Asiatic, a loose category of language families including Mon-Khmer, Thai and Austronesian, to which the Munda peoples of India belong, as well as the Andamanians. The oldest surviving race are no doubt the Vedda or Weda people in the hills of Sri Lanka. If any people then the shy Veddas could claim India by right of precedence. The argument 'we were here before you' should always be used with circumspection lest later data reveal yet older inhabitants.

Nor is it likely that the Aryans invaded as a single organized body.

As we have seen, the political units before the Harappa period were extremely small and peoples on the move are always composed of smaller groups than the sedentary peoples, by necessity. The Aryan peoples, like their predecessors, entered India in small clans, trickling in over a very long period, perhaps 2,000 years, between 5000 and 3000 BC. Nor could they have climbed the Karakorum from the north, they must have come from the west, from what is now Iran.

Literature

We are not well informed about the chronology of early Indian history even though we have a wealth of linguistic material, in Vedic, Sanskrit, Magadhi, Pali and Tamil; Tamil literature began in the first century AD, Vedic literature is usually dated from *c.*1500 BC, though some of the hymns might be much older. It is the oldest Asian literature of a continuing tradition, for the Vedic hymns are still studied by Brahmins, as well as recited. Sanskrit literature is usually dated to begin from *c.*1200 BC.

The most famous works of the post-Vedic period are the *Upanishads*, philosophical treatises, some of considerable length, some only a few pages, but all of fundamental importance for world philosophy. This literature was composed until *c.*200 BC. It is followed by the *Puranas*, versified narratives of the creation and the mythical lives of the gods. Several Puranas will be quoted in this work. The most voluminous single work (though composite in structure) is the great epic *Mahabharata* (see further on) of over 200,000 lines, which is the fountain of Indian mythology. It was completed no later than the fourth century AD. The *Ramayana* epic which has 'only' 48,000 lines (of eight syllables each) was composed in the second century BC by the famous poet Valmiki. It relates the history of Rama, Sita and Hanuman.

During the Middle Ages several other large collections of long narrative songs were composed, the best-known among them being the *Katha-Sarit-Sagara*, 'the Story-River-Ocean' — that is, the Ocean in which all the Story-rivers have been collected, by the poet Somadeva around AD 1000. Famous prose collections of fables are the *Pancha Tantra*, 'Five Books of Wisdom', a series of tales illustrating deplomacy and sagacity. The *Hitopadesha* contains similar fables but with Buddhist lessons. The *Shuka-Saptati* or 'Seventy Tales of a Parrot' are intended to entertain women and teach them morality as well as resourcefulness.

In Pali literature, which is entirely Buddhistic, the mythologist will find a great deal of interest in the *Jataka* tales (q.v.), a collection of parables which form part of the *Sutta-Pitaka*, one of the three early Buddhist textbooks.

Numerous tales have been collected in the modern spoken languages of India. They already fill many volumes.

The Sources

Our greatest single source for the mythology of India is and remains the magnificent Sanskrit epic of *Mahabharata*, 200,000 lines long. It is a vast storehouse of Indian lore, culture, manners and morals. This great work was the product of the labours of many poets and a compiler *vyasa* (and several editors), who created the structure of the epic by arranging the numerous almost unrelated ballads dealing with different episodes into 18 books of very different sizes and contents. Some of the books contain only dialogue, others deal exclusively with morality, courtesy and good manners for noblemen and sportsmen. The oldest passages are composed in the language and metre of the late Vedic period which ended about 1000 BC. Other long passages seem to have been composed and inserted in the early centuries of the Christian era. Thus this greatest of all oriental epic poems took more than a thousand years to compose. The most famous philosophical insertion is the *Bhagavadgita*, the Sermon of Krishna, that is Vishnu himself, before the great battle. This has been very tentatively dated in the fifth century BC.

The *Ramayana* coincides partly with the later parts of the *Mahabharata*, dating from the third century AD or earlier. Yet, what makes the *Mahabharata* one of the greatest epics in world literature is neither its venerable antiquity nor its enormous size. It is the fact that the entire life of India in Antiquity is in it. Not only warfare, but sport, hunting and travelling. Religion with its sacrifices and liturgies, its priests and ascetics, is prominently explained. The forests, rivers and mountains of India where the poets were at home, are vividly described with the traveller's open eye. But there is more. The *Mahabharata* is world literature because of its nobility and its human-ness and humane-ness. It is noble because its heroes have to obey an elaborate code of highly ethical rules of behaviour. For example when the eruptive hero Bhima is unable to contain his very justified wrath, his older brother Yudhisthira reprimands him saying that such behaviour is unworthy of an Indian nobleman, and Bhima obeys his brother. The Pandavas are the five noble heroes, whose behaviour is impeccable, contrasting sharply with the despicable dishonesty of their jealous cousins, the Kauravas, one hundred scoundrels. The *Mahabharata*, however, is more than a textbook of ethics full of dull tales with a conspicuous moral lesson in them. It is a great romance about human beings full of normal, almost modern feelings of love and hatred, devotion and jealousy, revenge and forgiveness, faithfulness and treachery and a hundred other emotions that we can all share.

It is also a work written by very humane authors. There is much forgiveness in it, even for depraved characters, after they have perpetrated malicious acts. There is understanding for the feelings of women which in European and Islamic literature arrives in the foreground only much later in history. There is a gentleness of attitude in the heroes demonstrating that the *Mahabharata* was created in the country of non-violence, of Buddhism, Jainism and other noble philosophies, enjoining restrained behaviour.

The *Mahabharata* contains much more the stuff of a genuine epic than the *Ramayana*. Whereas the latter has more the character of a fairy-tale for Rama's devotees — for whom it is recited, the *Mahabharata* contains in essence the desperate struggle between Man and his destiny, between human beings and the immutable decree of the gods. In addition, as Homer says so eloquently, we mortals suffer more than the gods intend us to suffer, as a result of our own short-sightedness and our inability to contain our passions. At the same time the epic contains great scenes of bravery and human self-sacrifice, the heroes displaying the highest virtues of which men and women are capable. Whereas the Homeric epic describes only a brief period in the heroes' lives, the *Mahabharata* relates their complete lives with those of all their ancestors.

The Hindi *Ramayana* by Tulsi Das is still used in ceremonial sessions as a textbook for recitals. The reciters know the text by heart; they can cantilate it or sing it for hours on end, while the people listen enthralled since for them Rama is God. Thus the *Ramayana* relates the happy episode of history when God walked upon earth to defeat the demons and liberate the people of the earth from the evil which had accumulated at that time. Thus the student of mythology studies more than myths of epic tales; religion and philosophy are his twin subjects at first. After that he has to study the society of the believers, the people who *live* in that world which we call mythical. For the reality of one community is a fairy-tale world for others. The Indian philosophers are well aware of this relativity of all human thinking and knowledge. They call it Maya (q.v.) 'illusion'. The world we think we live in, the gods we think we have seen, are all images in our minds. The essence of reality cannot be seen by human eyes. This notion gives Indian myths a playfulness which other nations' myths lack, except perhaps Homer's own versions, in which it is evident that he does not take the gods seriously. Only his human heroes suffer truly. Thus there is always the changing relationship between the poet, the story-teller, their audience, and the gods who populate their ever-changing world of beautiful images.

History

India's history is too long for this Introduction. Like Chinese history, India's history is, if summarized, a list of dynasties with only a few truly great emperors who ruled at different times in different capitals. Often there were several kingdoms at the same time in the vast spaces of the sub-continent. Each dynasty is also known for its typical art: its architecture, sculpture, painting, and so on.

Some places in India are pointed out as being the sites of the seven most ancient capital cities of India. Hastinapura on the River Ganges is now a small village but was once the capital of a kingdom in epic times. Indraprastha is believed to be under part of the present New Delhi on the bank of the Jumna (Yamuna). Ujjain, Ujjaina in the Vindhya district still has substantial ruins. Kapilavastu in the north was the kingdom of Buddha's father. Ayodhya near the present Oudh, was Rama's capital. Kosala, further north, was the capital of the once extensive kingdom of Shravasti. Finally Rajagriha east of Varanasi, which is also called Girivraja, became the capital of Magadha in what is now Southern Bihar, under King Sisunaka or Shishunaga, the founder of the Shaishunaga dynasty c.650 BC.

His descendant the famous King Bimbisara may have been a patron of the Buddhist monks and their monasteries. King Bimbisara reigned in c.500 BC and so is the first historical ruler of India. His contemporary, Darius I of Persia, extended his empire down to the Indus valley and even sent a fleet to India, perhaps the first navy in history. The Indus remained the frontier between India and Persia until Alexander the Great arrived. Bimbisara was succeeded by his son Ajatashatru, 494–467 BC. He built the fortress of Patali on the River Son which later developed into the imperial city of Pataliputra. He conquered or absorbed the kingdom of Kosala where his queen had been born. He was succeeded by his son Darshaka (467–443 BC), who was succeeded by his son Udaya.

The Persians brought the so-called Aramaeic alphabet which was later also used for Persian. In India it was developed into the Kharoshti alphabet which became the mother of all the Indian alphabets up to modern times. The only exception is the Arabo-Persian system of writing which came to India with Islam and is now in use for Urdu and Sindhi in Pakistan. The Kharoshti alphabet spread beyond the borders of India to China. The early alphabet of the Uyghur language of the Buddhists of Turkestan was based on this script.

Buddhism brought the Indian scripts to South-East Asia where the writing systems of Burmese, Thai, Laotian, Cambodian (Khmer), Balinese and Javanese are still based on a form of ancient Indian script.

It seems that King Bimbisara was related to Vardhamana Mahavira, the founder of Jainism, and that his son Ajatashatru (also known as Kunika) visited Gautama Buddha who died c.480 BC. It is quite possible that the rise of those two philosophies (which had not yet grown into religions with institutionalized adoration of the founders) was caused by the Brahmins' overemphasis on ritual, which had led to elaborate ceremonies dominated by the priests who, of course, had to be full-blooded Brahmins. These priggish officiants insisted that there was no other religion than that based on their Vedas, and their power may have caused the reaction in favour of a philosophy without priest or ritual, for individual seekers of the Truth. The popularity of Buddhism and Jainism continued growing especially among the Kshatriyas, the ruling classes, until the onslaught of the Turkish–Muslim invasions destroyed the whole framework of the old Hindu society and Hinduism was reduced to a religion for peasants. Curiously, the priestly class survived and when the British conquered India in the nineteenth century, destroying Muslim power in its turn, the religion of Hinduism reclaimed its proper place as the oldest religion of India and with that, the oldest surviving Indo-European religion.

It then appeared that the Hindus, like the Parsis, were intellectually much more adaptable than the Muslims, so the new spiritual leaders of India gave Hinduism a modern philosophy. It would take too long to discuss here what these new Indian scholars adapted from Western thought and what they took and reinstated from ancient Hindu cosmology. The process is still going on, since on the one hand Western (now American rather than British) ideas put 'mental pressure' on Indian minds to adapt to the age of science, technology and mathematics, which the Indians do much better than most other nations. This happens no doubt because Hinduism is by its nature a multiple cosmology without a fixed monolithic dogma like Islam. In Hinduism there is room for an exchange of views while Buddhism regards all our views as illusion. The true reality cannot be found on this earth. Such persuasions leave latitude to tolerance and spiritual development. On the other hand ever more ancient Sanskrit texts are discovered, published, translated and interpreted. There are an estimated 500,000 manuscripts in India, composed in a dozen languages; the majority still await publication. In this way Hinduism and Buddhism may survive into the modern world precisely because they are flexible philosophies, and so, like Christianity, they are open for debate and so, for evolution. Islam on the other hand tends to turn in upon itself preferring to return to the original oldest forms and dogmas.

The Later Dynasties

The Shaishunaga dynasty comprised 10 kings; the last two were the so-called Nanda kings. After these a new dynasty composed of nine more Nandas came to power, the 'new' Nandas, i.e. King Mahapadma and his eight sons. They reigned in Magadha from c.400 to 320 BC.

The last Nanda king was overthrown by Chandragupta, the first king of the Maurya dynasty who succeeded just after the invasion of Alexander the Great in Western India in 326 BC. Chandragupta's chief minister was Chanakya Kautilya the first political scientist.

Chandragupta Maurya died in 297 BC and was succeeded by his son Bindusara (297–272 BC), who was succeeded by his son Ashoka, one of the most famous emperors who ever ruled India (272–232 BC), so he was a contemporary of the Egyptian ruler Ptolemy II Philadelphos (285–246 BC), who founded colonies on the Red Sea coast and patronized the great mathematician Euclid. Ashoka knew of him and other rulers of his time. Towards the end of his reign a great Buddhist council was held in Pataliputra (now called Patna).

The last prince of the Maurya dynasty, Brihadratha, was assassinated by his commander-in-chief Pushyamitra or Pushpamitra Shunga in 185 BC, founder of the Shunga dynasty. It seems that the Shungas, like the Mauryas, were Buddhists. Several famous *stupas* remain from the Shunga period. A *stupa* is a monument in the shape of a pyramid erected (originally in earth, later in sculpted stone) over the sacred relics of a Buddhist saint, a tooth or a bone, to be venerated by pilgrims. The last Shunga ruler, Devabhumi, was poisoned (?) by his chief minister Vasudeva in 73 BC, initiating the Kanva dynasty. The Kanva dynasty lasted only till 28 BC, When Augustus was already a Roman emperor. But whereas Augustus created a system of paid officials which outlasted him for four hundred years, the Indian rulers were not normally so capable to create an enduring state. The following centuries witnessed the invasions of various peoples whose leaders set themselves up as rulers of large areas of northern India. The most famous of these kings are Kanishka and his son (?) Huvishka who ruled during the second century AD. They are known as the Indo-Scythians, who spoke an Iranian language. They are mainly famous for the great Buddha statues which can still be admired in what is now northern Pakistan.

The one great and famous dynasty of Hindu India is that of the Guptas, which lasted from AD320–647. Their greatest emperors were: Chandra-gupta I (320–335), his son Samudra-gupta (335–376), Chandra-gupta II (376–415), Kumara-gupta (415–455), Skanda-gupta (455–467) and Budha-gupta (477–495). For almost two centuries there was stability in Central India so that the arts flourished. Apart from sculpture and painting the Gupta period was remarkable for the renaissance of the classical Sanskrit language and the creation, or recreation, of the great Sanskrit literature as we know it today. Apart from the completion of the great epics, Kalidasa must be mentioned, the greatest dramatist India ever had. The Chinese Buddhist scholar who visited India in the years 399–414, of the Gupta period, Fa Hien, regarded India as the sacred land of the Buddha, but the Gupta emperors referred on their coins to the deity as Bhagavad or Vishnu. Their reign was apparently marked by complete tolerance, long before there was any suggestion of this in Europe. The Gupta period saw the final redaction of the oldest Purana works, which are a mine of information of Hindu mythology and belief. The fine fabric of the

Gupta state which covered most of North India, was destroyed by the invasion of the Huna, known to the Greeks as Ephthalites and to European historians as the White Huns. They overran the Sassanian empire of Iran (in 484), which was later restored, but the Gupta empire was never resurrected. The Gupta dynasty of Magadha survived but it was probably not the same family. The political unity of Hindu India was broken for ever. We learn of isolated able kings like Harsha (604–647), who regained the empire of North India in five years of bitter warfare. We then learn of local dynasties ruling separate kingdoms. Some of these developed an art form entirely their own, such as the Chalukya dynasty of what is now Maharashtra and Gujerat founded by Pulakeshin I, c.550 near Bombay, lasting till 757.

The Pala kings of Bengal, beginning with the election of Gopala in AD750, ended with the defeat of Govindapala by the Muslim Turks in 1199. The kings of Kanauj (Kanyakubja) beginning with Pratihara of Bhoja (840–890), Mahendra Pala (890–908) and Mahipala (908–940) ended in the sad debacle of the Muslim victory of 1193 when Jayachandra (Jay Chand) was defeated by Muhammad Ghuri, who occupied Gujerat in 1197. The Pallava dynasty of Kanchi (Conjeeveram) in what is now Tamil-Nadu lasted from c.550–850 when the Chola kings took over. The Chola dynasty ruled in what was later called Coromandel from King Vijalaya (c.850–880) to Rajendra III (1252–1267).

The last great Hindu kingdom of India was Vijayanagara. Its dynasty was created by King Harithara I (1336–1354), and his brother Bukka, (1354–1377). The kingdom lasted until its last ruler, Ramaraja, was killed by the Sultan of Ahmadnager in the battle of Talikota in 1565. Vijayanagara was destroyed but a small Hindu kingdom survived in Madura. The last Hindu king in India was Ranga II (1642–1684); after him the kingdom was annexed by Aurangzeb.

The Muslim Conquest

While the Hindu kings fought petty wars, the dark clouds of Islam gathered on the Western horizon. Sindh was Islamicized from the eighth century, Peshawar fell to Islam in 991. Mahmud of Ghazni (997–1030) conquered the Panjab, but Multan fell to Islam only in 1175. Until that time the Rajas of India could pretend that Islam was not there. It is true that some Afghan chiefs raided Indian cities not so much for the sake of spreading Islam but rather for amassing fabulous treasures. Mahmud's raid on Somnath (Sorate) in 1022–6 was the most terrible of these plundering expeditions. However, Muhammad Ghuri was yet more ruthless. He lost the first battle of Tarain (1191) but won the second (1192). India lay open to the onslaught of Islam. Delhi fell in 1193, Ajmer in 1197, Bihar in 1193. In this last city, thousands of unarmed Buddhist monks were put to the sword and the great library of the oldest Buddhist college in the world was totally destroyed. All the priceless works of Buddhist philosophy went up in flames. Buddhism as an organized religion ceased to exist in India after 1200. In 1202 Muhammed Khilji overran East Bengal, which is still a Muslim state. Delhi became the capital of a sultanate and from there further expeditions were sent out to subjugate the hapless Indians to Islam. In 1301 the Rajput fortress of Rauthambor was stormed by the Muslims and its defender, Hamir Deva was killed. The proud, virtuous Hindu women threw themselves into the flames rather than become the slaves of the invaders. Malwa and Ujjain fell in 1305. In 1310–11, the eunuch Kafur (eunuchs are known for their cruelty and ruthlessness) raided the Hindu kingdoms of Warangal and Hoysala. He returned to Delhi with untold treasures and became the Sultan's favourite. Gujerat was conquered in 1297, but was never completely Islamicized. It became an independent sultanate. Further south Zafar Khan founded the Bahmanid dynasty at Daulatabad in 1347. In the same year a Muslim ruler took over in Kashmir.

We will not follow the endless raids of the Muslim leaders, mere bandits some of them, who set themselves up as petty sultans in what remained of India. They soon started quarrelling among themselves, just like the Hindu rajas before them, so that again India became exposed to attacks from outside.

The invaders from outside this time were first the Mongols under Jengiz (Chinghiz) Khan himself. They contented themselves with plundering the Western Panjab but did not ride further east. Instead they turned west, but came back later and sacked Lahore in 1241, then Sindh and Multan in 1242. A prince of Delhi was killed in a battle against the Mongols in 1285. The Mongols raided the Panjab again in 1296, 1297 and 1299. In this last year the Mongols were defeated near Delhi.

A century later, in 1398, a descendent of Jengiz Khan, Timur Lang ('Tamerlane'), stormed into India and took Multan. He defeated the Sultan of Delhi, Mahmud Tughluq and took the city where he massacred thousands. Thousands more were transported all the way to Samarqand as slaves to build his capital for him. There, Timur 'Steel', died in 1405. It took 45 years before the sultanate's throne in Delhi was occupied by a good organizer, Buhlul Khan, who was proclaimed sultan in 1451. He founded the Lodi dynasty of Afghan origin. He died in 1489 and was succeeded by his son Sikander (1489–1517). His son Ibrahim had to face a new invader who claimed to be a descendant of Timur, Babur, King of Kabul, who crushed Ibrahim in 1526 at Panipat, one of the famous battles of Indian history.

Babur made himself not only sultan of Delhi but called himself Padishah, emperor. He founded the famous dynasty of the Moghul emperors. The word Moghul has the same meaning as Mongol, for the Moghuls were Mongols. Before he died in 1530, Babur 'the Tiger', defeated the rulers of Rajput, Chanderi, Bihar and Bengal, so that he died a real emperor. His son Humayun had great trouble defending his empire against Shere Khan, who defeated him in 1539 and again in 1540. Humayun sought refuge at the court of the Shah of Iran, who sent him back with an army to reconquer his empire; after Shere (or Sheer 'lion') had died in 1545, he succeeded. Barely 10 years later, in 1556, Humayun died and the consolidation of his empire was left to his son Akbar. This task took Akbar 20 years, after which he lived almost 30 more years, during which he enjoyed his power. He was succeeded by his son Jahangir (1605–1626), who was in his turn succeeded by his son Shah-Jahan (1626–1657). These three rulers were the great lovers of art who together created the golden century of Moghul India: 1556–1657. Never before or after has so much splendour been displayed in India. Painting, carpet-making, architecture, jade cutting, music and every other aspect of art flourished.

Akbar made history not only with his conquests which made him the greatest Indian emperor in a thousand years, but also became so powerful he could do what he liked, even criticize Islam. He created his own religion, the Din Ilahi, the Divine Religion. Several courtiers including the scholar Mubarak and his son Abu'l-Fazl, elaborated the details of this religion. India, of course, is the country of religions. Many religions were born in India: Hinduism, Buddhism, Jainism, Sikhism, Ahmadiism, Sufism and others. Yet others found refuge there and prospered, for example Ismailism and Parsiism. It is said that it all began when Akbar was on a hunting expedition. He rode into a landscape that was so beautiful that he wanted to be by himself to enjoy this moment of elation. He dismissed all his beaters, hunters and houndsmen and called off the hunt. He dismounted and walked in the splendour of Indian nature.

Akbar entertained two Jesuit priests at his court who were sent by the King of Portugal. One of them, Fr. Monserrate, left us a description of Akbar's empire and his new religion. Akbar built a special verandah-type room in Fatehpur where he would invite scholars of several religions to debate their respective doctrines. In this he was far ahead of his time, if we remember that at that time (c.1580) the wars of religion were raging in France and the Netherlands; Spain and Portugal were united by the fanatic Philip II. Akbar was perhaps the first prince whose religion could be called syncretistic. No one knows exactly what he believed except that his own ego was very important to him. Nor is it surprising that a man of his intelligence was disaffected by the futile but fierce debates he heard, in which scholars of repute defended their petty dogmas. A man with so much power could not be forced to accept only one belief. He also knew that the religious differences in India had been the cause of innumerable wars in the lands where he had to keep the peace. He has been called the mystic emperor and he was no doubt influenced by some of the many forms of mysticism in India, but whether he was a mystic himself is doubtful.

To him is attributed the tale of the elephant: Akbar blindfolded some scholars and made each one touch a part of the elephant, then debate what it was they had touched. They argued for a long time until the emperor showed them that they had all touched parts of the same big animal. The emperor's approach to religion — if this tale is true — was more Hinduist than Islamic. He may even have been a Buddhist. The most likely hypothesis is perhaps that, like Alexander in the East, he fancied the feeling of being adored as a royal incarnation of a god.

Akbar's great-grandson Aurangzeb, who called himself Alamgir 'World-seizer', was the last great emperor of the Moghul dynasty. He came to power after slaying his three brothers and their sons in a series of battles involving huge armies campaigning right across India from the Indus to Bengal. Aurangzeb imprisoned his father Shahjahan for nine years (1657–1666) while he ruled in his own name. Aurangzeb Alamgir is praised by all Muslim historians because he was an orthodox Muslim who sought to impose Islamic law in all its details. Naturally this aroused opposition in a sub-continent which had always been multi-religious and totally tolerant. In this respect the Indian mind was centuries ahead of the rest of the world. In Europe persecution for the sake of religion was still going on, led by Louis XIV abolishing Protestant freedom in 1686. Two non-Islamic, one might say, anti-Islamic nationalities, the Sikhs and the Marathas, survived his reign as did the Rajputs. In 1669, Aurangzeb destroyed the two greatest Hindu temples, the one in Mathura dedicated to Vishnu, the other in Varanasi which was dedicated to Shiva.

After Aurangzeb's death in 1707 the same fratricidal war erupted as he had himself initiated half a century earlier. His four sons disputed the throne. The one who first reached Agra with its treasure chamber won because he could buy weapons, pay soldiers, bribe officials, and behave munificently to the nobles. The winner was Shah Alam Bahadur. He did not live long to enjoy his vast crime-won empire: he died in 1712. His four sons then began yet another war for the succession. The winner died in 1713... His successor was murdered in 1719. The grandeur of the Moghul empire was dead.

In 1739, Nadir Shah, ruler of Persia, invaded India, routed the imperial army and staged a massacre in Delhi. He returned to Iran with untold wealth, including the imperial peacock throne which is still in Tehran. Soon, the provinces made themselves independent, such as the governor (nawab) of Bengal (1740). In 1757, Robert Clive won the battle of Plassey and so, became master of Bengal. It marked the beginning of modern times in India.

The history of India in the last two centuries has been very well described and is not really relevant for the study of Indian

mythology except in one important aspect: the collection of the
sources in the form of the Indian literatures, oral as well as written
in a dozen languages. The collection of manuscripts was initiated by
Sir William Jones in *c.*1780; his favourite languages were Sanskrit
and Arabic.

It is often said that oriental manuscripts should be left where they
are, that they should not be buried in European and American
libraries, but the opposite is true. In properly funded libraries where
the latest technology is available, old manuscripts are stored at the
right temperature and humidity. They can be photographically
copied for scholars in other places so that the chance of loss is
minimal. Many old manuscripts need chemical treatment because
they are badly damaged by the many enemies that attack them in
tropical countries. In India, as elsewhere, most manuscripts are still
in private hands, kept in attics, lofts and other unsuitable corners
where white ants and cockroaches have free access to them. Many
village people move to the industrial centres, leaving their
manuscripts behind, together with other family possessions. The
old house must be sold and in a city flat there is no room for piles
of old papers. In 1970 Dr R. D. Gupta saw an old night watchman
lighting the fire for his teakettle with some old papers. Picking up
some of these old papers, Dr Gupta found himself reading Sanskrit
poetry. He asked the old man where he had found those papers and
the latter took him to a room in an old building which was stacked
to the ceiling with piles of manuscripts in half a dozen languages,
some dating from the sixteenth century. Such old manuscripts are
extremely rare in India. This was the beginning of the library of the
Brindaban Institute which is now already brimming over with
manuscripts of every kind. Numerous texts have already been
printed from manuscripts, collated and edited by competent and
patient scholars. In the old days it was believed that manuscripts
contained a part of the owner's soul so that his son and grandson
were enjoined to preserve them piously. However, some sons burnt
the manuscripts with their father's body, or let the papers float
down with the body on the Jumna and Ganges rivers, believing
that this act would purify their father's soul. When Dr Gupta
opened his library, which contained many manuscripts which
several old gentlemen had donated to him, they hailed him as 'our
son who piously preserves the material and spiritual remains of our
family.'

Sir William Jones founded the Asiatic Society of Bengal in 1784
with the aid of Charles Wilkins, administrator of the East India
Company in Calcutta. The Society published a journal, *The Asiatic
Researches*. That was the beginning of oriental studies by
Europeans. Before that, only missionaries such as Fr. Hanxleden (*c.*
1730) and Fr. Coeurdoux (*c.*1767) had studied Sanskrit and other
Indian languages. Charles Wilkins published the first English
translations of the *Bhagavadgita* (1784) and the *Hitopadesha* (1789).

Jones translated Kalidasa's *Shakuntalaa* (1789) and the *Gita-Govinda* (1782).

One of the leading Sanskrit scholars of the next generation was Horace Hayman Wilson (1789–1860) who was given the first chair of Sanskrit in Britain, at Oxford in 1832. Alexander Hamilton (1762–1824) was the first to teach Sanskrit in France; Friedrich Schlegel and Franz Bopp (1791–1867) were the first German scholars of Sanskrit. It was Bopp who published the first comparative grammar of Sanskrit, demonstrating that it was related historically to Persian, Greek, Latin and Gothic. The first French scholar in this field was Anquetil-Duperron, who in 1786 published a translation of the *Upanishads* from a Persian manuscript. Otto Böhtlingk was the chief author of the great *Sanskrit Dictionary* (1852–75); Friedrich Max Müller (1823–1900) was the editor of the *Rig-Veda* publication and the great series of annotated translations, the *Sacred Books of the East*, at Oxford, continuing till today. James Prinsep succeeded in deciphering the Brahmi, script, so that he could read the 'Seven Pillars of Wisdom', the famous edicts of Ashoka (1837). The greatest and earliest archaeologists of India were Alexander Cunningham who worked there from 1821 to 1885, and Sir John Marshall, who was appointed in 1901, and who excavated the first two of the great cities of antiquity, Harappa and Mohenjo Daro.

Further Reading

Arnold, Sir Edwin, *The Light of Asia, The Indian Song of Songs.* Calcutta 1949.

Bancroft, Anne, *The Buddhist World.* McDonald, London 1989.

Basham, A. L., *The Wonder that was India.* Sidgwick & Jackson, London 1954.

Boyce, Mary, *Zoroastrianism.* Manchester University Press 1984.

Conze, Edward, *Buddhist Scriptures.* Penguin Classics, Harmondsworth 1959.

Cowell, E. B., et al., *Buddhist Mahayana Texts.* Dover, New York 1969.

Davids, T. W. R., *Buddhist India.* Motilal Banarsidass, Delhi 1971.

Dowson, John, *Classical Dictionary of Hindu Mythology.* Kegan Paul, London 1961.

Dubois, J. A., *Hindu Manners, Customs and Ceremonies.* Clarendon, Oxford 1906.

Elwin, Verrier, *Myths of Middle India.* Oxford University Press 1949.

Garratt, G. D., *The Legacy of India.* Clarendon, Oxford 1937.

Ghosh, O. K., *Tales from the Indian Classics.* Bombay 1961.

Gupte, R. S., *Iconography of the Hindus, Buddhists and Jains.* Bombay 1972.

Humphreys, Christmas, *Buddhism*. Penguin, Harmondsworth
    1951.
Ions, Veronica, *Indian Mythology*. Hamlyn, London 1967.
Jash, P., *History of Shaivism*. Calcutta 1974.
Jones, J. G., *Tales and Teaching of the Buddha*. Allen & Unwin,
    London 1979.
Knappert, Jan, *Islamic Legends*, 2 vols. E. J. Brill, Leiden 1985.
    Myths and Legends of Indonesia. Heinemann, Singapore 1977.
Larousse Encyclopaedia of Mythology. Hamlyn, London 1965.
Mackenzie, Donald E., *Indian Myth and Legend*. Gresham, London.
MacNicol, Nicol, *Hindu Scriptures*. Everyman-Dent, London 1963.
Mahabharata and Ramayana, condensed ... by Romesh C. Dutt,
    Everyman, London 1963.
Narayan, R. K., *Gods, Demons and Others*. Hamlyn, London 1967.
O'Flaherty, Wendy, *The Rig Veda, an Anthology*. Penguin Classics
    1986.
Penzer, N. M., *The Ocean of Story*, being C. H. Tawney's translation
    of Somadeva's *Kathasaritsagara*. London 1924.
Roy Chaudhuri, P. C., et al. *Folk Tales of India*: 20 vol. Sterling,
    Delhi 1969.
Ryder, Arthur W., *The Panchatantra*. University of Chicago Press
    1956.
Smith, Vincent A., *The Oxford History of India*. Clarendon, Oxford
    1958.
Thapar, Romila, *A History of India*. Vol. 1. Pelican, Harmondsworth
    1966.
Thomas, E. J. and Francis, H. T., *Jataka Tales*. Jaico Publishing
    House, Bombay 1956.
Thomas, P., *Epics, Myths and Legends of India*. Taraporevala,
    Bombay 1973.
Upanishads, The, trans. from the Sanskrit by Juan Mascaro.
    Penguin, Harmondsworth 1965.
Valmiki, *The Ramayana*. Trans. Hari P. Shastri, London 1952.
Vitsaxis, Vassilis G., *Hindu Epics, Myths and Legends*. Oxford
    University Press Delhi 1984.
Vyasa, Dr S. N., *India in the Ramayana Age*. Delhi 1967.
Wilson, H. H., *The Vishnu Purana*. London 1840, Calcutta 1961.
Zaehner, R. C., *Hinduism*. Oxford University Press 1962.
Zimmer, H., *The Art of Indian Asia*. New York 1954.

A Guide to Pronunciation

The Sanskrit language possesses 12 vowels and 35 consonants.
These cannot all be represented in the Latin alphabet, since Latin
was a much simpler language. Scholars add dots and other
diacritical signs to their transliterations of Sanskrit words but for
ordinary readers these are not useful without lessons in phonetics.
The result is that in this book (and many other works), words are

spelled identically which sound differently when pronounced by Indians.

The following very general rules might be observed:

1. **Aspirates**. The sequences *kh*, *gh*, *th*, *dh*, *ph*, *bh* are pronounced separately, the *h* being heard after the consonant. Similarly there is a distinction between *ch* and *chh*, the former being pronounced without aspiration, the latter with the *h* clearly sounded. English speakers have difficulty pronouncing *k*, *t*, *p* and *ch without* aspiration when beginning a word, as in kit, tit, pit, chit.

2. **Long vowels**. These are not shown except in a few cases by doubling the vowels, as in Krishnaa, to distinguish this name from Krishna, Hidimbaa from Hidimba.
There are three words Brahma, one with the first vowel long, one with a long last vowel, and one with two short vowels.
E and *o* are always long, and so are double vowels and *ai* and *au*.

3. **Stress**. In words of two and three syllables, the stress is usually on the first syllable, except when the second syllable is followed by two or more consonants, when it attracts the stress, e.g. Vidarbha. Long vowels will normally have the stress.

4. **Modern languages**. Sanskrit died out before *c*.500 BC. Buddha already spoke Pali, the language in which the Buddhist scriptures are composed. A further development away from Sanskrit was Magadhi, the language of King Ashoka, which he used for his famous inscriptions. Most of the modern Aryan (= related to Sanskrit) languages display the following characteristics as far as mythological names are concerned: *B* represents both *b* and *v*. Some consonant clusters are simplified, e.g. *Jnyana* has become *gyana* 'knowledge'. The final vowels are inaudible. *S* and *sh* are no longer distinguished.
Z occurs only in Persian words.

A

Agni

Abhaya 'Have no fear', one of the hand-positions of the Buddha.

Abhimanyu Son of Arjuna by his 'own' wife Subhadra and so he is often called Saubhadra. In the great battle of Mahabharata, he killed Lakshmana, son of Duryodhana and was himself killed on the thirteenth day of the battle after fighting heroically. His wife was Uttara, daughter of the king of Virata. Their son Parikshit succeeded to the throne of Hastinapura.

Abhirati Wife of Panchika with whom she had 500 children, the youngest of whom, Priyamkara, was her favourite son. She is shown in sculpture surrounded by children, one of whom she is breastfeeding. She holds a pomegranate and a vase full of jewels, symbols of fertility. She is accompanied by a mongoose, the gold-vomiting animal. She is worshipped as a mother-goddess.

Abjaja, Abjayoni 'Born from a lotus'. Epithet of the god Brahma, who is represented as seated on a lotus rising out of the navel of Varuna, later of Narayana-Vishnu, by a long umbilical chord shaped like a flower-stem. This well-known image symbolizes divine purity as well as divine power, for the lotus is the world. Nor is it true to say that Brahma was born then. That is only part of Vishnu's Maya. The essence of Brahma (*sat*) which is the same as the essence of Vishnu, was never born, nor will it die.

Acharya A spiritual teacher or guide. A title of Drona.

Adharma 'Law-less'. Name of a son of Brahma.

Adi A demon who can take the shape of a bird or a snake; an incarnation of Vasishtha.

Adi-Buddha The original, essential, primeval Buddha, from whom all the later Buddha — and Bodhisattva — essences emanated.

Adipati See *Yama*.

Aditi 'Free, unbounded'. Infinity, space, heaven. The goddess of the firmament, often invoked for protection, forgiveness, children and cattle. She is also called Deva-matri, 'Mother of the Gods'. She is addressed as the 'Supporter of the Sky, Sustainer of the Earth'. She is the daughter of Daksha, wife of Kasyapa and mother of Vishnu, although the texts differ on these relations. She is even called the mother of Indra by some. She had a total of 12 children; she threw one of them out into the sky, Marttanda — the Sun. Indra gave his mother a pair of earrings which came to the surface when the gods churned the ocean. They were once stolen by the demon Naraka and brought back by Krishna. Devaki, the mother of Krishna, is an *avatara* of Aditi. Her children are called Adityas: her 12 sons led by Varuna.

Aditya An Aditya is a son of Aditi. Astrologers give the number of her children as 12, identifying them with the position of the Sun in each of the months of the year, i.e. with the signs of the zodiac. Aditya is one of the names of the Sun. Aditi meaning 'infinity, eternity', the Adityas were the immortal gods whose element was the eternal light. Their names are: Mitra, Aryaman, Bhaga, Varuna, Daksha, Ansa, Indra, Savitra, Aditya, Dhatri, Vishnu and Marttanda.

Agastya The Star Canopus; a great sage who conquered the Vindhya Mountains. Priest and poet, author of several hymns of the Rig-veda and a great personality. Mitra, one day staring at the beautiful heavenly nymph Urvasi, lost his seed, which fell all the way from heaven to earth into a water-jar, where it became a fish, so small that he was called Mana, 'little'. Finally he was born as a child. Hence his name Kalasi-suta, 'Son of a Jar'. He became a giant and a god who commanded the Vindhya mountains to bow before him, and when the ocean offended him, he drank it up, to find his enemies the Dityas who were hidden under the water. He was a medical scholar and ancestor of the Rakshasas. He is the ruler of Canopus, the South Star. When he needed a wife he took the most elegant parts of various animals and moulded them into a beautiful girl whom he placed in the palace at Vidarbha, making the King believe that she was his, the King's, daughter. When she was nubile he claimed her as his wife. She was called Lopamudra and the King loved her dearly. Later, Agastya lived in a hermitage up on the forested slopes of the Vindhya. One day Rama, Sita and Lakshmana arrived as exiles from their palaces. Agastya received them kindly and hospitably. In South India, Agastya is venerated as the divine teacher of science, Sanskrit literature and the religion that we now call Hinduism.

Agneya 'Son of Agni'. A name of Karttikeya. (See also *Skanda*.)

Agni Fire. The same as the Old Slavic god Ogoni or Agoni. Agni is born wherever a fire is lit, especially a sacrificial fire. Agni is also the endless fire that destroyed the magnificent forests of ancient India to make room for the plough, because Agni is the friend of Man. Agni is also the fire of the Sun, and the fire of lightning. Later, Agni was identified with Shiva in his aspect of Rudra, the roaring god of destruction. Agni is also sometimes identified with his son Skanda or Kartikeya, the god of war whose commonest appearance is fire. However, Agni also has his good aspects, since he is a friend in every household. Indeed if there is no fire in the house, the mother must be ill or have died. Agni is also the god of marriage, since on their wedding day, bride and groom walk around the fire seven times, to sanctify their marriage. Centuries later the mystic philosophers conceived of the fire as the divine presence and saw the human soul as a beautiful night-butterfly, a moth, who, in its consuming devotion, flew right into the fire and disappeared in a few brilliant sparks. Agni is represented with an extended stomach because the fire devours whole villages. He is coloured red and rides a ram. His tongue is a flame which licks up the sacrificial butter. He has two faces: the Sun-fire and the Earth-fire, seven arms which can reach the seven continents, and three legs representing the three fires of a person's life: the sacrificial, the nuptial and the funerary fire.

One day the sage Bhrigu carried away the wife of a man. The aggrieved man prayed to Agni to tell him where his wife was. Agni, the fire, has access to all homes, so he even knew the house of Bhrigu. Agni is also honest, because the fire is pure. So he told the man where his wife was. The man then went to Bhrigu's house and took his wife back. Bhrigu in his anger cursed Agni: 'You, fire, will consume every piece of dirt on earth.'

Agni remonstrated that gods must always speak the truth and that he, Bhrigu, was the impure one. Bhrigu admitted his fault and added to his curse (which could not be removed) that the fire would make all things pure, even dirt. This is why the Hindus burn the bodies of their dead: Agni will purify them. The alternative is to throw them in the purifying Ganges. In art, Agni is represented as having three heads growing red flames.

Agnimukha 'Fire-face', a type of Yakshas who live in Hell. They have fiery faces, hands and feet with which they torture the sinners.

Ahalya 'Night'. Name of the first woman ever created, by Brahma. She was given in marriage to the saintly priest Gautama. One day, Indra, the Sky-god with-a-thousand-eyes, saw her and fell in love with her. He persuaded the moon to assume the shape of a cock and to crow while it was still night. The moon did so and the devout Gautama, hearing that it was morning, as he thought, rose to go and perform his matutinal prayers and devotions. No sooner had he gone than Indra entered Ahalya's room, assuming the shape of Gautama and seduced her. Ahalya, who appeared to suspect his true identity, begged him to protect her against her husband's wrath. However, Indra could not even protect himself. As he left Ahalya's house, Gautama appeared, his body still shining with the holy bathing water. Having accumulated strong merit with his long asceticism, and having *dharma* (justice) on his side, Gautama cursed Indra: 'Thou shalt be impotent!'

At once, Indra's testicles fell off. To Ahalya Gautama spoke: 'You shall lie in the ashes for ten thousand years, eating only wind, until Rama comes here to release you of my curse.'

Years later, Rama arrived, restored her to her visible form and reconciled her husband with her. The hidden meaning of this myth is that Indra, as the Sun, sweeps away the shadows of the night after cock-crow.

Ahimsa Not hurting, not harming, gentleness towards all living beings.

Ahmadiya The Ahmadiya movement commenced in Kadian, a small town in British India which after partition remained just inside India. The Ahmadis maintain that they are good *Sunni* (orthodox) Muslims but the *Sunni* Muslims maintain that it is a new religion outside Islam. Yet all the teachings of the Ahmadiya are based on the Holy Koran, just interpreted differently from the Sunni tradition. Hasrat Mirza Ghulam Ahmad (1835–1908) was a serious scholar of Islam. He published a four-volume vindication of Islam. In 1889 he began to enrol student members for his movement. He announced that he was God's appointed Messiah, who may (according to the Koran 4, 159) come back to be present at the 'Last Judgement'. Other Muslims deny this, maintaining that God will send clear signs to give evidence that the true Messiah has come. The Ahmadis believe that the Messiah is Jesus who came to India from Palestine and 'was hidden' by God until His appointed time. Hazrat Ahmad has himself written about his experiences of visions of the other world, in which he saw, among other things, the sinners being beaten in Hell as punishment. He also wrote: 'I have been raised to this spiritual eminence. Almighty God has favoured me with his certain Word and has chosen me that I may give sight to the blind.'

He taught that the human soul grows in the body and is then

'given another form' by God, that in all man's actions there is, therefore, a soul hidden, subject to Divine Law; when fully developed it is like a light which only some can see. In its body the soul lives in this world. It will lose its first body at death and be given a second body for life in Barzakh, the second world. If the person has been a sinner his second body will be black and will be punished in Hell-fire, a smoky world. If, however, the soul has, in the first life, sought to perfect itself by study, devotion and abstention from evil, then the second body will be white and live happily in a bright spiritual world. When God calls the Resurrection, the souls, 'virtuous or wicked', will be given a third 'visible body'. The Day of Resurrection will be the day of the complete manifestation of God's glory. The good souls will thereafter live in the Janna, 'the Garden', and drink the Water of Life, i.e. immortality, while spiritual nourishment will be served to them. They will live in blissful proximity to God.

Ahriman The Evil One, the Uncreated Spirit of deceit in Zoroastrianism.

Ahura Mazda Great God, from the old Persian Ahura 'God', and Mazda 'great'; in the Parsi (Zoroastrian) religion Ahura Mazda is the Creator, the Good God whom all people must worship.

Airavata From Iravat, 'child of the water'. Airavata was a colossal elephant produced by the churning of the ocean and given to Indra.

Aja 'Unborn'. Son of Dilipa, father of Dasharatha. Aja was chosen by Indumati, daughter of the king of Vidarbha to be her husband. On his way to the tournament (see *Svayamvara*) he was waylaid by a wild elephant whom he wounded mortally. Out of the dead elephant there came a handsome young man, a Gandharva, who had been condemned to live as an elephant by a holy man whom he had mocked. By killing the elephant, Aja had terminated the punishment for the Gandharva who, as a token of his gratitude offered him a quiver full of magic arrows which would never miss. Aja took them to the tournament where, in the archery competition, he won all the prizes, and the hand of the princess Indumati as well. Their son was Dasharatha.

Akshamala A rosary, i.e. a string of beads, seeds or flowers. When carried by Brahma it represents time, i.e. continuous Creation without which the earth would perish. Buddha and the Bodhisattvas also hold rosaries symbolizing the chain of *samsara* (q.v.).

Akshobhya The second of the Dhyani-Buddhas or Buddhas of meditation. He represents the spiritual element *vijnana*, discernment, distinction, judgement, the faculty of understanding. He represents the winter season of introvert reflection, and the colour blue.

Amaravati 'Full of Ambrosia'. The capital city of Indra's heaven, situated near Mount Meru, also called Devapura 'City of the Gods'.

Amba (1) 'Mother'. An epithet of Uma-Parvati.

(2) Daughter of the king of Kasi. She was carried away by Bhishma, but he had to give her to the king of Salwa, because she was already betrothed to him. However, the king rejected her, since she had been in another man's house. Dejected, she went to the forest to do penance with such austerity and persistence that Shiva appeared to her and granted her a boon. She asked for her revenge on Bhishma. Shiva granted her that in her next life. She mounted the pyre, died and was reborn as Sikhandin who slew Bhishma in the great battle. (See *Mahabharata*.)

(3) The mango fruit.

Ambi, Ambika 'The Mother', a moon-goddess. Name of Uma or Parvati-Kali. Wife of Agni. (See *Devi*; *Durga*.) Also: a mango.

Ambrosia The food of the gods in Heaven. (See *Amrita-Kumbha*.)

Ameretat Immortality. (See *Zoroastrianism*.)

Amida The Buddha in his incarnation of compassionate spirituality.

Amitabha The oldest of the Dhyani-Buddhas, i.e. Buddhas in meditation. He resides in Sukhavati, the Happy Land of Eternal Bliss, presiding silently over our present period of history (*kalpa*), the Bhadrakalpa. He represents the cosmic element of insight, *sanjna*, self-knowledge, which leads to compassion with other human souls. This is the vital fluid in soul and society, so Amitabha represents the summer season, vital for the fruits, and the colour red. It was Amitabha (Japanese: Amida) who incarnated in Gautama.

Amoghasiddhi The fifth of the five Buddhas of meditation. See Dhyani-Buddha. He represents the important philosophical concept of *sanskara*, literally 'composition, synthesis'. This may refer to a work of art; we speak of a musical composition, or a literary composition. It can also mean 'decoration', when referring to visual art. *Sanskara* thus also means 'refinement', since art requires the composition of the best of everything. Hence the word Sanskrit, literally 'refined synthesis', the exquisite language of philosophy, consciously selected and composed by scholars from the best elements of the Aryan dialects. For a human being, *sanskara* means 'education, refinement, erudition', since that is the decoration of the soul, making a gross mind into a spiritual work of art, the highest intellectual achievement.

Amrita-Kumbha A *ratna* (q.v.), a precious treasure, the one object the gods were looking for when they decided to churn the ocean; the vial containing Amrita, the Elixir of Life.

Amrita Surabki The original begging-bowl of the Buddha. (See *Grail*.)

Anahita Aredvi Sura Anahita, ancient Iranian goddess of the waters, especially of the World River which supplies all the fresh water people need. She is invoked in Yasht 5 as the one 'who increases corn and increases herds', the one 'who purifies the seed of males, the wombs of females, the milk of mothers'.

Ananda 'Joy, happiness'. An epithet of Shiva (q.v.). Ananda (also called Nanda 'bull') was a half-brother of the Buddha who became his bosom friend. One day Ananda told Gautama that there would soon be a feast when he would marry. The Buddha told him that for him his whole life was a feast since he had overcome all desires and acquired enlightenment, so that he knew, saw and heard more than ever before; indeed he knew Absolute Truth. Ananda was converted and remained a lifelong friend and follower, becoming the Buddha's most devoted disciple to whom he addressed many sermons. He never married but slept in the woods together with the Buddha.

Ananga 'Bodiless'. Epithet of the Love-god Kama (q.v.).

Ananta 'Endless, infinity'. Epithet of Shesha the world sea-serpent used by the gods to churn the ocean in order to find the water of immortality, and on which Vishnu sleeps.

Ananta-Shayana 'Sleeping on Ananta'. Epithet of Vishnu (q.v.).

Anasuya 'Charity'. Wife of the priest Atri and mother of Durvasas. She received Sita hospitably when the latter sought refuge with her, and he gave her an ointment for lasting beauty.

Anatta *Anatman*, soul-less, in Buddhism the ideal condition of extinction.

Anga A vast land including the Ganges delta, now Bengal and Bangladesh.

Angiras One of the seven Maharishis or high priests, and one of the 10 Prajapatis or Founding Fathers of humanity. He was the priest of the gods and the Lord of the Sacrifice. He was a law-giver and astronomer, but first and foremost a poet of Vedic hymns. He was a son of Agneyi, Agni's daughter, but some say he was the father of Agni, Brihaspati and Utathya. He had four wives called Memory, Faith, Truth and Sacrifice.

Angirasa One of the Luminous Race, the descendants of Agni. They are deities of the fire, of the light, the heavenly bodies, celestial phenomena (e.g. meteors) and divisions of time. They were especially charged with protecting the sacrificial fires.

Anjali Supplication, greeting the deity by placing the palms of the hands together, signifying reverence for all beings, human and divine.

Anjuman, anjoman Religious community or congregation, pious society.

Annapurna Goddess of Daily Bread. The name Annapurna means filled (*purna*) with food (*anna*). One day Shiva, who was a mendicant priest, found no food so he felt hungry. He asked the sage Narada for the cause of his hunger. Narada explained: 'It is all on account of your wife. An auspicious wife brings good fortune to her husband. Look at Vishnu! He married Devi Sri and ever since he has been living in plenty.'

Having said this, the sage repaired to the kitchen, where he saw the starving Parvati sitting in a melancholy mood. She asked the wise old man why she was condemned to poverty. Narada explained: 'It is all on account of your husband. A capable husband supports his family by earning plentifully. Look at Devi Sri! Ever since she married Vishnu she has lived in heaven.'

Parvati brooded over this and the next morning when Shiva had gone out she took her children and left the house. When she had gone some way, Narada appeared and taught her how to persuade people to give her food. She paid visits to many families and came home with a basket full of food. When Shiva came home hungry and empty-handed she fed him until he was satisfied. He was so grateful that he embraced her until he became one with her. This unification in total love has often been cast in sculptures known as Ardhanari, half-man and half-woman.

Annapurna is a well-known mountain, one of the highest in the world. It is called Annapurna because from its slopes many streams descend to feed the fields and pastures, so that people have food. Parvati the Mountain-goddess is identified with this great mountain, just as Demeter, her Greek equivalent, is identified with the snow-clad Mount Ida.

Anugraha Acceptance of a person's prayers, offerings or austerities by a god, grace from the god given to such a person, special divine favour.

Anumati The moon just before it is full, worshipped as a goddess.

Apala A woman whose husband did not love her because she had a skin disease. She went in search of good luck and found a *soma* fruit. She pressed it between her lips and Indra appeared to her. She offered it to him and he made love to her. She begged him to restore three things: her skin, her father's potency and the fertility of his cultivated fields. Indra took her and pulled her through the axle holes of his chariot. The first time her skin sloughed off and became a hedgehog. The second time her next skin was stripped off and became a crocodile. The third time her next skin became a chameleon. After that treatment her skin became smooth, shiny and bright like the sun. Her husband then loved her again.

Ape See *Hanuman* and *Sugriva*, the Ape-gods that are still worshipped.

Apsaras 'Water-stream'. One of a race of beautiful nymphs who live in Indra's heaven. One of them is called Urvasi, but few of the others are known by name even though they are little love-goddesses. Some scholars say that they rose up from the ocean when it was being churned. They are too voluptuous to be called fairies; houris would be a more fitting term except that they are not sent to men to reward them for their virtue but on the contrary to prevent them from attaining such a high degree of saintliness that they become the equals of the gods. They are used by the gods to test a man's steadfastness (see Mara's daughters). They do function as houris when they are given by Indra to the heroes who fall in battle. They are also the Gandharvas' wives. They can bring a man good or ill luck in gambling. They can change their shapes as they wish. They can make a man mad.

Arahat, Arhat A Buddhist ascetic who has attained the highest level of self-control so that he is exempt from having to be born again.

Ardhanari Shiva together with Parvati or Durga. Durga, the impenetrable fortress, is also the loving mother Ambi Annapurna, who finds food for her children and for her husband even in times of famine. Annapurna is the great mountain in the Himalayan range, from which the holy river, the Ganges (Ganga) descends towards the plains of India. Ganga is the sister of Parvati, and descends through Shiva's matted hair to the parched plains. Thus millions of farmers' families depend on these gods of the Himalayan waters; without water, people and cattle starve.

The Hindu philosopher knows that these myths describe only the outside appearances of the gods, which are nothing but colourful illusions. The gods are one god, our own spirits are one spirit and in the most essential nucleus of our spirits is God himself. Thus teaches Shiva himself, who is the god of meditation and guru of all gurus, the very fountain of Veda (knowledge).

After receiving food from Parvati, Shiva loved her so much that he embraced her totally and became one with her. This conjugal unity is often depicted as the statue of Ardhanari: half-man, half-woman.

Ardhanari-Ishvara 'The Lord who is both male and female'. While Brahma was engaged in creating the universe, the earth, the animals, demons and human beings, he perceived that for the creation of living beings male gods were not adequate. Thus he called Shiva, who appeared to him as Ardha-nari 'half-woman', with the left side having all the attributes of a woman, while the right side was that of a man. This new inclusive form had been the result of Shiva and his devoted wife Devi loving each other with such passion that they merged and became one person for the purpose of creation.

Argha A stone ring, or a small basin, built in the ground or on a stone table in a Shaiva sanctuary, where Shakti is worshipped. Shiva's Linga usually stands in the middle of the basin which often contains water for the ablutions of the worshippers.

Arhat *Arahat*, a *bhikkhu* who has reached enlightenment.

Arjuna One of the Pandava brothers, chosen as husband by Draupadi (q.v.). (See also *Bhagavadgita*.)

Aruna 'Rosy-coloured'. The dawn-god, described as a charioteer of the sun. Also called Rumar, son of Kasyapa.

Arundhati 'The Morning Star'. Faithful wife of the priest Vasishtha. She does not come near the fire (of the sun) while bathing in the cold mountain morning, knowing that the fire (Agni) will make her an adulteress with its hot sparks.

Arupa-Loka 'The World of the Formless'. One of 10 heavens where only the Arhats and Buddhas live who are exempt from returning in physical form.

Arusha, Arushi A red stallion and a red mare belonging to the Sun-god. Epithet of the rising sun.

Arya (1) (Last syllable long). 'The noble goddess'. (See *Devi*; *Durga*.)
    (2) (First syllable long). In Buddhism, a saint or holy person, one who controls all his desires.
    (3) An Aryan, a person speaking an Aryan (Indo-Iranian) language. This group of languages includes old and modern Persian, Kurdish, Ossetic, Pashto, Beluchi and Scythian, as well as the languages more closely related to Sanskrit: Assamese, Bengali, Bihari, Cutchi, Gujerati, Hindi, Kashmiri, Magadhi, Sinhalese (on Sri Lanka) and Urdu. In the Veda, Arya is the name by which the authors refer to themselves and their own people. The other people in India are called Dasyu.

Aryaman 'Bosom friend'. One of the Adityas (q.v.).

Arya Samaj A society of modern Hindu Indians who have formulated what they see as the essence of Hinduism without the emphasis on ritual. The following are their beliefs:

1. First, they believe in God, 'the Primordial Root, the Eternal, Unseen, Supreme Sustainer of all true knowledge and of all objects made known by true knowledge'.
2. He is the Personification of existence, the Intelligence and Bliss. He is Formless, Almighty, Just, Benevolent, Unborn, Endless,

Immutable, Incomparable, Omniscient, Omnipresent, Undecaying, Creator of All, to whom alone worship is due.
3. The Veda is His word. It is the scripture of true knowledge.
4. We should always be ready to accept truth and abandon untruth.
5. All our deeds should be in accordance with *dharma*, righteousness.
6. The Arya Samaj, the Vedic Church, intends to promote the physical, spiritual and social good of every sentient being.
7. Love and Justice should guide our conduct towards all people.
8. *Avidya* 'ignorance' must be combated and *vidya* 'knowledge, science' promoted.
9. No one should be content with promoting his own good only, on the contrary one should seek to do one's own good by promoting the good of all people.
10. All People should subordinate themselves to the laws of society.

Ashoka Emperor of India, 273–232 BC. In 242 BC, Ashoka erected the so-called Seven Pillars of Wisdom, metal posts with long inscriptions in the Magadhi language. These inscriptions have been deciphered; they contain prescriptions for Life, admonitions for honourable conduct and laws based on his Buddhist convictions. The extent of the positions of these pillars (though some have been moved by later rulers) indicate that Ashoka's rule was recognized over almost the entire Indian Subcontinent. He left us nine (not seven) inscribed pillars, eight rock edicts and fifteen minor rock inscriptions, the oldest original written documents surviving in India.

Ashoka was the son of Bindusara (298–273), son of Chandragupta (322–298). All three were great emperors of the Maurya dynasty. Here are some of the main points of conviction of this emperor-philosopher: Honour thy parents. Respect all living beings. Speak the Truth. Keeping the *Dharma* is a virtue. Treat all servants kindly. Health of the body must be preserved: medicinal herbs must be planted. Tolerance towards the 'tribes' and protection to all sects is guaranteed. Liberality, almsgiving, and the study of Buddha's works are recommended. Those who do wrong and rebel will be forgiven but the Beloved of the Gods (the Emperor) is not only compassionate but also powerful so he tells them to repent or they will be executed. The Beloved of the Gods desires peace, self-control, justice and happiness for all beings.

Ashoka regarded his subjects as his children and admonished his administrators to observe more gentleness in their dealings with them. He supported *ahimsa*, love of duty and the *Dharma*, and condemned schisms in Buddhism to which end a Synod was held in Pataliputra. He was strongly against animal sacrifices and urged his courtiers to become vegetarians. Purity, self-examination and hard work were enjoined. Through his reign of morality the gods would manifest themselves on earth, he believed.

Ashtapatha The Eightfold Path in Buddhism: Right Views, Right Resolve, Right Speech, Right Conduct, Right Livelihood, Right Effort, Right Recollection, Right Meditation. This is the Middle Way, *Madhyapatha*.

Ashvamedha 'The horse-sacrifice'. When in Vedic times a king had no son, he would resort to sacrificing his finest stallion. The king's wives then had to spend the night in close proximity to the carcass. It was evidently expected that the spirit of the noble animal would make the queens fertile. (See *Dasharatha*.) This sacrifice of Man's most precious domestic animal was believed to be so magically powerful that a hundred such sacrifices would make a king emperor over the whole world.

Ashvatthaman Son of Drona and Kripa. One of the last surviving members of the Kaurava warriors with Kripa and Kritavarman. They entered the camp of the Pandavas, where at that time everyone was asleep after the battle, and killed all the men they found, including Dhrishta-dyumna and Sikhandin, the sons of Drupada and the five little sons of Draupadi. With his secret weapon, Ashvatthaman killed Parikshit inside Uttara's womb, but Krishna cursed him for his injustice. The next morning he fled but was captured by Arjuna who took his priceless jewel from him since the son of a Brahmin could not be killed.

Ashvins The Asvinau. The twin horsemen, Gemini. These Dioscuri were the sons of the Sky-god Surya. They are young and handsome, bright, agile and swift as falcons. They ride in a golden chariot drawn by horses or birds, preceding Ushas (= Eos), the Goddess of Dawn, Aurora. They were sons of the Sun by his wife Sanjuna, who had secretly assumed the shape of a mare. Their names were Dasra and Nasatya, although other names too are given to them in the Vedic hymns. They were benevolent dispensers of medicine and restorers of youth. They may have been day and night but it seems more probable that they were the two appearances of the planet Mercury.

Asipatra 'Sword-wing', a type of bird with wings like swords and claws like knives. These birds live in trees whose branches are spears in Yamapura, the City of Death where the sinners are tortured for ever after.

Asura Anti-god, demon. In the oldest Vedic texts, this word means just 'god', like the ancient Iranian cognate *ahura*, as in Ahura Mazda 'great god'. In the Veda, the gods Agni, Indra and Varuna are referred to as Asuras. Later the term changes its meaning, like the Greek *daimon*, which originally meant 'deity', but is the same word as demon, in a similar development of meaning. The *asuras* were born from Brahma's groin and they became the enemies of the gods. A new word, *sura*, was formed to mean 'god', so that now *asura* means 'non-god'. The *asuras* are titans, sons of Kasyapa, Danavas and Daityas. (See also *Demon*.)

Asvath The fig-tree, *Ficus religiosa*, dedicated to Brihaspati, Jupiter.

Atman (Pronounced: *aatman*). Soul, spirit. Originally this word meant 'breath', then, in the sense of 'last breath' its meaning develops into 'spirit'. Yet the concept of an individual spirit or soul is curiously underdeveloped in Hinduism if one compares its evolution in Christian thinking. From a Western point of view, on the other hand, the abstract concept of *atman* is very difficult to grasp, precisely because it is *not* limited to an individual soul or spirit. *Atman* is our innermost self, so deeply hidden inside our minds that most people never even discover it. The sages, however, (Plato's 'philosophers') recognize in the innermost nucleus of their psyche that which is identical with the divine world-soul, the cosmic all-soul out of which all moving life and thinking perception emanates, the Universal Consciousness, *atman*. Indian teachers illustrate this by an old parable of the father giving his son a nut and asking him what there is in it. In the nut is the kernel. What is in the kernel? In essence: the nut-tree which may one day grow up out of it. And what is there even deeper inside the nut? The essence of life (as we would say), that which causes the growth the fructation of all living things, the secret of Nature, the evolution of all living things. And what is there inside that? When the son has no answer, the father says: '*Tat tuam asi*: that is you.'

This is the famous phrase containing the essence of Hinduism, which is the philosophy of self-identification. Not what distinguishes me from other beings, but that which unifies me with the Essence of Life of the Universe itself, that is me, that is my own essence, the element of all the elements, out of which the entire creation grew like a tree growing out of a seed, the seed containing the essence. *Atman* thus means 'world-spirit, the limitless ocean of the soul-universe', as well as 'individual soul, my own spirit'. Whoever can think through these two absolutely contradictory concepts and see them as one, that person has begun to grasp the essence of Hinduism. It explains why the Hindus can worship a multitude of gods and yet maintain that God is one, in essence, but appearing in many shapes, like Nature, which appears in a thousand life-forms. The soul of a dying person merges with the universal Atman and yet remains an individual ready for reincarnation. (See *Brahma*.)

Atma-Yukta having a soul, animated, possessing vital intellect.

Aurobindo, Sri A Guru in South India, believed to have been an incarnation of God.

Avalokita 'Looking down' with compassion to earth. Compassion personified, and, in Mahayana Buddhism, deified. (See *Bodhisattva*.)

Avalokiteshvara The most prominent of the Bodhisattvas, who is popular throughout the Buddhist world. He resides in Patalaka, which is situated in the south near Amaravati, although we have to think of a heavenly Amaravati rather than the famous ruined *stupa* in South India. Avalokiteshvara is the manifestation of the Dhyani-Buddha (q.v.) Amitabha (q.v.) on earth. One day when Amitabha's meditation was particularly intense, a ray of white light issued from his right eye which brought Padmapani-Avalokiteshvara into existence. Amitabha blessed him, whereupon Avalokiteshvara pronounced his first prayer: *Om Mani Padme Hum*, which means: The Jewel of Creation in the Lotus. Avalokiteshvara is thus the child of Amitabha and his *shakti* (female energy principle) Pandara. Together with his 'parents', he presides over the present period of history (see *Kalpa*) called Bhadrakalpa 'the Age of Prosperity'. He will rule the universe from the Paranirvana ('departure', q.v.) of the Buddha Gautama to the appearance of the future Buddha, Maitreya, five thousand years later, when this, the Fourth World, will have come to an end. Then Vishvapani will create the Fifth World and become its ruler as Maitreya, when all people will acquire *bodhi* (enlightenment, q.v.). For the present time therefore, the fourth Buddha Avalokiteshvara is ruler of our world and its living Buddha, though not living in the earthly sense. For that he would have to incarnate, which, according to some schools, he does from time to time. It should be stressed that, as with the Hindu deities, the spiritual essence of the Buddhas and Bodhisattvas is always identical. Thus, Avalokiteshvara is described as 'the Bhagavan' (i.e. the Lord), who takes the form of a Bodhisattva and whose duty it is to look around (*avalokita* = looking around) for the purpose of the welfare and happiness of the people on earth and to teach them the way towards enlightenment. He, Padmapani, created this world himself: from between his shoulders sprang Brahma, from his two eyes the sun and the moon, from his mouth the wind, from his navel the water, from his knees Lakshmi (the earth), from his hair Indra, from his teeth Sarasvati. There are 19 Bodhisattvas of whom Avalokiteshvara is the most revered. He in turn is presented in sculptured form in 15 different *rupas* (shapes). He is known as the Bodhisattva of compassion and instruction since he has sacrificed his *nirvana* for the sake of the people he wants to lead. Some say there are 333 known incarnations of Avalokiteshvara during the past 2,500 years since Gautama Buddha went into *paranirvana*. Avalokiteshvara has been worshipped as a god from perhaps as early as the third century AD, hymns have been composed in his honour, describing his numerous appearances. Avalokiteshvara is often depicted accompanied by the goddess Tara. She too appears in a confusing number of different forms, including the so-called

'Colour-Taras': green, yellow, white, red and blue. One of her many names is Vidyarajni 'Queen of Knowledge'. She is full of compassion and devoted to alleviating the suffering of people on earth. Indeed, gradually she became the personification of compassion (*karuna*) and love (*maitri*). So, Tara was elevated to the status of mother of all the Buddhas shown with the royal *vajra* in her hand and a crown on her head. As Queen of Heaven she is lauded in many *stotras*, hymns. Avalokiteshvara has vowed that he will not accept the eternal peace of Nirvana until all human souls have found enlightenment because he decided that it would be selfish to enjoy peace and knowledge while the people are still suffering in ignorance. Their misery is his misery, he sheds tears in his sorrow for their pain. It is believed by the people that when they pray to invoke him: 'Hail Saviour, Deliverer, Compassionate Padmapani Bodhisattva', he will come and help them in their need and distress, and deliver them from fire and war, from slavery, wild beasts, disease and death. Thus, Avalokiteshvara is the continuation of the Universal Spirit of the Buddha, looking after the well-being of humanity, omnipresent in nature, worshipped as Padmapani, i.e. residing on the World-lotus like Brahma and later Buddha himself, hence his *mantra*: *Om Mani Padme Hum*, in which *Om Mani* refers to the 'divine jewel', i.e. the essence of God. In Tibetan, Avalokiteshvara is called Chenresi. In China, Avalokiteshvara is venerated as a goddess, which may lead us to assume that she was a development from the Indian Tara, the companion or *shakti* of Avalokiteshvara (and, according to some, also of Amoghasiddhi and Akshobhya). In China she is called Kwan Yin (Guan Yin), goddess of compassion and also goddess of agriculture, i.e. the rice-goddess, equivalent of the Indian Lakshmi.

Avatara Avatar. Literally this word means 'descent', picturing the divine spirit as descending from heaven to earth and taking up its abode in a human body or other material form. Later writers have distinguished different types of Avatara. (See especially Vishnu.) Firstly, some Hindu theologians maintain that Krishna was not an avatara of Vishnu, he was Vishnu himself, but that his brother Balarama was an avatara of Vishnu, suggesting that he had only part of Vishnu's divine spirit within him, whereas Krishna had all of it. This seems contradictory if one compares the myth of King Dasharatha (q.v.), whose four sons together shared the total 'nature' (*prakriti* or *swarupa*) of the god Vishnu, Rama getting half of it, yet Rama is also called an avatara of Vishnu. Meanwhile, having enclosed his total nature in a vessel of nectar, does not prevent Vishnu from appearing to the king carrying that vessel, the contents of which subsequently 'become', or are instrumental in causing, the embryos of the four princes inside the three queens. Nor does this prevent Vishnu from appearing in other forms elsewhere, nor indeed does he have to interrupt his eternal sleep in the limitless ocean of the not-yet-created universe. Thus we should distinguish the 'true' *avatara* or incarnation, when the divine spirit is born inside the flesh of a child or the young of an animal, and appearance, or manifestation, when the god shows himself in visible form and speaks to a chosen person. Meanwhile the divine spirit may linger anywhere in space unmanifested, unseen, unborn. This spirit is divisible in the sense that part of it may live in a human body, yet indivisible in the sense that the god 'himself' is not separated from that part of his spirit in that body but is conscious of its existence, continues to communicate with it and wills its actions, e.g. by making that body fly through the air or perform other miracles. The Hindu philosophers always end by saying that God is one (see *Atman*) and that all physical appearance is *maya* (q.v.) i.e. illusion, the result of our limited thought-capacity.

Avesta 'Teaching', the works of Zarathustra (q.v.) as far as they have been preserved in Old Persian, by the Zoroastrians, the largest group of whom live in India and are known as Parsis. The great collection of holy books in Persian was compiled before AD600. The oldest texts, the Gathas or hymns, date from the second millennium BC. The Avesta contained all the sacred texts of the Zoroastrians. Three-quarters of this vast thesaurus has been lost, destroyed when the Arabs invaded Iran in AD641. The Parsis of India have preserved about a quarter, namely the books that are in constant use for their holy liturgy so that many passages are still recited by heart. The Avesta is composed of two major parts, the Gathas (q.v.), composed in a very old (*c.*3000 years) form of Persian, and the younger Avesta some of which is also believed to have been inspired by God. These texts contain rules for life, especially the Laws for Purity. The 'Little Avesta' or *Khorda* is the Parsi Book of Common Prayers.

Avici In Buddhist cosmology, the lowest hell for those who mock Buddha and *dharma*.

Avidya Ignorance, the main cause of suffering, the first Nidana.

Ayanagosha The husband of Radha. When he surprised Radha with her lover Krishna, Krishna quickly assumed the appearance of Durga, so Ayanagosha worshipped her.

Ayodhya The capital city of Rama. Modern Oudh is not on exactly the same site.

Ayudha-Purusha A person used as a weapon, or a weapon with a spiritual individuality. The chief weapons (*ayudha*) of kings and gods in India and Indonesia are people (*purusha*), either male (e.g. *vajra*) or female (e.g. *gada*). A god or a demon can use a person as a weapon in war. (See also *Chakra*.)

B

Buddha's birth

Babhru-Vahana Son of Arjuna and Chitrangada. He became king of Manipura when his mother's father died. When his father Arjuna arrived with a horse for an Ashva-medha sacrifice, the two quarrelled and Arjuna was accidentally killed by his son. Full of remorse, Babhru-Vahana was ready to kill himself, but his stepmother, the Naga princess Ulupi, gave him the Jewel of Life which revived Arjuna miraculously.

Balarama, Baladeva, Balahadra, Halayudha, Langali Eldest brother of Krisha, the seventh incarnation of Vishnu. Or it is said that Vishnu took two of his own hairs, a black one and a white one and created Krishna out of the black hair, and Balarama out of the white one, then caused Devaki to give birth to these pieces of himself, in succession. As soon as he was born, Balarama was carried to Gokula out of danger, for the tyrant Kansa had been told that he would be killed by those boys. It was pretended that he was Rohini's child and he was nursed by Nanda. When he had grown up he slew the demon Dhenuka who had taken the form of a big ass. Another demon giant picked Balarama up and carried him away on his shoulders, but Balarama beat his brains out with his fists. He helped Krishna to defeat and kill Kansa the tyrant of Mathura. He also killed the great ape Dvivida who had stolen his weapons.

Before the great war of the Mahabharata, Balarama taught both
Bhima and Duryodhana the use of the mace. They were destined to
use their skills against one another in the final combat of that
terrible cataclysm. During the war, when Duryodhana had locked
up Krishna's son Samba in Hastinapura, Balarama demanded his
release and when Duryodhana refused, Balarama took his plough
Hala and started ploughing under the walls of the city, pulling the
ramparts down like brushwood. Duryodhana had to release Samba
to save his city. Balarama married Revati, daughter of King Raivata.
They had two sons, Nishatha and Ulmuka. Balarama did not have
Krishna's inclination for love affairs but he was called Madhu-
priya, 'a friend of the wine'. Although he sometimes quarrelled
with Krishna, he was basically of a pacific nature and refused to
participate in the great war between cousins described in the
Mahabharata, even though the Pandavas were his own full cousins,
as sons of Kunti, sister of Vasudeva, Balarama's earthly father,
being the husband of Devaki. Balarama's tools and emblems are the
club Saunanda, the ploughshare Hala, and the pestle Musala. These
symbols demonstrate that Balarama was the god of the ploughmen,
Langali, the peaceful farmers, while Krishna was the *gopala*, the
cowherd. Balarama died just before Krishna, while sitting under a
Banyan tree in Dvaraka. When he died, Shesha, the immortal sea-
serpent, appeared from his mouth and flew away, back to Vishnu's
ocean.

Bali (1) Monkey prince, half-brother of Sugriva, whom he drove
into exile, making himself king of monkeyland. Bali was a giant ape
with a long tail that could tie demons, He was killed by one of
Rama's arrows. Also: Balin.

(2) King of Mahabalipura, son of Virochana, grandson of
Prahlada, husband of Vindhyavali. Bali was so virtuous and
righteous, he performed such austere devotions, that the gods had
to yield to him their authority over the three worlds (Triloka).
Vishnu later appeared to him as the dwarf Vamana and asked a
boon of him: could he please have as much land as he could
encompass in three steps? Bali could not refuse, but Vishnu
suddenly resumed his cosmic size, took one step from one end of
the earth to the other, then another step from one side of Heaven to
the other, then with a third step he would easily have arrived at the
farthest frontier of the Underworld, but out of respect for the high
merits of King Bali, Vishnu refrained from taking the entire
kingdom. Bali was left with Patala, the lowest region. Thus the gods
tricked King Bali out of the world empire which he had acquired by
sheer strength of character and purity of soul. Of course Bali should
never have claimed the empire of Heaven and he should have
perceived that Vamana was no ordinary dwarf.

Bana (Also called Vairochi). Eldest son of Bali. This demon had a
thousand arms and was an enemy of Vishnu. When his daughter

Usha fell in love with Aniruddha, a grandson of Krishna, Bali transported Aniruddha by magic through the air to be united with Usha. Krishna and Balarama came and attacked Bana, who was defended by Shiva and Skanda. Skanda was wounded, Bana's arms were chopped off by Krishna's missiles and Krishna overpowered Shiva. Shiva pleaded for Bana's life and Krishna relented.

Banyan (1) The sacred fig-tree, *Ficus Indica*, under which women pray in the hope of having children.
(2) An Indian trader.

Bear See Jambavan the bear who fought for Rama who gave him the assurance that he, the bear, could only be killed by Vishnu. Decades later, Krishna fought the bear and wounded him mortally, so that he, Jambavan, perceived that it was Vishnu he was fighting.

Behula Behula is the very model of the devout wife. When her husband died of snakebite his body was placed on a raft, which she boarded. It was pushed from the shore so that it slowly floated down the stream. After many days she saw a woman beating her son to death, then reviving him with water from a jar. Behula begged the woman to give her some of that water to revive her husband. The woman led her to the goddess Manasa (q.v.), who ultimately revived Behula's husband.

Bha Venus, a star.

Bhaarata A descendant of King Bharata. One of the Pandavas.

Bhachakra The 'star-circle' or zodiac. Indian astrology places less emphasis on a person's Sun-sign than on his Moon-sign. In this and other significant ways it is completely different from Western astrology.

Bhadra Prosperity.

Bhadraa A cow.

Bhadracharu A son of Krishna and Rukmini.

Bhadrajina The last of the Tirthamkaras who still lives in the Devaloka of the Jains.

Bhadrakali See *Durga*; *Kali*; *Parvati*.

Bhaga The god of good luck, strength, prosperity, beauty, love and happy marriage.

Bhagavad, Bhagavan, Bahagavat God, usually Krishna (q.v.).

Bhagavadgita 'The Song of God', i.e. Krishna. One of the finest pieces of world literature ever written. It may date from the first century AD. Its author is unknown but he was no doubt one of India's greatest philosophers. The poem, consisting of 606 verses arranged in 18 cantos, has been incorporated in the Bhishmaparvan

of the Mahabharata epic, but is of a much later date. It is believed
by the faithful Vaishnavites that the god Krishna himself composed
it while he was Arjuna's charioteer. Krishna, although a kinsman of
Arjuna, had declined to join him in battle, but his very powerful
presence in the Pandavas' camp assured them of victory in spite of
the odds being against them. Krishna, being God, knew that. So
when Arjuna, being a kind-hearted righteous prince, hesitated to
ride into battle against the Kauravas, his own cousins, feeling the
approaching battle and bloodshed weighing heavily on his
conscience, Krishna consoled him by saying: 'Do your duty as a
Kshatriya [warrior], and do not fear to kill: I have already killed
them.'

This is the nucleus of Hindu philosophy: everything that happens
is the manifestation of immutable universal laws. The warrior must
kill, the victim must die, both should do so resignedly, since it is
their destiny. The sweeper sweeps, the farmer ploughs, the king
reigns, that is their destiny since birth. All those things were created
by me, says Krishna, they are in me, yet I am distinct from them. In
the eleventh canto Arjuna insists he wants to see Krishna the god in
his true form. Krishna at last consents, terrifying Arjuna with what
he sees: Vishnu, God. So Arjuna prays:

> I see in Thy body all the gods and all the created beings, Lord
> Brahma seated on his Lotus Throne, the sages and all heavenly
> beings.
> I see Thee infinite in form on all sides of me with countless
> arms, bellies, faces and eyes. I see no end and no beginning, O
> Lord of all Forms, Lord of all Things.
> I see Thee with Crown, Mace and Discus [Vishnu's
> emblems] ...
> A glowing mass of light dazzling radiance on all sides ...

Thus a man sees God by exceptional favour, but remember that
even this vision is an illusion, it is the powerful essence of the
universe wrapped up in earthly phenomena to make it visible. The
poem teaches *shraddha* 'faith', *bhakti* 'devotion' and the pantheistic
theology of the Vedanta. In verse IV, 8, Krishna speaks: 'For the
protection of the good, for the destruction of the wicked and to
establish righteousness, I come into existence from time to time.'

Vishnu is 'normally' dormant in the endless ocean of non-
creation, but when God is needed because the world is in danger of
being overpowered by the forces of evil, then Vishnu is aroused
from his slumber, assumes visible form on earth and exterminates
evil so that the good may prosper again.

Bhagavan, Bhagavat 'The Lord'. Title of a guru believed to be
divine.

Bhagavata, Bhagavat, Bhagavan, Bhagavant, Bhagvan God,
the being who is worthy of worship. Some Hindu sects believe that

a god (usually Vishnu) is wholly or partly incarnate in a saintly person, so that person receives worship like a divinity.

Bhagavata-Purana 'The Old Book of Divinity'. It is composed of 12 books, divided into 332 chapters and has a total of 10,000 verses. It is dedicated to Bhagavata or Vishnu. The tenth book narrates the history of Krishna; it is so popular that it has been translated into many languages. It was composed by the grammarian Vopadeva who lived c.1300 in Devagiri (now called Daulatabad) at the Raja's court.

Bhagavati 'The Goddess'. Epithet of Devi–Uma–Kali (q.v.).

Bhagiratha Great-grandson of King Sagara who performed asceticism for so long that Shiva granted his wish to allow the great River Ganga to flow through India, whose earth thirsted. To this end Shiva guided the river-water through his thickly matted hair, lest it should destroy the earth by falling on it with too great a force from Heaven. Bhagiratha named the river Sagara, and dug a bed for it, more than a thousand miles long. All those who have bathed in it have become purified of their sins, and some have even entered a better new life, either in this life or in the next.

Bhairava A name of Shiva in his terrifying aspect which has eight manifestations including Kala (q.v.), Asitanga (with black limbs), Sanhara (destruction), Ruru (hound), Krodha (anger, see *Bhuta*), Kapala (skull), Rudra (storm) and Unmatta (raging). He is depicted in sculpture and painting with frowning, angry eyes and sharp tiger's teeth, stark naked with garlands of skulls and a coiled viper round his neck, carrying weapons in his four hands: *pasha* 'noose', *trishula* 'trident', *damaru* a drum to accompany his dancing, a skull-cap and flaming hair. A dog accompanies him.

Bhairavi Terrifying female. A name for Durga-Kali in the Tantras (q.v.).

Bhakti 'Devotion, dedication, love', of God to his creatures and of a human being to God. There are two main forms, the monkeys and the cats. The baby monkeys cling to their mother; in the same manner the devotee clings to his God in his need for divine love and protection. The mother cat carries her baby with great care to a safe place; in the same way, the devotee believes, God carries his faithful believer lovingly towards a safe and protected life.

Bharadvaja, Bharadwaja A sage and arch-priest. One of the greatest poets who ever lived; the majority of the magnificent hymns of the Veda are attributed to him. He was the son of Brihaspati and the father of Drona. He was the *guru* of the Pandavas. He received Rama and Sita in his hermitage at Prayaga, which became a place of pilgrimage. Thus he participated in both of the great epic histories.

Bharata This is a common name leading to much confusion.

(1) Bharata was a king of the Bharata people in Vedic times.

(2) Bharata was a hermit who meditated on the bank of a river. One day a pregnant doe fell in the river and gave birth there. The doe drowned but Bharata rescued her young faun and brought it up with great love. When he died he saw tears in its eyes and so he was reborn as a stag, since while dying he had concentrated his thoughts on this animal instead of on his god, Vishnu. However, because of his merits as a saint he was allowed to remember his previous life in his existence as a deer. He led an abstemious life in the forest so, when he died again he did not have to be reborn in another earthly existence again. He would have no more future.

(3) Bharata was the son of King Dasharatha of Ayodhya (Oudh) and Queen Kaikeyi and so, was Rama's half-brother. He was taught by his maternal grandfather, King of Kekaya. He married Madavi, a cousin of Sita. His mother was responsible for Rama having to go into exile as she wanted Bharata to be king but he refused, for he was a righteous prince. When his father died, Bharata dutifully performed the funeral ceremonies, then went in search of Rama, whom he found near Chitrakuta. He offered Rama the throne but Rama wished to fulfil the vow he made to King Dasharatha, of staying in exile. So, Bharata returned to Ayodhya, where he placed Rama's sandals on the throne and reigned in his name, as a faithful regent.

(4) Bharata was the son of Dushyanta and Shakuntala. He became the ancestor of Kuru and Pandu and thus of the Kauravas and the Pandavas, the heroes in the great war who together are known as the Bharatas, the descendants of Bharata. Hence also the name of the country; Bharata (Bharat), India, and of the epic, the Mahabharata (q.v.).

Bharatavarsha India, the kingdom of Bharata. It has nine *khandas*, regions: Indradwipa, Kasherumat, Tamaravarna, Gabhastimat, Nagadwipa, Saumya, Gandharva, Varuna.

Bharati A name for Saraswati (q.v.).

Bhattara Guru 'Venerable Teacher'. Respectful term of address for the Supreme God, usually Indra or Shiva.

Bhava Existence. A name for Rudra – Shiva as the god of knowledge.

Bhavaja God of Love. (See *Kama.*)

Bhavani (Bhowani). A name for Parvati (q.v.), or Devi-Uma.

Bhikkhu A Buddhist monk, a student of Scripture.

Bhikkhuni A nun. Like monks, nuns make a vow of abstinence.

Bhikshu *Bhikkhu*, a monk or mendicant, literally: a disciple studying Buddhism.

Bhima 'Terrible'. (1) A name for Rudra (q.v.), or Shiva.

(2) The second of the five Pandava brothers, after Yudhisthira. He was the son of Vayu in one myth. He was a giant of great strength, jovial, irascible, fierce, brave, coarse and cruel. He was called Vrikodara 'wolf's belly' because of his appetite. He ate half the family's food, the other half sufficed for his mother and four brothers. He was trained as a warrior in the use of the club by Drona and Balarama; there were strict rules for the use of every weapon. A jealous cousin of his once poisoned Bhima and threw his dead body into the River Ganges, where it sank to the bottom. There, however, it was found and revived by the serpents who lived in the water. He abused Karna, who became an enemy for life. When Purochana conspired to burn the Pandavas in their palace, Bhima, warned in time, burnt Purochana in his own house. He killed the demon Hidimba and married his sister Hidimbaa. He tore the demon Vaka into two pieces and killed so many other demons as well that the Asuras agreed to molest human beings no longer. As son of Vayu the Wind-god, Bhima could fly; he flew to Kubera in the Himalayas with Hanuman. He pursued Jayadratha, who had tried to rape Draupadi, overtook him and beat him till he agreed to be a slave of the Pandavas. Another accoster of Draupadi, Kitchaka, was likewise overtaken by Bhima and beaten into pulp. When Draupadi was sentenced to be burnt, it was Bhima who saved her, disguised as a demon so that the executioners fled. Bhima took a prominent part in the great war of the Mahabharata. On the first day he fought Bhishma. On the second he slew the two princes of Magadha. On the seventeenth day he killed Duhsasana and drank his blood as he had vowed. On the eighteenth and last day he fought Duryodhana and smashed his thigh, again just as he had vowed. The sly King Dhritarashtra invited Bhima to his palace but Krishna quickly made an iron statue in Bhima's stead and placed that before the king, who crushed it in his embrace. Bhima had a son named Ghatotkacha by Hidimbaa, and another named Sarvaga by Balandhara, a princess of Kasi.

Bhimadevi 'The terrifying goddess'. Epithet of Devi–Uma–Kali. (See *Kali*.)

Bhishma 'The Terrible'. Son of King Shantanu and the river-goddess Ganga, so he is also called Gangeya and Nadija 'river-born'. He was a devoted son and faithful half-brother who always kept his word. His old father wanted a young wife, so Bhishma found him one, Satyavati. When her parents objected that their daughter's son, if one was born, would never be king, Bhishma vowed that he would never be king and never marry. So, Shantanu married Satyavati, who bore him two sons. One succeeded as king but was soon killed in battle, the other, Vichitra-virya, was then made king by Bhishma who found two wives for him, princesses of Kasi. Vichitra-virya died young, so Bhishma asked Satyavati's first son (see *Vyasa*) to 'raise seed' for him. Both princesses of Kasi had sons as a result, Dhritarashtra and Pandu. Bhishma brought them up and administered the kingdom of Hastinapura. He also educated their sons, the Kauravas and the Pandavas. When war threatened, Bhishma did his best to keep the peace but when, despite his efforts, it had started, he tried to lay down rules for its mitigation. However he took the side of the Kauravas, who made him their commander-in-chief. On the tenth day of the great battle. Bhishma was goaded into an attack on Arjuna, much against his wish. Arjuna shot so many arrows into his body that the dying Bhishma lay on a couch of arrows all sticking into his back. Since Bhishma could, by divine power, fix the day of his death, he lay thus for 58 days, during which time he gave lectures on morality and other subjects. He had lived a life of altruism, self-denial and fidelity.

Bhogavati 'Full of Treasures'. The voluptuous Nagas or serpents had their capital city, which was full of treasures, in the nether region.

Bhramari 'The Bee'. Epithet of Devi–Uma–Kali. (See *Kali*.)

Bhrigu A high priest (*rishi*) and sage. One of the 10 patriarchs instituted by Manu, sole possessors of the knowledge of how to kindle the sacrificial fire, so that they are closely associated with Agni. Hence the name Bhrigu 'bright'. Such a man alone can perform the ceremony of the sacrifice which keeps mortal men on pacific terms with the immortals. These ancient priests had formidable power and cosmic influence as a result of their controlling the sacrificial rites which regularly kept open the lines of communication between gods and men. Once, when Agastya had been made into a slave by the tyrant Nahusha, Bhrigu crept into Agastya's hair to protect himself from Nahusha's killing eyes. When Nahusha kicked Agastya's head, Bhrigu cursed him, turning Nahusha into a snake. One day the Rishis decided even to test the highest gods, wanting to determine which god was the most deserving of men's worship. Bhrigu was delegated to carry out this hazardous investigation. He went on his way until he found Brahma and approached him, but he did not perform the humble greeting and bowing that is necessary for men when confronting gods. Brahma reprimanded Bhrigu, who quickly did make the necessary gestures, whereupon Brahma forgave him. Next, Bhrigu travelled up into the Himalayas until he finally reached Shiva on Mount Kailasa, seated in profound meditation. Bhrigu tried to catch the god's attention, hoping that the god would not open his third eye, capable of emitting a ray of light-energy that burns to ashes any mortal being standing in its path. Fortunately, Shiva opened his 'normal', eyes, looking disturbed. Bhrigu had to propitiate the god with soothing words and prayers. He then hurried away, down to the depths of the limitless ocean. There Vishnu resided on Shesha the primeval serpent. Vishnu was lingering in his deep pre-creation sleep which may last many thousands of years. Bhrigu kicked the god, trusting in his kindness. He was not mistaken. Vishnu woke up and asked gently, 'Did you hurt your foot?' (He had. A god's body can be like marble.)

This myth is obviously tendentious, created by the priests of Vishnu to prove that his worshippers will be best rewarded.

Another version of this tale goes as follows. Bhrigu went to find Shiva but the god was embracing Parvati and was surrounded by darkness ('Kali'). Having found no access, Bhrigu travelled on to Brahma, who was surrounded by sages and too elevated to be concerned with the worship of mortals. So Bhrigu then went in search of Vishnu, who was asleep as usual. Having seen voluptuousness, arrogance and now sloth, Bhrigu became indignant and stamped on Vishnu's chest. Vishnu, aroused, took Bhrigu's foot in his hand and massaged it, saying that he hoped the honourable Rishi had not hurt his foot and that he was happy and honoured to receive his visit. Thus Bhrigu declared Vishnu to be the only god worthy of worship. The significance of this myth is the moral that a god, to be worthy of worship, must be a model of humility and kindness, like Jesus.

Bhrihad-Aranyaka One of the great Upanishads (q.v.).

Bhu The Earth, a goddess who, before Creation, rested at the bottom of the primeval ocean. Here Brahma found her and raised her to the surface in the shape of a many-petalled lotus flower (*Nymphaea stellata*) which opened magnificently as soon as she reached the light. Brahma Prajapati the Creator, is often depicted seated on the rising lotus absorbed in meditation.

Bhudevi 'The Goddess Earth'. She is shown in art with a blue lotus in her right hand. She is associated with Vishnu. (See *Bhu*; *Bhuvaraha*; *Sita*.)

Bhumi The earth. (See *Bhu*; *Bhuvaraha*; *Prithivi*.)

Bhumisparsha The *mudra* in which the right hand is turned with the palm towards the spectator, touching the ground below the right knee. The Buddha is often sculptured in this *mudra* position which represents the moment when he called the earth to witness (*sparsha*) that he had never interrupted his severe asceticism and was never seduced.

Bhuta A ghost, imp or evil spirit which haunts cemeteries, lurks in trees and deludes people with visions in the night. Bhutas are ghosts of men who died violently and who hate the living. A *bhuta* can enter a corpse so that the dead body 'comes to life', rises up, attacks human beings and devours them, cracking their bones. They speak in a nasal voice which should arouse the suspicion of whoever meets them in a more or less human appearance. The test is that they hate fire, the element of purification which was not used to burn their bodies in the funeral rite. They also have no shadow. The Bhutas' mother is Krodha, 'anger'. They serve Shiva.

Bhuta-Nayaki 'Leader of Demons'. Epithet of Devi–Uma–Kali. (See *Kali*.)

Bhuvaraha This was the episode in Vishnu's *avatara* of Varaha (q.v.) often shown in medieval Indian sculpture such as can be admired at Ellora (q.v.). Vishnu appears as the great Boar of cosmic size, standing up on the bottom of the world ocean, with his snout near the bosom of a comely goddess, Bhu, the Earth. He has just nuzzled her up from the sea bottom where she had been imprisoned by Hiranyaksha, 'Goldeneye', a destructive demon who claimed her for himself and held her at the bottom of the sea. Vishnu descended as Varaha and liberated her by slaying the demon and raising the earth up from the dark depths. She looks joyfully and gratefully at her liberator, standing on the Boar's raised knee. His left leg stands on the sea bottom while his right foot rests on Shesha's head. Bhu, the Earth is clearly an incarnation of Lakshmi, Vishnu's consort in all his earthly existences. As Sita she is also the earth, 'the furrow', rising from, and, at death, returning into, the earth.

Bija-Mantra In the Tantrist tradition, the followers have to repeat certain mantras, formulas which contain compressed magic power. Bija ('seed-pearl') mantras are single syllables, each of which represents a god or goddess, *is* the deity. So, by repeating *klim*, *hrim*, *shrim*, the devotee conjures up the godhead's appearance.

Bodhi 'Awakening', enlightenment. The ultimate goal in life for which every true Buddhist spends many years of austerities. Bodhi comes only to those who have mastered all their thoughts, suppressed their fantasies and who control all their desires, so that they are never jealous, disappointed or angry. Bodhi is the insight that human life is only suffering.

Bodhidharma Buddhist scholar, the first to leave India to teach *dhyana* in China.

Bodhisattva, Bodhisatta A Bodhisattva is, in Buddhism, a person who has achieved complete enlightenment, *bodhi*, and who could, for that reason, enter Nirvana, a state of complete detachment from suffering. Originally the word Bodhisattva, literally 'the one who is destined for Enlightenment', referred to the Buddha before Buddhahood, usually the Buddha in his previous lives. However, out of pure altruism, the Bodhisattvas have decided to postpone their departure and to remain in this world of suffering in order to help and guide the human beings who have not yet attained enlightenment. The Bodhisattvas are often represented in sculpture, often in groups of five, seated in their *dhyana* attitude of profound meditation (except Manjushri and Maitreya, who are often shown seated as kings on a throne). During the evolution of Buddhism, especially in its Mahayana form, the belief arose that there were several Bodhisattvas, the living 'spirits' of those who had been walking on earth once, and who now deferred their complete transience into Nirvana in order to help people. In accordance with the Mahayana principle that ordinary people need the guidance of the Masters of the past on their way to salvation, the Bodhisattvas have been given the function of the saints in Christianity. Buddhist people worship the Bodhisattvas by praying to them in the temples where their statues can be found. These statues are manufactured (in bronze) or sculpted (in stone or wood) according to the fixed rules of Buddhist iconography. The most prominent of the Bodhisattvas are listed below. The first five in the left-hand column are followed by the names of the primal Bodhisattvas whose emanation each is.

Samantabhadra	Vairocana
Vajrapani	Akshobhya
Ratnapani	Ratnasambhava
Padmapani = Avalokiteshvara; Kwan Yin in China)	Amitabha (Amida in Japan)
Vishvapani	Amogasiddhi

The last of the Bodisattvas is Maitreya, who lives in 'heaven' and will descend on earth when the end of times is approaching, to lead all people to salvation.

The Bodhisattvas are the saviours of humanity because of their charity (*karuna*), which has motivated them to suspend their own 'ascension' into Nirvana in order to help other human beings who are still wandering in darkness. They help us because their merit, accumulated by their asceticism, is transferred to lesser humans, and their enlightenment (*bodhi*) helps others to find their way. The basic philosophy feeding this belief is the concept of identity (*tat tuam asi*) according to which we all form part of a cosmic system of merits and faults in which the merits or demerits (i.e. the *karma*) of one being affects those of all the others. Likewise, kindness and compassion may 'flow' from highly advanced beings to those who are anxious to receive it. It is this philosophy which has made Buddhism a world religion. (See *Mahayana*.)

It is difficult to speak about the 'spirit' of Gautama or Buddha in the context of Buddhist beliefs, since the concept of an individual spirit, already complex in Hinduism (see *Atman*; *Spirit*) is purely philosophical in Buddhist thinking. (For the Buddha's previous lives see *Jataka*.) Although he could have entered the state of Nirvana many times during his preceding lives, the Buddha chose to remain on earth and even to be reborn in a new body when his old body died, in order to help the people who lived in ignorance

and needed knowldge of the Way, because their suffering aroused
the Buddha's compassion whenever he saw people erring.

According to another tradition there are eight principal
Bodhisattvas whose names are: Adi-Buddha Vajradhara;
Avalokiteshvara; Inanaketu; Maitreya; Manjushri; Ratnapani;
Vajrapani; Vajrasattva. From these, many other minor
Bodhisattvas have emanated in the way that light reflects ever
further from object to object.

Bonze Japanese for Bhikkhu.

Brahma (1) (First syllable long). A man of the highest caste of
Hindu society, a Brahmin. A Brahmin feels superior to all other
created beings, since they all — animals, foreigners and all people in
India who are not Brahmins — have to await rebirth as Brahmins
before they can hope to break the chain of births and enter into a
higher form of existence. Brahmins enjoy privileges in India, since
many Hindus believe that some Brahmins are gods walking upon
the earth. Brahmins never do manual work except for the
preparation and arrangement of the sacrifice and starting the fire
for the burnt offering. Indeed only the Brahmins can do this;
without their presence and knowledge of the exact rites and correct
formulas no sacrifice is valid. As a result of the invalidity of
sacrifices, the gods will cease to be interested in the human race,
which would lead to disaster. The Brahmins study the Vedas, the
holy scriptures of Hinduism, which they memorize, in so far as it is
necessary, to recite all the correct prayers and hymns during the
ceremonies that form the chain or links between gods and men in
this life. For instance the funerary rites offered by a son to his
deceased father. All Brahmins aspire to be scholars; the cycle of
their lives is fixed thus:

1. *Brahmachari*. The student stage, during which a young man
studies and lives with a Guru and serves him in every way.
2. *Grihastha*. The stage at home during which the Brahmin lives a
married life, raises a family, teaches and officiates.
3. *Vanastha*. The stage at which the Brahmin retires to the forest
vana, which occurs as soon as his eldest son can take over the
responsibilities of the family. There he will study further, meditate,
meet with other scholars who are even higher, more advanced on
the path to enlightenment and disengagement from earthly affairs.
The Brahmin at this stage will live an austere, abstemious life.
4. *Sannyasa*. Having attained complete detachment from the body,
from worldly needs and desires, the old Brahmin returns to the
world to teach but mainly to wander about, living on alms.
Insensitive to pain and hunger, the Brahmin lives in spirititual
union with the deity, until he is completely absorbed by the divine
spirit.

(2) (Last syllable long). God, the Creator, the Supreme Being. The first conscious mind in the universe, who himself grew from the Golden Nucleus (Hiranyagarbha), which germinated after being 'sparked off' by the mysterious First Cause. As Creator, Brahma is called Prajapati, or rather, the two gods have become merged in the course of history. Brahma is the Creator in the sense that he causes the world and all that is in it to exist, but not in the sense that he forms every detail consciously and deliberately, as in Genesis 1. Brahma sleeps while nothing exists. When he awakes, the world takes shape. Some philosophers tell us that when Brahma 'breathes out', the universe comes into existence. Brahma then stays awake for a day, which lasts for two billion human years; after this Brahma gradually falls asleep again, or 'breathes in', which means that the entire phenomenal world will end, will lose its visible form and be withdrawn into the divine essence, everything going back to its own nucleus. The elements from which all the existing beings are composed, each by its own set of laws, remain, as do the spirits, i.e. the individual essences of the gods and sages, the great minds of the universe. They will lie dormant until Brahma awakes once more. Brahma's consort is Sarasvati, the goddess of learning and music, also called Brahmi or Vach (Vac) the goddess Logos, the Word, language. Brahma creates by procreation (as do the other gods), by embracing Vach-Sarasvati, who is also his daughter, but gods do what men may not do. Gods have their own laws. In later literature Brahma does become more the deliberate creator; he created the gods, Soma (moon), Surya (sun) and placed them in the sky. He created Agni (fire), Vayu (wind) and Varuna (water). He placed the Hiranya-garbha, the Golden Seed, in the water where it germinated and became Brahma himself, now in created form. Or it is said that he was a stag and with the doe Rohita, procreated the animals. Furthermore, he became a boar and with his snout pushed up the mountains of the earth. Brahma rides on Hansa, a goose or swan. Brahma, in brief, is every being at the same time as being *in* every being. In Indian art, Brahma is represented with four faces, one looking to each of the points of the compass. These faces represent the four Vedas or books of sacred hymns. Brahma is dressed in the skin of a black antelope. He is seated in the yoga position in a chariot drawn by seven swans. He carries water in a *kamandalu* 'vase, jar' (or *kalasha*, q.v.). He has a rosary for counting the times of the gods and humans. The swans represent the seven *lokas* (worlds or continents). The lotus flower on which Brahma is seated, is *mani*, the earth.

   (3) (Short vowels). Also Brahman, the soul of the universe, self-contained, eternal, from which all existing things emanate and to which they return when they cease their individual existences. This divine essence is immaterial, invisible, uncreated, unlimited, all-pervading. It manifests itself in a million forms within nature, both the living world and the physical cosmos. It lives in all the gods as well as in the smallest creatures on earth. No one worships this

Brahma but the sages meditate upon it until they are completely absorbed by it, gaining complete mental illumination through it.

Brahmachari A Brahmin student, who follows his guru.

Brahmadatta King of Kasi (Varanasi) when the Bodhisattva was born on earth, many generations before he was born as Gautama Buddha.

Brahman See *Brahma*.

Brahmana One of a series of extensive scholarly works said to have been inspired by the gods. They are a series of commentaries on the Veda and Upanishad texts.

Brahmanda 'The egg of Brahma'. The nucleus of world history, the mythical egg out of which past, present and future are steadily being born. (See *Hiranyagarbha*.)

Brahmapura The city of Brahma on Mount Meru in the Himalayas, enclosed by the River Ganges, Brahma's heaven.

Brahma-Purana 'The Old Book of Brahma'. Also called *Adipurana* 'the First Purana.' It is believed that Brahma himself dictated it to the sage Marichi. It is a poem of over 7,000 verses. It begins with the creation of the world by Brahma and continues with a description of the universe, a cosmology. The later chapters deal with the veneration of Vishnu-Krishna as Jagannatha in Orissa and were not composed before AD1200.

Brahmaputra 'The Son of Brahma'. The great river which springs from Mount Kailasa (Kelas) where Shiva resides, then flows east through Tibet (now occupied by the Chinese) past Lhasa, then turns south and finally joins the Ganges in Bengal and Bangladesh to form the earth's largest delta. Thus the son of Brahma and the sister of Parvati are united.

Brahma-Sutra A work on Vedantic philosophy.

Brahma-Yuga The first of the four ages of world history.

Brahmin A man belonging to the priest class, the highest caste. (See *Brahma (1)*.)

Brihaspati Jupiter. Literally the Great Father, the god of the priests, also called Purohita, the family priest. His wife is Tara, who was once abducted by Soma, the Moon-god. A war ensued in which Rudra, the Daityas and Danavas sided with Soma, but Indra supported Brihaspati. This war so distressed the earth, Bhumi, that she appealed to Brahma, who ordered Soma to let Tara go back to her husband. She gave birth to a son and when Brahma questioned her she had to confess that the father of the child was Soma. The child's name was Budha (q.v.). Brihaspati as the Planet Jupiter is called 'the gold-coloured one', 'the shining one'. He rules Thursday.

Buddha Gautama (Gotama) was born *c*.563 BC as the son of Suddhodana the king of Sakya (Shakya), hence his praise-name Sakyamuni 'Sage of Sakya'. His other praise-name is Siddhartha 'the one who has achieved his purpose', as indeed he has in his life. The name Buddha means the Awakened One, i.e. the one who has found insight and enlightenment, *bodhi*, bright wisdom. He is also often referred to as Tathagata — the one who walks the same path as his predecessors, the earlier Buddhas, his previous incarnations. *The* Buddha was the last incarnation of this great teacher, though many believe that he will come back at the end of time, others that he was one of the 10 incarnations of the god Vishnu (q.v.). Some believe that Buddha was an incarnation of the Sun-god.

Numerous myths are related about the birth of the Buddha in human form. How Queen Maya had a dream in which she saw a white elephant descending from heaven; how she saw the full moon landing in her lap, bright and shining. The actual birth took place in a most unearthly way, when the child emerged from her side, signifying his divine origin. Many of these myths have been beautifully represented in sculpture and painting, a sample of which is shown in the illustration at the opening of letter B.

Prince Gautama was born in Kapilavastu, the capital of Shakya just on the southern border of present-day Nepal. In the garden palace of Lumbini his mother Maya had a dream of a white elephant, a royal symbol, entering her side. Some time later, Gautama was born out of her side. The young prince was surrounded by all the luxury of a royal household. When he learned to walk he suddenly took seven steps to the north, east, south and west, signifying his spiritual conquest of the earth. He was trained to handle all the weapons of a warrior, for an Indian ruler had to defend his realm constantly against invaders by force of arms. At 16, in an armed contest, he won his wife Yasodhara, who bore him a son, Rahula. Besides his wife, he had concubines or pleasure girls, like every prince. His father also gave him a chariot of his own. Its driver, or charioteer, Channa, became one of the prince's confidants. Like Krishna, Arjuna's charioteer, he taught his prince many useful things. As they were riding through the city one day, the prince saw a very old man. He asked what had happened to the poor man who was shuffling along leaning on his stick. Channa answered: 'We shall all be like that one day.'

Then, one day, Gautama saw a man who was lying ill and asked what had happened to him. Channa said: 'This suffering comes to all of us.'

On a third day Gautama saw a man who had died. Channa commented: 'That too will happen to all of us.'

Reflecting on all this when he came home, Gautama lost his desire to enjoy the luxuries of his three palaces, even the pleasures of his female companions. He concluded that there was no lasting pleasure in life and decided to live a life of solitude and meditation.

One night he ordered Channa to saddle his faithful horse Kanthaka, and together they left the palace precinct. The gods held the hooves of the Buddha's horse lest their noise wake up the guards. Thus, Prince Gautama's horse walked on the hands of the gods because they favoured the future Buddha. Here, the myth emphasizes that with the rise of Buddhism the gods would lose their status and become servants of the Enlightened One. When he arrived at the edge of the forest, that is, at the end of the cultivated fields and the inhabited world, the Buddha dismounted, said goodbye to his faithful Channa, took off his princely garments, and walked away from the world. He was 29.

He spent six years in the wilderness. As he was meditating in the well-known cross-legged position, *padmasana*, of concentration, *samadhi*, the gods became concerned lest his great will-power and severe abstention would cause the Buddha to accumulate divine status, so they sent Mara, the god of seduction, who told his shapely daughters to perform sensual dances in front of the seated Buddha, but by that time the Enlightened One had all his emotions under complete control, and was unmoved by the erotic prancing of the girls. The vision disappeared and the Buddha completed his meditation. He came to the conclusion that excessive fasting is not useful for the acquisition of merit. Seated under the famous fig-tree, where there is now the sanctuary of Bodhigaya in Bihar, he finally achieved complete *bodhi*, Enlightenment, hence his name. He perceived that desire is the root of all evil, of worry, anger and violence. It is desire that makes us want to live again after death, so that a person who cannot control his desires goes through an endless chain of existences, represented by the 'wheel' *chakra*, symbol of ceaseless repetition. Thus, life moves from birth to death, from being to non-being in a never-ending chain (*samsara*) of suffering (*duhkha*). He who can suppress his desire can break out of the chain and instead of being reborn enter Nirvana after death. At this moment, the Buddha could have passed into the state of Nirvana, ending all suffering for himself. However, he chose instead to go back to the world and preach his new-found wisdom (*prajna*) to the people who needed deliverance (*moksha*) from suffering and desire. Thus, out of compassion (*karuna*) for humanity, the Buddha decided to remain on earth as a teacher (*guru*).

On his way out of the forest he saw a ferocious elephant ready to attack him but the Buddha spoke soothing words to the wild animal, inducing it to feel *metta*, loving-kindness towards his fellow creatures. The great elephant, the king of the forest, knelt down respectfully before the Buddha, honouring the Teacher of all the creatures. Thence, the Buddha walked to Varanasi where, in Sarnath, in the famous deer-park Isipatana, he preached his first sermon. At last he returned to Kapilavastu, and appeared to his own people as the teacher of a new philosophy of life, dressed in yellow robes indicating the sunlight of his wisdom, and surrounded

by his followers. His son Rahula joined him. In his sermon the
Buddha often made use of parables, the first of which was the
comparison of desire to a wildfire.

After 45 years of wandering and preaching the Buddha, at 80,
decided to end his earthly existence and go into Paranirvana, the
highest state of absolute bliss. His last words were: 'All bodies are
composed and so they will one day decompose. You can by your
own effort be freed.' (c.480 BC).

Buddha-Avatara The concept of the Buddha being an incarnation
of Vishnu is not acceptable to the Buddhists. They regard it as a
misguided attempt to fit Buddhism into a small compartment of
Hinduism whereas in fact Buddhism has an entirely different
philosophy in which the many gods play only a subordinate role.

Buddhaghosa Buddhist scholar who lived in Sri Lanka in the fifth
century. He compiled the Theravada in Pali from scattered older
traditions.

Buddhi Intelligence, comprehension, which makes *bodhi*,
enlightenment, possible.

Buddhism Whether Buddhism is in its original form, a religion or,
as some scholars maintain 'only' a philosophy, is a question that
must be left to the philosophers of religion. As the Buddha taught
it, it was a way of life which would lead to salvation, i.e. to the
liberation from suffering, *duhkha*. Life is suffering, therefore the
only way to definitive happiness (*sukha*) is the liberation, *moksha*,
from the repeated imprisonment (*samsara*) of the self in a succession
of bodies, symbolized by the *dharmachakra*, the wheel of destiny, to
which all human beings are chained by their own desire, *trishna*, or
tanha in Pali, also referred to as *lobha*, greed. This desire causes
jealousy, anger and so, hatred, *dosha* (*dosa*) as when a man feels
passion (*kama*) for a woman. All these harmful emotions are the
result of *moha*, stupidity, and *avidya*, ignorance, i.e. entanglement
in the illusory images (*maya*) of this world. The elimination of all
one's desires is therefore the necessary condition for salvation. To
this purpose a man has to obey the Buddha-*dharma*, the law of
Buddha or the Buddha-*sasana*, the teaching of Buddha. Buddha
taught the Eightfold Path, the *Ashtapatha*, i.e. Right Views, Right
Attitude of Mind, Right Speech, Right Conduct, Right Means of
Livelihood, Right Effort or Purpose, Right Mind Control and Right
Meditation or Serenity. This Path leads from selfishness, *ahamkara*
to compassion, *karuna*. Most people have so much desire left at the
end of their lives that their *karma*, their accumulated deeds, will
cause (*karma*, also means causation, action-reaction in physics)
their conscious selves to be reborn in another body and start the
cycle of desire and sorrow all over again by *jati*, birth, *bhava*,
existence and *upadana*, attachedness. The purpose of Buddha's
teaching is to help the suffering millions to break out of this chain

of rebirths, old age, infirmity and death by right living through adherence to the five precepts, the *Pancha Sila*:

1. Refrain from injuring living things.
2. Refrain from taking that which is not given.
3. Refrain from all forms of *kama*, sexual desire.
4. Refrain from all falsehood, in word and deed.
5. Refrain from worldly enjoyments: no drugs, no drink, no sloth.

The Buddhist should ultimately strive to raise himself to a state of *brahmavihara*, divine dwelling by observing the four rules of:

1. *Metta*, loving kindness; as a result of his complete understanding of his fellow beings the Buddhist regards them as his own kin whose suffering he knows.
2. *Karuna*, compassion. The knowledge that we are all part of the union of existence and the resulting understanding of all living beings, leads to our wish to help them in their suffering.
3. *Mudita*, sympathetic joy. Buddha said repeatedly: 'Let all be happy.' Gladness should be shared with all those who are in need of it. There should never be hatred or jealousy. Each of us can become a Buddha and approach our fellow beings with the mood of empathetic harmony that causes Buddhas to smile.
4. *Upekkha (Upeksha)*, equanimity. Nothing must be allowed to disturb the crystal clarity of the Buddhist mind. All strong emotions are harmful; suffering is to be expected anyway; death is not frightening for those who are not attached to life. A Buddhist fears no enemies since he hates no one.

Such are the rules of life for the Buddhist. Its purpose is Nirvana (Nibbana) the state of neither being nor not-being, that is the state of being without opposites. As long as there are opposites there are conflicts, there is a chain of action and reaction, and a man is the slave of *karma*, the endless causation of further reactions in contrast to existing things. So, Buddhism is the opposite of Marxism: the endless reactions of thesis and antithesis leading to 'necessary' revolutions must be overcome and replaced for every individual by a state of perfect calm and serenity of neither desire nor negativity: the only possible state of perfect peace in which even the individual dissolves into perfect unity with the universe.

Although Buddha preached to individuals at first, soon his followers began to organize themselves in a *sangha*, community, which grew into a *vihara*, a monastery, as several rich persons gave the young Buddhist community land and buildings to live in. When the Buddha died there were already several established monasteries. The young men entering them become *bhikshus* (*bhikkhus*) 'disciples, students'. After they have been *samaneras*, novices, for some years, they take a vow to abstain from all luxuries and to obey the rules of the *sangha*. They do not have to vow to remain monks forever: they may relinquish the monastic life whenever they wish. They are ruled by the Elders (*Sthavira*, *Thera*) who are in turn administered by the *Mahathera*, the Eldest. They are mendicants, i.e. they go out daily with their begging bowls to receive food from the villagers, even though the monasteries often own good land. They spend their days meditating, reciting Buddha's teachings and teaching the *dharma*. In India, Buddhism declined during the Muslim invasions of the Middle Ages, but today it is rapidly gaining adherents. Not all Buddhists are philosophers who can understand the beautiful logic of this 2,500-year-old system of thought which is still an inspiration for intellectuals in both East and West. The common people in the Buddhist countries have turned Buddhism into a real religion, no longer applying its pure logic in their lives, but worshipping the Buddha as a god, and the Bodhisattvas as demigods beside him. They came to regard the Buddha as a benign, compassionate Saviour to whom prayers are due and for whom joss-sticks are burnt, for whom temples were built and whose relics (e.g. his teeth) are kept religiously in reliquaries. Tantrism (q.v.) has created a new branch of Buddhism by introducing magic and quasi-erotic images and practices. Some Buddhists even believe in a heaven for the virtuous and a hell for the wicked, a totally alien concept to the original Buddhism.

Budha The planet Mercury. Budhavara is Wednesday, French Mercredi, 'Mercury-day'. English Wednesday is originally Wodansday, because Wodan was identified with Mercury, the Greek Hermes, the god of occult wisdom. Budha = wisdom. Budha was the son of Soma and Tara who may be identified with Hera–Juno. Budha's wife is Ila, a woman who becomes a man every other month. Buddha's influence is neither favourable nor nefarious, but can only be assessed in relation to that of the other planets. According to some scholars, Brihaspati is Budha's true father.

Buffalo The vehicle of the goddess Chamunda when fighting demons. (See also *Yama*.)

Bundahishn Old Persian for Creation. (See *Zoroastrianism*.)

C

Chandraprabha

Caste See *Varna, Dwija*.

Chadanta One of the appearances of the Bodhisattva in a previous life. As Chadanta he had the form of a white elephant who had six tusks and two wives. One of his wives was jealous of the other, so she prayed that she might be reborn as a human princess. She was, and when she came of age she was married to the king of Varanasi. As soon as she was queen she, remembering her previous life, called all the king's huntsmen and ordered them to find a white elephant with six tusks and bring her back the tusks. One of the hunters, Sunottara, caught Chadanta in a pit-trap. The hunter tried to kill him but the elephant asked him: 'What wrong have I done?'

The hunter replied: 'The queen desires your tusks.'

Chadanta then remembered that this queen was once his wife. Now she wanted him dead. He lay down resigning himself to his fate. The hunter started sawing the tusks but the ivory was too hard. So, Chadanta did the work for him, taking the saw in his trunk and sawing off his own beautiful tusks for his jealous ex-wife. Finally he collapsed in a pool of his own blood. The queen too died when she was told of what had happened.

Chaitanya A guru of the nineteenth century, believed to be an incarnation of Krishna, i.e. Vishnu.

Chaitya Buddhist *stupa*, which distinguishes Maitreya's headdress.

Chakra Wheel, symbol of the sun, which is often depicted with a hub and spokes. It was given by Shiva to Vishnu as a weapon to destroy the demons. Vishnu throws it in such a way that it emits sparks while rotating. It never misses its mark.

Chakravala 'Circular Enclosure'. The Buddhist universe divided into three sections: the 136 hells below, the 26 heavens above and in between the worlds of the animals, ghosts, demons and people. The centre is Mount Meru.

Chakra-Varti 'The wielder of the wheel' (i.e. the orbis of the entire world). The universal emperor. No man has the right in Hindu myths to claim the empire of the earth as his right unless he has Vishnu's *chakra* (disk) in his hand at birth, or is born with the disk of the full moon shining on his forehead or on his chest, as a clear sign to all humanity that the gods wish him to rule.

Chakshusha Son of Tvashtar, the sixth Manu.

Chamunda The goddess Durga in her manifestation as slayer of the demons Chanda and Munda. She is black with blood-red eyes and her tongue hangs out of her wide-open mouth. She is armed with sword, mace and noose and is clad in an elephant skin. (See also *Parvati*.)

Chanakya See *Kautilya*.

Chanda, Chandi, Chandika 'Fierce'. Durga-Kali as a terrifying goddess when she slays Mahisha.

Chandaka, Channa Buddha's charioteer in Kapilavastu.

Chandra The Moon, a male deity. In India the moon is inhabited by a hare, Shasha. (See *Soma*.)

Chandragupta Founder of the Maurya dynasty, grandfather to Ashoka.

Chandra-Kanta 'Moon-stone'. A precious stone of clear transparency but with a blueish-white or silvery colour. I never met anyone who had seen it, but it is said that it is formed by concentration of moonrays falling on the surface of a pond of absolutely pure and crystal-clear water. It has to be recovered at midnight by a diver valiant enough to brave the water-nymphs who live in the pond and who might put a spell on the intruder. Moonstone is much sought after by Indian doctors since it has a soothing effect on feverish patients, cooling throbbing headaches and other symptoms.

Chandraprabha The eighth of the 24 Tirthankaras (literally 'fordmakers'), trailblazers or forerunners of the Jain religion.

Chandraprabha is the Lord of the Moon and ruler of the present age. He also accompanies the Bodhisattva Manjushri. In sculpture, Chandraprabha is represented with five faces: the new moon, the first quarter, the full moon in the middle, and on the other side the last quarter and the waning crescent.

Chandra-Vamsa The Lunar Race. In epic times three great clans claimed descent from the moon (Soma, son of Atri), the Yadavas, the Pauravas and the kings of Kasi. Their ancestors were respectively: Yadu, Puru and Kshatravriddha, great-great grandsons of Budha (q.v.) son of Soma (q.v.).

Chanura A wicked wrestler employed by Kansa (q.v.). Krishna slew him.

Charaka A famous medical scholar who lived in Vedic times, believed to be an incarnation of the sea-serpent Shesha. He received his vast knowledge from Agnivesha, son of the Fire-god Agni. His famous book on medicine was translated into Arabic.

Charumati A daughter of Krishna and Rukmini.

Charvaka A wicked Rakshasa who fought a battle in the Mahabharata and entered Hastinapura in triumph. However, the Brahmins discovered he was an impostor so they killed him with the deadly rays from their eyes.

Chatur-Bhuja 'Four-armed'. (See *Vishnu*.)

Chaturanga The chess game. Literally, the four corners, referring to the four divisions of a traditional Indian army: the infantry (pawns from peons, pedons 'foot-troops'), the cavalry, the archers (now called 'bishops' because of a misinterpretation of their medieval helmets) and the elephants which used to carry wooden structures on their backs called 'castles', from which the warriors could take aim at the enemy. In Europe the elephants were omitted, but the remaining 'castles' were still moved across the board as the elephants had been, even though the true 'castle' in chess is formed by the 'rochade' move (castling).

Chetana 'Consciousness'. In Buddhism this is the source of individualism and so, of desire which leads to sin, because desires never stop luring.

Chhaya 'Shade'. A handmaid of the Sun. Sanjana, the Sun's wife, was overcome by her husband's heat, so she told Chhaya to take her place. The Sun-god begot three children by her: Shani, the planet-god Saturn, Savarni and a girl, Tapati. Chhaya loved her children so much that when death (Yama) came, she cursed him, so his leg became worm-eaten. According to some, Chhaya was Sanjna's sister.

Chinta-Mani 'Thought-gem'. The philosophers' stone, made by the god Brahma himself. It is also called Divya-ratna 'divine-jewel'. It contains all the world's knowledge.

Chinvat The Bridge to Paradise in the Parsi religion. It is very narrow except for the virtuous souls who have kept their thoughts, words and deeds pure. Others will be vexed by evil monsters as they try to climb up the endlessly long and high bridge.

Chitrakuta 'Bright Peak'. The modern city of Chitrakote stands on the River Pishuni. It has numerous temples and shrines. Its history is closely linked to Rama and Sita, who took refuge here at the hermitage of the great poet Valmiki.

Chitratha King of the Gandharvas.

Chola Name of a dynasty of kings in South India. Their kingdom was called Chola-mandala, hence 'Coromandel'.

Churning the Ocean See *Kurma*; *Lakshmi*; *Shesha-Vasuki*; *Vishnu*.

Chyavana Chyavana was one of those mysterious sages whose fame goes back to Vedic times. They are demigods. Puloma, wife of Bhrigu, was pursued by a demon and while she was running a baby fell out of her womb but survived and was called Chyavana, 'the one who fell'. When he came of age, Chyavana began to perform asceticism by standing motionless for many months until his body became shrivelled and white ants had built their anthills all around him. One day an inquisitive girl, Sukanya, a princess, peered through a hole in the anthill and saw two eyes looking at her. Not realizing they were human eyes, she put her hand through the hole to grab those shining objects. The sage, disturbed, demanded satisfaction from her father, King Saryata, who agreed to give Sukanya to Chyavana as a wife. Since she was very beautiful, she attracted the attention of the Ashvins, the twin gods (Gemini), who approached her as two good-looking young horsemen, hoping to seduce her, saying that her husband was too old to give her children. She remained faithful to her husband and told them:
'You Ashvins are not even proper gods!'
'How can we become gods?' they asked.
'How can my husband become young?' she asked.
It was agreed that they would exchange answers. The Ashvins took Chyavana to a secret pond where the old sage bathed and became a young man again. He in his turn told them: 'You are excluded from the sacrifices given to the other gods, but I will sacrifice to you now.'
This transgression enraged Indra, the Supreme God, who arrived to bury Chyavana under a mountain. Unafraid, Chyavana created a huge monster which took Indra gently in its mouth, with the mountain still in his hand. So enormous was this monster, whose name was Mada, that Indra the great God, was swimming like a fish in the saliva under the monster's tongue, together with the other

gods. The entire earth and the sky were also in the monster's mouth. Not surprisingly, Indra granted the wishes of Chyavana, and the Ashvins were permitted to drink Soma, the wine of immortality.

Cremation See *Dahakriya.*

D

Durga

Dadhicha, Dadhyancha Son of Atharvan. A famous scholar who was taught by Indra himself on condition that he would never part with the secret divine knowledge he possessed, or risk losing his head. The two Ashvins, hoping to become gods, prevailed upon Dadhyancha to teach them and in order to prevent him from losing his head they took it off, kept it in a safe place and put a horse's head on his shoulders. Soon, Indra appeared and struck the horse's head off. Happily, the Ashvins put the human head back on the sage's neck. Indra used the skull of the horse's head to defeat the Asuras.

Daeva, Diu, Div Spirit, usually wicked, in old Persian mythology. In its modern form, as *diew* or *div*, the word denotes a fantastic being, like the Arabic *jinn*, capable of taking any shape (especially in Pakistan).

Dagoba, Dagarba Originally Dhatugarbha, literally 'womb of objects', i.e. a repository of relics, of the Buddha, around which a *stupa*, later a temple was built and around which a *vihara* arose. (See *Temple.*) 'Dagoba' later became 'pagoda'.

Dahakriya, Dahasanskara Cremation of the deceased. In ancient times dead people were just left in the bush where wild animals and

birds would eat them. Later, it seems that dogs were pemitted to eat
their dead masters' flesh. In the oldest historical times the Aryans
buried their dead; mighty kings were buried with their wives,
slaves, horses and chariots. It is said that widow-burning (*suttee*, see
Sati) is a relic of this custom. Cremation of the body is symbolic for
the dissolution of all flesh into its constituting atoms or elements
according to Hindu philosophy, which teaches that composition
and decomposition is Brahma's breathing: he creates and dissolves
alternately. For the Persian fire-worshippers and many Hindus as
well, fire is the element that purifies (indeed 'Purifier' is one of
Agni's names). So, burning the dead is an alternative to casting the
bodies in the holy rivers Ganga and Jumna (Yamuna) which also
have a purifying and sanctifying power (Yamuna is the sister of the
god of the dead, Yama, and Ganga is a sister of Parvati). When a
man has died, particular herbs are strewn on his body (Basilicum)
and clay from the Ganges should be applied to it, while certain
hymns of the Veda are being chanted. Wreaths of flowers will cover
the body, which is carried by the nearest relatives (preferably the
sons of the deceased) to the place for the funerary pyre. The fire
must be lit from the consecrated fire which the deceased should
have maintained while alive. The attendant priest should pray to
Agni as follows: 'Fire! You have been lit by him, may he therefore
be brought forth from you again, may his soul attain celestial bliss
for all eternity.'

All the mourners who followed the bier will walk around the fire
three times but they may not look into it. Afterwards they will
proceed to the river and, after bathing, they will present oblations
with their cupped hands to the souls of the dead, reciting: 'May this
oblation reach you.'

Hymns like the following are sung:

> Only a fool believes this life will last for ever
> It will soon disappear like foam on ocean waves.
> A body, which is made of the five elements, when it dissolves
> again into five elements, what reason to lament?

If the proper rituals are observed, the souls of the ancestors will
cause prosperity to their descendants, while the living may save the
dead from hell by pious works. In antiquity some peoples believed
that the fire gave a man immortality and youth if he survived a bath
in it.

Daitya One of a race of Titans, the sons of Diti, a formidable
goddess, and Kasyapa. They were gigantic demons who made war
against the gods, pressing them hard more than once. They are
similar to Danavas.

Dakini One of a species of female demons, who serve Kali. They
thrive on human flesh, so they are called Ashrapa 'drinkers of
blood'.

Daksha 'Brilliant'. The Divinized Spiritual Power. Son of Brahma, leader of the Prajapatis; a patriarch. Daksha was a demigod who was born and killed in every generation. He was instructed by Brahma to create all the creatures that move as well as the immobile ones; those that are born from sloughed skin (snakes), from eggs (birds), from sprouts (plants) and from sweat (insects). He made Gandharvas, ghosts, Yakshas, animals — wild and tame. Daksha emerged from Brahma's right thumb, his wife Prasuti from Brahma's left thumb. They had 24 daughters, of whom 10 married the god Dharma and 13 married Kasyapa. They became the mothers of gods, demons, men, birds, reptiles and of all other living beings. One daughter, Sati, was an incarnation of Uma, so she became the wife of Shiva and later mounted a pyre and burnt herself. The second time Daksha was born, he was the son of the moon-daughter, Marisha. In that life he had seven sons, including Krodha 'anger' and Tamas 'darkness'. Some scholars relate that Daksha was continually reborn because he was cursed by Shiva, his son-in-law. Others narrate that it was Vishnu who was incarnated through him, in order to create all living beings. Yet others believe that Daksha, who was the first man, recreated himself as a woman, whom he liked so much that he married her. They had many beautiful daughters, who married the Moon-god Soma and became his light-days. Daksha instituted a great sacrifice for the gods, but Shiva, incensed because he deemed his share too small, shot an arrow through this original sacrifice so that the world trembled. Hastily the priests agreed to enlarge Shiva's share. Another version of this myth relates that Narayana (Vishnu) was hit by Shiva's trident, almost causing a cosmic war to start but Brahma reconciled the two gods, who were, in 'fact', identical to him. The Purana text relates that Shiva was not invited to this first sacrifice. He became so angry that he created Virabhadra, a ferocious demon of colossal size who rushed to the altar and scattered the gods who were there to receive the sacrifice as invitees of Daksha. Chandra, the Moon-god was beaten in the face so badly that the bruises are still visible! Daksha quickly propitiated Shiva and acknowledged his supremacy. Shiva thus pacified, called the monster Virabhadra off and restored all the victims of its rage to their former status. However, the version of the Vishnu-worshippers is different: they relate that Vishnu seized Shiva by the throat, telling him to stop the raging monster, which was only a materialization of his (Shiva's) wrath, and to acknowledge Vishnu as a superior.

Dakshina (1) A present made to a Brahmin as an honorarium for officiating at a sacrifice as a priest. Also the name of a goddess. (2) 'Right, competent, liberal'. Praise-name of Vishnu (q.v.).

Dakshina-Murti 'Facing South', a name of Shiva as teacher of all the yogis while he is seated on Mount Kailasa looking towards India at his feet. He teaches the *Shastras* as well as music.

Dalai Lama Da-Lai-La-Ma literally means 'Great Ocean Superior One'. When Tibet was an independent state, the Dalai Lama was its ruler, ever since Tibet ceased to be a kingdom. It has been said that the Dalai Lama was not democratically elected, but a ruler does not have to be elected to be acceptable to his followers. As the Pope is elected by the cardinals, so the Dalai Lama was elected by the Regent and Council who used to govern Tibet during the time after a Dalai Lama had died and until the new Dalai Lama came of age. The Dalai Lama was not (unlike the Pope) chosen from among the electors, but was chosen from among the Tibetan people on the basis of a complex set of qualifications. The state investigators may have to visit distant villages in order to find the one child who was born at exactly the right time after the demise of the last Dalai Lama. He had to have certain features of appearance and character in common with the deceased ruler, and furthermore, the child had to show he recognized some of the objects which the old Dalai Lama once possessed. This would assure the Council and the people that the old 'spirit' of the Dalai Lama had indeed returned to this world in a new body, as a child. This child would then be taken to the Potala palace in Lhasa and be educated with the greatest care so that he would be well prepared for his task as leader of the Buddhists of the world. Unlike the Pope, the Dalai Lama does not have to be obeyed and many groups of Buddhists have their own doctrines and rules of life. Nevertheless, the Dalai Lama has enormous prestige as a spiritual master and millions gladly accept his authority on matters of belief, doctrine, morality and daily conduct. The present Dalai Lama, though exiled from the Potala, his 'cathedral', is universally recognized as a religious leader of the first rank, a great scholar and a spirit endowed with profound charisma.

Dama Descendant of King Marutta whose father left his throne to Dama when he retired to the forest. There he was killed by the demon Vapushmat, who was later slain by Dama. Dama rescued his bride Sumana.

Damayanti A princess, wife of King Nala, one of the great characters of the Mahabharata, even though she appears only in one of the moralistic tales told by a saint to King Yudhisthira. The leading theme of the tale is her loyalty, devotion and virtue, a theme of which Indian writers are still very fond. She was the daughter of King Bhima of Vidarbha. She is described as having very fine features, graceful and of rare beauty, 'like lightning shooting through the clouds'; perhaps she was an incarnation of Sri Lakshmi — Sita.

While talking to her ladies-in-waiting she heard of the handsome King Nala and decided she wanted to marry him. Once, as they were playing near a lake, a flamingo walked up to Damayanti and spoke to her with a human voice about King Nala's secret love for her. Damayanti asked the beautiful bird to tell the king that her feelings were the same towards him. The flamingo promised to carry her message to King Nala and flew away. Thus Nala and Damayanti were destined for one another. Since that day Damayanti could think of nothing else, so that she became pale and thin. Her friends went to her father, King Bhima, and told him this. King Bhima perceived that it was time for her *svayamvara*, the great feast held by the Indian kings of antiquity during which their daughters were permitted to select the prince of their choice from the invited noblemen. Riding chariots, horses or even elephants, the rulers of the Indian kingdoms arrived. Not only rajas came, even the gods Indra, Agni and Varuna appeared, such was the fame of Damayanti's virtue and beauty. The gods saw Nala and told him to instruct Damayanti that she should choose one of them, a god. Nala protested but Indra simply commanded Nala to enter the woman's quarters of the palace, invisible to the guards through Indra's protection. Thus Nala suddenly appeared in front of Princess Damayanti in all his male beauty and informed her of the will of the gods. But precisely by sending Nala to Damayanti the gods had made her even more determined to choose that handsome man as her husband. She did, even though all the gods had disguised themselves as Nala. She even prayed to them to resume their true shape, which they did, for the gods play fair. Now she could see that no sweat appeared on their foreheads nor did they suffer from gravity: their 'bodies' floated in the air. The gods had garlands round their necks, made of flowers that never wilted, and they never blinked: their eyes were always open, nor did they have any dust on their 'bodies'. She could now recognize Nala as the one human being among them. Damayanti chose Nala by hanging a garland of fresh flowers round his neck. This was an act of great courage, for not only the gods, but the many powerful maharajas who were present, could also have taken their revenge. However, the gods played fair again: they congratulated the bridegroom and sent presents for the wedding. Agni and Varuna promised that Nala would always have fire and water if he wanted it but that he would never be burnt or drowned by their two elements. Thus Nala and Damayanti were married. Damayanti gave birth to twins: a boy Indrasena and a girl, Indraseni.

Kali, who was a demon (no connection with the goddess Kali, q.v.), had also intended to marry Damayanti, but he arrived too late. Furious, he decided upon revenge. He went to Nala's palace and stayed there, invisible, for 12 years, lurking until he saw his opportunity: Nala forgot, for once, his ablutions before his evening prayers, and at once Kali had power over him. The demon made Nala covet the game of dice (in reality the nut *vibhidaka* is used for this complicated game) and when his no-good brother Pushkara

invited him to a game, Nala gambled away all his possessions,
including his palace and his kingdom, while Damayanti stood there
imploring him with tears in her eyes to stop. He ignored her, but
when he was sent into exile by his merciless brother, she followed
him into the wilderness as a faithful wife. She had already sent her
two children away to the safety of her father's palace, seeing her
husband's addiction to the gambling nuts. Pushkara, now king,
decreed that no citizen was allowed to give food or shelter to Nala
and Damayanti who were now refugees and outcasts. Dejected,
Nala humbly proposed to Damayanti that she should go back to her
father's palace, while he should join the hermits in the hills who
lived on wild fruits. Damayanti would not hear of it, saying: 'There
is no better medicine for a sad man than a good wife. I would be
ashamed of myself if I did not stay with you in poverty.'

That night they found an empty hut in the forest and, overcome
by fatigue, they fell asleep there. That night Nala deserted
Damayanti, hoping she would go back to Vidarbha once she found
herself to be alone, for he was too ashamed to share his poverty with
her and because the demon still had power over him.

In the 11th canto of the epic, Damayanti sings a sad lament after
waking up and finding herself deserted. Walking through the forest
alone she sings of her fears of the wild animals. At last she came
upon the hermitage of two virtuous ascetics, who predicted that her
life would one day be happy again. However, it was only *maya*, an
illusion which vanished leaving Damayanti alone again in the
forest. Finally she joined a caravan, but when in the encampment
all the tents were upset by a herd of mad elephants, she was accused
of bringing ill luck upon the travellers, many of whom had been
trampled to death. At last Damayanti arrived in the city of Chedi
where King Subahu ruled. The king's mother happened to look out
over the square from a palace balcony and saw this tired young
woman dressed in a torn sari, surrounded by mocking children. Yet
she seemed so noble and even familiar. The Queen Mother ordered
a lady-in-waiting to go and invite the young woman into the palace.
When she arrived the Queen Mother asked Damayanti to tell her
who she was and how she had come to be in Chedi. Damayanti told
her story without giving her husband's name. When she was offered
the position of lady-in-waiting to the princess Sunanda, she made
three conditions: 'I must never be forced to eat other people's leftovers, to wash other people's feet, or to speak to unknown men.'

Meanwhile, Damayanti's father, King Bhima of Vidarbha, called
his Brahmins together and asked them to go in search of his
daughter and son-in-law. Indian rajas used to employ Brahmins
whose profession it was to gather knowledge about people and
countries. One of these Brahmins, Sudeva, arrived in Chedi. As is
good custom, he paid his homage to the king in the palace. There he
saw the king's daughter Sunanda and her lady-in-waiting,
Damayanti. Sudeva recognized Bhima's daughter at once. He

addressed her thus: 'My name is Sudeva, I am one of the hundred Brahmins whom your father, King Bhima, sent out in search of you. Your father and mother are both in good health, so are your three brothers and your two children: they are growing up prosperously.'

Tears streamed down Damayanti's cheeks when she recognized the old man, her father's counsellor. At the Queen Mother's behest, the Brahmin told her the story of Damayanti, except of course of her adventures in the forest. He added that Damayanti could be recognized by the tiny crescent on her forehead with which she had been born. Sunanda rubbed off the ashes, which Damayanti had put on her face as a sign of despondency and to avoid questions. Sure enough, the crescent was there on her forehead. The Queen Mother embraced Damayanti because Damayanti's mother was her sister. She invited her to stay but of course Damayanti begged permission to go home to her father's palace, to rejoin her parents and her children. King Subahu ordered a company of armed men to escort her palanquin. As soon as Damayanti had arrived home and had embraced all her loved ones, she asked her father to renew the search for her husband. The king agreed and soon the Brahmins were on their way again with precise instructions. One of the Brahmins, Parnada, returned to Damayanti to tell her that he had met a deformed charioteer who had told him how he had lost his wife . . . 'and it was exactly your story, princess!'

Deeply moved, Damayanti decided to hold a second *svayamvara*. She told the trusted Sudeva to go and tell the king who employed the deformed charioteer that Princess Damayanti was preparing a maiden-choice at which she would select a second husband, the first one having disappeared long ago. The king, Rituparna by name, called his charioteer (Nala) who selected the best horses and drove to Vidarbha with such speed that the chariot took off and flew over the forest. When they arrived at Vidarbha, Nala's own horses, who were in King Bhima's stable, could smell their master and neighed joyfully. Damayanti, hearing this, knew that her husband had arrived. When King Rituparna told King Bhima that Damayanti had proclaimed a *svayamvara* which was the reason for his arrival, the latter was very surprised since his own daughter had left him ignorant of the fact, and so, unprepared for any guests. Meanwhile, Damayanti sent her maid, Keshini, to watch the charioteer closely. Keshini went and soon came back excited: she had seen that the charioteer did not have to light a fire, it lit itself for him. When he needed water for his ablutions, his jars filled themselves. Then Damayanti gave Keshini a dish telling her: 'Go and ask the charioteer to give you a piece of the meat he is cooking.'

In those days it was quite normal for a king to entrust the cooking of a royal meal to his own charioteer since no one else could be trusted. So, the disguised Nala gave Keshini a piece of the meat he had prepared. As soon as Damayanti tasted it, she knew that only her husband could have cooked it, as it tasted so good. She wept and then she called her two children to her saying: 'Go to the man who is cooking outside the stable gate and say ''Father'' to him.'

When Nala saw them, he too wept. Keshini brought the children back and reported what she had witnessed. Now, Damayanti asked her parents' permission to invite the charioteer into her room, to which request they consented. Nala, still in his deformed state, appeared. Damayanti asked him: 'Do you know King Nala who left his faithful wife behind in the forest?'

He answered: 'It was not my fault, I was possessed by the devil Kali. But how is it possible that Queen Damayanti wants to choose a new husband? Has she forgotten Nala?'

Trembling, Damayanti knelt down at his feet: 'Forgive me, it was only a ruse necessary to get Nala to come here. Only Nala can make the horses run 100 miles in a day. Have you forgotten that I chose Nala, spurning even the gods! I swear by the Wind-god that I have always been faithful to you.'

Suddenly they heard the voice of the Wind-god: 'She speaks the truth, O King Nala. Hold her close to your heart!'

Nala, deeply moved, resumed his own shape, helped by Indra. Seeing her husband in his old splendour, Damayanti cried out aloud and embraced him lovingly, having missed him so much throughout their long separation.

Damodara Tied with a rope (*dama*) around his belly (*udara*). A nickname of Krishna whom his foster mother so tied, when he had secretly eaten the butter.

Damodbhava A king who was so proud that he attacked the sage Nara with his army. The sage picked up pieces of straw and threw them up in the air, where they multiplied and sharpened until the sky was white with the flying projectiles. These hit the soldiers in their eyes until the king fell down at Nara's feet and begged for grace.

Danavas A race of titans, giants who battled against the gods. Similar to Daityas.

Dandaka A vast forest which once stood to the south of the Yamuna river. It was full of Rakshasas and wild beasts. Many hermits, too, lived there in solitude under the trees. Rama and Sita experienced many adventures in Dandaka.

Danu The mother of the Danavas, wife of Kasyapa.

Darsana, Darshana 'Demonstration, teaching, doctrine'. One of six schools of Hindu philosophy, including Yoga and Sankhya.

Dasa, Das Slave, servant. One of a race of black, snub-nosed infidel demons who hate gods and people. Kalidas(a) means a slave of Kali.

Dasha-Bhuja 'Ten-armed'. A name of Devi-Durga. (See *Durga*.)

Dasharatha, Dasarata Son of Aja of the Solar Race, king of Ayodhya. He had three wives but no sons. He performed the horse-sacrifice, after which the first queen (the senior wife Kausalya) lay near the slaughtered horse for a night with the other two queens beside her. After the sacrifice Vishnu appeared to Dasharatha in radiant effulgence and gave him a vessel full of nectar to divide between his wives. Dasharatha gave half of the nectar to his senior wife and a fourth each to Kaikeyi and Sumitra; the latter divided her share again into two portions. The nectar was the divine essence itself. In due course the three queens gave birth to four sons. Kausalya bore Rama, Kaikeyi bore Bharata, after which Sumitra, the youngest queen, gave birth to Lakshmana and Satrughna. Rama received half of the essence of Vishnu, Bharata a quarter and the twins shared an eighth each. All this was the consequence of a promise made by Vishnu that he would destroy the evil demon Ravana. (See *Ashvamedha*, *Avatara*, *Bharata* (3).)

Dasras 'Handsome'. One of the two Ashvins (q.v.).

Dasya Service, devotion as worship, out of love. This is the true feeling of Krishna's devotees towards their god, the essence of religion.

Dasyus Evil beings, enemies of people and even of the gods. They look like people but they are dark and ugly, robbers and thugs.

Dattatreya The incarnation of the Hindu Trinity. Anasuya was a lady of perfect virtue. She married the sage Atri Maharishi, and adored her husband. She performed severe austerities for a long time until not one but three gods appeared to her: Brahma, Shiva and Vishnu, disguised as *sannyasins* (ascetics). They asked the good lady what she would like to have and she replied: 'Three sons, one like Brahma, one like Shiva and one like Vishnu.'

The three gods fulfilled her wish there and then by becoming three boy babies. Suddenly Anasuya felt milk flowing into her breasts. When her husband arrived she did not have to explain anything since he knew everything already. He embraced his three sons together. They then became one child with two feet, three heads and six arms. The three gods told Atri Maharishi that this three-headed child would grow up to become a great sage who would possess the combined knowledge and power of the three gods. Dattatreya was soon worshipped by many sages and taught the Vedanta doctrine of Self-realization. He was a person of gentle, peaceful and loving character. His *Jayanti* (birthday) is celebrated on the full moon in the month of Margasirsha.

One day, Dattatreya was asked why he was so happy and cheerful. Here is part of his answer:

The Earth taught me patience and generosity.

The Ocean taught me to remain the same in spite of storms.
The Fire taught me to give myself so that I would shine brightly.
The Air taught me to move freely anywhere and not stay in one
    place.
The Water taught me how much purity is needed for good
    health.
The Sky taught me to be above everything and yet embrace all
    things.
The Moon taught me that the Self remains the same even when
    the appearance changes.
The Sun taught me that a luminous face is reflected by all smooth
    surfaces.
The Dove taught me that love means feeding one's family.
The Bee taught me to collect sweet wisdom from places where no
    one suspected it to be.
The Arrow-maker taught me to be purposeful and always
    concentrate to one point.
The Snake taught me to be content to live in a hole or cave and
    build no house.
The Fish taught me never to take the bait and so destroy myself.
The Owl taught me to sit peacefully and be content with little
    food.

Death Mrityu, is a goddess born from the fire of Brahma's wrath
when he saw that there were too many people burdening the Earth
so that she complained to Brahma. Death was told by him that she
must kill all creatures immediately, but she refused, saying that she
would do nothing unjust, *adharma*. Brahma who created all life,
answered that it is only just for all creatures to die. Since then Death
became the companion of Dharma (q.v.). Only the gods are *amara*,
immortal. Yama (q.v.) is the ruler of the dead.

Deluge See *Vaivasvat*.

Demons As in most countries of Asia and Africa, numerous
demons inhabit secret places in India, where they are referred to not
by a collective term like 'demon' but by a specification, such as
Asura, Danava, Pishacha, Gandharva, Rakshasa, Yaksha or Dasyu.
The Jains have different demons, (see *Heli*); many of the Buddhists'
demons have non-Indian names, they are Tibetan, Burmese, etc.
Some demons are just imps and evil sprites of little power who can
make a nuisance of themselves by teasing us, to try our patience.
Others are races of sexually voracious devils, like the Gandharvas
and their female counterparts the Apsaras, who will seduce lonely
travellers of the opposite sex and generate offspring of doubtful
humanity with them. The Yakshas live in the forest with their
females the Yakshis. They are not really dangerous, just delusive.
Yakshis can appear as lovely naked women who, when the traveller
has followed them into the dense forest, will change into trees so

that he has lost his way and his illusions as well. The Asuras are by far the most dangerous and the most powerful demons, they are a race of anti-gods, as their name implies, who will wage war against the Devas, the good gods, and often almost win. The Rakshasas are the most vicious of the demons. Their king, Ravana, is a wicked and cunning character who enjoys doing mischief in a big way. Vishnu has had to incarnate himself on earth more than once in order to combat and defeat this nasty demon with his criminal armies.

Demons, when they appear in visible form, are horrifying, ugly, misshapen, terrifying, enormous and inescapable. Only the gods can defeat them. The Islamic regions of India have their own demons, some called *div*, which may be a ghost or a giant; some are *djinnies* or *jinns*, who can take any size or form, usually with horns. Their females can appear as lovable women, marry mortal men and have families with them, but they live much longer than people. *Shetans* are always dangerous and never friendly. They will tempt people to sin by whispering in their ears, or frighten them with their huge size, sharp claws, long horns, hairy skins and fiery eyes.

Deva or Sura A god, a good deity who is worshipped. Their number is variously given as 8, 12 or 33 — 11 for each of the three worlds. Fem. Devi.

Devadatta (The name has the same meaning as the Latin Deodatus.) A cousin and lifelong enemy of Gautama the Buddha. One day the young Buddha was absorbed in watching the flight of seven swans over the bank of a river. Suddenly one of the swans fell down, hit by an arrow belonging to the treacherous Devadatta. Overcome by compassion, Gautama knelt down, patiently disengaged the vicious barb from the swan's tender flesh, washed the wound and dressed it with a piece of his own garment. Soon Devadatta arrived in search of his victim. He claimed the swan he had wounded as his property, but the Buddha refused to give it to him. Devadatta then took him to court in the Council of Elders. There, the Buddha argued that the animal does not become the property of the hunter who wounds it, but of the friend who looks after it. It was then that he formulated the Principle of Property: 'A living being belongs to the one who loves it.' This had already been stated by King Vikramaditya in his debate with the Vetala (q.v.): the revived princess must marry the man who stayed with her all the time. It is essentially the same principle as the one implied by King Solomon in 1 Kings 3:27.

Devaki Daughter of Devaka, wife of Vasudeva, mother of Krishna. Vishnu took one of his hairs and placed it in her womb, where it grew and became Krishna (or Kesava, from *kesa* 'hair'), who was born as a blue baby. The tyrant Kansa had locked Devaki in a room in his palace because the sage Narada had told him that she would give birth to the child who would kill Kansa. But when

Krishna was born all the soldiers guarding the palace lay fast asleep because the gods had willed it so. Vasudeva took the child and carried him out of the palace whose doors were unlocked by the gods. Vasudeva escaped with the child from Mathura and brought him to Nanda, a cowherd who lived across the River Yamuna. Nanda's wife Yasoda had just been delivered of a girl. Baby Krishna was given to Yasoda and the girl was taken, by Vasudeva, to Mathura and given to Devaki. Kansa, upon learning that Devaki had had a girl, set the family free, but ordered all the baby boys in the city to be killed.

Devaloka The world of the gods, Swarga, Indra's heaven.

Devamatar, Devamatri Mother of the gods. (See *Aditi*.)

Devata, Devataa Any deity or godhead.

Devayani Daughter of Shukra, priest of the Daityas. (See also *Kacha*; *Shukra*.) She confessed her love for her father's student Kacha to him but he rejected her. She cursed him but he cursed her in return. He said: 'You, daughter of a Brahmin, will marry a Kshatriya, a man of lower rank.'
   One day Devayani went bathing with Sarmistha, daughter of the Daitya king. The Wind-god Vayu came and blew their clothes around so that they changed places. After their bath the girls quarrelled over their saris. Devayani abused Sarmistha, who picked her up and dropped her in a deep, dry well. There Devayani lay until she was discovered by a passing traveller who turned out to be a king, Yayati by name. He took her to her father's house and proposed to her. She agreed to marry him, although even a king was not as good as a priest. She insisted that her father claim Sarmistha as a servant for his daughter, as satisfaction for her hardship in the well. Thus Sarmistha lived at the court of King Yayati in a little house of her own, where the king saw her whenever he walked in his park. She begged him not to let her go to waste as a woman so he visited her and she bore him three sons. When Devayani discovered that her husband had a second wife (which was quite normal in those days) and that it was none other than her enemy and servant (there was always hatred and rank-pulling between co-wives) she left the court, leaving behind her own two sons Yadu and Turvasu (the children of a divorced wife belong to the father). She complained bitterly to her father, who cursed Yayati saying: 'Thou shalt be old and impotent.'
   He mitigated this curse later by adding that the curse would be transferable to one of Yayati's sons. (See *Yayati*).

Devi The word for a goddess, feminine of *deva*. If Devi is used as a name by itself, it refers to Kali, Parvati, Uma, Durga.

Devi-Mahatmya 'The Greatness of Devi'. A poem of 12 cantos, 700 verses, forming chapters 81–93 of the great Markandeya

Purana. It is one of our main sources for the mythology of the Great Goddess, Maha-Devi, celebrating Devi-Uma's victories over the demons and sung by the goddess herself. It is the ancient textbook for her worshippers and is recited daily in her temples. It is also called Chandipatha. Here is a sample, the twelfth hymn:

If you continue all your life   to sing these hymns to me
I will preserve you all your days, you will live happily.

The poet who has written it,   the scribe, the devotee,
the pious who recite this song   will be well kept by me.

And all those who will listen to the bards when they recite
will be preserved from poverty   and suffering day or night

No one will fear an enemy   nor fire, floods or war
nor evil spirits nor bad kings   nor weapons, never more!

No dread of sickness or disease; demons I will cast out.
Whoever will recite this hymn   will never be alone.

Whoever builds a shrine to me   a sanctuary in stone
I will reside for ever there   with those who are devout.

With those who come and listen
there,   the simple and the wise
with them I will united be   in love without disguise.

In autumn, in October when   ripen the fruits of rain
come to me and perform *puja*:   I give children and grain.

Those who have listened to this
hymn   will know me where they look
they know my triumphs of the
past   recounted in this book.

Recite my victories at night   when waking from a dream
after a horrifying sight   when stars ill-boding seem.
When children wake up terrified because they heard a bird that
                                         cried
Recite this poem and their
minds   will soon be pacified.

Yes, all you need is recitation of my exalted celebration
to gain the power of expulsion   of all the demons of convulsion.

If anyone of you has sinned   and needs propitiation
let flowers, perfume and incense precede this recitation.

My poem will efface the sins   and it assures good health
for it destroys all evil ghosts;   it gives good luck and wealth.

To give an offering is good   provide the holy men with food
share with the poor what you
have won,   I witness all that you have done.

Your soul will live in happiness	your spirit will be pure devotion
if you recite with tenderness	with love and pure emotion.
When you are lost, imprisoned, or	exhausted, near starvation,
Recite this poem and I will	work for your liberation.
If you are on a ship at sea	in danger and distress
Recite this hymn and I will be	near you in happiness.

Markandeya, the sage who dictated the Purana (an ancient textbook on the nature of the gods), recounts the periods of cosmic history to his disciples. Each period has its regent and the regent of the eighth period was Savarni, an incarnation of King Suratha, who lived in the preceding *antara* or cosmic period. It was his great accumulation of merit in that seventh period, on behalf of Devi-Kali, which earned him that high station in the divine world of regents.

The epic is composed in classic Sanskrit, in *c.*600 slokas, i.e. stanzas of 32 syllables, divided into four hemistichs of eight syllables. Its oral tradition is very much alive today, especially in South India, and this epic is both recited and sung, in temples and homes.

The story begins at the hermitage of the sage Rishi Medhas in the jungle, where two persons meet with the purpose of retreating there for study and meditation. The first to arrive is ex-king Suratha whom a usurper has ousted from his kingdom. The second is a businessman called Samadhi who has lost his wealth through the deceit, trickery and corruption of those nearest to him. Neither of these gentlemen bemoans his lot; on the contrary, both are most concerned about the well-being of those who have robbed them. The ex-king is worried over the gloomy prospects of his ungrateful citizens. The businessman frets over what will happen to the family fortune, not because he wants to have it back but because the new owners, his own relatives, will dissipate it so that his grandchildren will be disinherited. While discussing their common experiences, a question arises in the minds of the two men: why should this be so? Why does a philosopher worry about the lives of people to whom he owes nothing and who show no signs of gratitude for his work on their behalf, on the contrary, who have taken all that he had collected for them and expelled him for his trouble? Is this not *moha*, folly? Is it not better to turn away from this wicked world and devote oneself to pure meditation? They decide to go and see the wise Medhas together. The sage answers them with a parable: Is it not known that a parent bird will continue feeding its young even when he or she is weak with hunger? This phenomenon, continues the sage, is the expression of the cosmic activity of Devi-Kali, who possesses many shapes. These numerous aspects in which she manifests herself, are together called *mahamaya*, the great magic, by which this world is created.

The present writer should here add an explanation for those readers who are not familiar with Hindu philosophy, a subject that baffles even some of the most intelligent scientists. The reason is that science is based on the assumption that the physical world which we study is the real world, but that our mental images of it are not real. So, when I see the sun, I believe it is actually there, but when I shut my eyes, I can still see the sun; however, that is called an optical illusion caused by the retina being exposed too long to the sunlight. Hindu philosophers disagree with the first assumption. They teach that all our observations are based on illusion, *maya*. This illusion is created by the gods who *think* the universe as a result of which we see it, so the creation is a collective illusion. Buddhism has accepted this philosophy and taken it a step further by concluding that human life and suffering are also an illusion, from which we must liberate ourselves to attain salvation. Moreover, contrary to Christianity and Islam, Hinduism does not regard this creation as the only one but as one in a series of existences. When the god Brahma is breathing out, there is existence *antara*, but as soon as he begins to breathe in, all things disappear and withdraw into their essences. During that period of non-existence, Vishnu is in a state of *yoga-nidra*, 'concentration-sleep', meaning that there is no creation to be upheld, so Vishnu can concentrate his mind on spiritual matters. In this way the two gods are in perfect co-operation, while Shiva too, as we have seen, often resides in a state of yogic meditation before the time of creation. Of course, the student of Hindu philosophy knows that the three gods are identical in the spirit; their very separation into distinct images is an illusion. 'That which can be observed is not essential; that which is essential cannot be distinguished, it is one, it is you.'

The Devi-Kali is herself responsible for this illusion, indeed she *is* the illusion when she is 'playing' creation. At the same time Devi-Kali can liberate us from this illusion once we have seen through it, because it is this illusion that is responsible for our desire to return after this life in another body and start a new life. It is desire that causes illusory images in our brain. Knowing this will enable us to liberate ourselves from this desire and so liberate us from the suffering of existence which is the price of desire.

Suratha and Samadhi now beseech the sage to evoke the goddess; the Rishi complies and to this end begins the recitation of the epic poem Devi-Mahatmayam. Suratha and Samadhi decided to devote a cult to the goddess, which meant that they developed a new form of worship, within the religious structure of Hinduism, aimed at Devi. The two first devotees of the goddess fashioned a sculpture of her from clay and meditated for three full years, fasting severely, in order to obtain a boon. Finally the goddess appeared and granted each a boon. King Suratha wished that he might reign over a kingdom of justice, while Samadhi wished to be delivered of egotism and possessiveness. Note which wish is the wisest!

The first episode of the epic of the great goddess Devi-Kali recounts that at the beginning of a new period in the cosmic cycle of existence (*kalpa*) two demons appear; demons of the most dangerous type are called Asuras. The two evil beings conspired to destroy creation. Vishnu, still half asleep (i.e. absorbed in yoga) appealed to the Great Goddess Devi for assistance to combat them. To this end, Vishnu recited a hymn in praise of Devi which he had composed himself. Shortly after, the goddess appeared out of the darkness, coming into existence as a result of the god's magic hymn, out of himself, for she is is dream, his illusion in the night of non-existence. She is herself the tangible darkness, Tamasi Devi.

Meanwhile, the two Asuras, who were nothing but miserable rejects creeping out of Vishnu's ears, discovered that there was nothing on earth yet except the beachless ocean. So, thinking that they were clever, they asked the god not to kill them anywhere where water had been present. Contemptuously, Vishnu, owner of the conch and club, killed them with his razor-sharp disc which had been hovering above the waters for countless centuries. This first victory over the forces of evil, however, was only the beginning of the great war between the gods and the titans, or Asuras.

The leader of the Asuras is Mahisha, 'buffalo', who, with his host of evil spirits wins one battle after another, until finally the gods are vanquished and expelled from their rightful abode, *Swarga* 'heaven', so that they have to go and live on earth like common mortals, a terrible degradation for gods.

The number of gods is given as 30 or 33, but only eight are mentioned by name: Indra, the Supreme god, Surya the Sun-god, Agni the Fire god, Vayu the Wind-god, Chandra the Moon-god, Yama the Death-god, Varuna the Rain-god, Kumara the War-god (he is, characteristically, a bachelor, *kumara*; he is later identified with Karttikeya). In addition there is, of course, the 'Hindu Trinity' (though not really comparable to the Christian Trinity), Shiva, Vishnu and Brahma, and finally there is the Goddess, Devi Durga or Kali. The Hindu pantheon has thus 12 major gods, like the Greek tradition.

The buffalo god, Mahisha, installed himself in Heaven as the successor of Indra, King of the Heavens, by right of conquest. Shiva, Vishnu and the other gods were so furious about this affront that their faces became luminous with rage and out of this fire of their furore they created a goddess, a new being composed out of their combined anger which is potential energy, *shakti* 'divine power'. As we have seen, the goddess already existed as a deity, as a spirit, working as *Maya*, but now the gods had given her a share of their tremendous energy so that she became perceptible matter, since matter is energy, or is perceptible because it is energy. Thus, Shiva's energy became her face, Vishnu's became her arms. Yama's became her hair, Chandra's became her breasts, Indra's became her waist, Brahma's became her feet, Surya's became her toes, Agni's became her eyes, Vayu's became her ears; her teeth grew from the energy of Prajapati, the Creator, a manifestation of Brahma; Kuvera, the god of wealth, here mentioned for the first time, gave her a nose; Bhumi the earth, gave her beautiful hips; the eight Vasus — deities of the times of day and night, ruling dawn, midday heat, dusk, moonshine, pole-star and other phenomena — gave her her hands; thus Devi is depicted in iconography with eight hands, each of which holds an object, usually a weapon, such as a bow and arrow, disc (or wheel), javelin, noose, shield and sword. The eighth object, the conch, is not a weapon but is blown like a bugle in medieval warfare, to summon the warriors into battle. Thus Devi is the goddess of defence and warfare, like Athena-Minerva, and like her, she is also the goddess of wisdom and knowledge. Both goddesses inspire terror (Athena by means of the lethal Medusa head on her shield) and are at the same time faithful helpers of their worshippers, giving rich boons to devout supplicants.

When Devi had been created to perfection, she uttered a cry of great joy, of superabundant energy and the gods exclaimed: *'Jaya*: Vanquish!'

That was to be her work in this world: to overcome the enemies of the gods. To that end they all gave her a weapon or an ornament from their own treasuries, as a birthday present. As she was standing there in the primeval cosmos, which had already partly fallen into the hands of evil beings, she, the one who would save the gods from servitude, radiated light: the energy which they had given her, all fused into one. Shiva gave her his trident, Krishna (Vishnu) gave her his disc; Varuna gave her his conch from the western shore; Agni gave her a flaming spear; Maruta (Vayu) gave her a bow and arrows in a quiver; Indra gave her his *vajra* or thunder-hammer; Yama gave her a copy of his own Staff of Fate (Kala-danda); Ambupati, the Lord of the Waters, gave her a noose (or lasso, *pasham*); Prajapati gave her a rosary, a necklace of lovely beads; Brahma gave her a water-jar for the performance of her daily ablutions (since even the gods have to follow all the Brahmanic rituals: they *are* all Brahmins); the Sun-god planted his own rays in all the pores of her skin (particularly those from which her hair grew), which shone like gold; Kuvera gave her a cup of wine; Shesha, the Snake-god of the Himalayas, gave her a lion to ride on. Thus they all made a contribution to her victory over the forces of evil in the world.

Note that the poet, eager to show his knowledge of the teeming pantheon of India, introduces gods which he has not mentioned previously; some of these are local deities, others have later been absorbed or identified with Shiva (Kala, Agni) or Vishnu (Krishna, Surya), so that their presence depends on the period of history in which the text was composed, written down or copied. The Hindu period was preceded by the Brahmanic period, which in its turn followed the Vedic period, which again came after the Aryan times! As different dynasties favoured different gods and as one tribe of the Aryan family dominated another, so it imposed its god on the others, who worshipped the same gods as their ancestors, but henceforth under different names. Thus new (or, rather, old) aspects were added to the Vedic gods, as the Aryans settled in the great plains, gradually spreading out from west to east, and mingled with the peoples who were already there. Gradually they changed, their culture, their habits and their preferences for certain gods. Their greatest creation, the Sanskrit language, had already ceased to be spoken in the days of the Buddha in the fifth century BC.

The god Brahma-Prajapati composed a hymn for Devi and sung this:

You are the source of heavenly milk from which the gods must drink!
You are the mother of the Word, the syllable of Life!
You are the mother of the gods, of man and woman too.
You are the one who made this world, who carries it along;
You are the one who keeps this world, your form is life itself;
You will one day destroy this world and call it back to naught;
You are yourself the sciences, wisdom, enlightenment;
You are both demon and divine, magic and sorcery.
Darkness and light are both in you, error and truthfulness,
You are the night, and foolishness, nature in all its grace,
The splendour of awakening, of honesty and modesty,
Of patience and prosperity, intelligence and peace!

The hymn is much longer in the original text, but a translator of poetry must be aware of the differences in culture between the speakers of the two languages he is translating from and into. Only the most devout English-speaking people would enjoy the full text of the endless praises in honour of the great goddess Devi-Kali. Of course, the authorship of Brahma himself warrants the sanctity of this hymn.

The goddess received a new name, Chandika, 'the terrible', before riding into battle on the fierce lion, her new *vahana* (vehicle). Chandika and the Asuras (literally 'anti-gods'), or demons, waged war for a hundred years. It was like a cosmic display of fireworks, as all the skies were full of the fiery projectiles which the gods and demons launched at each other. The goddess came into her own as the battle raged. She rained arrows down on the demons who were massed together in their millions; she sliced limbs and heads off by the thousand. But the demons could fight on even with missing limbs. Some demons could continue without heads, swinging their great swords blindly. The entire earth became a battlefield and was soon made impassable as piles of corpses, dead horses and smashed chariots lay on the ground as far as the eye could see. Rivers of blood flowed between the armies, so deep that only the elephants could be seen above them. Chandika was to the demons what fire is to dry grass: total destruction. Mahisha had a general called Chiksura, who now approached the goddess with a rain of arrows like an avalanche tumbling down from the slopes of the Himalayas, but Chandika cut all his arrows in half before they could fall, killed his horses and his charioteer, so that Chiksura had to fight on foot. He ran up at her and struck her faithful lion on its head, but Chandika raised her club and shattered his skull into a thousand pieces. In this way she destroyed many other generals of the demon army, until finally Mahisha himself approached her, in the shape of a buffalo, trampling his enemies, the good gods, under him. His enormous hooves crumbled the earth, while his long and dangerous tail swung out towards the ocean, whipping up mountainous waves. With his great terrifying horns he tossed entire mountains up into the air as if they were clods of earth. The blast of his hot breath blew away the hills which in falling buried the gods. Finally, the goddess took out her lasso and caught this wild bull in its noose, tying him fast. But he quickly changed into a lion. Quickly, Chandika drew her sword and slashed through his neck. The lion fell down dead, but out of his neck came the demon in a new form, becoming a man with a sabre in his hand. She pierced him with a hundred arrows, killing the man, but the demon took on yet another shape, that of a huge elephant, red-eyed with rage. With one swing of her sword, the goddess cut off his trunk. Mahisha then resumed his original shape, that of the big buffalo, shaking the earth, the heavens and the underworld with his terrifying rage. But Chandika was unafraid, she leaped up and put her foot on his neck, crushing him down and stamping on his neck, laughing all the time. Then she cut off his head with her sword, finally killing him for ever.

Immediately the gods cheered loudly across the earth and the heavens, proclaiming everywhere the greatness and glory of Maha-Devi. However, the troubles of the gods were not over yet. Two more demons arose out of nothing, it seemed, or out of the lap of evil itself. Meanwhile, Chandika had retired to her own country, the Himalayas, where she resides as Parvati 'the lady of the mountains'. The gods lined up to sing a hymn to her valour, hoping to induce her to prepare for another battle with the two new demons, whose names are Shumbha and Nishumbha. The goddess, here also called Kali ('the black one', i.e. darkness) and Durga ('the impenetrable one' like a dark forest or a steep mountain), agreed to fight the two demons with their innumerable armies. The battle lasts for four cantos, 5–8. After many vicissitudes the goddess was finally confronted by Nishumbha, whose heart she pierced with her lance, whereupon he himself came out of his own body in the form of a man, but she immediately cut his head off.

Then only Shumbha remained, the fiercest and strongest of all the demons ever to face the great goddess. After smashing all his weapons one after another, she waited a moment, so he attacked her with his bare hands, punching her, but she beat him down. Alas! the contact with the earth revived the villain magically, so that he jumped up again, assaulted the goddess, took her by the shoulders and flew up into the sky with her. There the demon Shumbha and the goddess Maha-Devi continued their cosmic battle to the great surprise of the celestials, the inhabitants of Heaven, the sages and perfect men. Finally, the goddess disengaged herself from her attacker and threw him down, quickly piercing him with her lance through his heart. He died at once.

Suddenly, after the evil spirit (duratman) had thus been removed from the universe, peace returned to it, the light regained its strength, where previously it had been almost totally dark.

The Apsaras (river-nymphs) began to sing and dance together, to celebrate the new era of goodness. The sacrificial fires flamed cheerfully again after the rituals for the gods had been badly neglected during the long time of war. The gods, restored to their normal functions and reinstalled in their rightful homes in Heaven, together approached the goddess, led by Indra, and intoned a hymn to her, in which they praised her strength and her valour, and implored her to protect them from evil for ever after. They burst out into a song of praise for the goddess in the eleventh canto, a magnificent ode to Devi (Narayani namo 'stu te). In it she is praised with many other names, Chandi 'radiant', Ambika 'mother', Bhadrakali 'the goddess of the auspicious time', Kali 'black', Durga 'impenetrable like a forest', and so, 'invincible'. After the hymn-singing by the gods, the goddess promised that she would arise and intervene each time the Asuras returned to the world to resume the fighting in their efforts to revive the forces of evil in the cosmos. The gods already knew that one day the demons Shumbha and Nishumbha would be reborn. The loyal goddess would then return in order to combat the two evil ones. To that purpose she would be reborn in the Vindhya mountains in central India as a simple shepherd's daughter.

Devi Sri Noble goddess. One of the names of Lakshmi (q.v.).

Dhamma (Pali), in Theravada Buddhism the word for 'the law' derived from Dharma (Sanskrit) (q.v.). It can also mean: duty, norm, right, what one cannot avoid, destiny, fate. Often it is the word for the collective teachings of the Buddha.

Dhanada 'Giving Wealth'. Epithet of Kubera (q.v.).

Dhanu Sagittarius, a sign of the zodiac (q.v.).

Dharani The Earth. Wife of Parashu-Rama.

Dharini In Tantrayana Buddhism, a goddess who assists the memory.

Dharma (1) An abstract Sanskrit term which is not easy to grasp. The general meaning is 'that which is right', referring not only to a person's rights but first and foremost to his duties. These duties devolve neither from divine decree nor from a person's own resolve, but from the position in life and society into which he is born. Thus a warrior must fight and a sweeper sweep, a farmer must plough and a woman give birth, that is *dharma*. There is neither punishment nor reward in *dharma*, but the wisdom of this concept is that it helps people to accept their condition. A woman will never be a man, a man can never be a child again. Accordingly we have to act in harmony with our state, since rebellion against *dharma* is like wishing to delay a sunset. *Dharma* in this sense can be translated as 'law,' as in *dharmashastra*, a textbook of law. The difference is that in Western countries law is made by people and abolished by people. *Dharma* cannot be changed. Dharma is also a god who appears where men are being tested for their righteousness, strength of character, sense of honour, generosity and readiness for self-sacrifice. Those are the qualities Dharma likes to see in men, their willingness to bow to the eternal laws of *dharma*. The epic saga of the Mahabharata is based entirely on the heroes' acceptance of Dharma's immutable rules of behaviour.

(2) In Buddhism the word means:

1. The Ultimate Reality;
2. Buddha's teaching, his doctine, and the scriptures in which this doctrine is laid down. Dharma (the Dhamma) in the formulation of Buddha's teaching as laid down in the *sutras* (q.v.). The basic points are:

(a) Knowledge is indispensable. Ignorance is the cause of suffering.

(b) Birth, and the life that follows, are evil, since they cause suffering.

(c) Suffering is pain, sickness, old age, death, sorrow, war, poverty.

(d) Suffering is also parting from friends and meeting enemies.

(e) Suffering is the impossibility of what we want and the arrival of what we do not want.

(f) Removal of suffering is only possible through suppression of all desires, detachment from all earthly goods and beings, giving up all ambitions.

(g) We must be indifferent to suffering, hardened to pain and hunger.

(h) We must be entirely pure and chaste, and leave to others what they desire.

3. The Truth.

4. Quality, virtue, propriety, righteousness, the correct way of life. (See also *Buddha*, *Buddhism*, *Karma*, *Yoga*.)

Dharmaatma A Saint, a person who never sins, whose spirit (*atma*) always walks with the god of justice, Dharma.

Dharmachakra The wheel of the law, hand-position of the Buddha, *vairocana* or *maitreya*. It signifies the never-ending cycle of suffering caused by ever-returning births and deaths, which is in turn caused by desire. Only the total suppression of desire can break this cycle.

Dharmakaya One of the three aspects of the Buddha's cosmic body, *kaya*, which is the ultimate, universal reality. Dharmakaya, literally 'the Body of the Law', is the substance of the Law, which is Buddha himself, being pure Truth. This substance has no shape so that it is not in any place, nor is there a place where it is not. It neither comes nor does it go anywhere. The Buddha is like the blue sky: it is all around us, encompassing everything, lacking nothing. He never dies.

Dharmaketu 'Whose Banner is Justice', praise-name of Buddha.

Dharma-Raja Ruler of Justice. Epithet of Yama (q.v.).

Dharmashastra The textbook of Hindu law composed by Manu who was inspired by Vishnu, and other sages.

Dhenuka A demon who owned a fruit garden. When Krishna and his brother Balarama were picking fruits there, Dhenuka took the form of a big donkey and started kicking Balarama. Balarama picked the donkey up by its hind legs and swung it round until it died. Many other donkeys came running up to the brothers and attacked them but they all met the same fate, till the orchard looked like a donkey graveyard.

Dhrishta-Dyumna Son of Drupada, brother of Draupadi, commander of the Pandava army. He killed Drona, who had killed his father, so he in turn was killed by Drona's son, the coward Ashvatthaman who stamped him to death as he lay asleep after the last battle of the war of Mahabharata, in the camp of the Pandavas.

Dhrita-Rashtra Eldest son of Vyasa (Vichitra-virya) and Ambika. He married Gandhari, who bore him 100 sons, the eldest of whom was Duryodhana, the leader of the party called the Kauravas in the war of the Mahabharata, against the Pandavas, the sons of Pandu who was Dhrita-rashtra's brother. Their father, Vyasa or Vedavyasa, was also called Krishna Dvaipayana.

Dhruva The pole-star. Once upon a time there was a king, who had a queen called Suniti. He also had a 'younger wife' who, by her beauty, exercised great power over the king. She even persuaded the king to send Suniti and her little son Dhruva out into the forest.

When Dhruva reached the age of 7 he asked his mother: 'Who is my father?' Suniti wept and told him that his father was the king. When the boy asked permission to go and see his father, his mother blessed him and let him go. When the king saw his son, he was overjoyed and put him on his knee, but as soon as the stepmother saw the prince, she snatched him from his father's lap and turned him out of the palace. Young Dhruva went back to his mother and asked her:

'Is there anyone more powerful than the king?'

'Yes,' said his mother. 'Narayana is the most powerful.'

'Where is he?'

'In the mountains.'

The boy said nothing, but that night he left the house very quietly and set out towards the mountains. He walked through forest and jungle, fearing no one. The bears and tigers ran away from him.

Finally he met the sage Narada and asked him: 'Where can I find Narayana?'

The sage answered: 'Stay right here. You have reached the edge of the northern sky. Concentrate all your thoughts on Narayana and have patience.'

The boy did so and there, standing on the same summit under the starry sky, he meditated, concentrating his mind on Narayana. Finally Narayana came down from heaven and revealed himself to Dhruva. Narayana is an epithet of Vishnu. Vishnu re-created the boy Dhruva as the Polar Star, because, he said, Dhruva had shown steadfast perseverance.

Dhumavarna 'Smoke-coloured'. King of the Sea-serpents, a kind of semi-human aquatic creature. When Yadu, son of King Yayati, went for a walk one day along the beach, Dhumavarna suddenly appeared and carried him off to his palace in the ocean. There he married his five beautiful daughters to Yadu. These sea-princesses must have looked like beautiful mermaids. All five had children with Yadu.

Dhundhu An Asura who caused flames to burst out from a mountain of sand while the saint Uttanka was meditating there. King Kuvalayaswa arrived with his 21,000 young sons to dig Uttanka out but only three of his sons survived the flames. They killed Dhundhu. Perhaps Dhundhu is to be equated with the Roman god Vulcanus.

Dhurjati 'Having matted, uncombed hair'. An epithet of Shiva (q.v.).

Dhyana Meditation, religious contemplation. *Dhyana-yoga*, complete absorption in thought, exercises in concentration. *Dhyana*, a Sanskrit word from the verb *dhyai* 'to think, reflect', is the origin of the Japanese word *Zen*, via Chinese *ch'an* 'deep meditation, Buddhism'. *Dhyana* is more than sitting in a certain position while thinking. *Dhyana* is concentration on spiritual spheres to the exclusion of all that happens in the world around. Even an attack by thugs or tigers must not break the concentration of a Buddhist ascetic for whom nothing matters except the total purification of the mind from life-wish.

Dhyanaloka One of 10 heavens where Buddhist ascetics enjoy eternal meditation.

Dhyanamudra Or *Yogamudra*. A position of sitting in which the palms are turned upwards, the right hand is placed on the left hand and both are resting relaxed in the meditator's lap, ready to receive enlightenment. This is the *mudra* signifying *yoga* or *dhyana*, a state of concentration.

Dhyani-Buddha *Dhyani* means profound meditation so the *Dhyani-Buddhas* are represented in sculpture as absorbed in profound contemplation. The Buddha himself was not in favour of images of gods because it would distract the worshippers from the real goal of Buddhism. The Theravada (q.v.) branch of Buddhism has adhered to this principle, so they never show the Buddha in their art. The Mahayana (q.v.), however, which began to flourish in north-west India (in what is now north-west Pakistan) just before the beginning of the Christian era, place no such restriction on depicting the Buddha. Fine sculptures show a high form of art and Greek influence, the so-called Gandhara school which represented the Buddha as standing up, like Apollo. Soon however, the *padmasana* was introduced, i.e. the seated position with crossed legs which we all associate with the Buddha in sculpture. The first Buddha, whom Buddhist philosophy projects back into the dawn of history, is the Adi-Buddha, the spiritual principle from which all the later Buddhas of all times and places, evolved. It should be stressed here that only one Buddha ever existed on earth, and that all the other Buddhas are purely philosophical concepts, imagined as spiritual brothers of the historical Buddha, and sculptured with such talent that each of them is individually recognizable. These images are made to help our meditation along, they are not statues of gods intended to be worshipped but points of mental concentration for the seeker of enlightenment. See also *Bodhisattva*.

The Dhyani-Buddhas emanate from (one could say they are manifestations of) the Adi-Buddha, who is Svayam-Bhu, self-existent, i.e. his existence is not conditioned by matter, time or space. There are five Dhyani-Buddhas, representing the five cosmic elements, not including Adi-Buddha. They can all be easily recognized. They sit in the lotus position with the soles of their feet turned upwards and the palms of their hands likewise facing upwards (*dhyana-mudra*), with or without a cup resting on the opened hands, signifying receptivity. The Dhyani-Buddha is often accompanied by his consort representing the unification of the twoness, or the merging of the opposites. The names of the five Dhyani-Buddhas are Vairocana, Ratnasambhava, Amitabha, Amoghasiddhi and Akshobhya. Apart from meditation, they represent the attitude of beneficence, instruction and protection. The Dhyani-Bodhisattvas are in turn emanations from the Dhyani-Buddhas. Originally there were five Bodhisattvas, but with the centuries they multiplied. They were responsible for creation. Each Dhyani-Buddha inspires a cycle of world-evolution (see *Kalpa*) and they may incarnate as a Buddha living on earth in each of these periods of history, through manifestation as a Bodhisattva, i.e. a saint who postpones his final absorption in Nirvana out of compassion for the human souls still living in the darkness of error who must be helped.

Digambara 'Clothed in space, dressed in air'. A naked ascetic or mendicant. An epithet of Shiva. (See also *Jainism*.)

Dig-Gaja, Dikpala One of eight gods in the shape of elephants who support the eight corners of Dik, the universe. Their names are Airavata, Pundarika, Supratika, Vamana, Kumuda, Anjana, Pushpadanta, Suryabhauma.

Dirgha-Tamas 'Long darkness'. Name of a blind king who performed severe asceticism until Agni gave him his eyesight.

Diti A goddess, mother of the Daityas. She was the daughter of Daksha, son of Brahma. With her husband Kasyapa she had many children but they all died, for which she blamed Indra. So she begged her husband for a son who would be indestructible so he could defeat Indra. While she was pregnant with her latest child, Indra arrived late in the night and divided the embryo with his *vajra* into 49 pieces. Each of the parts survived and was born, crying loudly. This was the origin of the 49 Maruts, fast-flying deities.

Divali A Hindu feast. From *deepavali*, 'cluster of lights', because the people used to hang lamps in the trees to guide the *pitris*, the spirits of the dead on their way to the land of bliss. On this day Vikramaditya was crowned king of Ujayyini, about the time when Augustus became Roman Emperor. He was victorious against the Shaka invaders and a celebrated patron of the arts and the *nava-ratna*, the nine gems of literature. He himself became a hero of romantic poetry. The date of the festival, late October — early November, makes it likely that there may be links with All Souls in pre-Christian Europe, when the dead souls were commemorated and prayed for. At that time or a little before, the sun enters the sign of Scorpio, which is ruled by Diana the Moon-goddess. The Hindus worship Lakshmi on that day, which has been compared to New Year's Day. The shop-keepers whitewash their shops and open new account books. It is considered an auspicious day for gambling as Shiva and his sons themselves gambled on that day, Shiva losing everything and his sons winning it back. People dress up, meet in the streets, go to the fair and give each other presents and sweets. Fireworks are lit. Some scholars maintain that Divali celebrates Mahabali or King Bali (q.v.) of Mahabalipura, whom the gods admired for his devotion and austerity. Vishnu took his earthly kingdoms from him leaving him only Patala, the Kingdom of the Dead, which points again at Divali being the day to commemorate the souls of the dead and care for them. The women in Maharashtra make effigies of Bali from dough and pray that Bali's kingdom may be restored. Another myth relates that on this day Vishnu finally killed the demon Narakasura and took back the jewels he had stolen. Narakasura was a rapist who kept 10,000 women in his impregnable castle Prag Jyotisha in the mountains. The liberation from this wicked Naraka-Asura (hell-demon) is well worth celebrating.

Doab 'Two Rivers'. The region covering the vast plains of Hindustan that lies between the two holy rivers Ganga (Ganges) and Yamuna (Jumna) which 'become one' near Allahabad ('City of God'), called in antiquity Prayaga 'sacrifice'. In the Gupta period the king was represented in sculpture as standing between the two goddesses who protected his realm.

Dog When Brahma created the dog he told him to go and serve the most powerful being on earth. After serving the elephant and the lion, the dog discovered they both feared the hunter so he served man. When a dog howls it is believed in India that it can see its owner's death approaching.

Doomsday See *Samvarta, Kalkin* (Vishnu). In the Dvapara age Shiva himself will become the Doomsday fire. Other books (of the Purana tradition) state that a white horse, Kalkin, will arrive and stamp on the earth, so that the entire earth will fall off the hood which Shesha the world serpent has been carrying all these years. The earth will fall into the endless deep with all its sinful people. Bottomless darkness will hold the earth enveloped for ever after.

Dragon See *Naga*.

Draupadi Wife of the Pandavas. Daughter of Drupada king of Panchala, Draupadi was a woman of great beauty and of a fierce spirit. Indeed she was the Helen of the Indian epic, and more than that, for whereas Helen was passively taken by Paris, and then taken back by Menelaus, Draupadi actively interfered in the war which was started for her sake, and incited her men to take revenge. Yet there are many parallels in the tales of the two loveliest women of their time. Each was wooed by many suitors and each was allowed by her father to choose her own husband from the circle of princes who had come to seek her hand. Both had five husbands but whereas Helen had them in succession, Draupadi was married to the five Pandava brothers in one ceremony, each husband spending

two successive nights with her in rotation. She had a son and a
daughter by each husband, so she had 10 children. It was Kunti, the
Pandavas' mother, who, when Draupadi chose her son Arjuna, told
him to share Draupadi with his four brothers. Arjuna obeyed, being
a good son. The saint Vyasa confirmed that it was the gods' will that
Draupadi should be married to all five brothers. One fatal day the
eldest brother Yuddhisthira gambled with Indian dice against his
cousins the Kauravas. He lost everything, including his wife and
even his own brothers. So Draupadi became a slave. The leader of
the Kauravas, Duryodhana, told her to sweep the floor. When she
protested that she was the daughter of a king and not of a sweeper,
Duhsasana pulled her down by her hair and tore her clothes off. A
miracle happened: the god Krishna came and put her clothes back
on her as fast as Duhsasana tore them off. Draupadi screamed to
her husbands for revenge but Yuddhisthira reminded them that
they were slaves. It was, however, arranged that the five Pandavas
with Draupadi should go into exile for 13 years.

For 12 years they lived in the forest. One day another cousin, King
Jayadratha of Sindhu, called at the Pandavas' house while they
were hunting. Finding the beautiful Draupadi alone, his passion
was kindled by her beauty and he tried to seduce her. When she
repulsed him scornfully, he dragged her to his chariot and drove off
with her. When the Pandavas heard about this they pursued
Jayadratha, who could not escape. Bhima beat him unconscious but
Yuddhisthira reminded him that a cousin must not be killed. Bhima
gave Jayadratha's jewels to Draupadi. This pacified her so she
released Jayadratha.

After those 12 years in the forest, the Pandavas spent one year as
servants of the king of Virata. Draupadi became the queen's lady in
waiting, stipulating that she should not have to eat other people's
leftovers and not have to wash other people's feet. When the queen
expressed the fear that Draupadi's beauty might excite other men,
Draupadi said that she was protected by five Gandharvas (a race of
demigods). However, General Kichaka, the queen's brother, was so
excited by Draupadi's beauty that he tried to seduce her. Again,
Draupadi complained to Bhima, who, when he met Kichaka, beat
the general so badly that later only a ball of flesh was found.
Draupadi told the queen that one of her *gandharvas* had done it. She
was nevertheless held responsible and sentenced to die by fire.
Bhima disguised himself as a *gandharva* and all those present fled.
Quietly Bhima untied Draupadi. Finally, after their 13 years of exile
had ended, they returned to their country and the great war of the
Mahabharata began. On the eighteenth and last night of the battle,
the victorious Pandavas invaded the enemy camp. Meanwhile
Draupadi was alone in their own camp with her five sons. At that
moment, Ashvatthaman, the only surviving general of the
Kauravas, invaded her camp and killed all five of her sons.
Draupadi clamoured for revenge, so Bhima and Arjuna went in

pursuit and captured Ashvatthaman. Bhima was ready to kill him but Yudhisthira pointed out that Ashvatthaman was a Brahmin and so, could not be killed, but he had to hand over the famous jewel which he wore in his hair. It was given to Draupadi, who gave it to Yudhisthira as he was head of the family. So he wore it in his hair, even though he was responsible for all the misfortune that had befallen the family. Finally, the Pandavas decided to withdraw from the world and went on their journey to the Himalayas where the sages meditate. Draupadi followed them but died on the way. Draupadi's own name was Krishnaa, suggesting that she was of divine nature and descent, or simply that she was dark-skinned, although that is less likely.

Drona 'A bucket'. A Brahmin who was generated by his father Bharadvaja in a bucket. He married Kripa, half-sister of the hero Bhishma; their son was Ashvatthaman. He was an instructor in the martial arts to the Kauravas and the Pandavas who lived at the court of King Dhritarashtra. In the great war of the Mahabharata, he took sides against the Pandavas and killed their father-in-law, Drupada, even though they had once been friends, and so he was in turn attacked by Dhrishtadyumna, who had sworn to revenge his father Drupada, on the fourth day of the great battle. During the combat, Drona was told that his own son had been killed. Overcome by grief Drona laid down his weapon so Dhrishtadyumna hewed his head off, but he paid for that later. Other scholars relate that Drona travelled up to heaven in a bright light.

Drupada Son of Prishata, King of Panchala. He once denied that the high priest Drona had been his classmate. Drona never forgave him. Drupada performed a powerful sacrifice to Vishnu in order to obtain children. Two children were born 'out of the altar', Dhrishtadyumna and Krishnaa. The latter was a daughter who is better known as Draupadi (q.v.), who married the five Pandava princes. In the great battle of the Mahabharata, Drupada fought with his sons-in-law until he was killed by Drona, who, the next day, was killed by Dhrishtadyumna.

Duhkha See *Dukkha.*

Duhsasana, Dushasana The name means 'hard to rule'. One of the hundred sons of King Dhritarashtra. When the Pandavas had lost their wife Draupadi to the winners in the Indian dice game, the Kauravas, Duhsasana pulled her down by her hair (a married woman's hair is sacred) and abused her. This sparked off the great war of the Mahabharata at the end of which Bhima drank Duhsasana's blood. (See also *Bhima*; *Draupadi*; *Mahabharata*.)

Dukkha, Duhkha Sorrow, unhappiness. Suffering is, according to the Buddha, inherent to ordinary life. It is caused by desire for more than what one needs. It is removed by removing desire.

Durga (1) (Long final vowel). The goddess Kali is called Durga 'impenetrable' like a mountain fortress (see *Haimati* and *Parvati*). Durga is depicted as an attractive woman, but riding her fierce tiger and herself being of the same yellowish colour as the tiger. (See also *Chamunda*; *Devi-Mahatmya*.)

(2) (Final vowel short). A demon who conquered the Three Worlds and humbled the gods by sending them to live in the forest, and compelling them to worship him. Thus the water in the rivers stopped flowing to the sea, the fire could no longer burn, and even the stars fled away. The gods beseeched Parvati to defeat the demon, who owned a hundred million chariots with horses and men and as many elephants. Parvati took the form of a warrior woman with a thousand arms. Her terrifying battle with the giant is described in detail: how he became an elephant as large as a mountain, whereupon she with her nails as long as swords tore him to pieces, whereupon he took the shape of a buffalo. Finally she killed him and took his name so she became known as Durga. (with a long final vowel).

Durga-Mahatmya The legend of the goddess Durga. (See *Devi*; *Kali*; *Uma*.)

Durvasas Son of Atar (Atri) and Anasuya, a sage and Brahmin of a viciously proud and irascible character. When the nymph Shakuntala did not greet him at once because she was full of the thoughts of her love, her cursed her saying that her lover would forget her. When Krishna omitted to wipe the crumbs from Durvasas' feet, the sage predicted angrily how Krishna would die. Even Indra was cursed by Durvasas, who foretold him that the Asuras would subvert his kingdom. Durvasas, who may have been an incarnation of Shiva, had kinder moments too. Kunti, daughter of Yadava, showed such deep devotion to Durvasas that he gave her a charm by means of which she could have a child by any god she wished. So she had sons by Surya, Brahma, Indra, Vishnu and the Ashvins.

Duryodhana The name means 'hard to conquer'. Duryodhana was the eldest son of King Dhritarashtra and the leader of the Kauravas in the great war of the Mahabharata. Dhritarashtra had invited his dead brother's five sons, the Pandavas to come and live at his court to be educated. Constant rivalry and friction resulted in Duryodhana poisoning Bhima who, however, survived. Then, Duryodhana tried to burn the Pandavas in their own house, but they escaped. Finally, Duryodhana persuaded his father to invite the Pandavas to a gambling match in which he, with the help of the cunning cheat Sakuni, defeated the weak-willed Yudhisthira, eldest of the Pandavas, who lost his freedom and gambled away that of his brothers and their common wife, the beautiful Draupadi. Mockingly, Duryodhana called her to come and sweep the floor for

him. When she, a king's daughter, refused, he told her to come and
sit on his thigh. Draupadi screamed for revenge and Bhima,
Yuddhisthira's brother, swore he would smash that thigh. Thirteen
years later, after winning the great battle of the Mahabharata, he
did just that. Duryodhana, seeing that the battle was lost, hid in a
pool. He could stay underwater for a long time, so he had to be
made to emerge with taunts and mockery. It was then decided that
he should fight it out with Bhima, using clubs. The duel lasted a
long time until Bhima remembered that he had vowed to smash
Duryodhana's thigh, so he did. Left wounded and alone in the
field, Duryodhana was visited by Ashvatthaman and told him to
bring the heads of the five Pandava brothers. Ashvatthaman went
and killed the five young sons of Draupadi, and brought their heads
to Duryodhana who did not recognize them as it was already dusk.
So he asked Ashvatthaman which one was Bhima's head. When
Ashvatthaman pointed at one of the boys' heads, Duryodhana
crushed it with his hand. Then he knew that it could not be Bhima's
head, which could not even be crushed by a mace. So, Duryodhana
told Ashvatthaman: 'It was the Pandavas I hated, not those
innocent boys!' Then he died.

Dushkriti The sum of one's sins, all the evil a person has
perpetrated during his life.

Dushyanta A king, descendant of Puru. In the forest he met the
nymph Shakuntala by whom he had a son, Bharata.

Dvaraka, Dwarka A celestial palace built by Visvakarman for
Krishna, who settled the Yadavas inside its strongly fortified wall,
where Kansa could do them no harm.

Dvarakala 'Time is the Doorkeeper', name of the guardian at the
crossroads in the Other World. One road, going north and up to the
hills, leads to the abode of Kubera, where the heroes live who fell in
battle and where they now enjoy luxury. The road to the west will
take one to Buddhapada, 'Buddha's Foot'; there lives Mahadeva
(Varuna) with the pious souls who practised giving generously. The
road to the east leads to the habitation of Ishvara (Indra) and the
blessed palaces of the monks who have acquired supernatural
power by means of asceticism. Finally, the road to the south leads
the intrepid traveller to the sinister abode of Yama-Adipati, the
Archlord of Death, from whence none return.

Dvija, Dwija 'Twice-born'. The three (upper) castes of Hindu
society. The Brahmins, Kshatriyas and Vaishyas, who are believed
to live second lives, after their first lives in the lowest caste (or: as
out-castes) have already ended. Only reincarnations, i.e. old and
experienced souls who possess understanding and civilization,
qualify to be reborn into a caste family. This is where caste differs
fundamentally from social class in Europe. Caste has nothing to do

with wealth or professional skill. It is a religious concept.

Dwaravati, Dvaraka A fine city built by Krishna on an island in the ocean (Bombay?) It was submerged by the ocean a week after Krishna died.

Dwarka, Dvaraka A celestial palace built by Vishvakarman for Krishna, who settled the Yadavas inside its strongly fortified wall, where Kansa could do them no harm.

Dwipa One of the seven continents of early Indian cosmology. Mount Meru in the central Himalayas was regarded as the pivot of the world or rather as the hub of the World Lotus from which the continents stretch out as the petals, resting on the surface of the seven oceans. Each ocean contains a different liquid: milk, curds, ghee, wine, syrup, salt water and fresh water. The continent called Jambu-dwipa, 'rose-apple land', is the one on which we live: its central part is Bharata, India.

Dyaus 'Light, the sky'. Dyaus is also the Sky-god, often referred to as Dyaus-pitri or Dyaus-pita, the Sky-father. He may, with some reservations, be identified with Uranus of Greek antiquity. His wife is Prithivi, the earth, the goddess of nature, the mother-goddess who can be identified with the Greek Gaya. Together the couple are called Dyava-Prithivi and are regarded as the parents of the gods and human beings. It is not clear which of them was born first. Did Dyaus create the earth, his wife?

E

Ekadanta

Earth The greatest earth-goddess of India is Lakshmi (q.v.), with her incarnations Devi Shri (Sri), Sita, Trishnavati and Tulsi. Many people in India worship the earth as a tree-goddess, a Yakshi. Parvati as the mountain-goddess is also worshipped by some as the earth-goddess, though she is also identified with the moon. Savitri is also worshipped by some Indians as the earth-goddess since she conceives children from her husband after he has died, like the Egyptian Isis: the earth receives the dead and gives life. (See *Bhu*; *Bhumi*; *Prithivi*.) Prithivi is the wife of Dyaus, the sky.

Eclipse An eclipse of the moon occurs when the monster Rahu devours it.

Ekadanta 'Having one tooth'. Appellation of Ganesha, one of whose tusks was knocked out by Parashurama.

Eka-Pada One of a fabulous race of one-footed men or 'hoppers'.

Elixir The water of life, the secret potion of power. (See *Amrita-Kumbha*.)

Emptiness Pali: *sunnata*, Sanskrit: *shunyata*. This often misunderstood Buddhist concept refers to a state of the mind which must be arrived at from several directions before complete enlightenment, *bodhi*, is achieved. Firstly, through concentration, *samadhi*, the mind must be taught to shut out all disturbances from outside, all the noise and turbulence of the world must be kept from perturbing the mind, so that neither weather nor war may distract the ascetic from his concentration. This is the opposite of Western culture, with its radio, television and numerous other distractions. The latest news and fashions are shunned by Buddhists. The next stage is more difficult: all the *internal* disturbances must be stilled and the 'chain of thought' broken. All the images which desires and memories, fears and wishes project on the screen of the conscious mind must be abolished because they prevent concentration on what really matters: enlightenment. The third stage is yet more difficult since it is now necessary to abolish the ego itself. This concept *ahamkara*, literally the ego-maker, is based on an illusion, namely the belief that there is such a thing as I, me. These words are simply the morphemes in the verbal system of the language used to express the first person in conjugation. The ego is in the way of enlightenment, which means the conciousness of our relationship with all beings great and small, the unity of all living consciousness in the universe. Upon examining, in the fourth stage of meditation, all the ideas which we have learned in the past, in short, all our knowledge, we shall find that it is not knowledge but illusion or prejudice. Many things we believe we know about other people, other countries, past or present, are not based on facts but on hearsay. All this quasi-knowledge has to be abolished, so that the mind becomes gradually empty. This explains the great tolerance of the Buddhists: they have no preconceived judgement of other people. It also explains the complete peacefulness of Buddhists: they refuse to harbour thoughts of envy, anger or aggression. Just as only the still pond can reflect the sky, so only the stilled mind can receive enlightenment.

Emusha A black boar which pushed up the earth. (See *Bhu; Varaha.*)

F

Fakir

Fakir This is the Arabic word for an ascetic. Literally it means 'a poor man'. The Sanskrit word is *sannyasin*. Fakirs hope to acquire merit by undergoing self-torture such as lying on a bed of nails or holding up one arm until it has become stiff and rigid. This merit is a favour from God or the gods which gives fakirs (as some believe) the power to levitate (lift themselves up in the air) since their detachment from earthly desires has made them so light as to be free from gravity. Thus many tales are told about the ability of the fakir to climb a rope that stands up in the air attached to nothing. The moral of this myth is that no one can reach heaven that way; only virtue and prayer can lead us to heaven. The fakir deludes the public, proving that illusion rules the minds of most people who see what they want to see. (See also *Yogi*, *Yoga*.)

Fig Tree The genus *ficus* of the *moraceae* family contains over 900 species. The *ficus carica* is the fruit tree; the *ficus benghalensis* is the Indian Banyan tree. It is sacred because it is believed that women who pray in its shade will have children. Gods and spirits are said to live in it. (See also *Banyan*.)

Firdaus Paradise for the Muslims, usually called Janna (Jannat) in the Koran, or Adan, Eden. It is described as a pleasant garden (*janna*) with many streams and shady trees. The virtuous souls drink fresh water, milk, honey and wine which does not intoxicate. Paradise is surrounded by a high wall with 12 gates, each of which bears the name of a virtue or pious act by means of which the soul may enter it: 'Prayer', 'Giving Alms', 'Fasting', 'Faith', 'Repentance', 'Pilgrimage', 'Patience', 'Compassion', 'Generosity', 'Perseverance', 'Vigils', Wakefulness', and 'Holy War'. There is no fear that Paradise will ever be full of people for it is hundreds of times larger than the earth. Every inhabitant has a palace there, the size of which depends on his saintliness on earth. Horses and camels enable the Chosen Ones to ride through its verdant landscapes to see friends and relatives if they are also there. For the young heroes who died in a holy war, i.e. the obligatory struggle for the propagation of Islam, there are special female spirits, *Huri l'Aini*, with shining black eyes, who will receive their souls as soon as they die on the battlefield and carry them on their wings to Heaven.

Fire This is a sacred element, since it is essential firstly in the sun, secondly in the sacrificial fire which is lit to make the sun rise, thirdly in the fireplace in the homes where the food is prepared, fourthly in the funerary pyres on which dead bodies are purified, fifthly in the Indian oil-lamps without which no one can see at night, sixthly in lightning and seventhly in the distant stars. (See also *Agni*.)

Fish See *Makara*; *Manu*; *Matsya*; *Vishnu*.

Five-Fold Buddha The five types of knowledge needed for perfect *bodhi*:

1. The pure knowledge of the Dharma.
2. The knowledge which reflects the facts like a mirror.
3. The awareness that all existing things are appearances of the essential sameness.
4. Perceptive knowledge.
5. Knowledge of what is necessary, both of things and activities.

See also *Bodhisattva*; *Dhyani-Buddha*; *Pancha-tathagata*.

Flood See *Vaivasvata*.

Form See *Kaya*; *Rupa*; *Dharmakaya*.

Four Kings In Buddhist cosmology, King Dhritarashtra rules the East, Virudhaka the South, Virupaksha the West and Vaisravana the North.

Four Signs Before the young Prince Gautama was driven through the streets of Kapilavastu by his charioteer Chandaka (Channa) his father the king had all the sick beggars removed, but the gods acted in their stead. One god showed himself as a feeble old man, so Gautama asked Chandaka what old age was. During the second ride he saw a sick man, then a dead man on a bier, and finally a monk, standing calm and serene in complete self-control. Each time Chandaka explained whatever it was young Gautama wanted to know.

Frashegird 'Making wonderful'. Restoring the world to goodness. It is the duty of every Zoroastrian to help, by his own spiritual purity, advance the arrival of the *Shoshyant* who will begin the work of *Frashegird*.

Future Buddha See *Maitreya*.

G

Ganga

Gada Club or mace, a weapon used by Vishnu and Bhima in battle.

Gadhi Son of King Kushamba, father of Vishvamitra, an incarnation of Indra.

Gajadevi Image of Lakshmi being bathed by two white elephants.

Gana One of nine groups of minor deities or demons all attendant on Shiva and Parvati, and presided over by his son Ganesha (q.v.) or Ganapati. They are sometimes described as dwarfs. They punish wrongdoers and word-breakers.

Gana-Nayaki 'Leader of Ganas'. Epithet of Devi-Uma-Kali (q.v.).

Ganapati Lord of the Ganas. See *Ganesha*.

Ganapatya Member of a sect of worshippers of Ganesha.

Gandhari Princess of Gandhara, daughter of King Subala, wife of King Dhritarashtra of Hastinapura and mother of a hundred sons. Vyasa (= Krishna Dvaipayana) offered Gandhari a boon when she had received him hospitably, so she asked for 100 sons. Soon afterwards she became pregnant and after two years she was delivered of a lump of flesh. Vyasa divided this into 101 pieces. He placed each piece in a jar which he sealed. The first son to emerge was Duryodhana, whose 'birth' was accompanied by such frightening omens that the counsellors advised the king to abandon the baby in the forest. If only he had done so, war and endless suffering would have been prevented, but King Dhritarashtra refused. A month afterwards, 99 further sons were born and one daughter, Duhsala, who later married Jayadratha. Gandhari later perished with her husband in a forest fire.

Gandharva One of 6,333 minor deities dwelling in the sky who possessed the secrets of heaven, including the single most vital secret for the gods: the secret of preparing Soma, the celestial wine. They are also experts in medicines and love-potions. They can appear on earth as handsome men who are irresistible to women. Hence the term 'Gandharva marriage' is used for love at first sight as a result of which a woman yields to a man at once. The Gandharvas are also singers and musicians in heaven. They were born from Brahma and suckled by the goddess of speech so they are eloquent love-makers. Their chief was called Chitra-ratha, and their wives were the Apsaras. At one time the Gandharvas attacked the Nagas in their subterranean country. The Nagas begged Vishnu to help them. They sent Narmada (the river now called Nerbudda) to guide him. On her back Vishnu floated down to the nether-world, where he defeated the Gandharvas. It is said that there is a race of wild men in India still known as Gandharvas.

Gandharva-Veda Musicology, including the arts of drama, singing and dancing, supposedly taught by the Gandharvas.

Gandiva Arjuna's famous celestial bow which once belonged to the god Soma and which he wields in the great battle.

Ganesha, Ganesh Lord of the Ganas, or dwarf-demons. One of the most popular gods of India, whose long-trunked, pot-bellied statue can be seen in most Indian towns. Similar statues from the early Middle Ages can be seen as far away as East Java. Ganesha is the god of all good enterprises so that Hindus — and even some others, will place some offerings near the statue before setting off on a journey or opening a new business or wedding negotiations. Ganesha is the god of practical wisdom, the remover of obstacles. He is the god of scribes who is invoked at the beginning of books. He is also called Heramba, Lambakarna 'long-eared', Lambodara 'hang-bellied' or Gajanana. There are many legends about the reasons for Ganesha having an elephant head. The most probable explanation is that in the most ancient times of human history, when the gods were still theromorphic (when Apollo was still a wolf, Athena an owl, Diana a bear and Zeus a bull), Ganesha was an elephant, just as Hanuman the monkey is now represented as a man with a monkey head. The peoples of antiquity in India and also in Africa, regarded the elephant as the wisest of all animals because the elephant lives longest. The elephant's huge size demonstrates his noble birth: he is by right king of the jungle. He knows its secrets since he was not born yesterday. In philosophy, Ganesha represents the unity of man, the individual, the microcosm, with the universe, the macrocosm, which is symbolized by the elephant, the king of the animal world. Devout Hindus often pray to Ganesha hoping he will intercede on their behalf with the redoubtable Shiva. The elephant pushes his way through the thickest and thorniest jungle; likewise Ganesha makes a path for the traveller wherever he wants to go. Ganesha's mount is a mouse, the animal which slips through the smallest hole, or gnaws its way through obstructions.

One day Parvati wanted a guardian to prevent Shiva from spying on her while she was bathing. So she took her bath oil and other secret substances, and formed the body of a man with a fat belly. Then she sprinkled her bathwater (Ganges water) over him, so he came to life. When Shiva arrived, Ganesha would not let him come near her. In his wrath, Shiva cut off Ganesha's head, then looking quickly around, saw an elephant, cut off its head and put it on Ganesha's shoulders, in which form he can still be seen today.

Another myth relates that the gods decided it was too easy for people to attain heaven, because all their pious enterprises succeeded. The heavens were crowded with meritorious people whereas hell was empty. They went to Parvati to ask for help. She rubbed her already shining body with a miraculous oil and in a short while she gave birth to a fat man with four arms and an elephant's head. This monster is always an obstacle to people's enterprises, unless he is properly propitiated. His fat lazy mass is in the way of all human spiritual energy. In heaven, Ganesha was appointed by his father Shiva as guardian or gatekeeper of Kailasa. One day Parashurama arrived, wanting to see Shiva, but Ganesha would not let him, because Parashurama always behaved in a proud, high-handed manner. Of course, he was Vishnu's sixth incarnation, so he was not a nobody. Yet, he was of a violent disposition and tried to force his way into Shiva's palace. A scuffle ensued in which Parashurama knocked out one of Ganesha's tusks. Parvati was about to curse her son's attacker, but the other gods pleaded with her not to start a war amongst the gods. Brahma promised her that although having only one tooth (hence his name *Ekadanta*), Ganesha would be worshipped by all men and even by the gods.

Ganesha is also the god of the sciences and skills, in the first place of writing. He is the first scribe and it was to him that Vyasa dictated the Mahabharata epic. As a man with an elephant's head and belly, Ganesha has an elephant's appetite and is always pleased with abundant offerings of fruits and vegetables, as well as other foodstuffs. Ganesha has two wives, Siddhi 'achievement' and Buddhi 'intelligence'. He won them by his encyclopaedic knowledge. One day he agreed with his brother Kartikeya that whichever of the two of them won a race around the world would marry both these beautiful girls. Kartikeya started running but Ganesha just sat there until Kartikeya came back. When he challenged Ganesha the latter gave him an exact description of the whole world, pretending that he had seen every detail of it himself. He had read all the books of science, so he knew the whole world and won the women.

Another myth relates that Ganesha was Vishnu, reborn as a son of Parvati, but that she defied Shani to look at the newly born babe. Shani, or Saturn, was known to have eyes that radiated immediate destruction and when Parvati foolishly invited him to look at her baby, its head was burnt off, but Vishnu quickly replaced it using the head of an elephant that he found sleeping on a riverbank.

Ganesha-Chaturthi One of the most popular Hindu festivals, it is celebrated on the fourth (*chaturthi*) day of the bright first fortnight of the moon-month Bhadrapada, towards the end of August. Statues and figurines of the elephant-headed god are made of clay, cloth or any other substance, which, after being worshipped for 10 days, are thrown into the sea or a river. Without the blessing of Ganesha no one can attain his purpose. Even the teacher on his pupils' first day in class will make them repeat the mantra: *Om Sri Ganeshaya Namah*, Hail to Holy Ganesha, Honour! Only then will he begin teaching the alphabet. It is said that Ganesha has such a round belly because he is given sweet rice puddings and balls of flour with sugar on his birthday. One day he mounted his mouse but it stumbled because it was frightened by a snake. Ganesha fell onto the ground in such a way that his belly burst open and all the delicious puddings and sweetballs came rolling out. Ganesha quickly picked them up and put them back in his belly. Then he picked the snake up and wrapped it around his belly to keep it closed. The full moon laughed to see such sport, but this made Ganesha angry so he took off one of his tusks and threw it at the moon. He never got it back. On his feast-day no one may look at the moon.

Ganga The Ganges. The mighty Ganges winds its way east right through the middle of India, through the immense plain called Hindustan, which was made by the Ganges out of the earth which she brought down from the Himalayas since before the Ice Age. In the beginning there are the two rivers, the Ganges and her sister Yamuna, now called Jumna, gracefully curving down from the Himalayas first running south, then bending eastwards. The twin rivers flow ever closer together until they finally merge at Allahabad, City of God, which was once called Prayaga. Gigantic canals have been built for the irrigation of the endless square miles of farmland. The Ganges and her sister rivers keep India alive. With their precious Himalayan waters the millions of farmers patiently irrigate their plots. Without that water no wheat, no maize, no millet would grow, and India would die. In the dry season the Ganges is too small for her wide bed. Yet, at one time she was so abundant that Shiva had to make her flow through his matted hair lest she drown India. Ganga was the daughter of the mountain-god Himavan, 'Owner of Snow', and sister of Parvati, spouse of Shiva. In the earliest times the gods kept her all to themselves, for they considered her too precious and too beautiful to share her with terrestrials. It was Bhagiratha, son of Dilipa, son of the pious Ansuman, King of Ayodhya, who, with his prolonged asceticism, induced Brahma to grant him a boon. Bhagiratha prayed that the sacred river Ganga might be allowed to descend to earth, so that the 60,000 burnt brothers of King Ansuman might be brought back to life. Brahma warned him that it was only possible if Shiva consented to let Ganga flow through his hair. After a long period of asceticism, Bhagiratha finally persuaded Shiva to agree. Roaring and foaming she came down and would have drowned India, but Shiva's hair was like a dense forest where she became the gentle river we know today. (See *Bhagiratha*.)

Gangadhara 'Carrying the Ganges', praise-name of Shiva, shown protecting the earth by 'restraining the torrential river in his hair'.

Ganga-Dwara 'The Gate of the Ganges'. The southern end of the gorge through which the Ganges pours onto the plain of Hindustan, near modern Hardwar, or Haradvara, 'Shiva's Gate'.

Garuda A sacred bird, a demigod who carries Vishnu. Garuda is so famous that he is well known in Indonesian tradition, so much so that they made him the symbol of their airlines. He is sometimes represented as a peacock with a long tail, but he belongs to the eagle family. He is variously described as having a golden body, like the golden eagle, or a white head like the 'bald' eagle. Perhaps Garuda was once the famous lammergeier, which can still be seen wheeling over the Himalayas. Garuda is the king of the birds serving Vishnu. Often Vishnu and Lakshmi are shown seated together on the Garuda's broad back flying up to their heaven of love. Garuda was the son of Kasyapa and Vinata, and he glowed so beautifully when he was born that the people worshipped him thinking he was an incarnation of Agni. With his red wings he can hit and kill bad men and he is the enemy of snakes. Perhaps he was originally the lightning, for he is still called Taraswin, the swift one. He once stole Indra's thunderbolt and Indra had to give battle to recover it. When Garuda soars up into the sky he is the symbol of the human spirit. He is thus the symbol of every thinking person.

Garudi A female bird of prey, one of the secret forms of Shiva.

Gatha Song, hymn, other than the Vedas. Also one of 17 hymns in Old Persian composed by the Prophet Zarathustra, inspired by Ahura Mazda, who makes the Prophet see visions of God and his purpose, prophecies of things to come. These psalms express a wonderfully profound devotion, full of passionate feeling and conviction, full of subtle allusions, and profound meaning. It is true poetry composed by a great seer, who, through study and meditation, reached communion with the divine world.

Gati Type of life, sort of existence. There are only six possible *gatis*:

1. Suffering in Hell.
2. Life as a ghost, *preta*, always hungry.
3. Life as a demon, *asura*.
4. Life as a mammal, bird, reptile, fish or insect.
5. Human life.
6. Life as a god, immortal life.

Only the last two are desirable.

Gauri 'The Shining One', 'the Golden Lady'. The first name for Parvati or Kali, when she rides on a tiger. (See *Sati*.)

Gayatri 'Singer'. Poetry personified as a goddess, wife of Brahma and mother of the four Vedas. She is depicted with five heads and ten arms, seated on a lotus, and holding a lotus in her hand, as well as an axe, a whip, a conch, a bowl, a mace, a bracelet and a crown. She is herself a hymn made visible: the famous Hindu hymn to the rising sun, which all the Brahmin priests have to memorize and sing every morning beginning just before sunrise, to the Saviour Sun. It is found in the Rig-Veda and so it is one of the oldest prayers on earth.

Gayatri Japa (*Japa* = a muttered prayer), a feast for the goddess Gayatri who is 'the divine power that transforms the human into the divine, granting us the blessing of the highest spiritual illumination'. A Gayatri *japa* should be prayed every day. The Para Brahma Gayatri Mantra is the most important of all *mantras*. Every Brahmin, at every stage of his life, repeats it daily. It is repeated while the mind is concentrated on any feminine form of the Deity. Originally Gayatri was simply the name of the metre and not the deity of the Mantra. That deity is the personal absolute Brahma. Here is the mantra with interlinear translation (*Om* encompasses all gods):

1. *Om*   *Bhur*   *Bhuvah*   *Svaha.*
   Brahma   Earth   Sky   Heaven.
2. *TAT*   *Savitu*   *Varenyam.*
   The Essence,   the Creator   is worth worshipping.
3. *Bharga*   *Devasya Dhimahi.*
   Upon the Glory we meditate.
4. *Dhiyo*   *Yo*   *Nah Prachodyaat.*
   The Intellect which us may guide.

This mantra should be repeated 1,008 times on Gayatri day, which falls at the end of July.

Ghritachi An Apsaras who had love affairs with gods and men.

Girija (1) 'Mountain-born'. Epithet of Devi-Uma-Kali (q.v.).
(2) A name for Vishnu in his incarnation as Narasimha.

Girisha 'Lord of the Mountains', a name for Rudra as Storm-god.

Gita A song or hymn. (See also *Bhagavadgita*.)

Gita-Govinda A long poem by Jayadeva on the life of Krishna as a cowherd, Govinda. It is both amorous and mystical because readers can interpret it in such a way as is in accordance with their own nature. It describes especially beautifully the feelings of Radha while she is waiting for Krishna, whom she loves. This is interpreted as the love of the human soul for the divine presence.

Gita Jayanti The birthday of the Bhagavadgita, is celebrated throughout India on the eleventh day (*Ekadashi*) of the bright (first) half of the moon-month, Margashirsha, which is around Christmas. It was on this day that Sanjaya recited the Bhagavadgita for the first time, more than 5,000 years ago. The first recital, by the Lord Krishna himself, was accompanied by an effulgence of light as bright as a sunrise, when he showed himself at Arjuna's insistence in Canto XI, 9. The Gita is for millions of Indians the most sublime work of world literature, dictated by God himself so that its language has divine power. Reciting it is reliving the experience of divine proximity. The faithful repeat with devotion verse XVIII, 66:

> Abandoning all duties, come to Me alone for shelter.
> Be free of care, for I will liberate you from all evils.

God See *Deva*.

Gods (See also *Deva*.) To what extent the gods of India can be equated with the classical gods of Greece and Rome is still being debated. Here is a list of those gods of the two civilizations as well as ancient Egypt which can be equated without too much doubt:

Indian	Function	Greek	Roman	Egyptian
Ashvinau	Twins	Dioskouroi	Sign of Gemini	–
Brahma	Creator/Artisan	Hephaistos	Vulcanus	Ptah
Dyaus	Ancient Sky-god	Ouranos	Uranus, Coelus	–
Indra	Lightning-god	Zeus	Jupiter	Amon
Indrani	Sky-goddess	Hera	Juno	Mut
Kali-Uma	Fertility/Death	Demeter-Rhea	Cybele-Ceres	Isis
Kama	Love-god	Eros	Cupido	–

Indian	Function	Greek	Roman	Egyptian
Kartikeya-Skanda	War-god	Ares	Mars	Onuris
Lakshmi-Radha	Love-goddess	Aphrodite	Venus	Hathor
Ratri	Night-goddess	Athena	Minerva	Neith
Rudra	Fury, inebriation	Dionysos	Bacchus	–
Sarasvati	River and Swan Goddess	Leda	Leda	–
Shiva	Ancient god of the Other World	Kronos	Saturnus	Osiris
Surya	Sun-god	Apollo-Helios	Sol	Horus
Ushas	Dawn-goddess	Eos	Aurora	–
Varuna	Ocean-god	Poseidon	Neptune	Sebek
Vayu	Wind-god	Aiolos	Ventus	–
Vishnu	God of Communication	Hermes	Mercurius	Anubis
Yama	Death-god	Hades	Pluto	Thoth

Gokula A district near Mathura where Krishna once lived.

Goloka The 'private' heaven of the cowherd god Krishna.

Gopa, Gopala, Govinda 'Cowherd'. (See *Krishna*.)

Gopi Cowgirl, female of Gopa, a cowherd. Radha was one of the Gopis who were secretly watched by Krishna while they bathed.

Govardhana Once, while Krishna was trying to persuade the people of Vrindabana to worship him, Indra sent a rainstorm. Krishna picked up the mountain called Govardhana and held it over the heads of the people who were there in the fields so they all remained dry.

Govinda 'Cowherd', a name for Krishna as Radha's beloved.

Graha 'Seizure'. One of a type of rapacious evil spirits who cause eclipses of the moon and fits or convulsions in children. They live in lakes.

Grail What is the original meaning of the Grail? Many theories have been propounded about it. The word grail comes ultimately from the Greek *krater*, 'mixing bowl', for wine. In the European Middle Ages it was believed that the Grail was the plate or platter from which Jesus shared out, and from which he ate, at the Last Supper. This simple dish was given special magic power by God, so it could heal the sick and provide abundant food for all the people. In Buddhism, Amrita Surabhi was the original begging bowl of the Buddha which provided food for him and his followers. The country where it was taken would always have enough water and food. But most of the time it is hidden in the water of a lake, from which it emerges annually on Buddha's birthday. It rises up and flies toward the virtuous lady, Manimekhalai, who will receive it and travel with it to a town where there are many destitute people because of drought, disease and other disasters. At once, Indra will order rain to fall so the crops will grow. Out of the one bowl Manimekhalai will feed all the hungry townspeople, and all the sick and suffering will be healthy and happy as soon as they touch the bowl.

Grandfather Worshipful term of address for Brahma, from whom all beings spring: gods, human beings, animals and even demons.

Grihapati 'Lord of the House', name of Agni as the Family Fireplace.

Guga A serpent-god, sometimes depicted with a human head.

Guha 'Secret', 'brought up secretly'. Epithet of the War-god Karttikeya, Skanda-of-the-six-heads.

Guhyaka One of a race of cavemen, treasure-keepers for Kubera (q.v.).

Guna One of the three elementary principles which pervade all creation: *sattva* — being, light, goodness; *tamas* — darkness, inertia, weight: *rajas* — movement, desire, sense.

Guru Spiritual master, especially the one who is destined to become one's guide to enlightenment.

H

Hanuman

Hades See *Hell*; *Bali*; *Patala*, the city of serpents and demons. See also *Yama*; *Yamapura*; *Naraka*.

Haimati 'The Snow Queen', 'Daughter of the Owner of Snow'. A name of Parvati-Devi as goddess of the high Himalayas and wife of the Mountain-god Shiva.

Halayudha 'Whose weapon is a ploughshare'. An epithet of Balarama.

Hamsa, Hansa Originally a goose, later a swan. Brahma's mount. In pre-Aryan times when the Indo-Europeans still wandered across the steppes of Russia, the Wild Goose was a holy bird, a god himself. Its sad cry when flying in V formation to the warm South in November marked the beginning of winter. In Sanskrit, *Hamsa* means swan. The swan is dedicated to Sarasvati, spouse of Brahma and goddess of beauty.

Hanuman Commander-in-Chief of the monkey warriors of Sugriva's kingdom. Still venerated as a god in India. As son of Pavana, a wind-god, Hanuman possessed the faculty of flying. Hanuman is one of the chief characters in the Ramayana, where he is the faithful general of Rama. He jumped from India to Sri Lanka in one leap, he had the power to seize clouds and tear up trees and rocks. Unlike the Hanuman-monkeys of today he was of gigantic size. He had yellow fur and a red face, while his tail was many miles long and his voice was as loud as thunder. The Rakshasas, hoping to play a trick on him, put tar on his tail and set it alight, but Hanuman used his flaming tail to set fire to the entire city. He flew to the Himalayas where he found medicinal herbs with which he cured the wounded on the battlefield. He fought many battles with great bravery against Rakshasas and Gandharvas and even against the monster Kalanemi whom he slew. Apart from pharmacology and medicine, Hanuman had mastered grammar and many other sciences, including poetry.

Hara Shiva (q.v.).

Harappa Pre-classical civilization at a city of that name, now in Pakistan, abandoned *c.*1500. Its beginnings may date from as early as 2500 BC. Other sites (over 70 in total) where the same civilization was discovered, include Mohenjo Daro, Lothal, Kalibangan, Rupar, Sutkagen Dor. The inhabitants had a script which has not been deciphered as yet, so we do not know their language. They may have been worshippers of Shiva.

Hare (See also *Shashi.*) As one of the Jataka Tales relates: One day the Bodhisattva came to life as a hare. The hare lived in a wood with three friends: a monkey, a jackal and an otter. They chose the hare as their leader because he was the most intelligent among them. He taught his friends the need for charity, contentment and self-sacrifice. One day Shakra (Indra) came down from heaven to test the hare's charity. Disguised as a beggar he asked the hare for food. The hare had nothing to offer except the grass he ate himself, which was unsuited for a human being. So the hare lit a fire, then shook himself repeatedly so that all the lice and fleas in his fur could escape and finally, he jumped into the fire, intending to cook himself as the only meat suitable for his guest. However, the fire froze because Agni would not let it burn. Indra was so impressed by this extreme hospitality, that in order to honour his host he reassumed his divine stature, picked up a mountain, squeezed it out like a fruit in his gigantic hand and with the juice painted the figure of a hare on the face of the moon. The picture of the hare still adorns the moon, or so say the Indians.

Hari The sun. A name for Vishnu. (See also *Harihara.*)

Haridwara A town now called Hardvar, where the great River Ganges emerges from the Himalayas onto the open plain of Hindustan. It has been a place of pilgrimage since early antiquity.

Harihara The twin-gods Vishnu and Shiva, merged into one great god, signifying the oneness of the divine essence. When Shiva saw Vishnu in his appearance as Mohini, even he fell in love with that beautiful woman, so he embraced her and merged with her, i.e.

with Vishnu, who, at that moment resumed his 'true' form. This myth illustrates again the Hindu philosophy that multiplicity is an illusion of the human mind but that all forms are delusive whereas unity of essence is the only true principle.

Haripriya 'Beloved of Vishnu', praise name for Lakshmi (q.v.).

Harischandra Twenty-eighth king of the Solar dynasty, son of Trisanku, famous for his piety and scrupulous adherence to justice. For his boundless generosity and his numerous sacrifices to Indra the latter invited him to live in his own heaven. One day while the king was riding through a forest, he heard loud lamentations, as if from oppressed women. When the king, who saw it as his duty to defend the oppressed, came closer, he saw the fervid sage Visvamitra who was master of all the sciences, and the sciences themselves, shaped like beautiful women, who were being overpowered by the great scholar, for whom no science was safe. The holy man was so provoked by this intrusion into his daily work that he demanded satisfaction from the king. Harischandra, who regarded it as his duty to honour all Brahmins and sacrifice to them all he owned, offered whatever the Brahmin asked for, unquestioningly. Visvamitra took all the king's possessions, his palace, his treasures and his whole kingdom, leaving him only a vest of bark-cloth.

With his wife and son the ex-king left his kingdom and went on a pilgrimage to Benares. Alas! Visvamitra was waiting for them there, and demanded also the queen and the prince as his right. Harischandra ceded, for which treasures are eternal? His wife and child were sold, weeping bitterly. Then the relentless Visvamitra sold the king himself into slavery, to a greedy slave-dealer called Chandala, who beat his slaves daily. The ex-king was sent every night to a cemetery to steal treasures from the dead. After a year Harischandra suddenly saw his wife, who told him that their son had died of a snakebite and that she had come to the cemetery to perform the last rites. She proposed to him that they die together on their son's funeral pyre. He agreed but he felt that he had to ask permission of his owner because he was not his own master but a slave.

At this point of utter conscientiousness, Harischandra was finally rewarded for his scrupulous uprightness. The gods Indra and Vishnu appeared to him, which is a sign of exceedingly great honour after long suffering. The harsh slave-trader transformed himself, taking his true shape as Dharma, God of Justice, who often descends and appears on earth in disguise in order to test a person with a reputation for great justice, such as the king. Indra invited Harischandra to Heaven but the king-slave protested that he could not go to heaven without permission of his master. Dharma then revealed himself as the same person as Chandala, and Visvamitra likewise renounced all claims on the king's property or family.

Harischandra was king once more, and his wife was queen again. However the good king objected that he could not go to Heaven without his faithful subjects. This request was granted by Indra, who brought Rohitaswa, the king and queen's son, back to earthly life, whereupon Visvamitra inaugurated the young prince as king in his father's place. Harischandra was now free to go to Heaven with his followers. Indra created a special city for them, suspended in the sky where Harischandra lives together with his wife in eternal bliss. It is said that on clear nights the city in the sky is just visible.

Hariti 'The one who snatches away'. Originally the name of the goddess of smallpox, wife of Panchika. She is the mother of the Yakshas, the nature deities. She is represented as an ogress, a terrifying monster with a horse's head, who was said to devour people's children. Until one day she met Buddha, who had taken and hidden her youngest son, Pingala, to teach her a lesson. Suddenly she realized what she had done to other mothers and she felt contrite. She was converted by Buddha and decided to compensate people for the suffering she had caused. She became Nanda, 'Joy', the goddess to whom people pray when they hope to have children, bringing her offerings of food to replace the human flesh that used to be her sustenance. (See also *Apsaras*; *Makara*.)

Harivamsa A long epic poem about the life of Krishna.

Hastimukha Elephant-face. (See *Ganesha*.)

Hastinapura The capital city of central India in the days of the great war of the Mahabharata. It was founded by Hastin, son of Bharata, the first ruler of India.

Hayagriva Vishnu with the head of a horse, as the god of learning.

Heaven Each god has his own heaven in which the souls of his devotees live happily.

Hell According to Jain cosmology, the nether region has seven hells, the seventh being the lowest, called Mahatuma 'deep darkness'. Each hell has its own name and a special type of torture is applied in it by a special category of gods: the Amba scrape the sinners' nerves, the Ambaras carve the flesh from the bones, the Sama beat them with sticks, the Sabala tear out pieces of flesh with hot pliers, the Rudra stick spearpoints into the sinners' flesh, the Maharudra mince their flesh in grinders, the Kala roast the sinners on a grid, the Mahakala pull out pieces of their bodies, the Asipala cut them with big knives, the Dhanu jab arrows into them, the Kumbha rub chilli powder into their wounds, the Valu bury their victims in hot sand in Valuka, a hell reserved specially for that purpose. Furthermore the Vetarani dash their victims against the stones and the Kharasvara push them naked into thornbushes.

According to the Hindu work Bhagabata, there are 28 hells for various sinners. Tamusra is a region of darkness where robbers and adulterers are tortured, Raurava is the hell where sadists ('those who wantonly hurt people') are torn to pieces but not killed. Kumbhika is a hell where cruel men are boiled in oil. Those who have killed a Brahmin will be fried in the fires of Kalasutra. Asipatravana is for heretics, and kings who have oppressed their subjects are crushed like oilseeds between two rollers in the hell called Sukramukha. Krimibhoja is a room full of worms where the inhospitable, selfish house-owners, having been transformed into worms, will eat one another. Those who have married outside their caste will be thrown into Vajrakantaka where they will be forced to embrace red-hot metal statues. Those who have given false testimony will be thrown into Avichimat from a great height, before being hoisted up and thrown down again. Misers reside in Suchimukha, where barbed wire is wound round their bodies. Those who cause disagreement among the religious scholars are thrown into Vaitarani River, which is a stream of boiling urine, blood, excreta, pus and other filthy liquids, though of course they do not die in it.

Hemakuta 'The Golden Peaks'. A mythical mountain range lying to the north of the Himalayas towards Mount Meru.

Hidimba An *asura* or demon cannibal who lived in the forest where the Pandavas fled after their palace was burnt down. He sent his beautiful sister Hidimbaa to lure them to his bone-cave, but when she saw Bhima, she fell in love with him. She offered to carry him to safety, but he refused. He was attacked by Hidimba but killed him in a terrible fight. Hidimba's sister was terrified and fled but later came back to claim Bhima as her husband. Bhima married her and they had a son named Ghatotkacha.

Himachala The Himalayan mountains.

Himalaya 'The Abode of Snow', personified as the mighty Mountain God, father of the great goddess Parvati. It contains the sources of all the great rivers of India: Indus, Yamuna, Ganges, Brahmaputra and the five rivers of the Panjab. All the major gods live in these mountains: Indra, Brahma, Kubera, Vishnu, Shiva, Parvati and others.

Himavan or **Himavat** 'Owner of Snow'. The god of the Himalayas, whose wife was Mena. They had two daughters, Ganga and Uma.

Hinayana The 'Lesser Vehicle'. The earliest form of Buddhism, which survives as Therevada (q.v.).

Hiranya-Garbha 'The Golden Seed'. It has also been translated as 'the Golden Germ' or 'the Golden Egg'. *Garbha* literally means 'womb'. Hiranya-garbha is the Vedic symbol for the secret of

Creation, the essence of life which all created beings share. It is sometimes equated with Brahma (see *Brahma 3*), the soul-essence of the universe, that out of which the god Brahma (see *Brahma 2*) created and creates all things, the only eternal thing in the cosmos where all visible things are transitory. It is inside every living being, inside every fruit or nut, which — one should remember — can grow into a tree similar to the one it grew on. The god Brahma himself lived inside this 'golden womb' for one of his years, then he divided it into two parts, one male and one female, one above (heaven), the other below (earth). Thus heaven's vaults above us are like an empty eggshell. We are all inside its resplendent dome. The 'golden egg' is the sky we know and inhabit, with the sun, the stars, the land and the oceans in it. It is like one golden seed in the vast spaces of the universe.

'All those things I created out of myself and yet I remain distinct from them,' says the Lord in the Bhagavadgita. The 'golden germ' is God so that we are both in Him while He is in us, yet He is always uncatchable like the golden sunlight. It is this of which the sage said to his son: *Tat tuam asi* 'it is you'. The essence of existence is what we all have in common.

Hiranyaksha 'Gold-eye'. A demon who drowned the earth. He was killed by Vishnu as Varaha, who raised the land again.

Hitopadesha The Book of Sound Counsel. A collection of fables, partly based on the Panchatantra, but with alterations in the morals of the stories under Buddhist influence. Whereas the Panchatantra contains practical lessons for young princes and diplomats, the Hitopadesha teaches morality and other-worldliness.

Holi Holi is a famous Hindu feast which is celebrated when the sun enters the sign of Pisces late in February, in the Indian month of Phalgun. Some people say that on this day Kama the god of love was burnt to ashes by Shiva's third eye so that he had to start looking for a body, which he finds wherever husband and wife embrace in love. In some towns the women sing dirges, songs of lament to commemorate Rati's grief at losing her husband. Rati is the Hindu equivalent of Venus, Aphrodite, the goddess of love who rules the zodiacal sign of Pisces, of spring. Others maintain that Holi is celebrated to commemorate Krishna's victory over the demoness Putana, the goddess of winter and death. During the Holi festival people sprinkle each other with water (often scented and coloured pink) or even blow red powder over each other. I am told that women and girls seek out the man they love secretly and blow red powder over him as a secret sign. At no other time could a girl express her feelings in any way whatsoever. Red signifies love. At Indore and some other towns huge statues of a giant Nathurama, another enemy that Krishna destroyed, are erected and burnt at night, for fun. Socially, Holi is an off-time celebration, a time during which official social relations and strains are suspended. Things are done with impunity that would be inconceivable during the rest of the year; there is even a reversal of relationships in which the lowly can abuse the high-born. Holi celebrates the dalliance of Krishna and his *Gopa* (cowherd) friends with the Gopis, the lovable cowgirls who bathed naked in the river, secretly watched by Krishna hidden in a tree. Radha is his favourite. She awaits him all night. He, the god, comes at dawn.

Hotar, Hotri The priest who performs the sacrifice. Agni was the first Hotar and remains the perfect example as the 'One Who Lights the Fire'.

Hotra The sacrifice of burnt offerings in the fire, Agni's true self. Oblations with prayers.

Hrada A demon-serpent, son of Hiranyakashipu, who stole the people's sacrifices from the gods. The gods were in despair, as Hrada and his fellow demons were performing asceticism too. The gods sent Vishnu to mislead them, which he did with his power of *maya*. He seduced them away from the Veda and the Dharma so they became ignorant and could be defeated.

Huvishka A central Asian ruler who reigned in north India in the middle of the second century AD. He was said to be a Buddhist.

I

Indra

Ida *Ida* originally means food. Also food for the gods, i.e. libations of milk which are poured over the gods' statues. Then also: food for the soul, i.e. praise. With perceptive intuition the Indian mind knew that what each of us needs most is encouragement in the form of a laudatory ego-boost. Food is subject to rules. What we eat, how much, when and in what combination, it all has to be regulated so that we may lead healthy lives. Over the centuries, Ida gradually became the goddess of food, of offerings and of eloquence; then also she became the goddess of law. She taught Manu the Law which he proclaimed among his fellow human beings. Ida is also a goddess of the earth, i.e. of the land, the cultivated field. She arose and appeared first when Manu performed a sacrifice, the rules for which are Ida's laws. The purpose of knowing the rules is to have success, and success in antiquity was one thing: to beget a healthy family. The sacrifice pleased her so much that she remained faithful to Manu, a mere man, although the gods Mitra and Varuna proposed to her. Ida and Manu had many children. According to another myth she is Manu's daugther and married Budha, the planetary god Mercury. She led a curious double life, being a woman for one month (Ida), then changing in one night and living as a man (Ila) during the next month. This double life probably symbolizes the alternating phases of the moon.

Idol See *Murti; Form.*

Ikshvaku Son of Vaivasvat, grandson of Vivasvat the Sun-god. The great demigod Manu sneezed and Ikshvaku was born. He became the first king of Ayodhya, founding the dynasty of Suryavansa, the Sun-clan. He had a hundred sons; the name of the eldest was Vikukshi. A younger son named Nimi founded the dynasty of Mithila.

Imam Ar., originally a leader of a tribe or nation. In Islam, the leader of the prayers in the mosque and so, the rector of the Islamic parish. Some imams in history have been acclaimed as kings. In Shiah Islam, the imam is a descendant of the Prophet Muhammad who possesses miraculous powers. The Prophet's grandson Husayn, the third imam, is still widely venerated and is said to appear in dreams. Many Indians want to visit his tomb in Kerbela in Iraq. The seventh imam is venerated by the Ismailis (Khojas). The twelfth imam was hidden by God in AD 940. On Doomsday he will reappear and lead the armies of Islam to victory against the enemies of God.

Incarnation See *Avatara; Vishnu.*

Indira 'Lotus'. A name for Lakshmi (q.v.).

Indra One of the most ancient and prestigious gods of India, the supreme god of Vedic times, the god of the skies, of rain, of lightning and thunder which he creates with his *vajra* (q.v.). Thus Indra has been equated with the classical god Zeus–Jupiter. Indra's colour is golden or reddish, and he has long arms which span the skies. He rides in a golden chariot drawn by bay horses with flowing manes. His weapons are the thunderbolt, bow, net and *anka* or hook. He is the Weather-god, sending rainstorms when and where he wishes. He is thus the God of Life, battling against Vritra (Ahi) the god of drought and death. In this respect Indra is co-functional with the Roman Jupiter Pluvius. Indra is often at war against the evil demons, the Asuras and Daityas, but his battles do not always end in triumph. He did kill Vala who had stolen the heavenly cows. Indra also destroyed the fortified cities of the Asuras. Like all the good Hindu gods, Indra has a wife, Indrani or Aindra, the Queen of Heaven, like Hera, whom he loves dearly. Indra's heaven is called Svarga or Suarga, the Good Kingdom, where Yudhisthira and his brothers hope to arrive when they die. Like Zeus, Indra had many love affairs. One must not forget, however, that gods are not men and do not live by men's laws. Gods are immortal and so they always outlive their mortal sweethearts. Indra is also called Sahasraksha 'thousand eyes', with which he can see the whole universe in one glance. He is the god of the Garden of Delight for the souls who have led a meritorious life and now live on golden Mount Meru. He is also the god of a hundred sacrifices and many of the earliest hymns are sung in his worship.

The beautiful twelfth hymn of Book II of the Rig-Veda sings Indra's praises as 'the one who had insight when he was born, who protected the gods with his power of thought, before whose breath the two world-halves tremble at the greatness of his manly powers ... He who made fast the tottering earth, who made still the quaking mountains ... who propped up the sky ... who gave birth to the fire between two stones (i.e. Indra made lightning flash) ... He freed the cows (for the benefit of the people) which (the demon) Vala kept hidden ... He killed the serpent and so, released the seven rivers (of India, thus ending the great drought) ... He drove away the Dasas (the enemies of the Aryans) to outer darkness ... He encourages the weary and the sick ... He made the sun and the waters ... He is invoked by both armies locked in battle, he without whom people do not conquer ... He who kills the sinners.'

Indrajala The magic arts, taught by Indra, the god of lightning.

Indrani Queen of Indra, goddess of the sky, famous for her golden skin and great sensuality, the ideal of the Indian woman; beautiful and devoted to her husband. She knows that she will never be a widow, so she is the happiest of all wives. Also called Paulomi or Aindra.

Indra-Prastha The capital city of the Pandava princes. Remains of it have been found in New Delhi along the River Jumna.

Indra-Pura The City of Indra, a name for Paradise.

Indrasena Son of Nala (q.v.) and Damayanti (q.v.).

Indu The Moon. (See *Chandra* and *Soma*.)

Indu-Mani Moon-gem. (*See Chandra-Kanta*.)

Indumati 'The full moon'. Princess of Vidarbha. She chose Prince Aja to be her husband at her *svayamvara* (q.v.). She died when a multitude of flowers completely covered her, while she slept in her orchard.

Iraja 'Born in the water'. An epithet of Kama (q.v.).

Iravat Son of Arjuna and Ulupi, princess of the Nagas.

Isha 'Lord'. An epithet of Shiva.

Ishana 'Lord'. One of the appellations of Rudra-Shiva, guardian of the North-east.

Ishani 'The Great Lady'. Epithet of Devi–Uma–Kali (q.v.).

Ishvara, Iswara 'Lord'. An epithet of Shiva (q.v.).

Isipatana The Deerpark near Varanasi where Buddha preached his first sermon so the deer, anxious for enlightenment, could hear him.

Itihasa An epic poem dealing with legendary heroes.

J

Jnana-Dakshina (Shiva)

Jaganmata 'World-mother'. A name of Devi-Uma-Durga-Kali (q.v.).

Jagannath (Juggernaut). This name means Lord (Nath, Naut) of the world (Jagan). The celebrated temple for Jagannath, an appearance of Vishnu, stands at Puri in the State of Orissa, although some scholars maintain Jagannath was Buddha, others that he was really Krishna, which is another name for Vishnu. It is related that one day Vishnu had assumed the form of an animal and was killed by a hunter who left the body to rot. A devout king named Indradyumna or Indradhumna was directed by Vishnu to collect the bones and place them in a coffin, to build a temple, to have a statue made and place it inside the temple. The great artist Vishvakarma promised to make the statue on condition that the king would not look at it before it was finished. Alas, the king could not control his curiosity: he stole a look at the statue and the sculptor stopped working. The king prayed to Brahma, who promised to give the statue eyes and even a soul.

During the festival of Snana-yantra in the month of Jyaishtha, the great statue of the god is washed ritually with milk, of which Krishna is known to be fond. During the festival Ratha-yatra 'car-feast' in the month of Ashada, the statue of the god is placed on an enormous wheeled vehicle which is pulled through the streets of the city by numbers of devotees. Some believers become so excited by seeing the statue of the god (which is normally hidden in the temple) that they are overcome by a holy desire to see the god himself, who is believed to be nearby at that moment. Since no man can see God while he is alive, these believers, in a state of utter surrender to the love of God, throw themselves under the wheels, where they are crushed by the juggernaut, which weighs many tons. This is the meaning of the cryptic expression; 'to go and see the god' which people use for 'to worship god'. It is believed that a man who so dies will be totally sinless.

Jahnu A sage whose meditation was disturbed by the Ganges overflowing. His response was to drink up all its water. The gods persuaded him to relent so he let it escape out of his ear.

Jainism The Jain religious movement, founded by Vardhamana Mahavira called Jina, who lived c.540–468 BC, in what is now the state of Bihar. The word *Jain* originates from *Jina*, 'victor', since the Jains claim to have vanquished all human passion and desire. Even the ancient Greek writers had heard of the Gennoi, the 'naked philosophers' whose asceticism they highly admired.

The Jains have a chronology of their own which begins in the year 527 BC, which, according to their time-reckoning, was the date of Mahavira's death, aged 72. He is said to have been a prince in Bihar who, at the age of 40, was dissatisfied with life. After 12 years of severe asceticism, he attained enlightenment. He was preceded in history by a series of 23 *tirthankaras* or trail-blazers; the last one of these, Parshva, may have lived in the late eighth century BC.

The early Jains spread from Bihar, especially to Gujerat and South India. At an early stage, a division arose between the Shvetambaras 'dressed in white', who permitted themselves a white loincloth as their sole possession, and the Digambaras 'dressed in air', who walked about stark naked being without any possessions. Since they had vanquished all their desires, their nakedness could not be associated with any form of libido.

The Jains' holy scripture is laid down in 12 books (the last one is lost), called Angas, in the Prakrit language. The Digambaras (now few in numbers) maintain that the *Angas* were never composed by Mahavira. They use instead the books composed by later religious Jain leaders. This is the so-called Secondary Canon, which in turn is followed by an extensive dogmatic and theological literature. In it, the Jain is admonished to practise the virtues of poverty, humility, purity, truthfulness, self-discipline, suffering, tolerance, reasonableness, innocence, abstention and asceticism. By conquering all his desires a person may 'break out' of the *sansara* or chain of rebirths and so end all suffering.

The cosmology of the Jains teaches that the world is eternal and space immense, though limited, and empty. In the centre of the disk-shaped earth there is the great mountain Meru. Under the earth there are the strata of kingdoms ruled by demons where the doomed suffer long but not eternal punishment. Above the earth rise layers of skies and, higher still, lovely heavens where different classes of gods enjoy power and pleasure.

The gods are great and may grant boons to mortals, but they are not themselves immortal, being subject to karma and the chains of reincarnation. Higher even than the abode of the gods, beyond a disc which acts like a lid closing off the mortal realms, there lies the realm of those who have gained enlightenment and are therefore exempt from rebirth. The regions beneath and above the earth remain unchanged, but on earth ascending and descending epochs of history cause the earth's peoples to grow taller and better, or smaller and meaner. At present we live in an era in which people grow gradually more wicked and immoral. This deterioration will last for another several thousand years before there is an improvement in the moral standards on earth.

All the individual souls together form the spiritual substance of the universe. They are in essence knowing and wise, but their wisdom is clouded by their own desires, which in turn are caused by their bodies, which are infected with physical pollution and with ignorance. This condition causes the souls to travel from one mortal body to the next, like a person drowning in a torrent who is incapable of getting out of the current. The *karma* 'activity' of a soul causes vibrations which attract particles of matter towards it. Only through complete control of all its desires can the soul attain peace, stillness and so, lucidity and insight into its condition. Only when that is achieved, then the enlightened ascetic may end his life by ceasing to take food. When he dies, his liberated soul will rise to the summit of the world where it will live for ever.

The Jains deny the existence of a creator. The world has always existed and is subject to the eternal laws of karma, the causality of recompense and punishment. The Jains do not worship the gods but they venerate the Tirthankaras, the 'pioneers', the early saints and precursors of Mahavira, who first broke out of the *sansara*, the chain of existences. Many legends circulate about them. This cult is practised in temples where their colossal statues are venerated by hymn-singing. Only the sect of the Sthanakavasis rejects all temple cults and concentrates only on studying the scriptures.

Jainism is characterized by vegetarianism and complete *ahimsa*, i.e. that its members take care not to harm any fellow creatures to the extent that some Jains even walk with brooms to sweep away the insects from their path lest they tread on them. There are less than four million Jains in India and in a few Western countries. Jainism was very important in India in the eleventh and twelfth centuries, before the Islamic conquests. (See also *Mahavira*.)

Jaladhi-Ja 'Born in the Ocean'. The moon; epithet for Lakshmi (q.v.).

Jala-Hastin or Jalebha A water-elephant, an aquatic spirit.

Jala-Shayin 'Sleeping on the water'. Epithet of Vishnu (q.v.).

Jala-Turaga A water-horse, an aquatic spirit.

Jambavat King of the bears. He once fought a lion and, on killing it, found a precious jewel in its mouth. It belonged to Krishna but Jambavat did not know this. So, when Krishna appeared in the bear's den, he fought him fiercely. The battle lasted for three weeks before Jambavat surrendered and gave up the jewel. Discovering that he had been fighting a god, he gave Krishna his daughter Jambavati, his only precious possession. Jambavat and his army of formidable bears faithfully helped Rama, another of Vishnu's incarnations, in his war against Ravana in Sri Lanka.

Jambha 'Jaws', a demon killed by Vishnu.

Jambhala The god of wealth in the Buddhist tradition (see *Kubera* for the Hindu tradition). He is shown carrying a bag of gold. He also sometimes holds a mongoose, the animal that fights snakes, *nagas*. The *nagas* are the keepers of the treasures in the earth so Jambhala wins gold with his mongoose. He also holds a *jambhara*, a lemon; its seeds are the seeds of the world.

Jambudwipa 'Sweet fruit island'. The name of one of the seven continents, the best, because it is the one of which India forms part. In its centre stands Mount Meru, where Indra resides. India, Bharata-varsha, is the southern part.

Janaka King of Videha, known for his knowledge, charity and sanctity. Through his pure and righteous life he became a Brahman and a Rajarshi, a priest-king. As he was childless, he performed the ceremony of ploughing the earth. Out of the earth sprang Sita 'furrow', an incarnation of Lakshmi, who became Rama's wife. By his saintliness, King Janaka prepared the way for Buddha.

Janguli The Buddhist serpent-goddess who is recognizable in sculpture by a *sarpa-kundala*, an ear ornament of a coiled cobra in each ear, and a *sarpa mekhala*, a snake-necklace. She is also shown playing with a long cobra. She cures snakebites and can prevent them. Special mantras are dedicated to her, which can extract snake poison if properly recited. She plays the *vina* or another musical instrument and her colours are white and gold. She is one of the oldest goddesses of India.

Janna The Garden of Paradise. (See *Firdaus*.)

Jara-Sandha Once upon a time there was a king of Magadha called Brihadratha ('big carriage'). This king had two wives who gave birth to two half-babies on the same day. These two halves of a child were thrown out in the forest where they were found by Jara, a demoness who loved human flesh. She put the two halves together, presumably hoping they would together become one fat live baby. They did and the baby cried lustily, alerting King Brihadratha, who arrived on the scene at once. He was preparing to kill the demoness when she explained what she had done. He realized that it was his son. Taking the child from her he gave him the name of Jarasandha, 'put together by Jara'. Jarasandha became a great warrior but was later killed by Bhima, after many wars.

Jarita A very big female bird. The saint Mandapala had to return from the Land of the Dead because he had no son. He took the shape of a male Jarita-bird (Sarangika) and married Jarita. They had four sons, after which he had to return to the Land of the Dead. Later, a terrible fire broke out in the forest where Jarita lived. Mandapala pleaded with Agni, who diverted the fire from the Jaritas' dwelling.

Jataka Birth, incarnation. A previous incarnation of the Buddha; part of the history of his previous lives, i.e. as a Bodhisattva. A legend about one of these lives. (See *Chadanta*; *Hare*; *Mahasattva*; *Yasapani*.)

Jatavedas See *Agni*.

Jatayu A big bird, son of Garuda and king of the eagles. He joined Rama in the war against Ravana in which he was killed by Ravana. His soul went up to heaven as a favour from Rama (i.e. Vishnu), because Jatayu had once saved Dasharatha (Rama's father) when the king was falling from his flying chariot, which was in flames.

Jayadeva Poet of the Gita-Govinda, the finest love-poem of India, describing Radha and Krishna's romance.

Jayanti 'Victorious', a daughter of Indra, who sent her to seduce Kavya (see *Shukra*), who had suspended himself head down over a sacrificial fire-pit, inhaling its smoke. He persisted in spite of her massaging. After a thousand years Shiva granted him a boon: he gave him all his knowledge, invincibility, wealth and dominance of all created beings. Finally, Shiva vanished but Jayanti was still there. With his infinite knowledge, Kavya knew her wishes and he withdrew with her, invisible for all creatures because of his magic power of illusion which only gods possess.

Jhana See *Dhyana*.

Jina See *Jainism*; *Mahavira*.

Jiva Life, the soul of a person, his principle of life.

Jivatma The animating soul, the immaterial part of a person.

Jnana Knowledge, insight, the most desirable acquisition in both Hindu and Buddhist philosophy. Without it there is only ignorance, *ajnana*, the cause of suffering and evil. Only knowledge enables us to follow the correct path.

Jnana-Mudra The Buddha is often shown with the *jnana-mudra*, the 'sign of insight', holding up his hand with the thumb touching the tip of the middle or index finger, forming a circle signifying all-round knowledge of the three worlds.

Jupiter See *Brihaspati*.

K

Kali

Ka This meditation-syllable represents for some the creator, the unknown God who created Existence itself and all the gods after him. It is uncertain whether he created the primal waters or arose out of them. He or she is identified with Hiranyagarbha and later with Prajapati-Brahma; she may also be the Goddess. (See *Aditi*; *Bhu*; *Uttanapad*.)

Kabandha Name of a Rakshasa whom Rama killed. He was an ugly giant without a head but with a large mouth surrounded by sharp teeth, set in his belly. He was hairy all over and each of his eight arms was a mile long. He had only one eye, which was in the middle of his chest and no legs so that he walked on his eight long arms like a spider. This deformity was caused by Indra, with whom the foolish Kabandha once quarrelled. Indra hit him with his lightning (*vajra*), striking his head, which sank into his body, and his legs which came off his body. Kabandha met Rama when the latter was on his way to Sri Lanka and begged him to burn him alive. Out of the ashes he rose transformed as a good Gandharva and offered to help Rama in his battle against the tyrant Ravana. Kabandha or Danu was a son of Devi Sri.

Kacha Son of Brihaspati (q.v.). His father sent him to become the student of Shukra, the chief priest of the Asuras, to learn the secret charm that brings the dead back to life. Only Shukra possessed the knowledge of that charm. The Asuras came and killed Kacha but his teacher revived him because he loved his pupil. So did the guru's daughter, Devayani, who pleaded with her father to restore Kacha's life each time the Asuras killed him. Eventually the Asuras decided to burn Kacha's body and mix the ashes with Shukra's wine. So, unknowingly, the old guru drank his own student. Devayani, discovering that Kacha had been murdered yet again, begged her father to pronounce the secret formula which would bring her lover back to life. He did so and Kacha revived but as a baby inside his old teacher's stomach. Now the sagacious Shukra had no option but to teach his pupil the secret mantra of life. He then allowed a surgeon to carve the young Kacha out of his stomach, Kacha came out alive and well, but Shukra died on the operating table. This was no problem as Kacha now knew the secret charm, so he brought Shukra to life again. Unfortunately this was not a happy ending. As Kacha had just been born from Devayani's father, he became her brother and could therefore not marry her. (See *Shukra*.)

Kadru Daughter of Daksha, married to Kasyapa. She became the mother of a dozen many-headed serpents, *nagas*.

Kaikeyi A princess of Kaikeya, wife of King Dasharatha and mother of Bharata, his third son. She lovingly looked after her husband when he was wounded in battle so he granted her a wish. Her wicked maid-servant, Mauthara, suggested that she should get Rama sent into exile so Bharata would become king. Dasharatha, unfortunately, could not refuse her wish.

Kailasa The 'Silver Mountain', where Shiva has his palace. (See *Brahmaputra*.)

Kaitabha Kaitabha and Madhu were two horrifying giant demons who conspired to kill Brahma, just as he was rising out of Vishnu's navel, while seated on the world lotus. They were just creeping out of their hiding places in Vishnu's ears, when Vishnu woke up and killed them. Whenever Vishnu wakes up, a new era, a new world epoch or aeon begins. So, at that moment in time, Brahma commenced creation. He took the two giants' bodies and created the earth out of their marrow (*medas*).

Kala The God of Time and so, the god of death, ruin, destruction and decay. Usually identified with Shiva but sometimes with Yama, Brahma or Vishnu. Kala also means 'black' as a name for Shiva, the god of the carbonized corpses, husband of the killing Kali.

Kalaka Daughter of Daksha. With her sister Puloma she became a wife of Kasyapa and bore him 60,000 sons, the Danavas. Her religious devotion had earned her, as a reward, the privilege of giving birth without pain. Her sons were powerful, ferocious giants.

Kala-Mukha 'Black-face'. The name for a special race of people who descend from the union of human men and Rakshasis, pretty female demons who seduced the men in the wilderness.

Kalanemi A Rakshasa, Son of Virochana, grandson of Hiran-yakashipu. He was also an uncle of Ravana's, who promised him half his kingdom if he, Kalanemi, would kill Hanuman. Disguised as a hermit, Kalanemi met Hanuman while the latter was searching for herbs in the forest. Kalanemi offered him food but Hanuman refused as he was fasting that day. Later, Hanuman went to bathe in a nearby pond. A large crocodile caught his foot but he dragged the ugly beast out, for Hanuman was very strong and accomplished in magic. He killed the crocodile and out of it came a beautiful Apsaras nymph who had been cursed by Daksha to be a crocodile until Hanuman killed her, and so, liberated her. She told her saviour that Kalanemi was looking for a chance to kill him. Hanuman went up to his intending murderer, picked him up by a leg and swung him up into the air, towards the south. Kalanemi landed in Sri Lanka. He fell down in his nephew's throne room in full view of the public. He was killed by Vishnu, but reincarnated as both Kamsa and Kaliya. Kalanemi had six sons who lived as embryos until Vishnu took them and placed them in Devaki to be born and thereafter to be killed by Kamsa, who, unbeknownst to himself, was their spirit-father.

Kalari Shiva in his aspect of Commander of Life (*vayas*), Time (*kala*) and even of the god of death (Yama).

Kalasha A vase or water-jar, symbol of Brahma, who is often shown with it, hence his identification with Aquarius. He created all things out of water, the primary element. Even he himself came forth from the water seated on a lotus. Thus the women's water-jar signifies the primeval ocean. (See also *Kumbha*.)

Kala-Yavana A foreign king who invaded India. Krishna met him and persuaded him to visit the cave of Muchukunda, the sleeping giant. Kala-yavana, imprudent barbarian that he was, kicked the giant, who woke up and, with his radiant eyes, set fire to the invader, who was burnt to ashes.

Kali 'Black' (the same as Syama). Devi-Uma in her ferocious and terrifying aspect as female world-ruler (Jaganmata), who leaves behind her a trail of death and destruction. She is depicted as a black woman of voluptuous appearance but with blazing bloodthirsty eyes, from which human blood drips and with her long tongue hanging out, ready to lick up her victim's blood. Human skulls hang on strings round her body, snakes writhe around her neck and there are weapons in each of her 10 hands. Her victims are sacrificed to her in the Durga-puja, the rituals due to her, in which, some say, human victims are sometimes sacrificed. She is painted dancing on her husband Shiva's dead body, swinging his head in one hand and a sword in the other. (One is reminded of Isis who pieces together her husband's limbs, then has intercourse with the dead body.) As goddess of death, Kali has to destroy everything, including her husband, since no visible thing is eternal. (See *Chamunda*; *Devi-Mahatmya*; *Durga*; *Parvati*; *Sati*; *Shakti*.)

Kalidasa One of the greatest poets of India, who probably lived in Ujjaini in the first century BC, at the court of the fabulous King Vikramaditya (q.v.), Kalidasa wrote many famous poems such as Raghu-vamsa and the Megha-duta. He also wrote dramatic works, the most famous of which is the moving Shakuntala (q.v.). Goethe wrote:

> If you wish to see spring flowers
> If you wish the fruits of autumn
> If you wish charm and excitement
> If you wish what feeds and quenches
> If you wish heaven and earth
> Only one name need I give you:
> Shakuntala says it all.

Kalika-Purana A Sanskrit poem of c.9000 stanzas dedicated to the worship of Kalika, or Kali, the bride of Shiva, as Devi Shakti, the potency of the god Shiva. It glorifies the adoration of the female powers of the deities, especially Sandhya-Sarasvati, who was loved by Brahma, and Parvati-Sati, whose marriage to Shiva is described in detail, followed by Shiva carrying the dead body of his beloved wife around the world in a cosmic act of mourning. It also describes the worship of Devi-Kali and some of the sanguinary sacrifices.

Kalinda A mountain in the Himalayas, from whence the Yamuna springs.

Kalindi The River Yamuna, daughter of Kalinda the Sun-god.

Kaliya King of the serpents with five ugly heads who lived in the River Yamuna, served by numerous dangerous serpents. The serpents' mouths spat fire and smoke so that many people died. One day Krishna went to bathe in the river and was nearly strangled by the monster, which was an incarnation of Kalanemi. Then Balarama reminded him that he was a god, so Krishna put his foot on the monster's central neck. Since a god's foot is immensely heavy, Kaliya had to beg for mercy. He was exiled.

Kaliyadamana 'Conqueror of Kaliya, the Serpent'. Praise-name of Krishna (q.v.).

Kali-Yuga 'The age of iron'. The period of the history of the universe in which we live. It began just over 5,000 years ago and will last for another 400,000 years. Like the philosophers of ancient Greece and Rome, so the Indian sages agree that this is the worst of

the four great periods of world history, the winter season of the
universe, the last epoch before a new cyclical year of Brahma
begins. This is the black period when there is little goodness left in
the world and even that is diminishing. Crime, vice and mendacity
are on the increase, there is less and less compassion or truthfulness
to be found. Even nature is crumbling and disintegrating, as
Brahma slowly breathes in, and will do so until all matter has
vanished.

Kalki or Kalkin The 'white horse'. The tenth incarnation of
Vishnu, when at the end of human time he will descend to purify
the earth of all evil. The Agni-Purana predicts that in the 'near'
future (meaning perhaps a thousand years after it was written) there
will be increasing ignorance so that men will marry daughters of
other castes, a major sin; the Vedic sacrifices will be forgotten;
foreign barbarians will occupy India and rule it. Then Vishnu will
appear riding a white horse, his shining sword raised aloft, and
destroy the barbarians, restoring order, purity and law.

Kalmasha-Pada 'Spotted legs'. The name of a king whose legs
developed black spots when cursed water fell on them; thus says the
tradition, though it is more probable that he was a leopard, because
it is said that he was a man-eater for 12 years. While he was still a
king Kalmasha-pada once met an aggressive tiger when he was
hunting in the jungle. He killed it but, dying, it changed into a
Rakshasa who swore revenge, then disappeared. Later, when the
king was sponsoring a sacrifice at which the famous priest Vasishtha
officiated, a cook offered his services for the banquet, which was
customary after a sacrifice. The cook was the Rakshasa in disguise;
he cooked human meat. The sage Vasishtha discovered it in time
and accused the king: 'I curse you that you will yourself become a
man-eater!'
    When it turned out that the king was innocent, the priest limited
his curse to 12 years. From that day for 12 years the king had to eat
a man or a woman daily.

Kalpa (1) A day of the god Brahma, equalling four billion human
years. According to Buddha, when a piece of cloth has rubbed away
a rock 16 miles high, long and broad, one second of Kalpa is past.
    (2) Kalpa and Kalpathitha are the two uppermost levels of the
universe according to Jain cosmology. The Kalpa region is divided
into 16 Devalokas or heavens, each one with a name and its own
inhabitants. The Kalpathitha region is divided into 14 abodes for
gods. (But see also *Siddha-Sila*.)

Kama, Kamadeva (1) The god of love. Kama 'desire' is equated
with the Greek Eros, the Roman Cupido, Cupid. The Veda says that
Kama was the cause of life because it was desire that made the first
being move; before anything lived desire arrived to start creation
moving. Some scholars say that Kama was the son of Sraddha, the

goddess of faith, others that he was the son of Lakshmi, the goddess of fortune. If the latter statement is correct we should equate Lakshmi with Venus, the mother of Cupid. Both goddesses arose from the ocean's waves. However, other sources point at Rati the goddess of desire as Kama's wife. Once when Uma wanted a child from her husband Shiva, she sent Kama to arouse the god from his centuries-long meditation. Kama approached the feared god who awoke but was so incensed by this disturbance that he opened his deadly third eye. This eye radiates death when opened. The poor Kama's body was burnt to ashes in an instant before Shiva realized what he was doing. Of course, gods do not really need a body: they can function without it or create one as and when they need it. Henceforth, wherever a husband and a wife embrace one another in true love, their two bodies become one, it becomes the god of love, Kama! It is from such a union that the future generation is created. This is the secret meaning of the expression 'to make love'. It must be taken literally: two lovers embracing in mutual surrender, by that act, cause the god of love to exist for one hour. Kama is king of the Apsaras or love-nymphs. He rides on a parrot, the wisest of all the birds, or the peacock, symbol of impatient desire. His symbol is Makara, the fish. He holds a bow made of sugar cane and flower-tipped arrows with bees on them.

(2) In Buddhism, Kama is (sexual) desire, obstructing enlightenment.

Kamadhatu This low world of earthly desires which causes delusion.

Kama-Dhenu 'Wish-cow'. This priceless cow was once owned by the sage Vasishtha. She was one of the miraculous treasures that emerged from the ocean when it was churned by the gods. Also called Savala, she was so powerful that she once produced an army to fight a war for Vasishtha.

Kamakhya 'Whose name is love'. Epithet of Devi-Uma-Kali (q.v.).

Kamakshi 'Love-eyed'. Epithet of Devi-Uma-Kali (q.v.).

Kamala Lotus flower. (See also *Padma*.) It is the symbol of water and of creation. It also symbolizes self-creation. Brahma resides on a lotus flower when he creates the earth, Bhu, from the primal ocean. Buddha too, is sculpted as sitting on a lotus. The Adi-Buddha arose as a flame springing up from a lotus flower. When the Buddha was born he at once took seven steps and fresh lotus flowers opened in his footprints. The lotus is the symbol of Divinity when used as a 'pedestal' by the gods. It signifies the soul rising out of the darkness of ignorance towards the light of knowledge, to rest serenely on the surface of the water.

Kamma See *Karma*.

Kampilya Modern Kampila, capital city of King Drupada of Panchala.

Kamyaka The forest near the River Sarasvati where the five Pandavas lived in exile for 12 years, with Draupadi.

Kanaka 'Gold', son of Varaha-Vishnu and Bhu, the earth.

Kandarpa 'The one who excites even the god Brahma'. (See also *Kama.*)

Kanishka A famous king, father of Huvishka, who ruled North India in about AD160.

Kansa A tyrant who oppressed the people of Mathura. He had deposed his father Ugrasena, so he was also a usurper. He was told that he would be killed by a son of his cousin Devaki, so he decided to kill all her sons, then perpetrated a massacre of the innocents in Mathura. Kansa is sometimes identified with Kalanemi. He was eventually killed by Krishna, Devaki's son.

Kanwa A sage who lived in the forest where he found the little nymph Shakuntala, whom he brought up as his own daughter.

Kanya Virgo, a sign of the zodiac (q.v.).

Kanya-Kumari 'The girl', 'young maiden'. An epithet of Devi-Uma. (See these.)

Kapalini 'The skull-owning woman'. Epithet of Durga-Kali. (See *Kali.*)

Kapi A monkey. Indrani accused Vrishakapi, Indra's pet monkey, of taking liberties with her. Her husband Indra praised her to pacify her with a song: 'Your arms and your fingers are so lovely, your hair so long, your buttocks so broad. You are the wife of a hero, Indra, Supreme above all.' (See also *Hanuman.*)

Kapila-Vastu A city on the River Rohini in North India, on the India-Nepal border, *c.*560 BC. Capital of King Suddhodana, birthplace of the Buddha.

Kapisha Mother of the Pishachas, a species of demons.

Karali 'Terrible'. (See *Kali.*)

Karma Karman. Literally 'act, deed', in particular, sacrifice. Later it included also the words and thoughts of a person during his lifetime. Karma is a total philosophy which pervades much of Hinduism and all of Buddhism. It is believed that a person's karma accumulates over the years, with bad deeds increasing the negative side and good deeds, such as charity, generosity, austerity and asceticism, increasing the positive side. Thus, karma was originally a sort of account of credits and debits, a reckoning to be settled at the end of a life. Here is where the philosophy of karma is based on

that of metempsychosis. In the next life a person is rewarded for his
virtuous behaviour in this life, by being born into a better family, a
higher caste, a richer and happier milieu. If his bad deeds surpass
the weight of his good ones, he will be reborn as a *shudra*, a
foreigner, an animal, a bird or even a reptile or insect. By means of
rigorous mortification of the flesh, a person may improve his
position in the next life — not in this one, for that has been settled
in the previous life. This leads people of such convictions not only
to be fatalistic, since every misfortune in this life can be blamed on
the sins of a previous life, but even to welcome suffering because it
accumulates merit for the next existence (*bhava*). This philosophy
thus presupposes firstly that there is an absolute good and an
absolute evil, since, to be just, the same law (*dharma*) of good deeds
and bad deeds must apply to all people. This *dharma* is to fulfil what
one's status in life predestines one for. Thus the man who is born as
a sweeper, must sweep all his life, the bearer carries loads until he
is old, the woman bears children since she is born a woman. In this
way an ordered society has developed in which people do not
protest against their status because it is not their employer's fault.
Secondly, karma presupposes the existence of a continuous part of
a person to survive his death. This is the *atman* or soul, which lives
on and is reborn in a new baby, loaded with the sins of its previous
life, 'stained by filth' and also partly cleansed by labour and pain in
the previous life. Thirdly, karma implies free will, the freedom to
choose one's actions individually; without this the system would
not be just. There is no deity charged with judgement, like Osiris,
presiding over the weighing of the good and bad acts, nor is there
a Last Judgement, winding up all human life once and for all. The
purpose of every soul is to be relieved of this *samsara*, this chain of
rebirths, and to achieve *moksha*, liberation from existence.

Karna Son of Kunti, also called Pritha, and Surya the Sun-god,
before Kunti was married to King Pandu. One day when Kunti was
still very young, she saw the famous sage Durvasas. She greeted him
with humility and devotion and she started bringing him offerings
of food regularly. To reward her for her humble services the sage
gave her a secret object, a charm, by means of which she would be
able to induce the god she loved to come and make her pregnant.
She chose the Sun-god Surya, the most radiant of all the gods. He
responded to her invocation and came down to earth in his full
brilliance. She became pregnant and had a son, Karna, 'causation'.
Alas, she feared the censure of her community so she put the
shining child, who was born in full armour, on the banks of the
Yamuna. There the little foundling was picked up by Nandana,
charioteer to King Dhritarashtra. Karna grew up to become a very
handsome boy. The god Indra, noticing the shining armour of the
Sun-child, persuaded him to hand it over. In exchange, Indra gave
Karna a spear that never missed. Duryodhana made Karna king of

Anga (an old name for Bengal). When he appeared as a suitor at the *svayamvara* (q.v.) of Draupadi, he won the contest with his javelin that never missed, but Draupadi spurned him as the son of a lowly charioteer. Little did she know that, as son of the Sun-god, only Krishna was his equal in that company. As a result of her contempt, Karna joined her enemies the Kauravas. When the great war of the Mahabharata broke out, he killed Ghatotkacha with his spear but was later killed by Arjuna, his half-brother. Finally, after his death, it was revealed to Arjuna that Karna was the eldest son of his own mother. The Pandavas then mourned their mother's firstborn with due funerary rites and showed kindness to his widow and dependants.

Karna-Moti 'With pearls in her ears'. Epithet of Devi–Uma–Kali (q.v.).

Karttikeya Skanda. The God of War; the planet Mars. Son of Rudra–Shiva with no mother. Shiva one day dropped his seed in the fire. The fire went out and the seed was received by the River Ganga, so the resulting child, Karttikeya, is called Ganga-ja 'born from the Ganges'.

Another story of his birth goes as follows. One day his father Shiva, who used to command the celestial armies in their endless wars against the evil demons, retired to become an ascetic and spend the rest of his centuries in profound meditation, foreshadowing the future lives of Brahmins who retire as soon as their eldest sons are fully grown. When Shiva no longer led the gods in battle, the demons conquered the world, and heaven too, so that even Indra was exiled from his palace and had to live quietly in the forest. One day he heard a woman's voice screaming that she was being attacked. No wonder: when the good powers of law and order cease to work, evil runs free. Indra hurried to the scene, where he found a lovely girl, Devasena, about to be violated by the demon Kesin. As soon as he saw Indra with his *vajra*, Kesin fled. The girl prostrated herself before her god and saviour, begging him to find her a husband and protector. Indra went up to heaven with Devasena, where they sought Brahma's wise counsel. Brahma decided that Devasena should marry Agni, the god of fire. They then had a son, Kartikeya. This is the 'nice' myth of Kartikeya's birth. Devasena means 'God's Army'.

Stranger still is the following myth: Agni saw the wives of the famous seven Rishis bathing in the Ganges. Their seven husbands had just lit the sacrificial fire in which Agni had come to life. He decided, however, that it would be immoral to seduce the wives of priests, so he went on into the forest. However, a young woman called Svaha, a daughter of Daksha, loved him and offered herself to him, but Agni rejected her. Svaha, however, had learned divine magic from her father, so she changed her appearance and suddenly looked exactly like one of the Rishis' wives. She seduced

Agni, who embraced her there and then. She came back to Agni six more times, each time looking like another of the Rishis' wives. In the end she gave birth to a boy, Kumara, or Kartikeya, a child with six heads. It was he who married Devasena and reconquered heaven for the gods. Six daughters of six kings came to bathe in the Ganges (they were the Pleiades) and, seeing the child with six heads, each of the ladies suckled one of his greedy little mouths. Kumara is a bachelor, hence his name. He made women into widows.

Roman Mars, too, is the god of the sacrificial fire and a god of great potency, lover of Venus herself. The god of war must be a god of fire, of terrifying experience, for nothing on earth is worse than war, when whole cities are destroyed by fire. We should also note that Parvati is herself a daughter of Daksha, who voluntarily destroyed herself in his sacrificial fire, and that her husband Shiva was later identified with Agni. Kartikeya is also regarded as their son.

Kartikeya rides a peacock called Paravani, holding a bow and arrow. His wife is called Kaumari or Sena. His other names are Sena-pati 'army-commander', Subrahmanya and Mahasena. He was born for the special purpose of killing Taraka, a demon. Taraka performed austerities so the gods decided he must die. One day Indra proposed to Skanda that they would race each other around Mount Kailasa. The mountain decided incorrectly that Indra had won, so Skanda threw his spear and split the mountain, opening a pass to the south.

Karuna Compassion, the wish to help others find enlightenment in suffering. Buddha taught compassion as the highest virtue.

Kashi, Kasi Old name for Varanasi or Benares. (See also *Nirvana*.)

Kashyapa, Kasyapa (1) A sage and poet of several hymns in the Veda. He was the son of Marichi, a grandson of Brahma. His son was Vivasvat, father of Manu, the father of Humanity. Kasyapa means the same as Kurma, a tortoise. One myth relates that Brahma assumed the shape of a tortoise and 'made the world', so all human beings descended from the tortoise, reportedly the most intelligent of all animals. Vishnu, too, incarnated as a tortoise in order to assist the gods at creation. A later incarnation of Vishnu, Vamana the dwarf, was born as a son of Kasyapa and Aditi. Kasyapa married the 13 daughters of Daksha. The children of Aditi and Kasyapa are called the Adityas. The eldest was no less a god than Indra, also called Vivasvat. By the other 12 wives Kasyapa had numerous progeny, some of them human beings, some Nagas, reptiles, demons, birds of all kinds and most other living beings. Kasyapa as the father of life is sometimes identified with Prajapati, the Creator. He was one of the seven Rishis and he was arch-priest for Rama.

(2) The third Manushi Buddha (q.v.) who lived on earth for 20,000 years preceding Gautama Buddha.

Katha-Sarit-Sagara 'The Ocean (*Sagara*) of the Rivers (*Sarit*) of Tales (*Katha*)'. This great work of mythology written by Somadeva in Sanskrit verse in the eleventh century, has been translated into English by C. H. Tawney and is published in 10 volumes.

Kaurava One of the 100 sons of King Dhritarashtra. The eldest two were Duryodhana and Duhsasana. Their wickedness caused the war of the Mahabharata.

Kaushiki See *Durga*.

Kautilya Also called Chanakya, the first Indian political scientist. Author of a book on the art of statesmanship entitled Arthashastra and so the creator of political science. He was prime minister of the Emperor Chandragupta and served his master well. One day the emperor, having built a new palace, wanted to enter it but Kautilya persuaded his ruler to wait until he had inspected the palace. When he had finished he asked the emperor for a regiment of well-armed soldiers. The emperor, surprised, but knowing that Kautilya was always right, placed a regiment at his command. Kautilya ordered the soldiers to surround the palace, then enter it and break the floorboards open. To everybody's surprise they found heavily armed men under the floor who were soon arrested, disarmed and executed. Their leader confessed that it was their intention to assassinate the emperor. Later Chandragupta asked Kautilya: 'How did you know what was under the floor of my palace?'

Kautilya explained: 'When I inspected the floor, I saw ants carrying breadcrumbs, which was strange, considering no one was supposed to have lived in the palace as yet. I then saw how the ants brought those crumbs up from beneath the floor, through the cracks between the boards. I concluded that there were people under the floor and moreover that they had been waiting there for some time and so, had brought bread to sustain them. No one would want to wait all night cramped under the floor of your palace unless they had evil intentions.'

This is an exemplary tale of how a prime minister should always be vigilant and how a ruler's life is constantly in danger.

Kavi Poet. All the peoples of India love poetry and song; they honour their poets. In the tenth book of the Rig-Veda it is even suggested that it was the poetic mind that sparked off creation, where it says (hymn 129, 4): 'Poets searching with wisdom in their hearts found the string of existence in non-existence.' (See also *Vak*.)

Kaya Body. One of three aspects in which the Universal Buddha dwells in the cosmos as a living spirit, motivated by compassion for our suffering, full of complete knowledge and wisdom. (See also

Dharmakaya; Nirmanakaya; Sambhogakaya.)

Keshi (Keshin) 'Long-haired'. A demon in the shape of a vicious horse, who is slain by Krishna, who pushed his arm into the horse's mouth and thereby choked him.

Ketu 'Comet, meteor', collective term for the ninth 'planet'.

Khasa Daughter of Daksha, wife of Kasyapa, mother of the Yakshas and Rakshasas, two types of demons.

Kinnara One of a race of men with horses' heads. They make music and sing beautifully at the court of Kubera.

Kirata One of a race of primitive people believed to inhabit the mountain forests north and east of the great plains of India. They can live in the water and eat raw fish. Some writers maintain that Kirata is a man-tiger, a man-eating monster, who has the appearance of a tiger from the waist up. A female Kirata can be a beautiful, gold-coloured maiden running naked in the forest and ever ready to seduce virtuous men.

Kirati 'The mountain woman'. Epithet of Durga-Kali.

Kirka Cancer, a sign of the zodiac (q.v.).

Knowledge (Jnana, Gnyana, Gyana) According to Jain philosophy there are five types of knowledge:

1. *Mati-Jnana*, simple knowledge, obtained through the senses; common sense. *Mati* means 'opinion'.
2. *Shruta-Jnana*, reflective knowledge, obtained through study and contemplation.
3. *Avadhi-Jnana*, 'time-knowledge', which is not limited to the present. Gods and demons possess this time-knowledge; people only rarely do.
4. *Manahparyaya-Jnana*, knowledge of the course of thoughts of other people, 'mind-reading', which only gifted people achieve.
5. *Kevala-Jnana*, 'pure, absolute' knowledge, i.e. omniscience, which only a *Siddha* and an *Arhat* can possess, after long exercises.

Kotari 'The naked'. Epithet of Devi-Uma-Kali (q.v.).

Kripa 'Pity, compassion', one of the virtues of a Buddhist. (See also *Karuna*.)

Krishna When Devaki was pregnant for the eighth time, the demon ruler Kansa doubled the guards of the prison in which he had locked her up, knowing that one of her sons would destroy him. On the evening before the child was due, Vishnu appeared to Vasudeva, who was imprisoned with his wife, Devaki, and commanded: 'As soon as the child is born, take him to Yasoda, wife of Nanda the herdsman. She too will give birth to a child. Bring that one here.'

At midnight the boy Krishna was born. Vasudeva took the child in his arms and miraculously the prison door opened itself. Outside, the guards were fast asleep. In fact nobody at all stirred in the whole town of Mathura. Vishnu sent his faithful serpent Shesha as a guard to accompany Vasudeva, who had to cross the Yamuna. The river was in flood, the waves seething and hissing, but Shesha, the god of the waters, commanded the river to let Vasudeva cross it. He found Yasoda, who had also just given birth, but agreed to exchange babies since it was the god's wish. When Vasudeva came back to the prison and gave the baby to Devaki, it cried, arousing the guards, who then warned Kansa, as he had instructed them to do. Kansa hurried to the prison, seized the child from Devaki's arms and would have dashed it to the floor if it had not escaped. It flew away, mocking him: 'Fool! You cannot kill me, I am Yoganidra, the Great Illusion. Your killer has been born and is safe!'

Kansa fled and locked himself up in his palace, trembling. Nanda took his wife Yasoda, baby Krishna and his brother Balarama to Gokula 'Cowtown', in the heart of the countryside, where they lived safely. Kansa started sending a series of agents with orders to kill Krishna. The first was Putana an innocent-looking demoness with full breasts which, however, were filled with poison. She gave baby Krishna a breast but he sucked all her life out of her, so she died. The second demon who was sent by Kansa to destroy Krishna was Sakta-Sura, who arrived by flying and alighted on a cart under which Krishna was sleeping. The cart collapsed under the demon's weight, as intended, but just in time Krishna kicked it away so it landed on top of the demon, crushing him instead. The third demon, sent by Kansa was Trinavarta, 'Whirlwind'. He swooped down, snatched Krishna from Yasoda's arms and flew away with him. Krishna, however, twisted him round and smashed him against a rock. At once the storm was silent. The fourth demon had the shape of a cow and was called Vatsasura. The fifth demon had the shape of a giant raven called Bakasura. He picked Krishna up and was about to swallow the child, but Krishna made himself so hot that the raven had to drop him from its beak. The sixth demon was Dhenuka (q.v.), who had the shape of a huge donkey.

In the River Yamuna there lived an evil serpent with many heads called Kaliya, which prevented the women from fetching water from the river. They asked Krishna what they could do to get water, so he immediately dived into the river, where the monster attacked him and proceeded to devour him. Krishna shook the monster so hard it had to release him. Then he stood on it so that it was crushed, since Krishna's weight is that of the universe. The serpent Kaliya and his wives, who were *naginis* — women with fishtails, finally recognizing the god, prostrated themselves before him and begged for mercy: 'Lord of the Worlds,' cried the serpent. 'You created me. I acted only in accordance with the nature you gave me. Please let me live!'

Krishna answered this beseeching thus: 'You shall quit the holy river Yamuna and live in the ocean. Whenever you are seen on earth, my companion, Garuda the serpent-eagle will fight you, but I grant you your life.'

One day, when Krishna was walking in the forest, a fire demon made a huge fire which encircled Krishna and his friends. Krishna swallowed the fire and saved his friends. One night Krishna met people who were bringing offerings to Indra. When Krishna demanded those gifts as due to him since he too was a god, Indra sent down a torrential rain, but Krishna picked up the Mountain Govardhana and held it over the people, balancing it on his little finger, giving shelter to everyone. These scenes are frequently shown in paintings: Putana with her breasts, the big bird, Kaliya and his wives, the people under the mountain.

Next, King Kansa decided to give a feast. Kansa sent Akrura, the only honest man left in Mathura, to invite Krishna and Balarama, and his nephews. Akrura warned them that it was a trap but they showed no fear and went to the party. Kansa then sent Keshin, another demon, in the shape of a horse, to waylay them. Krishna simply pushed his fist into the horse's mouth so it choked. Part of the festivities was a sports competition. Strong men were asked to bend a big bow for the archery competition. No one could bend it except Krishna, who broke it. Kansa sent an elephant called Kuvalayapida to trample Krishna but the god killed him and Kansa as well. Thereupon he freed Ugrasena the rightful king and placed him back on his throne in Mathura.

Krishna built a city of his own, Dvaraka, to live in with his parents. But yet more demons had to be killed: Shankha-Sura, Jarasandha, Kalayavana. Thus Krishna had to make war against the evil spirits all his life. Meanwhile he had numerous love affairs with the cowherdesses (gopis) who fell in love with the god without exception. Whenever the god played his flute at night the women would leave their husbands to go and join him in the forest. There they would dance the famous dance called lilarasa, in which each woman had the illusion that she was the one whom the god had chosen to dance with. This scene is often depicted in art, showing a circle of women dancing, each with Krishna. The god had divided himself into as many men as there were women wanting to dance.

The tales of the women's love for Krishna concentrate on one girl in particular, Radha, about whose yearnings for Krishna many poems and songs have been composed, complete with music, in the appropriate raga 'mood'. These poems in beautiful Hindi have been collected in books illustrated with colourful, refined miniatures, which describe every possible feeling in sophisticated metaphors. For example, the girl is seen one night quitting her home and running into the forest to meet her lover. At that moment a thunderstorm approaches, sending streaks of lightning across the sky, symbolizing her emotions (of passion) and fears (of punishment for her illicit affair). When she meets her lover, rain begins to fall (symbolizing his fertility) while two swans can be seen flying across the sky, the birds that are dedicated to Brahma and Sarasvati, the first couple, the gods who created humanity. The lover is always Krishna, the god, represented by a royal crown, a blue skin and sometimes with four arms. There is for the artist no doubt: the Beloved is God, not a man. Thus we must conclude that the loving woman is not a sensual, wanton adulteress but a devout worshipper, indeed the human soul herself. Without this knowledge neither the myths of India nor its art can be understood. The soul is constantly yearning to unite herself with God, the spiritual reality of the other, better world.

The next chapter in Krishna's history is his love for Rukmini, who, like Radha, is an incarnation of Lakshmi, Vishnu's faithful wife. Shiva and Brahma, disguised as beggars, told Rukmini of a handsome prince called Krishna so she fell in love with him before ever meeting him. Meanwhile, Rukma, Rukmini's brother decided that she must marry Sisupala, not knowing that Sisupala (Shishupala) was an incarnation of Ravana, who had so bitterly battled against Vishnu when he was still Rama and not yet Krishna. (Even before that, Susupala had been Hiranyakashipu, when Vishnu was Narasimha.) Rukmini was afraid of Sisupala although she did not know his spiritual identity. She wrote a secret letter to Krishna which had to be smuggled out of the palace where she lived with her tyrannical brother. Krishna received the letter and arrived on the morning of the wedding. He eloped with Rukmini but was pursued by Sisupala, Rukma and even Jarasandha, who had not been killed properly, with his army of demons. After exhausting battles all the demons were killed by Balarama and Krishna. Only Rukma's life was spared because Rukmini begged for it, kissing Krishna's feet. A sister always prays for her brother, even if he is bad, simply because she owes loyalty to him. Such is the moral of this myth.

Later Krishna married yet other wives: Jambavati, daughter of Jambavan, king of the bears, and Satyabhama, daughter of Satrajit, and Kalindi daughter of the Sun. This was possible as a god's life is long, spanning many human lives on earth, multiplied in space and time.

Later, Krishna had to fight Sisupala and Jarasandha once again, assisted by his cousins Bhima and Arjuna, whom Krishna rejoined later in the great epic battle of the Mahabharata, where Krishna, as Arjuna's charioteer, revealed himself as God in the Bhagavadgita.

Krishna-Janmashtami The eighth day of the dark fortnight of the moon-month Shravana (Sravan) or Bhadrapada, is the birthday of Krishna, the eighth *avatara* of Vishnu. He was born at midnight. A 24-hour fast is observed on this day by worshippers, which lasts until midnight. The temples are decorated, conches are blown, bells are sounded. At Mathura where Krishna was born, there are spiritual gatherings attended by pilgrims from all over India. Astrologers have calculated that Krishna was born 3,227 years before Christ. Scholarly worshippers will study the Bhagavata Purana on this day, convinced that there is no science better than devotion (*bhakti*) to Krishna. They explain that Krishna's 'birth' and 'death' are no more than an appearance and disappearance of Vishnu by means of his *maya* (q.v.). Statues of Krishna playing his magic flute inviting the souls to love him, are worshipped in numerous homes. Worshippers repeat his invincible mantra: *Om Namo Bhagavate Vasudevaya*.

Kritanta 'The end of work'. Fate, the god of death.

Krodha 'Anger'. Daughter of Daksha, wife of Kasyapa and mother of all the sharp-toothed and sharp-beaked living beings, i.e. birds of prey and four-footed predators.

Kshatriya A member of the second caste or hereditary class of warriors, the first or highest caste being the Brahmins. 'Warriors' usually included the cavalry and the officers of the Indian armies of antiquity, while the infantry was recruited from the peasants. A better translation for Kshatriya might be 'nobleman', since most of the kings belonged to the Kshatriya caste. The ministers were usually Brahmins.

Kubera, Kuvera The giant god of the spirits, guardian of the North. Like Pluto he is god of the dead and of wealth. He is also commander of the Yakshas and the Guhyakas. Son of Visravas and Idavida. Kubera's capital is Prabha, also called Alaka, in the Himalayas, with a lovely park on Mount Mandara. From his father Visravas, he inherited the kingdom of Sri Lanka, but he was expelled by his half-brother the malicious Ravana, which was the spark of the conflict resolved in the epic of Ramayana. Kubera owned the gold, silver and jewels of this earth. Brahma gave him Pushpaka, the famous flying vehicle. Kubera is always represented as very fat. His wife's names were Yakshi, Charvi or Kauveri, daughter of Mura, one of the Danavas. They had three sons and a daughter, Minakshi. Kubera was a white man and very ugly. He is called Dhana-pati 'lord of wealth' and Nara-raja 'king of men', because whoever owns wealth rules men. He is also known as Ratna-garbha 'jewel-belly' but he is not worshipped.

Kumara 'Youth'. A name of Skanda the War-god.

Kumari 'Princess'. A name of Devi.

Kumbha 'Water-jar.' Aquarius, a sign of the Zodiac (q.v.).

Kumbha-Karna 'Pot-ear'. A monster, brother of Ravana, who used to sleep for half a year at a time and then awake for only one day. He was 84 leagues tall, 420,000 metres — a good example of

Indian hyperbole since Mount Everest is only 8,848 metres high. When he breathed, storms arose on the earth. When Rama attacked Ravana in Lanka, Ravana sent messengers to wake Kumbhakarna. It took them hours to shake him from his slumber, after which he drank 2,000 jars of liquor; only then did he feel ready for action. He joined the fray in Lanka, beat Sugriva but was defeated by Rama, who cut his head off.

Kumudavati 'Owner of Lotuses'. Daughter of the Naga king, Kumuda. She married Kusha, elder son of Rama.

Kunjarakarna The Indian Dante who made a long journey through all the strata of Hell where he was shown round by Yama-Adipati, India's Hades.

Kunti Daughter of King Sura of Mathura, mother of the Pandavas. She had a love affair with Surya the Sun-god and had a son who was born in golden armour, (see *Karna*). Subsequently she married Pandu but (it is said) her next three sons were also begotten by gods, namely Dharma, who begot Yudhisthira, Vayu, who begot Bhima the giant and Indra, by whom she had the hero Arjuna. Her husband Pandu died early. After the great war of the Mahabharata, Kunti followed her brother-in-law Dhritarashtra into the forest where she died in a fire.

Kurma Vishnu in his early incarnation as a tortoise, living at the bottom of the sea, where he taught the essentials of life: duty and pleasure. (See also *Vishnu*.)

Kuru A king of the Kuru people in North-West India, grandson of the Sun, ancestor of both the Kauravas and the Pandavas.

Kusha A son of Rama and Sita. He built the city of Kushavati.

Kushamba Son of Kusha who worshipped Indra. He performed austerities wishing to have a son like Indra. At last Indra consented and *became* his son, by incarnation, being born as Gadhi.

Kusinara The place where Buddha lay down to end his earthly life. (See also *Paranirvana*.)

Kusumamodini Goddess of the flowers of the mountains. Flora.

Kusuma-Pura 'Flower city', also called Patali-putra, now Patna.

Kuvera See *Kubera*.

Kwan Yin See *Avalokiteshvara*.

L

Lakshmi

Lakshmana 'Lucky-omened'. Son of King Dasharatha and Queen
Sumitra, Rama's most faithful brother. One-eighth of his spirit was
divine, or — and here the texts are not clear — one eighth of the
divine spirit of Vishnu was in him, shared with his twin brother
Shatrughna. Other texts say he was an incarnation of Shesha,
Vishnu's sea-snake. Lakshmana is the Hindu ideal of the devoted
brother. He accompanied Rama to his exile in the forest. He
married Urmila, Sita's sister, and they had two sons, Angada and
Chandraketu. One dark day in the forest, Sita was attacked by a
jealous Rakshasi (female demon) called Shurpa-nakha, who was in
love with Rama. Rama and Lakshmana defended Sita and the
Rakshasi lost her nose and ears in the fighting. She then flew to her
brother the terrible Ravana and complained. Ravana then took
revenge by abducting Sita, which sparked off the great war of the
Ramayana. Lakshmana accompanied Rama tirelessly in his long
search for Sita and in conducting the war on Lanka where she was
held captive. He travelled home with Rama and the liberated Sita
when the war was won. When he felt his end approaching,
Lakshmana sat down by the riverside, where he ended his days by
meditating resignedly until the gods took him to Heaven.

Lakshmi Goddess of Fortune, later mainly of good fortunes and

vegetation. She was the daughter of Brahma-Prajapati and the wife
of Vishnu in all her incarnations: for Krishna she is born as Radha,
and later as Rukmini, for Rama she is born as Sita. There are also
numerous folktales in which she is born as a princess who marries
a prince who turns out to be Vishnu in disguise, whom she loves in
life after life! Her son is Kama and her daughter is Trisna or Trishna,
also Tisnavati, 'the one who desires'. Both goddesses, mother and
daughter, are better known among the people of South India and as
far away as Java, as the Rice Goddess Devi Sri, or Trishnavati, who
is reborn every year as the new rice, the harvesting of which is
surrounded with numerous ceremonies for the Devi Sri, the Mother
of Love. As Sita, when she says she wants to join her husband Rama
in exile in the forest, the question is raised: 'Sita, the princess who
was brought up on the finest prepared rice (karbi), how will she
survive on raw wild rice?'

For the fishermen along the south coast and the islands she is the
Empress of the Sea to whom sacrifices have to be made for securing
a rich catch and a safe home voyage. To her is dedicated also the
basil flower *tulsi* or *tulasi*, *Ocymum basilicum*, a medicinal herb. She
is also called Padma or Kamala, both names meaning lotus.

She was born from the waters when the gods churned the World
Ocean. Lakshmi rises out of the milk-ocean while the gods are
churning it. She is seated on her lotus throne; she *is* the lotus,
Padma, rising out of the water, serenely smiling. The River Ganga
serves her gladly; she has two elephants who shower bathing water
over her. The ocean of milk gives her a fresh garland of everlasting
flowers every day. She is also depicted as reclining on her husband
Vishnu's mighty chest, while he is seated on Shesha. Lakshmi gives
children and harvests, she protects the granary. Lakshmi is also, in
some regions, associated with cow dung, *gomaya*, which is used as
fertilizer and as fuel for cooking the family meal. Thus Lakshmi
lives in the homes of the people as Vriddhi, the goddess of growth,
as Matrirupa, the mother of all living things. She is Dakshina the
cow who transformed herself into innumerable daughters with a
womb, *garbha* in each one. She is the goddess of fruits (Ambika, the
mango goddess) and of all food, saying: 'Through me eats food
annam, whoever sees and breathes, or hears the spoken word,
uktam.' She is the earth, Bhu, the creation; she is devotion, altar,
donation and invocation. She is also the dark ocean, Sadana, the
waves and the moonshine. As the faithful wife of Vishnu, Lakshmi
accompanies him on all his *avataras* (descents, incarnations) to
earth. When he is born as Parashurama, she becomes Dharani;
when he is born as Rama-Chandra, she is born in a nearby kingdom
as Sita; when he is born as Krishna, he will meet her as Radha.
Then, later, Krishna will marry her as Rukmini. There are other
known incarnations of this divine couple as lesser, more human
persons. Rohini was another of Lakshmi's incarnations, as the
mother of Balarama. More than the wives of other gods, Lakshmi is

Vishnu's other self. Together they fly through the sky on the wings of Garuda, the Snake-eagle, the symbol of the sun, shown with a snake, the symbol of the waters, in its claws, visualizing the eternal struggle between water and fire. Vishnu is himself a sun-god, while Lakshmi is the water-born lotus flower Padma, on which she resides.

Lakshmi-Vrata (*Vrata* = devotion). The feast for Lakshmi celebrated on the Friday preceding the full moon in the moon-month of Sravan (late August, when the sun enters Virgo). Married women take a bath, put on new clothes, and paint a *mandala* (ornamental circle) on the floor with a lotus, Lakshmi's flower, in the centre. A *kalasha* (jar) is filled with rice and closed with fresh mango leaves; a coconut and a cloth are placed in the mandala. Mother Lakshmi is invoked in the mandala, with the scattering of fresh grains which remind us that Lakshmi is the goddess of growth and charity.

Lalita-Vistara A Sanskrit work on the life and teaching of Buddha.

Lambodara 'With hanging belly'. Appellation of Ganesha (q.v.).

Langali See *Balarama*.

Lanka Now called Sri Lanka, 'Holy Lanka' (the prefix Sri indicates that Lanka is a goddess, identified with Lakshmi, the goddess of vegetation, of whom Sita is an incarnation). It is the large island off the south coast of India. In the epic of Ramayana we read that Lanka was occupied by a horde of Rakshasas, evil demons who captured poor Sita, Rama's wife, so Rama had to recruit an army to liberate her, after besieging and storming the citadel. It is said that Lanka was formed when Vayu, the Wind-god, tore off the top of Mount Meru and threw it into the ocean.

Last Days, The When, according to Hindu scholars, the end of this era comes near, the spiritual life of the people will be totally degenerated. The leaders of men will give bad examples of living. They will be mean and greedy, short-lived owing to their debauchery, corrupt, mendacious and cruel. Even the Brahmins will have no sanctity left. The rich will cease to give alms. Truth and love will disappear from the earth. The reason for marriage will only be sensuality. Religion will be forgotten, nothing will be sacred anymore, nor will there be any true scholarship left. People will run around naked like animals because they will be too lazy to build houses or weave clothes and too lazy to raise crops, so they will eat wild fruits. At that moment, but in his own time, Kalkin (q.v.) will appear on earth.

Lava Son of Rama and Sita, twin brother to Kusha.

Lila Playing, sport, game. To the gods, creating the world is *lila*.

They create human souls and suffering, fate and fatality without regard to their human subjects. In this the gods are like the kings and dictators of later times who sent thousands to their death. The gods, however, have at least created this beautiful earth with forests and rivers, birds, stars, sun and moon. This 'game' is essentially a love-embrace (see *Shakti*), in which two divine spouses make love, setting in motion the next generation and with it the earth we live in. After their embrace they separate again and the material world disintegrates, for things can only exist as long as the gods will them, love them (see *Kama*). This philosophy is beautifully symbolized in the love-story of Krishna and Radha, who are Vishnu and Lakshmi, co-creators of the universe. Existence is only possible when there is love, being-together. Separation causes our world to fall into dust. We live as long as the gods love us and we love each other. (See also *Shiva*.)

Linga (Lingam). The 12 emblems of Shiva are listed under *Shiva*. The *Linga* is Shiva's most prominent symbol, to the extent that it represents the god himself. *Lingam* is often translated as 'phallus', though some Indian scholars deny that it is or ever was a representation of the male organ. Many ancient cultures worshipped a god with a phallus. Ancient Egypt had two: Geb and Min (whom the Greeks knew as Priapus). Osiris himself is shown with his phallus erect while he is lying in his coffin. The *Lingam* is often seen in India in the shape of a pillar with a hemispherical top, standing in a basin or round tank called a *yoni*, a word which also means vagina or womb. Sometimes the pillar has a niche in the middle in which a statue of Shiva stands. Such statues are still worshipped by the people. In some cases the pillar is simply a cylinder. Philosophers prefer this, saying that the abstract shape represents better the god's shapelessness, i.e. his ability to assume all shapes and enter all places. The statue needs no eyes or legs, since the god can see and move without those. Shaivas, i.e. worshippers of Shiva, sometimes carry a *linga* on their person, usually a round object like a soapstone globe, representing the total universal formlessness of the god. They know that a god is not a man who needs genitals for reproduction: a god can procreate by his will. Thus the *linga* and *yoni* become symbols of the procreative principles rather than of the divine couple Shiva and Parvati. Offerings are brought to the *linga* by supplicants hoping for offspring and abundant crops. For the believers, Shiva is the cause of causes and the *linga* represents him as the principle of fertility, i.e. creation, causation.

Lion Lions are now found in only one forest reserve in India. (See also *Nara Simha*.)

Lobha 'Lust, libido, greed'. One of the obstacles on the path to *bodhi*.

Loha-Mukha 'Iron-faced'. One of a race of men with iron faces and only one foot each. They eat human meat.

Loka World. According to Hindu cosmology, the universe is divided into three or seven worlds. The Tri-Loka or three-world universe encompasses the earth, heaven and the underworld. The Sapta-Loka, or seven-world universe, is structured as follows:

1. Bhur-Loka, the earth.
2. Bhuvar-Loka, the sky between the earth and the sun where the sages live, the Munis and Siddhas.
3. Svar-Loka, the heaven of Indra, between the sun and the pole-star.
4. Marar-Loka, where Bhrigu lives with the other saints. These four worlds were burnt in a terrible conflagration which ended the cycle of existence of all the nether worlds but from which the upper worlds were safe.
5. Jana-Loka where Brahma's children live.
6. Tapa-Loka, where the Vairagis live. Also called Vairajas, these demigods are the spirits of saints and sages who will not go back to a life on earth but have become immortals by their merits.
7. Satya-Loka 'Abode of Truth' or Brahma-Loka, where Brahma resides together with immortal gods for as long as a period of his life lasts.

In Hinduism nothing is eternal yet nothing ends definitively. All life, including that of the gods, is cyclical, progressing in endless spirals. The first three of the seven worlds are destroyed at the end of each *Kalpa* or cosmic epoch, which is a day in the life of Brahma, but many millennia in human time. Brahma, the Supreme God himself, lives for a hundred years of his time, which equals millions of human years. At the end of that time not only Brahma but all seven worlds will come to an end and history will begin anew, with a fresh creation and new unknown beings. The sixth world is also called Pitri-Loka, the world where the ancestors reside. There are yet other worlds where numerous species of deities dwell: Soma-Loka for the moon and the planets, Indra-Loka for the lesser deities, Gandharva-Loka for the spirits of heaven, Yaksha-Loka, Rakshasa-Loka for the demons and Pishacha-Loka for the imps.

Lokamata 'Mother of the World', a praise-name of Lakshmi (q.v.).

Loka-Pala World-guardian. One of eight gods who guard the eight main points of the compass:

1. Indra, east, with his elephant Airavata.
2. Agni, south-east, with his elephant Pundarika.
3. Yama, south, with his elephant Vamana.
4. Surya, south-west, with his elephant Kumuda.
5. Varuna, west. His elephant is Anjana.

6. Vayu, north-west. His elephant is Pushpa-danta.
7. Kubera, north, in Hima-Pandara, 'snow-palace'.
8. Soma, or Shiva, or Prithivi, north-east.

Each of these gods has his own named elephant as his vehicle for the defence of the region, also called Lokapala, and each of these elephants has his own female standing there with him.

Lopamudra The ideal woman. A girl of exceptional beauty who was put together by Agastya from the best and finest parts of the animals, so that she became the most perfect wife.

Love There are many words for love in Indian languages, which represent different types and aspects of love. The Buddhist form of love is the Sanskrit *karuna*, 'compassion, charity', which commands a man to work for his fellow creatures by deferring his own *nirvana* or *moksha* (salvation). The Urdu word *muhabbat* refers both to the love of God and the love between two people. The Hindi word *preman* is given as 'love, sport' in the dictionary, but the Sanskrit *prema* means love in the divine sense, cf. the name Premadas, 'servant of the God of Love'. *Pyara* is the Hindi word for love, from the Sanskrit *priya*, 'dear, precious', *priti*, 'love, favour'. The goddess of earthly love is Rati, identified with Lakshmi and Venus; she becomes the wife of one of Krishna's incarnations, and so she is also identifiable with Radha, who represents the double symbolism of the wife who is totally devoted to her husband, and the human soul who is absorbed in loving contemplation of Krishna, her god. Love is also the god Kama (q.v.) or Kamadeva (Eros, Cupido). The Kama-sutra ('Love-textbook') is the first systematic guide to a happy sex-life.

M

Mara's daughters

Mada (1) Intoxication, drunken madness.
(2) A terrifying monster with open mouth and long protruding teeth; it gobbles up anyone who is unfortunate enough to come under its spell.

Madhava The God of Spring, Madhu. An epithet of Krishna (q.v.).

Madhu Mead, honey-wine. Intoxication.

Madhyapatha The Middle Way of the Buddha: 'Follow neither the satisfaction of your cravings, nor extreme mortification. Lead a moral, well-ordered life.'

Madri Sister of the King of Madras, second wife of King Pandu. She had twin sons, Nakula and Sahadeva, actually fathered, it was said, by the twin gods the Ashvinau. Maybe her co-wife Kunti gave her the charm that attracts gods.

Magadha The state now called Bihar, where the Bodhi-tree once stood, where Pali was once spoken and where the Bodhigaya shrine now stands. There, Buddha preached his enlightenment.

Magic See *Mantra vidya*; *Tantra*; *Yantra*.

Mahabharata The great epic of the war between the Pandavas and the Kauravas. This is one of the greatest epics ever written. It is composed of 220,000 lines, compared with the 11,000 lines in Homer's *Iliad*. The final editor was Krishna Dvaipayana, or, for short Vyasa 'the Compiler', but he is himself a mythical character so that his authenticity is doubtful. The Mahabharata was certainly composed over a long period of time since there are pieces in it of very different linguistic and metric structure.

The name probably refers to the Bharatas, descendants of King Bharata, which most of the heroes in the epic were. Maha-Bharata also means 'greater India', but normally the name Mahabharata refers to the epic, a unique document of world literature. Although many of the characters in the epic are gods or demons, the majority are human beings with very human personalities. The epic is not only filled with terrifying battles, both single combats and wars on the plain of Kurukshetra, west of Delhi, but it is also full of human drama, of theatre, deep pathos, tragic encounters, and the consciousness of inescapable destiny.

The epic myths of India are like Russian novels. Not only are they filled with numerous characters, but these are also referred to by several different names, which makes summarizing the tales extremely complicated. In addition, all the chief characters are related to each other as cousins, uncles, in-laws, etc. A very condensed version is given below.

King Shantanu had a son called Bhishma Shantavana. King Shantanu in his old age fell in love with Princess Satyavati, but she refused to marry him because her son would only be second in line for the succession. Bhishma was a son of such noble character that he vowed never to be king so that his father could marry his beloved princess. Satyavati gave birth to two sons, who, in due course married but did not have time to raise children for they died young. Satyavati then invited Krishna Dvaipayana (= Vyasa the poet) to lie with the two widows so that he would raise seed for her two younger sons. Krishna was her son from a premarital affair. He was a demigod who had been living a life of asceticism in the forest. He looked so frightening that the elder woman shut her eyes when he approached her, so that her son, Dhritarashtra, was born blind. The younger widow turned white with fright when Krishna approached her, so her son, Pandu, was born pale. Since a blind man was not considered fit to reign in the east, Pandu ascended the throne of Hastinapura, now a ruined city on the Ganges north of Delhi. King Pandu had two wives and five sons, though those sons were in 'reality' sons of gods. They were Yudhisthira, Bhima, Arjuna, Nakula and Sahadeva. His half-brother, Dhritarashtra had 100 sons by special favour of Krishna-Dvaipayana. These hundred princes are the Kauravas while the five sons of Pandu are the Pandavas. Pandu retired early to the forest to do penance, for it was said that his whiteness was leprosy. He was followed there by his

two wives. He died while his sons were still children. Dhritarashtra
took them into his palace and brought them up with his own
children. They were taught the arts of war, as befits princes, by
Drona and Balarama.

When Dhritarashtra appointed Yudhisthira, the eldest son of the
late King Pandu, as *yuvaraja* 'heir apparent', his own sons were
jealous and this hatred led ultimately to the great war. The
Pandavas decided to go and live in the forest in a fine wooden house
but even there they could not escape the anger of their cousins.
Duryodhana, the eldest of the Kauravas, set fire to the house, but
the Pandavas had been forewarned by their paternal uncle, Vidura.
They escaped and disappeared into the forest disguised as
mendicants. Then they heard of the *svayamvara* that was being
planned by King Drupada for his daughter Krishnaa Draupadi.
They decided to go and compete for the princess with the other
princes. If only they had stayed where they were they would have
lived peaceful lives. As it was they easily defeated all the other
princes — Arjuna as an expert archer, Bhima with his mace and
Yudhisthira with his great knowlege of the law. Draupadi fell in love
with Arjuna but she married all five brothers, as their mother told
them to share her.

Now that the Pandavas had surfaced again, Dhritarashtra
summoned them to his court and divided his kingdom in two
halves: Hastinapura would be ruled by Duryodhana, and
Indraprastha (now part of greater Delhi) would be the Pandavas'
capital. Yudhisthira enlarged his kingdom considerably, then
started making plans for the Raja-suya sacrifice which would make
him emperor. These plans aroused, more than ever before, the envy
and hatred of the Kauravas. They had an uncle, Shakuni, who was
the most dishonest man in the kingdom and an expert at throwing
dice. Together they persuaded their father to invite the Pandavas
for a game of dice. Yudhisthira, for whom every action was a matter
of honour, came with his brothers, played the game and lost. He
lost his kingdom, the freedom of his brothers and himself and also
that of Draupadi. When Draupadi was told that she was now a
slave, she tried to run away but Duhsasana, brother of
Duryodhana, caught up with her and dragged her back by her hair.
Bhima, seeing this, swore that he would drink Duhsasana's blood.
Duryodhana added insult to the Pandavas' humiliation by inviting
Draupadi to come and sit on his thigh. Bhima swore that he would
smash that thigh. Dhritarashtra, however, persuaded his sons that
the Pandavas should be given back their freedom, their wife and
their kingdom. This was done; however Yudhisthira was taunted
again to throw the dice. If he lost he would, with his family, spend
12 years in the forest and after that one year in a king's service. Of
course he lost again for who can win against wicked minds? So the
Pandavas lived in the forest for 12 years. In the thirteenth year they
entered the service of the King of Virata, Yudhisthira disguised as a

Brahmin, Bhima as a cook, Arjuna as a music teacher, Nakula as a
horse-trainer, and Sahadeva as a cowherd. Draupadi called herself
Sudeshna and became the queen's lady-in-waiting. Her beauty,
however, drew the attention of Kichaka, the queen's brother and
commander-in-chief of the army. He tried to rape Draupadi but
Bhima killed him. The royal family then decided Draupadi should
be burnt with the body of Kichaka on the funerary pyre, but Bhima
appeared just before the fire was lit, disguised as a forest demon. All
those present fled in panic, whereupon Bhima quietly cut the ropes
that tied Draupadi to the stake. Later, when the King of Trigartta
attacked Virata, the Pandavas repulsed the invaders, so the King of
Virata had reason to be grateful and even more so when the
Kauravas attacked him and were likewise driven back by the
Pandavas. They did not recognize the Pandavas who were all in
disguise. Finally the Pandavas' days of service came to an end and
they decided to reconquer their kingdom. The King of Virata joined
them since he had every reason to wish to destroy the Kauravas.
Krishna, being a cousin of both parties, offered Arjuna and
Duryodhana a choice: one would get his army, the other would
have Krishna himself as an ally. Duryodhana opted for Krishna's
army, preferring to remain commander-in-chief himself. Arjuna
asked to have Krishna himself on his side. Arjuna chose wisely,
because having Vishnu on his side won the war for him. Arjuna
became the commander-in-chief of the Pandava army, Krishna
preferring the humble position of his charioteer. On the morning
before the battle he recited for Arjuna the famous poem
Bhagavadgita (q.v.) to reconcile Arjuna to the war. The Kaurava
army was at first led by their uncle Bhishma until Arjuna killed him
with a thousand arrows. Then Drona the old guru became
commander; after him Karna and finally Shalya, King of Madra.
The battle lasted for 18 days, at the end of which only three of the
hundred Kauravas were still alive, apart from Duryodhana.

At the end of the battle on the last day, the terrible fight between
the good but irascible Bhima and the well-controlled but malicious
Duryodhana took place. Bhima had already killed Duhsasana and
drunk his blood as he had vowed. Now it was Duryodhana's turn
and when after a long combat Bhima smashed his enemy's thigh, he
had done what he swore to do 13 years previously. He beat
Duryodhana, who fell down mortally wounded, but Yudhisthira
prevented Bhima from killing him: only a coward would do that.
However, the surviving Kauravas were, of course, cowards. They
sneaked secretly into the Pandava camp at night and killed the five
sons of Draupadi, still boys, in their sleep. Thus she too was terribly
punished for her pride. The five Pandava brothers remained the
victors. They went to the capital of Hastinapura, where Yudhisthira
was crowned maharaja. The Pandavas lived in peace and
prosperity. However, Yudhisthira was filled with remorse over the
massacre of his family, as indeed he should have been since his

weakness for gambling had led to all the killing. He decided to make the pilgrimage to Heaven, to Indra's palace on Mount Meru. His four faithful younger brothers followed him of course, as they had shared all their days of adventure and peace, of sadness and greatness together. Draupadi went with them, for she too had many reasons to propitiate the gods and she had always been ready for adventure. Arjuna's grandson Parikshit remained behind as maharaja of Hastinapura, with the blessing of the god Krishna. His son Janamejaya II, succeeded him as maharaja and it was to him that the Mahabharata was first recited.

The long exhausting journey of the Pandava princes, climbing the Himalayas to the palace of the gods, is another epic, contained in the seventeenth book of the Mahabharata. In this long episode accounts are rendered of what each of these formidable characters had done and why they had failed. Their defects of morale and morality proved fatal for them. Draupadi was the first to fall. She still loved Arjuna with undiminished love, but her pride could not face the long pilgrimage. Sahadeva too was full of pride, vanity and self-love, so he too fell. Nakula fell next; he was too full of his own handsomeness to possess the grim persistence needed for the arduous pilgrimage. Next, Arjuna fell by the wayside because his boasting had always been bigger than his achievements. He had once vowed that he would destroy all his enemies, but it was too late. Surprisingly the strong but inflammable Bhima was the last to fall along the way. He had cursed too many people instead of being a simple honest warrior. Alone with his dog, the persevering Yudhisthira reached the gate of Indra's heaven. He entered after he had insisted that his four brothers and Draupadi should be admitted with him.

The 'frame story' is the great battle of the descendants of Bharata against one another, cousins against cousins. Woven into this main narrative are numerous other tales: myths of the gods, sagas of heroes, legends of the saints, including the history of the world as seen by Hindu scholars of the early Middle Ages, both in terms of kings and battles, and the spiritual, divine history of the universe — the interminable battles between the good gods and the evil demons. Furthermore the Mahabharata contains long philosophical chapters, all in verse, including treatises on law, morality and virtue, religion and politics, medicine and many other subjects.

Mahadeva 'Great God'. Praise-name for Rudra-Shiva.

Mahadevi 'The Great Goddess'. Another name for Uma–Parvati–Kali (q.v.).

Mahakala Shiva as the god of irrevocable time, shown in sculpture in the caves of Elephanta as an executioner with a human body in one hand and an axe in the other. Shown too are a basin for receiving the blood and the sun which is setting behind him, ending life.

Mahakali 'The great black one'. An epithet of Devi–Uma–Kali (q.v.).

Mahalakshmi 'The Great Lakshmi', a name for Lakshmi (q.v.), mainly used in Indian art and sculpture. She is of course Lakshmi, spouse of Vishnu, in one of their many incarnations. She is normally shown with a *mahalunga* (a type of lemon), a mace and shield, a lotus (see Bhu), a bowl of petals, a vase, a *srifala* (coconut) and a *dindima* (drum).

Mahamari 'The great killer-woman'. An epithet of Durga–Kali. (See also *Devi*; *Mahisha-Mardini*.)

Maha-Purusha The Great Man, Vishnu.

Maha-Rishi, Maharshi Arch-priest, patriarch, great Rishi.

Mahasattva 'Great Truth', name of the Bodhisattva in a previous existence. He was born as the son of a mighty king, Maharatha 'big wheel'. One day, while walking in the forest he met a tigress who was so hungry that she was totally emaciated. She had two cubs but could not feed them, since her milk had long since dried up. Moved by compassion, the Bodhisattva lay down near the tigress inviting her to eat him, since for him physical existence was unimportant, while the tigress was suffering. However, she was too weak to kill him, so the Bodhisattva took his dagger and killed himself. When she smelled the blood, the tigress at last started to eat the prince. A variant to this tale relates that the Bodhisattva saw the tigress looking hungrily at her own cubs, so he offered himself to be her food, in order to prevent her from committing the sin of infanticide. This act would have caused her a bad *karma*, which would have set her back several stages at her next reincarnation, so it would have taken her many more lives to reach *nirvana*.

Maha-sena Chief — captain, Kartikeya, god of war.

Mahavira The 'Great Man' who lived peacefully in heaven for centuries until he decided to incarnate on earth in order to save humanity. He took the form of an embryo in the womb of Devananda, wife of the Brahmin Rishabhadatta, who lived at Kundapura. That night, while Devananda lay half asleep in her bed, she had a dream in which she saw 14 favourable omens: an elephant, a bull, a lion, the goddess Sri, a garland, the moon, the sun, a banner, a beautiful vase, a lake full of lotuses, the ocean, a palace, jewellery and an eternal flame. She told her husband what she had seen and Rishabhadatta was overjoyed, for he perceived that a son would be born to them who would become a great scholar and a famous religious leader. Then Sakra, the king of the gods in Heaven, decided that Mahavira should be the son of a Kshatriya by birth, so he gave instructions to the gods' messenger Haringamesi 'Deerhead', to transpose the new embryo from Devananda's womb to that of Trishala, wife of the Kshatriya Siddhartha, who was reclining on a luxurious bed in a palace full of flowers and vases of perfumes. Now it was Trishala's turn to see the 14 good omens in her dream. Her husband, Siddhartha, was accompanied by good fortune ever since that moment. He became ever richer in gold and silver, in land and grain, while his loyal army won victories and fame. In the night when Mahavira was to be born, the gods and goddesses descended from Heaven to share in the rejoicing. Flowers and fruits, gold and silver, rained from Heaven on Siddhartha's palace. When Mahavira (his heavenly name) was born, he received the earthly name of Vardhamana, 'he who grows and develops'. This event took place 2,590 years ago, according to the Jains' history.

For 30 years Vardhamana led a worldly life as a prince in Bihar, he married Yasoda and had a daughter called Riyadarshana. His parents, who were adherents of the doctrine of Parshva (see *Tirthamkara*), lay down one day and abstained from food until they died. Vardhamana, deeply impressed, decided that he would become an ascetic. He gave his wealth to the poor and began his wandering life without bonds. After 12 years he acquired *moksha*, liberation from all earthly desires and with it, enlightenment. Again the gods and demons assembled on earth around his person to exclaim: Victory! Thus Mahavira became Jina, the Victor (his followers call themselves Jainas or Jains after him). At that moment the sky was bluer than ever before, like a deep lake covered with blue lotuses, while heavenly music could be heard on earth. Mahavira, seated in profound meditation under a teak tree (*sala*), became *kevalin*, omniscient. He had overcome all evil and he now began to preach what he had practised for 12 years.

One day while Mahavira was meditating in a field a farmer arrived with his cows which he left in the field, telling Mahavira to guard them. Mahavira, however, was in such deep meditation that he did not hear the farmer nor see the cows. When the farmer came back the cows were nowhere to be seen. Furious the farmer screamed: 'You lazy useless idler!' to the noble saint, and started beating him.

He would have killed him if Indra had not descended from Heaven to protect the great ascetic whom he had watched all the time knowing what would happen.

Thirty years after becoming *kevalin*, he was ready to die, so he became *mukta* 'liberated', and *siddha* 'perfected'. When he was about to die Mahavira had himself carried to a throne made of diamonds in a large hall illuminated by heavenly light. He preached there until, in the small hours of the night, all his listeners had gone to sleep. Unseen, he died. Quickly many lamps were brought but the soul had departed to Heaven. This episode is commemorated by the Jains during the festival of Divali.

Mahayana The adherents of the Mahayana school of Buddhism call their doctrine the *Maha-yana*, the 'Great Vehicle', and all the other schools *Hina-yana* (q.v.) 'the Lesser Vehicle'. The Mahayana school of thought spread to China in the first century AD, to Tibet in the eighth century and to Japan in the sixth century. During this same period the Uyghurs, the Turkic-speaking people of what is now western China, were also converted to Buddhism and developed an original literature in their language. Mongolia was converted much later and Vietnam only partly. The northern provinces of what used to be British India, parts of Kashmir, Nepal, Sikkim, Bhutan and adjacent areas, still practise Buddhism, especially since the destruction of Buddhism in Tibet after 1962 caused an influx of refugees.

There is no antagonism between the two schools of Buddhism, no rejection of one by the other, just a difference of tradition based on the use of different books of doctrine. The Mahayana books are all based on the Sanskrit tradition of Buddhism (unlike the Theravada, q.v.); many works now in use in China are known only in Chinese translation, the Sanskrit original having been lost. These books are based on a reinterpretation of the older Buddhist doctrine of self-reliance. The Mahayana regards the Buddha as an absolute Being, immortal and universal. A person's life is ideally a process of self-realization of one's one-ness with all life in unison. The mutation of the original 'pure' Buddhism in China can partly be explained by the fundamental difference in structure between Sanskrit and Chinese. Sanskrit is composed of complex words which are strung together into long sentences with an advanced logical content. Chinese is composed of autonomous monosyllabic roots each of which contains endless reflections of semantic facets, which cannot well be understood without an older master. Thus Mahayana became the doctrine which has to be studied with a hierarchical superior, whereas the original Buddhism teaches spiritual independence. (See also *Amitabha*; *Bodhisattva*; *Dhyani-Buddha*; *Maitreya*.)

Mahendra Son of Ashoka, emperor of India 232–204 BC. It was during his reign that Buddhism was preached successfully in Sri Lanka.

Maheshvari 'The great lady'. An epithet of Devi–Uma–Kali (q.v.).

Mahinda (d. 222 BC). Son of the emperor Ashoka, became a Buddhist priest and led the expedition sent out by his father to Sri Lanka. There, he founded the monastery of Anuradhapura. In its garden he planted a branch of the original Bodhi tree brought from Bodhigaya by his sister, Sanghamitta, a Buddhist nun. The tree which grows there to this day is said to be the very tree which grew up from that branch. Branches from it have been taken to all the Buddhist countries.

Mahisha A buffalo-demon. (See *Kali–Durga*, who slew the demon.)

Mahisha-Mardini 'Killing Mahisha', the demon disguised as a buffalo. An epithet of Kali–Durga. Originally she may have been the one goddess of Hinduism, since she is a sister of Krishna, the wife of Shiva and a unification of three goddesses created to slay all the demons that threatened the world-order. (See *Chamunda*; *Durga*; *Kali*; *Parvati*.) She is the chief goddess of Hinduism, taking a central position especially in South India. She is sculpted with a belligerent appearance, holding a weapon in each of her eight hands: a javelin, sword, arrow, *chakra*, noose, shield, bow and conch. If she has 10 arms she also holds *chandra-bimba*, the moon-disk, and a skull, symbol of her function as the goddess of death. As the world-saving goddess she embodies the energy of all the gods.

Maitreya In Buddhism, the last of the five great Bodhisattvas, the one who lives 'in limbo' in the Heaven called Tushita, until the end of Time when he will come to earth to bring justice, liberation from evil and salvation to all. He arrived in Tushita when he 'died' on earth as Shakyamuni Gautama Buddha (see *Paranirvana*) after completing 550 preceding existences as animal, man and god. He will be born, after 5,000 years in Tushita, when the fifth world is created by the fifth Dhyani Bodhisattva (q.v.) Vishvapani. (Other authorities maintain that this period of Buddha-lessness will last only 4,000 or even 3,000 years.)

Buddha taught that at the end of time the water in the oceans will dry up, so that a man can walk from continent to continent. The mountains will be flattened so the earth becomes one vast plain. There will be no more criminals, people will do good for their own satisfaction. There will be no more thorn-bushes, only green grass. The trees will have flowers and fruits at the same time. There will be only one kingdom on earth, ruled by Shankha, a righteous king, who will make the Dharma law unto all. By that time the Bodhisattva Maitreya, who has been meditating upon the state of ignorance in the world and his future task, will descend to earth and enter the womb of Brahmavati, wife of Subrahmana, the king's prime minister. After 10 months she will give birth standing in a blossoming orchard. The Supreme Mind, Maitreya as Manushi Buddha (q.v.), will emerge from her right side as a little babe, entirely clean. At once he will walk and speak thus: 'This is my last birth.'

His father will perceive the 32 marks of the Buddhahood on his son. Wherever he places his feet, precious stones will appear. He will have a heavenly voice able to reach the corners of the world. He will wander without a home followed by thousands of disciples after having gained enlightenment while meditating under a dragon-tree. His preaching the Dharma will remove all evil, all sickness and suffering. Under his guidance hundreds of thousands will enter a religious life. He will teach them all the Law in a flower garden. In the end, all the people of the earth will follow the Teacher, even the demons, Gandharvas, Yakshas and Rakshasas will worship him, yes even the gods Brahma and Indra will praise him. People will no longer have doubts; they will be freed from illusion, *maya*. They will lead a holy life; they will no longer call anything their own; they will have no possessions — no gold or silver, no home, no family, no kinsmen. They will lead a life of chastity without passion, greed or envy. Happiness will reign until Maitreya himself enters Nirvana. His Dharma will last until all men lead pure lives. According to some, Maitreya is an incarnation of the Buddha himself, returning to earth to renew the Master's teaching. In the end, all people will have overcome their desires and with that, their suffering. They will all be a little like Buddha. No more children will be born since all men have left lust behind. Thus humanity will come to an end as all souls will be merged in the state of Nirvana, of equanimity, *samabuddhi*.

Many Buddhist sages seek communion with Maitreya and ask for his advice concerning their future thoughts and actions, because Maitreya is still alive and is concerned for humanity. The great Tantric sage Asanga succeeded, by his supernatural powers, in visiting Maitreya in distant Tushita, so Maitreya initiated him in the mysteries of Tantra. The Hinayana school also venerates Maitreya. Maitreya statues have been found from as early as the Gandhara period in what is now North Pakistan to as far away as medieval Java. Called in Chinese Mila-Fu, Maitreya is still worshipped in Korea, in Sri Lanka (Metteya) and is well known in Japan as Miroku, in Tibet as Maitri, in Mongolia and Manchuria as Maidari.

The origin of the name Maitreya is Mitri 'the one who has friendship'. Maitreya statues are recognizable by the *stupa* in his hair, symbol of future life, the flask of *amrita* (ambrosia), symbol of his life as a god in heaven, in one hand, and a lotus flower in the other, the symbol of self-creation, since the Bodhisattvas emanated from Adi-Buddha via the Dhyani-Buddhas. There is a legend relating that Maitreya was an existing person, a prince who met the Buddha and became his disciple. Thus he is often described as handsome, of golden hue and dressed in a golden robe, foreshadowing his future mission as ruler of the world, with a crown, *mukuta*, on his head. Maitreya will, when his time has come, descend to earth as the fifth Manushi Buddha and will first visit the *stupa* near Bodhigaya, where Kasyapa, the third Manushi Buddha, lies buried. The master's tomb will open by itself and Kasyapa will rise from the depths of the earth. He will give Maitreya the Buddha's robe of authority. It is for this reason that Maitreya is shown with the *stupa* in his crown. He towers 30 feet tall. He will then be recognized as Chakravartin, emperor of the world.

Makara (1) A *makara* is a water-monster; originally it was the large Indian crocodile, but later it functioned more like the Greek dolphin or the biblical Leviathan. In sculpture the crocodile tail is later replaced by a fish tail, later still by the root of the lotus plant. Only a valiant hero has enough courage to extract a priceless pearl from the Makara's mouth, and with that pearl he can make the lady of his heart fall in love with him. The Makara serves Varuna the Ocean-god, who rides it as his steed. The Makara is both a source of life and of death-terror. It gives the water of life to the good and death to the wicked. The Makara is also associated with Kamadeva, the god of love, because its *rasa* 'juice', will give men virility and make them irresistible to their sweethearts.

(2) Capricorn, a sign of the zodiac (q.v.)

Manasa (1) Manasa was the daughter of Kasyapa and Kadru. Shesha the serpent king was her brother, though some scholars maintain that Manasa is the daughter of Shiva. Manasa is the goddess who is worshipped especially in Bengal where her protection is invoked against snakebites. She is very jealous of the devotion of her worshippers, so that when a rich merchant called Chand refused to worship her she persecuted him for many years. Chand worshipped Shiva with dedication, so Shiva gave him the power to create plants and fruit-trees by magic. One day Manasa appeared to Chand as a beautiful girl and when Chand had fallen in love with her, she agreed to marry him on condition that he gave her his magic powers. As soon as he had done this, she destroyed his wonderful orchard which he could not now restore. Still Chand would not worship Manasa even when she appeared to him in her divine form. So she assumed her snake's appearance and bit the six sons of Chand, so that they died. She ruined his business by sinking his ships, leaving him marooned on a foreign shore. Still he did not adore her. After many hardships, Chand returned home and slowly rebuilt his life. A new son was born to him, named Lakshmindra. When he had become adult he was betrothed to a girl called Behula. The astrologer, who was consulted as is customary before a marriage, predicted that Lakshmindra would die of a snakebite on his wedding night. Chand at once began building a house of steel for his son to live in with his bride, in peace. However, Manasa frightened the builder so that he left an opening in the wall. Through it crept a dozen snakes but Behula gave each one a saucer of milk. However, when she finally fell asleep, yet another snake slid inside and killed the bridegroom. Behula prayed to Manasa, the snake-goddess, who promised to revive Lakshmindra if Behula could convert Chand. Finally, Chand worshipped Manasa and Lakshmindra, his son, was brought back to life by the goddess. The moral of this myth is that no one may refuse to worship the deity on meeting her.

(2) 'Spiritual', a lake on Mount Kailasa, where the wild geese nest.

Manasa-Putra 'Brain-Born'. One of seven (or ten) patriarchs whom the god Brahma created out of his brain as progenitors and rulers of men and women. They are also called Prajapati or Rishi.

Mandala 'Pivot, axle'. The mountain used by the gods for the churning of the milk ocean, as the pole around which the snake Vasuki was wound.

Mandira General term for a Hindu temple (now pronounced Mandir). Originally the temples were built of timber with elaborate wood carvings of animals and human beings as decorations. Later, when stone temples were built, the stone shapes imitated the earlier woodwork.

A temple is in essence the house where the deity resides, a building constructed around the statue of the god, the goddess or the two combined, such as Shiva and Parvati. The Hindu temple serves as a peaceful place where the devotees pray to the deity. These prayers are often sung hymns of great antiquity called *stuti*, *stotra*, *gita*, *devagana* or *isha-bhajana*. The music too has come down from an old tradition. Often groups of images are found in temples, e.g. Rama, Sita, Lakshmana and Hanuman, being worshipped together.

Mangala The planet Mars, good luck, happiness. Identified with the War-god Kartikeya, or Mars (Tiu in Germanic mythology). He rules Mangala-vara, Tuesday, in French Mardi, after Mars. His symbol is a copper triangle. Mangala is not an auspicious sign to be born under. Such a person will be prone to suffer, accident-prone, and likely to be imprisoned, wounded, and robbed of his money and cattle as well as his good name.

Mani (1) The Earth, symbolized by a lotus. (See also *Bhu*; *Padma*.)
(2) A jewel, the essence, a magic seed.

Manjushri, Manjusri The oldest of the Bodhisattvas, in terms of worship. He confers upon his worshipper wisdom, memory, intelligence and eloquence. In the beginning, Manjushri lived on Mount Panchashirsha ('five peaks') in the far north. One night he saw to the south a great flame of fire on a lotus. His intuition told him that this must signify the birth of the Adi-Buddha. At once he set out to find the source of the light and discovered that it burnt below the surface of a great lake surrounded by mountains. He drew his sword and carved a deep trench through the rocks. The water flowed away and exposed the beautiful valley which is now called Nepal, through which the River Baghmati still flows. Another legend relates that Buddha himself emitted a ray of bright light from his illustrious forehead. This ray hit a *jambu* tree from which at once a lotus flower sprouted. From the inner pistil 'sprouted a man, the beginning of the great master Manjushri, prince of sages'. 'Of golden hue, his right hand held the sword of wisdom, his left held a book attached to a lotus flower; his body was covered in ornaments'. Some Buddhists call him the founder of culture and learning in Nepal. He is venerated by some as the architect of the universe and the god of agriculture to whom the first day of the year is dedicated. With his Sword of Wisdom he destroys the dark clouds of ignorance.

Manmatha Vishnu in his aspect as the god of love with bow and arrows, associated with the goddesses Rati and Priti 'Love'. (See also *Kama*).

Mantra Originally any Vedic hymn which had to be recited by the priests for a particular purpose. Later, a portion of text which the guru gives to his pupil to meditate on, for life. Then it comes to mean counsel, good advice given by a Brahmin to those who come to consult him. Finally, since the Vedic hymns were believed to have magic power, *mantra* can mean 'magic formula', lines from an occult text which works wonders.

Mantravidya Magic, lit., the knowledge of mantras, which is what constitutes magic in India. A mantra, (q.v.), is a fixed formulation, originally of a specified prayer directed to a god mentioned by name. Later it was believed that by pronouncing the right formula in the required conditions, a god could be compelled to fulfil the wishes of the 'knower of the secret formulas', i.e. the magician. This latter has to be an accomplished ascetic since the best way to force the gods to fulfil one's wishes is a prolonged period of asceticism, *sannyasa*.

Mantri Mantrin, a counsellor, a Brahmin minister of state.

Manu One of 14 patriarchs, each of whom ruled the earth for one period of its history, called *Manu-antara* (*Manavatara*). (See also *Kalpa*; *Yuga*.) The first Manu was called Svayam-bhuva 'Existing by his own power', as an emanation from the god Brahma. He was the father of the 10 Prajapatis and the seven Maharishis. His wife was Shatarupa, an emanation of Sarasvati. He is the creator of the great Book of Hindu Laws called Manu-sanhita. The Manu of this our own age is Vaivasvata, the seventh Manu (q.v.). He was the Indian Noah.

Manushi-Buddha A Buddha who has (temporarily) taken the shape of a man in order to live and work in the world. There are seven Manushi Buddhas: Vipasyin, Sikhi, Vishvabhu, Krakucchanda, Kanakamuni, Kasyapa and Shakyamuni (Gautama). The last four belong to our present Kalpa.

Mara In Buddhism, the god of death, physical love, seduction and temptation, often compared to the devil in Christian lore. Both

Mara and Satan endeavour to destroy the devotee's concentration on his divinely ordained duty. Mara has numerous daughters, young ladies of lovable shape, whom he will send out to seduce saints and ascetics. They will dance voluptuously until the saint loses his concentration (see *Dhyana*). When the Buddha was being tempted in this way, however, he never wavered but remained aloof from all desires.

Mara's daughters Beautiful nymphs who danced lascivious dances before the Buddha's eyes, but failed to disrupt his profound meditation.

Maricha A Rakshasa, son of Taraka. Once when Rama met him, he shot an arrow at him which drove him away but did not kill him. Alas! Rama had made a vindictive enemy. Later, when Rama was in the forest, where he had to protect Sita, Maricha appeared to him in the shape of a golden deer which eluded Rama's arrows and lured him ever deeper into the forest, so that Ravana got his chance to capture Sita and fly away with her to Sri Lanka. (See *Ramayana*.)

Marichi Chief of the Maruts. One of the Prajapatis, son of Brahma, father of Kasyapa. One of the seven Rishis or archpriests.

Marisha 'Daughter of the Wind and the Moon, Nurseling of the trees'. She is the Dew, Tushara, which the cooling presence of the moon at night creates on the leaves. The Wind collected those beneficient drops into one body with fragrant and medicinal leaves, nurtured by the forest, supervised by the moon. She married Prachetas. Her son was Daksha.

Markandeya A sage who had acquired so much merit that he survived the dissolution of the universe and floated on the world ocean, until he was swallowed up by Vishnu. Inside Vishnu he saw the universe.

Markandeya-Purana A long narrative poem of some 9,000 verses, in which the sage Markandeya is the chief narrator. Some of the other narrators are fabulous birds which possess profound wisdom.

Martanda 'Born of an Egg', a name of the Sun-god as a skybird.

Marttanda See *Surya*.

Marut One of 49 storm-gods, servants of Indra. Sons of Rudra, they are armed with flashes of lightning and thunder-hammers, while riding on whirlwinds. Their mother was Diti who gave birth to them in one lump which Rudra-Shiva was asked to shape into handsome boys. Others relate that Shiva as a bull begot them with Prithivi as a cow. They had names like Wind-seed, Wind-flame, Wind-speed, Wind-force, Wind-circle (Vayuvega, Vayubala, Vayumandala, etc.).

Marutta A great emperor who once organized a sacrificial ceremony so lavish that both the gods and the priests were entirely satisfied. After this Marutta retired from the world and was carried up to heaven.

Matali Indra's charioteer.

Matanga A man whose mother was a Brahmin lady who, one day when she was drunk, enjoyed the embraces of a low-caste man. The fruit of this adulterous union was Matanga who was educated by his mother's husband as a Brahmin. One day he beat a young donkey, whereupon the donkey's mother said to her son: 'That is what you can expect from a low-class man.'

Matanga asked the she-donkey what she meant so she explained that he was not the son of his mother's Brahmin husband. From that moment Matanga became an ascetic, standing on one toe for a hundred years until Indra appeared and gave him the power to fly.

Matarisvan The first of the priests (Bhrigus, Rishis) who learned and taught the most precious human knowledge: the technique of sacrificing in fire. To this end he went and captured Indra's thunderbolt in Heaven.

Mathura An ancient and sacred city on the River Yamuna; the name is said to mean Madhu-vana, 'full of honey'. Here, Krishna was born and watched Radha bathing in the river.

Matrika Divine Mother. Originally there were seven divine mothers. They were the protectresses of human morality. In the world of human beings Knowledge (Vidya 'seeing') and Ignorance (Tamas 'darkness') are locked in endless battle for domination of our minds. One fine day Wisdom, symbolized by the gods, will win. In the following myth Shiva represents knowledge and Andhakasura, ignorance. Once upon a time the king of the demons coveted the beautiful Parvati. One of his demon-servants, called Nila, took the shape of a huge elephant wanting to kill Shiva. But Shiva's son, Virabhadra, was also ready for battle and ultimately killed Nila. Shiva hit the demon king with an arrow so that he began to bleed profusely. Every drop of royal demon-blood that fell on earth assumed the form of another Andhakasura. The gods needed more divine beings to help them prevent the demon's blood from falling on the earth. So, each of the eight gods present created a Shakti, a female deity capable of suppressing an evil character. Remember that mythology is in essence philosophy. Here are the names of the eight Shakti-Matrika goddesses with the sins or demons that are their special concern:

Goddess	Evil spirit	
Yogeshvari	Kama	Desire — Cupido
Maheshvari	Krodha	Anger — Ira
Vaishnavi	Lobha	Covetousness — Libido
Brahmani	Mada	Pride — Superbia

Kaumari	Moha	Illusion — Fallacia
Indrani	Matsarya	Fault-finding — Indicia
Chaumunda	Paisunya	Tale-bearing — Calumnia
Varahi	Asuya	Envy — Invidia

With the help of these powerful goddesses the demon army was defeated and the evil spirits prevented from multiplying. The demon king submitted to Shiva, praising him and worshipping him. The Divine Mothers can be seen in medieval sculpture in the great temples of Aihole and Ellora, as upright, dignified women of honour. Each of them represents the human resolve to overcome an evil aspect of one's own character.

Matsya 'Fish'. The fish incarnation of Vishnu (q.v.). There was also a country called Matsya; its people were called Matsyas. Vishnu, in the shape of the primeval fish, taught Manu (q.v.) the law. (See also *Vaivasvata*.)

Matsyadharma The law of the fishes, the most primitive of all the laws of humanity: the big fish eat the smaller fish and so forth. This is the 'right of the strongest' or 'might is right'.

Matsyapurana This text was dictated by Vishnu to Manu (q.v.). It is composed in verse and has a total of over 14,000 couplets. It is believed to contain the laws of Manu, the Indian equivalent of the Laws of Moses, but large sections are mythological rather than legal.

Maurya A dynasty of 10 Indian emperors who reigned altogether for 137 years, 324–187 BC. Their founder was Chandragupta and their capital was Pataliputra.

Maya (1) An architect, father of Mandodari who married Ravana. He lived in the Devagiri Mountains and he built a palace for the Pandavas.

(2) (With two long vowels). A Goddess. The Indian philosophers' conviction that what we see is not the real world, that we are constantly being deluded, has led the people to conceive of Maya as a goddess, smiling, seductive, fickle, treacherous, the goddess of what Western scientists call physical reality. She is, in later times, identified with Kali–Durga, the goddess of magic and spells, also called Maha-Devi 'the powerful goddess', or Maha-Maya. She is identified by the greeks with Cybele, who was also called Maia. Originally, Maya was the name for 'physical appearance, earthly form', 'deceptive exterior'. In Indo-European times Maya was an earth-mother goddess. In Greek and Roman mythology she was the mother of Hermes–Mercury, the Trickster-god, the arch-magician, the god of deceivers, Hermes Trismegistos, who appears in many forms. The name Maya was given to girls, like other names of goddesses, e.g. Janiki, Sarasvati, Sita, or in Europe, Diana. Maya was the name of Gautama's mother (see *Buddha*). Vishnu, to whom

Hermes may be compared as the god who most actively intervenes in the world of people when evil has to be combated, is the Creator of Maya in the sense of physical existence, the world of appearances. (See also *avatara*.) For the Indian philosophers, as for the Platonists, the real world was the existence of spiritual concepts, Plato's unchanging ideas. The changing physical world is not real but 'shadows of a distant fire' as Plato described it. Maya comes close to the Sufi concept of *ghurur* 'deception, illusion' as opposed to *Haq*, 'truth, god'.

(3) Illusion. Vishnu, in his incarnations, 'put on' flesh as if it were a garment wrapped around his invisible divine spirit. By their superior will, the gods can make mortals see what they, the gods, want them to see. The mirage in the desert is only a faint echo of the fairy-tales that the Indian gods could cause entire nations to live through. The sages are the only persons who, after many years of asceticism, have succeeded in breaking the spell of these divine illusions. They see that that which ordinary people regard as a normal experience, such as a body, is an illusion, because it will decay tomorrow. Only the eternal is genuine and the eternal is one. The people we see in the street are no more than illusory visions of plurality, emanations of the one unity: humanity, the human spirit, the essence of being human. Bodies will come and go but the spirit, the essence, Sat, continues to exist long after all the bodies have gone and only Brahma survives, invisible. Life with all its worries is Maya. Buddha accepted this important chapter of Hindu philosophy and made it part of his own. For the Buddhists, the illusion in our life is that we think we shall ever get pleasure out of it, that it is of any value.

'Have no illusion,' says Buddha. 'The sufferings of life will far overshadow the few pleasures that life lures us with. It is our own desire which makes us want to go on living from day to day until we are old and ailing. It is therefore our ignorance which causes the illusion that life, even if it is not pleasant now, will be so later. It never will be!'

One day a sage had performed so much asceticism that the god Vishnu appeared to him and granted him a boon.

'Teach me, great God, thy Maya!' thus prayed the sage.

'Very well,' spoke Vishnu. 'Dive into the river.'

The sage did. He descended to the bottom of the river, where he became she, a girl, a princess who grew up in a palace with a lovely park. When she came of age, she was married to a handsome prince and lived happily with him for many years until an enemy invaded the country. Her father, the king, her brothers and her husband had to go to war to defend the kingdom. Her husband was killed in battle and his body was brought home to be cremated. The princess, his faithful wife, agreed to be suttee (see *sati*) and be burned alive together with her dead husband. As she burned her body went up in smoke and her soul went up with it. Up and up she went until she came to the surface of the river and was again a man, the sage.

Vishnu was still there. He asked: 'Do you now know my Maya?'

Mayadevi, Mayavati She married Pradyumna a reincarnation of Kama the god of love, even though she could also be considered to be his mother. She is thus identified with Rati, the Indian Venus.

Mayamoha 'Illusion plus confusion'. Vishnu's great weapon against the gods' enemies whom he tempts away from their purpose, promising them whatever they ask for, then giving them the illusion they have it already.

Maya-Suta 'Son of Lakshmi,' (See *Kama*.)

Mayavati Goddess of Love. (See *Kama*; *Rati*.)

Mayura or Sharanga The peacock, a symbol of royal dignity.

Meda Marrow. Once after a war in which the gods had only just been victorious over the demons led by the horrific Madhu, the monsters' marrow covered the earth, who is since called Medini, the 'marrow-filled one'.

Meru The golden mountain, the great central mountain of the world, the navel of the earth, adorned by three luminous peaks. On its summit Indra has built his Swarga or Paradise where the celestial spirits live, the Hindu Olympus. Also called Deva-parvata, Sumeru and Ratnasanu.

Mesha A ram; Aries, a sign of the zodiac (q.v.).

Metta (Pali), a state of mind of benevolence which leads to generosity towards others, goodwill and friendship, love without emotion, kindness without vanity, charity, to treat one's neighbour as your loving mother would treat you. Sanskrit: *maitri*.

Metteya (Pali) see *Maitreya*.

Mina Pisces, a sign of the zodiac (q.v.).

Mira She was the youngest daughter of a king. One day when all her sisters were married she asked her mother if there was no husband for her. 'Here,' said her mother, lightheartedly pointing at a small statue of Krishna. 'Take him for a husband.'

Little did she know that both her daughter and the god would take her seriously. Mira took the statue and placed it in her room, after which she prayed to Krishna night and day, sang hymns to him and washed his statue regularly. Even when she did get an earthly husband, whom her parents commanded her to marry, all her true adoration was for Krishna, even though her husband, a kindly king, understood her devotion and loved her still. One day, as Mira was walking in her garden, praying to Krishna, the real god appeared to her and at once her soul left her body and merged with the divine spirit. For Hindu mystics this sad tale is in reality joyful, even though the kind king mourned his queen for the rest of his life. Beautiful songs are still sung in India to celebrate Mira's love for her god, a love so complete and consuming that her soul had no attachment to this world and cleaved to her god as soon as she saw him.

Mithila A city in northern Bihar once known as Videha, King Janaka's capital.

Mithra, Mitra The meaning of the word *mithra*, as we now know, is 'contract', 'covenant'. Thus the god Mithra represents and incorporates the structure of society on the basis of agreed relations between persons. Mitra is one of the oldest and also one of the mysterious gods of the Aryans. He is a sun-god; Mitra is one of the names of Surya (q.v.). From the meaning 'sun, sky', the word *mitra* acquires the meaning 'world' then 'community of people, village', the origin of the Russian word *mir* 'peace'. The essence of what keeps a human community together is what we would now call a 'social contract', a tacit agreement that makes it possible for people to live together without fighting.

In ancient Iran Mitra (spelled Mithra in Iranian) was the god of the contract, of mutual agreement, of the covenant between two nations. This pact was sanctified by the sacrifice of a bull to Mithra, followed by a sacrificial meal. As the sun-god, Mithra would supervise the keeping of the agreement. So gradually the Sanskrit word *mitra* came to mean 'friend', and the modern Persian word *mihr*, derived from *mithra*, still means 'the sun' and 'mutual love'. The essence of Mithra is that he sacrifices himself, he *is* the sun-bull which he slaughters himself, as can be seen in a famous sculpture. Mithra is thus the precursor of Jesus as the god who sacrificed himself for the sake of mutual love and peace.

We possess very different material concerning the adoration of Mithra in five distinct cultures:

1. Indo-Iranian or early Aryan cuture, with vestiges in the Veda.
2. Persian, divided into three successive cultures: heathen, Zoroastrian and Achaemenian cults of Mithra, linked to kingship rites.
3. Mithra in the Hellenistic period, mainly in Asia Minor.
4. The Roman Empire, where Mithra was revived in a new incarnation.
5. Armenia, quite possibly the birthplace of Mithra, at least of the Roman Mithra, if not of the older Persian Mithra.

Thus we find archaeological monuments of the worship of the same god, Mithra, from India (the Hymn to Mitra in the Rig-Veda), via Iran, Mesopotamia, the Greek world, Italy and Germany as far as Hadrian's wall east of Lancaster.

Who was this now extinct god who was so attractive to so many and so different people that he enjoyed an extraordinarily long career, from Indo-European to late Roman times? Other gods seldom survived the demise of the culture in which they originally functioned, e.g. Varuna, Mitra's twin-god in Vedic India, did not share in Mitra's triumphal march through antiquity, which lasted till the death of the good emperor Julian, which was also the death of classical culture and the beginning of the end of the Roman Empire. The reasons for this are complex, but some can be analysed. One is precisely this concept of Alliance, of Friendship (in Sanskrit, *mitra* means 'friend'); in Greek, *mitra* is a tie, a sash, a bandolier or headcloth (hence the English mitre, the bishop's headgear). This tying was actually made into a ceremony in which two or more persons engaged in an insoluble bond or covenant. Secondly, it must have been the mythology of Mithra, part Indian, part Iranian, part Greek and Roman, to which over the centuries many fascinating features had attached themselves. Mithra is the Sun-god who travels through the 12 signs of the zodiac, thus linking ancient with Hellenistic cosmology. Mithra was the white bull and the white ram. He was sacrificed (by himself in a sun-rebirth ritual) annually.

Finally the Romans drank wine during the Mithra feast after the sacrifice and that ceremony too goes back to Vedic times in India. Thus Mithra functioned in every aspect of daily activities, in food and beverages, in social and political relations, in sun and moon. The moon was associated with the bull, and also with the wine, or, in ancient India, the *soma*, that mysterious beverage which the gods extract from the *soma* plant, in Avestan *haoma*.

Mithuna, Mithun Gemini, the equivalent of the Zodiacal sign of the Twins (of different sexes). In classical Hinduism, Mithuna are the symbol of the ideal marriage, represented as man and wife, a couple in loving embrace. This is the central theme of numerous Indian myths: the blessings of holy matrimony. (See also *Zodiac.*)

Moha Ignorance, dullness, mental sloth, lethargy, a primitive state of mind from which both Hindus and Buddhists want to escape.

Mohini After long churning, the gods finally produced from the ocean the desired flask of ambrosia, the precious potion of immortality. But as soon as it became visible above the surface, in the hands of the famous physician Dhanvantari, both the gods and the demons rushed to get it. The demons won because they were quicker and more aggressive. However, being demons, they started quarrelling at once over who should drink from it first. It was at that moment that Mohini appeared, a goddess of exceptional beauty, smiling sweetly, with her anklets jangling and showing her heaving breasts. The demons, overcome by passion, forgot their draught of immortality and crowded around her. She offered to distribute the ambrosia equitably to all the demons. They all shouted approval, then she added: '... and the gods.'

The latter were invited to stand in an orderly row opposite the demons. Then Mohini served all the gods a draught of the priceless *amrita*, after which she disappeared. Pandemonium broke loose, but in vain. Mohini did not exist, she was only an appearance of Vishnu's *maya*, contrived to trick the demons out of immortality.

Moksha Liberation, release. (See *Buddhism*.)

Moon See *Chandra*; *Shashi*; *Soma*.

Mother-Goddess The Indians have worshipped mother-goddesses from prehistoric times (see *Matrika*). Shakti is the categorical term for all mother-goddesses, as the sole active, compassionate deities. The greatest Shakti is Parvati, also known as Uma, Mahadevi and Annapurna. Manasa, the snake-goddess, protects people from snakebite. Mariammai or Shitala protects children against smallpox. Bhu is the earth-goddess. Lakshmi, also called Devi Sri, and her incarnations, Sita and Devaki, are also mother-goddesses, as are the river-goddesses Ganga, Sarasvati and Yamuna. For the Buddhists, Tara and Pandara are the mother-goddesses.

Mouse The vehicle of Ganesha, because it can penetrate anywhere.

Mrityu Death, a god or goddess. (See *Yama*).

Muchukunda Son of Mandhatri, King of the World, who assisted the gods in their wars against the Asuras. They granted him a boon and he asked for eternal sleep. Whoever wakes him will be burnt to ashes.

Mudgala A saint of great virtue who used to treat his guests generously without telling them that he had to collect fruits and seeds in the forest in order to live. He never lost his patience with greedy guests when they ate all his food. When the messenger from heaven arrived to take him to the life of eternal bliss he refused to go, continuing his strenuous meditations in pursuit of pure knowledge, comprehension and peace.

Mudra Seal, signet, mark. In sculpture, *mudra* is the position of the hand and fingers of a statue, especially of Buddha, expressing one of 27 philosophical conditions, the best known of which are Abhaya 'fearlessness', Dharmachakra, Jnana, Dhyana and Bhumisparsha.

Mukhalinga Statue of Shiva, his face emerging from his *linga*.

Mukta-Kachha 'Liberated to the end', a Buddhist who has achieved enlightenment.

Mukunda 'Liberator'. (See *Vishnu*.)

Munda Bald. Name of a demon who opposed Durga (q.v.).

Muni 'Silent one'. A sage, a class of holy men, a scholar with divine nature, an ascetic, other than a Brahmin, who 'wears the wind as his girdle'. The power of their own silence enables them to fly like birds and gods. A *muni* knows what other people think, since he has drunk from the magic potion of Rudra-Shiva, which is poison to ordinary people.

Murti Figure, statue. Statues, images or pictures of the gods are 'teaching aids' for beginners, who need a physical object to concentrate their untrained minds on before they learn to meditate properly, by concentrating their minds directly on God. Worshippers will clean the statues, pour milk over them, rub them with *ghee*, place flowers around them and burn incense near them in the hope of establishing a close bond with the god. In this way believers can establish a loving relationship with God.

Muru A demon with 7,000 sons who were all burnt by Krishna.

Myths of Creation The world of existing things began when the god Brahma woke up one fine morning. He found himself seated on a splendid lotus flower which had just opened its pure white petals on the surface of the primeval ocean. Surveying the empty world of sea and sky, Brahma meditated: Where do I come from? He looked down into the water from where the lotus stalk that supported him had grown up. He saw to his surprise that it grew out of the navel of a person who was lying asleep on the bottom of the world ocean. That sleeper was Vishnu, who was resting his divine head on the coils of the World Serpent Ananta-Shesha.
  'Who are you?' the two gods asked each other, and started quarrelling.
  'I created you by thinking you,' argued Brahma.
  'I gave birth to you, so I am your father and your mother,' retorted Vishnu.
  Suddenly they saw a pillar of light rising from the bottom of the ocean to the top of the sky. Vishnu and Brahma agreed that this curious phenomenon must be investigated. Vishnu took the shape of Varaha, his wild boar incarnation and started digging the earth to find the root of the pillar, while Brahma took the shape of Hansa the swan and flew up into the sky to find its top. They both returned without success. Suddenly, the pillar opened a door in the middle and there appeared Shiva. The three gods were having a friendly competition before starting seriously on the creation. Each of them was the creator. They were not only brothers, they were identical, for there is only one god, who has a thousand names and as many shapes. Indian philosophers know that the divine reality will always elude our small minds.

N

Naga

Nachiketas Son of Aruni, who gave away all his possessions until his son Nachiketas asked: 'To whom shall I, your last possession, be given?'

Aruni answered: 'To Death.'

So Nachiketas set out in search of Death and stayed with Yama for three nights. Yama granted him a boon. First Nachiketas asked to be reconciled with his father, then he asked to be taught the true knowledge of the soul. The teaching of Death has been laid down in the famous Katha-Upanishad.

Nadi-Devata A river-goddess. Some forest people still worship the river-goddesses but in Buddhist art they are themselves shown worshipping the Buddha when he is bathing.

Naga (1) A snake, mostly the Cobra Capella.

(2) An elephant, so-called because its trunk is reminiscent of a snake.

(3) A mythical intelligent being with a human face and a long tail like a reptile. The Nagas are the descendants of Kadru, wife of Kasyapa. Their purpose in life is to inhabit the region of Patala under the earth. They have splendid palaces there and live in luxury. Some of their daughters have a completely human aspect and can even be beautiful, like Ulupi, who married Arjuna.

(4) A member of a tribe or nation still living in eastern India.

(5) A historical people, a clan or dynasty of kings who once ruled Naga-Dwipa.

Nahusha Son of Ayus, who was the eldest son of Pururavas. He had acquired so much merit by his asceticism that a thousand *rishis* carried his vehicle through the air. His toe once touched the sage Agastya, who was carrying him at the time. Agastya, incensed, exclaimed: 'Fall, you Naga!'

Nahusha fell to the earth and became a Naga, until Yudhisthira liberated him from that status enabling him to ascend to heaven.

Nakula The fourth of the Pandava princes, son of Madri, third wife of Pandu and one of the Ashvinau, Nasatya. He was master of the horse while employed by the King of Virata. He married Karenumati.

Nala (1) King of Nishadha whose history is part of the Mahabharata. Nala was famous for his bravery in battle, his handsome appearance, his righteousness, his sportsmanship and his scholarship in the Vedas, but he was addicted to gambling. One day he decided to try his luck at the *svayamvara* (husband-choosing ceremony) of the famous princess Damayanti, whose beauty and virtue were unequalled. On the way he fell into step with four very dignified gentlemen who, as it happened, were on their way to the same ceremony. They turned out to be the gods Indra, Varuna, Yama and Agni. As soon as they revealed themselves, Nala, even though he was a king, fell on his face to pay homage to the rulers of the universe. They accepted his reverence and charged him with a special task: to tell Damayanti that she ought to select one of the four gods as her bridegroom. Nala, wise king that he was, knew that he must hide his own purpose for travelling to Vidarbha and do the gods' bidding. What choice does a mortal have? So, King Nala presented himself at the court of King Bhima of Vidarbha with a message for the King's daughter, Damayanti. When she saw him, the princess fell in love with Nala, whose reputation was known to her. King Nala told her that four gods were on their way to her *svayamvara* and that they had instructed him to tell her to choose one of them. However, Princess Damayanti had a strong mind, and she was determined to have Nala for a husband. The gods knew her thoughts, so, when on the morning of the *svayamvara* all the leading kings and handsome princes of Bharata (India) stood in a wide circle, all adorned with fine jewellery, swords and regalia, there were five King Nalas: five mortal men all looking exactly like King Nala. Damayanti, however, wise princess that she was, knew what to do: she paid homage to the four gods who, she knew, were standing there in disguise, and prayed that they resume their celestial appearance. Even gods have their honour so, though they can override human wishes at any time, they showed themselves at that moment as the immortals they were, without, however, changing their resemblance to King Nala. Damayanti now inspected each of the five men very carefully until she had discovered who was a god and who was the mortal man. A man has to stand on the earth, a god does not; the gods float effortlessly above the ground not being subject to gravity. As a result Damayanti discovered that four of the figures she was studying did not have their feet upon the ground and so they had no dust on them; the gods are always clean. It follows that they were not standing upright either. Their 'bodies' (which in 'reality' were only manifestations, Maya, deluding mortals into seeing bodies) were suspended at an angle above the earth. Thirdly, the gods did not suffer the heat of the day, they did not pant like the other men who had travelled a long way, they did not breathe at all; gods need no air. As a result they did not perspire; there was no sweat on their faces, hands or necks. There was only one man standing in front of Damayanti, standing upright with his feet in the dust, and perspiration on his skin. Nala it was whom Damayanti chose as her husband, but the gods later made her pay for her self-willed behaviour.

Nala and Damayanti lived very happily. In time they had a son and a daughter, Indrasena and Indraseni. One day, Pushkara, Nala's younger brother, proposed a game of dice. Nala was irresistably tempted, but the gods had charmed the dice. In spite of entreaties from his wife, his ministers and his children, Nala gambled away his kingdom with all that was in it; even his clothes were lost. Pushkara, on winning the kingdom, proclaimed that none of his subjects might give food or shelter to ex-king Nala.

Nala wandered off into the jungle, followed only by his faithful wife. In the jungle a bird stole Nala's loincloth, his only garment, so, to spare his wife the disgrace of walking with a naked beggar, Nala left her sleeping in the forest and went on alone. He met the Snake-king, who bit him, his poison making Nala very ill. On his recovery he discovered that he had become ugly, pock-marked and bent like a little old man. He found his way to Ayodhya where the king agreed to employ him as a horse-trainer and cook.

Meanwhile, King Bhima had inquired after his daughter's health and when he was told that she had vanished in the forest, he sent out search-parties to find her. One of them discovered her and brought her back to her father's court where her children were also. She at once sent out messengers to search for Nala but they could not find him in his misshapen form. Yet one Brahmin suspected that the king of Ayodhya's cook was Nala and told Damayanti what he thought. She decided to hold a second *svayamvara* to see if he would appear again. He did, but as charioteer to Rituparna the King of Ayodhya, who had decided to try his luck himself. King

Rituparna was always lucky because he was an expert gambler. During the journey he taught Nala, his deformed horse-manager, all the tricks and details of gambling, including the game of dice, in exchange for a complete knowledge of horses. After their arrival at the court of King Bhima, King Rituparna, on greeting the king, saw no preparations for a *svayamvara*, so he did not reveal the reason for his arrival, being a man of wisdom. Damayanti meanwhile, looking down from her father's balcony, saw that the king was not her husband, but who was? Perhaps the charioteer? She had noticed that her husband's horses who were in her father's stable, were agitated, as if they could smell their master. But the charioteer was a deformed old man. Damayanti sent her trusted maid Keshini to have a closer look. The maid, observing Nala while he was preparing a meal for King Rituparna, saw him make water appear in a jar by simply wishing it and make fire by simply looking at a heap of dry grass. When he approached a low door the lintel raised itself up so that the deformed man did not have to bend down. When she told Damayanti this, the latter knew that the deformed man was indeed her husband, for she remembered that those miraculous abilities were wedding presents from the gods: Indra had given Nala uprightness so that he would never have to bend down, Varuna and Agni had given him each their own presence so that he would always have as much water and fire as he wished. Then Damayanti told Keshini: 'Now fetch me a piece of meat from the dish he has just prepared.'

Keshini quickly stole a piece of mutton, which had just been cooked by Nala and came running with it to Damayanti. When the latter tasted it she broke into tears for the food tasted exactly as Nala used to cook it for her. The art of cookery had been Yama's wedding present. She then sent her two children to the deformed cook. When he saw them he recognized them as his own, drew them towards him and wept. Damayanti, when her maid told her all this, wept too and knew now that King Rituparna's cook was truly her husband. She asked her parents' permission to summon him up to her apartments. They consented and Nala was accompanied to her room.

She addressed him reprovingly: 'You may know a man who left his wife asleep in the forest. She was innocent and she loves him to this day in spite of his desertion.'

Nala replied: 'I wonder what the reason is for the second *svayamvara* that will take place here tomorrow. Has Queen Damayanti forgotten her husband and is she looking for another?'

Damayanti replied: 'Never could I forget King Nala, whom I preferred even to the gods who wooed me. I decided on a second *svayamvara* because I thought that was the only way to make sure that Nala would arrive here, after he had abandoned me in the jungle. May the Wind-god take my breath away if I have not preserved my purity.'

At that moment they could hear the Wind-god whisper: 'She is pure! She is innocent!'

Nala now took the royal robe which the Snake-king had given him and put it on. At once he was Nala again in his regal appearance and Damayanti fell into his arms. A few days later, Nala rode back to his own palace, forced his false brother to a replay of the gambling match, staked his queen for his kingdom and won both.

(2) A monkey chief, an accomplished engineer who built the Ramu-setu, the Rama Bridge, from India to Sri Lanka. By his magic art he could make rocks float on the sea. Over these stones Rama's army marched to invade Sri Lanka and defeat Ravana's horde of demons. (See also *Rama*).

Namaskara Expression of adoration or worship by holding the palms together and bending the head.

Nanda (1) The faithful shepherd who brought up Krishna.
(2) Indra's own forest to the north of Mount Meru.

Nandana The Paradise of Indra full of lovely celestial nymphs.

Nandi Shiva's faithful bull which symbolizes *dharma*. On every painting and sculpture of Shiva, the white bull Nandi, or at least his head, is visible. Nandi is the guardian of all four-footed animals.

Nandini Female of Nandi. A cow which could fulfil all wishes.

Nandisha 'Lord of Nandi'. Epithet of Shiva. Once upon a time the demon Ravana was travelling to Sharavana, the forest that belonged to Skanda, when he met a brown dwarf with a monkey face who stopped Ravana.

The demon laughed mockingly: 'Who are you, monkey-face?'

Nandisha, for he was the dwarf, replied: 'You will be killed by monkey-faced beings.' Unafraid of the god, the demon went on boasting: 'I will show you who is stronger,' and lifted up a mountain, meaning to throw it into Nandisha's face, but the latter put his toe on the mountain, crushing Ravana's hands. Ravana had to sing hymns in praise of Shiva for a thousand years to propitiate the god.

Nara 'Man', primeval man in the service of Vishnu, carrying his bow.

Narada A famous sage, *rishi* or archpriest and *prajapati* or co-creator. He sprang from Brahma's forehead. He was at loggerheads with his colleague Daksha, who condemned him to be born from one of his daughters. This happened and the father was Brahma. Only gods can be born twice of the same father. Thus Narada was also called Brahma-deva.

Narada was the inventor of the *vina*, the Indian lute. He taught the Gandharvas to play music. He was also a friend of Krishna.

Naraka Hell, the lowest world, the place where the wicked are punished after death. Below the earth hung Patala, as the lowest abode of the old Hindu universe, suspended in space, composed of seven layers of hells, where the souls of the sinners lived in ever increasing misery as they went down. (See *Hell*.)

Narakasura, Naraka-asura A demon rapist slain by Vishnu. (See *Divali*.)

Nara Simha 'Man-lion'. An *avatara* of Vishnu when he appeared on earth as a living being with a lion's head and a man's body, in order to liberate the world from the tyranny of Hiranya-kashipu, a demon who could not be slain by a man nor by an animal. So, Vishnu appeared in this shape out of a stone pillar when the tyrant defied him after killing his own son, who was a worshipper of Vishnu.

Narayana 'Moving the Waters', 'whose place is in the water'. An epithet of:

1. Vishnu, who slept in the ocean resting on Shesha until Brahma started creating, then becoming 'Churner of the Ocean'.
2. Brahma because he was the creator of the waters out of which he then rose.
3. Narayana is the son of Nara, the First Man, a god identified with Vishnu.
4. Narayana was an ancient Rishi, son of the god Dharma and Ahimsa, who performed penance with such persistence that he alarmed the gods.

Narmada Now Nerbudda. A river in India, daughter of the Moon, sister of the Nagas. When they were attacked by the Gandharvas, she led her husband Purukutsa, an incarnation of Vishnu, to the underwater regions where the war took place. Purukutsa defeated the Gandharvas and the Nagas made Narmada's name a charm against snake-bite. Other names are: Induja, Makala, Reva.

Nasatya One of the two Ashvins (q.v.).

Nataraja Shiva is known by this name as king of the dancers. In the dance he conjures up the powers of magic, creating supernatural powers for the sorcerers on earth. The dance is itself an act of creation, the activation of the eternal energy in the cosmos. Whirling in the dance while playing his own drum, *damaru*, Shiva also maintains the stars and planets in their orbits, as well as the earth and all that is on it. Finally, as father of the fire and owner of the third eye with its killing ray, Shiva, by his dance, destroys the creation to make room for new things, just as the fire destroys the corpses on the *shmashana*, the cremation-field. At the end of our age, the Kali-yuga (q.v.), Shiva will thus destroy the whole world, by his funerary dance reabsorbing all the energy which he had released on the moment of creation. Thus existence will end. Shiva is seen dancing on the prostrate body of the dwarf, Apasmara Purusha, who symbolizes the darkness of ignorance. Thus, Shiva destroys ignorance by his knowledge of magic, *tantra* and *yoga*, the esoteric ('concealed') sciences of Mahayogi, the master of occult insight.

Natesha Lord of the Dance, Shiva, shown with his left leg raised, dancing.

Nauruz, Noroz 'New Light', the New Year of the Parsi religion, celebrated when the sun enters Aries, around 21–24 March.

Navagraha 'The house of nine', the seven planets plus Rahu and Ketu.

Navaratna The nine precious stones: diamond, pearl, ruby, sapphire, coral, emerald, lapis lazuli, topaz and cows' eye.

Nava-ratri 'Nine Nights', a great Hindu feast celebrating Durga or Kali, hence its alternative name: Durga-puja 'worshipping Durga'. It begins on the tenth day of the moon-month, Ashvayuga, usually in late September, when the moon is almost full. The faithful make an image of the mother-goddess which they will worship for nine days, after which it will be thrown into the water. The tenth day is called Vijaya Dasama 'Tenth (day) of Victory', or in modern speech, Dussera. Lord Shiva permitted his wife Parvati, daughter of the Himalayas, to go and see her mother only during these nine days once a year, after which her mother had to send her back. The women make images to which they attach themselves like a mother to her daughter, whom she has to let go to her husband. Worshippers make this feast into a series of spiritual exercises in which they confess their sins to the goddess, then ask her help in their enterprises.

Nidra Goddess of sleep, daughter of Brahma.

Nila or Nilagiri A mythical mountain range north of Meru.

Nilakantha 'Blue Throat', Epithet of Shiva, who agreed to take into his throat the ocean-poison which would otherwise have killed all the people of the earth. (See *Shiva*.)

Nimi A man whose body, after his death, was so well embalmed that it stayed fresh for years. The gods told the spirit of Nimi that they were prepared to restore him to life if he so wished, but he declined, saying that for the spirit to be separated from the body was such a painful experience that he did not want to go through it again, no matter how many pleasures he enjoyed while alive.

Nirgrantha 'Free from bonds', a member of a congregation of ascetics which was founded by Parshva and later transformed by Jina Mahavira into his own order, the Jains.

Nirjara In Jainism, the annihilation of *karma*, leading to complete *moksha*.

Nirmana-kaya One of the three forms in which the World-Buddha appears to us, different because people are of different character, though the Buddha's essence is immutable truth. *Nirmana-kaya* is the Manifestation-Body, i.e. the form in which the Buddha has shown himself to humanity, as human as possible, going through birth, old age and death. All the time he is motivated by his compassion for humanity, hoping that people will learn from his example and by following him, will find enlightenment, and an end to pain.

Nirrita The guardian deity of the South-West.

Nirruti An ancient god mentioned in the Rig-Veda, riding a lion surrounded by attractive nymphs and Rakshasas.

Nirvana Nirvana is the ultimate goal of every Buddhist intellectual (as opposed to the peasants in Buddhist countries for whom pure philosophy is of little value), it is the voluntary transition of a Buddha, i.e. a person who has come to *bodhi*, enlightenment, by means of *moksha*, liberation, from all illusions and desires. Nirvana is not heaven. Firstly it is not a place where the virtuous go, nor does one enjoy the earthly pleasures in Nirvana as one does in Janna (see *Firdaus*). Nirvana is a psychological condition which a monk who has become *arahat*, may attain, even in this life. It is a state in which the individual has no wishes left so that, by definition, he has achieved complete happiness. The official definition of Nirvana is: 'a state of neither being nor not-being'. As was said, this pure philosophy is of little help to ordinary people. Its meaning is that Nirvana is the condition of the removal of opposites, so that a state of peacefulness ensues in which the individual is suspended between conflicting contrasts. This means that what was once a person on earth has now lost the limitations of his existence as an individual and has widened his conscience as far as the frontiers of light. As a result his consciousness has expanded to include all other conscious minds who thus communicate by mutual 'feeling'. The 'Buddha' (for ultimately all thinking minds should become Buddhas) is thus in constant contact with the feeling-centres of all other beings on earth and elsewhere. The result is perfect compassion with all other beings, the effect of a total understanding of each of them. The Buddha's mind thus possesses total knowledge of all living things since they are all in his all-encompassing mind. This condition gives total happiness to the conscious mind: being in communion with all things. This happiness is Nirvana, the state in which all wishes have been 'blown out', so that illusion has been replaced by real knowledge. (See also *Buddhism*.)

Nishada, Bhil A person belonging to the peoples of the Vindhya Mountains. Their ancestors sprang from Brahma's thigh. The Bhil people have their own language.

Nishadha A kingdom and city in central India where Nala (q.v.) once ruled.

Nishumbha A demon, brother of Shumbha, both killed by Durga-Ambika-Kali. (See *Devi*.)

Nitishastra A series of books of fables in prose, containing parables with proverbs and aphorisms in verse.

Nivritti In Tantrism, the yearning for peace and withdrawal from the world.

Noah See *Vaivasvata*.

Nritta-Murti See *Nataraja*.

Nyaya Philosophy, logic, reason. Fitting behaviour, the proper way of achieving one's goal, the right method to arrive at a conclusion.

O

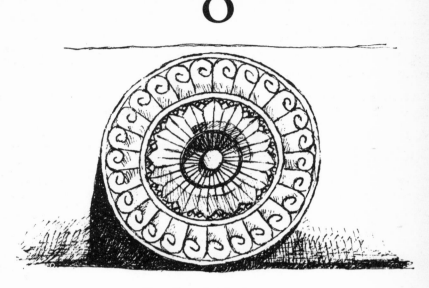

Om, the wheel of prayers

Obstacle There are five obstacles to enlightenment in Buddhism: lust and desire; ill will, anger; sloth, inertia; excitedness, worry; and doubt, wavering.

Odra The country now called Orissa. (See *Jagannath*.)

Om This syllable is combined of three elements: the open element represented by the letter A (alpha), which represents creation, when all existing things issued forth from Brahma's golden nucleus; the central element is the pronunciation of the letter U, which refers to Vishnu the god of the middle who preserves this world by balancing Brahma on a lotus above himself. It is the maintenance of the precarious condition of existence which may fall into ruin at any time, as soon as his vigilance falters. The letter U with the A, produces the sound of the long O (omega). The M produces the prolonged resonance of the nasal cavity with the mouth closed: it is the final part of the cycle of existence, when Vishnu falls asleep and Brahma has to breathe in so that all existing things have to disintegrate and are reduced to their essence in him. This is the M of Mahesha, the great Lord Shiva, whose long period of yoga begins so that the sensual world ceases to exist. For both Hindus and Buddhists this syllable is sacred and so laden with spiritual energy that it may only be pronounced with complete concentration.

It represents the absolute essence of the Divine Principle, the essence of God. The three components may be thought of as a condensation of the first three Vedas (Rig, Yajur, Sama), or as the Trinity of Brahma, the Creator. Vishnu, the protector. Shiva, the God of the End. Or as the three worlds, or the three steps of Vishnu as Vamana. For the Buddhist monk the syllable Om, if repeated often enough with complete concentration (*samadhi*) and abandon, will lead to a state of Emptiness (q.v.). To Buddhists it means the centrepiece of many prayers, veneration and awe.

Om Mani Padme Hum For the Buddhist meaning see *Avalokiteshvara*.

Oshadhi A medicinal herb. The science of healing by means of herbs (pharmacology) was highly advanced in ancient India.

P

Parvati

Padma The lotus flower, *Nelumbo nucifera*, of the *Nymphaeacaeae* family. The lotus is an aquatic plant, of which only the leaves and white flowers float on the surface. Its stalks grow under the water, where they are connected by nodes, thus forming a system of subaquatic roots which enable one plant to spread out across an entire lake. The blue lotus, *Nymphaea caerulea*, or Egyptian lotus, was imported into India at a later date. The white lotus became a symbol of purity and lucidity and finally the symbol of the earth itself as it floats on the primeval ocean. The god Brahma himself was first seen seated on a lotus afloat in this ocean. The node of that lotus was Vishnu's navel, as he is Lord of the Universal Ocean. Buddha too is seated on a lotus. It is the flower of Maitreya. (See also *Lakshmi*; *Sarasvati*.)

Padma-Nabha 'Whose navel is a lotus'. (See *Brahma*; *Vishnu*.)

Padma-Pitha 'Having a lotus as a throne or pedestal'. Gods are often depicted as seated on a lotus, e.g. Lakshmi, who is regarded by some as having risen from the Water of Origin. The lotus symbolizes the goddess' purity since the lotus petals never touch the water, nor are they ever soiled by mud.

Padma-Purana 'The Textbook of the Golden Lotus', a poem of over 50,000 couplets which describes the Creation, Srishti, of the World-lotus, of the Earth, Bhumi, of Heaven, Swarga and of the Nether-World, Patala.

Padmasana Lotus position, from *padma* (q.v.), 'lotus' and *asana*, 'manner of sitting'. Gods, including the Buddha and the Bodhisattvas, are often represented in the lotus position, absorbed in profound meditation, or in a state of supernatural beatitude, or enthroned as cosmic rulers.

Padmavati 'Owner of Lotus Flowers', Lakshmi, goddess of vegetation.

Pagoda The Buddhist temple, from *dagoba*, the tomb of a saint. (See *Dagoba*.)

Pahlava A hero from ancient Iranian times, born from a cow-goddess.

Pahlavas A nation of Iranian cattle-keepers and horsemen who lived to the north-west of India and speak Pahlavi, related to Sanskrit.

Pahlavi (1) The language spoken in Iran during a millenium between *c*.200 BC and *c*.AD800. Also called Middle Persian. It is the religious language of parts of the Avesta, Zand and Vendidad.
(2) Heroic. The word refers to the heroic days when the Persians beat the Turanians and others in the epic of Shahname.

Panchala The kingdom of King Drupada, father of Draupadi. The present-day towns of Ramnagar and Kampila formed part of it.

Pancha-Sila The five principles of virtue in Indian philosophy: Truthfulness, Self-control, Generosity, Fearlessness, Respect; or alternatively Faith, Civilized Behaviour, Harmony, Consultation, Justice.

Panchatantra 'The five formulas'. One of the oldest and most famous books of fables in world literature, a model for the fable books of the Persians (*Anwar-e-Suheili*) and the Arabs (*Kalila Wa Dimna*). The original fables were authored by a Brahmin prime minister called Vishnu-Sharman (corrupted to Bidpai or Pilpay in the translations). The purpose of the book was to teach unruly, uneducated princes good manners and diplomacy, what is now called 'public relations'. The five formulas are dealt with in the five books composing the work, namely: 'Loss of Friends'; 'The Winning of Friends'; 'How to Deal with Enemies'; 'Loss of Gains'; and 'Ill-Considered Actions'.
In many ways the Panchatantra is a textbook of political science and 'how to make friends and influence people', in the disguise of folk-tales which are easy to remember and each of which contain a

practical lesson. Some tales are almost identical to some of Aesop's fables and many are found in oral traditions from Indonesia to East Africa and the Far East. One of the best-known is the tale of the Brahmin who hears a tiger in a cage pleading to free him. He soon realizes his error in releasing the animal and a jackal finally helps the frightened Brahmin to get the tiger back into the cage. Moral of the story: once a dangerous criminal is in prison, leave him there.

Pancha-Tathagata The Five-Fold Buddha (q.v.), i.e. the five Dhyani-Buddhas: Amitabha, Amoghasiddhi, Akshobhya, Ratnasambhava and Vairochana. (See also *Bodhisattva*; *Dhyani-Buddha*.)

Panchayudha 'Having five weapons'. (See *Vishnu*.)

Pandara Shakti or 'wife' of the Dhyani-Buddha, Amitabha, and spiritual mother of Avalokiteshvara. She is shown as a very beautiful woman with a garland of flowers in her hair, two lotus flowers in her hands, seated on a lotus, with rich ornaments upon her and an aureole round her head.

Pandavas The five sons of Pandu's two wives, born of five gods. (See *Kunti*; *Madri*; *Pandu*.) When their parents retired to the forest, the Pandavas were invited by their uncle, King Dhritarashtra the Blind, to live in his palace at Hastinapura. Yudhisthira, the eldest was made Yuvaraja, 'heir apparent', which aroused the jealousy of Duryodhana, Dhritarashtra's eldest son. It was this jealousy which became the cause of the great war between the Pandavas and the Kauravas known as the Mahabharata (q.v.). (See also *Arjuna*; *Bhima*; *Yudhisthira*.)

Pandu 'The pale one'. Son of Krishna Dvaipayana, brother of Dhritarashtra, father of the five Pandavas, husband of Kunti and Madri. Dhritarashtra, the elder brother was blind and thus by ancient law deemed incapable to reign, so Pandu became king of Hastinapura. He did not procreate with his wives owing to his paleness, which according to some scholars was due to leprosy. His five sons were the offspring of five gods, three of whom, Dharma, Vayu and Indra, fertilized Kunti (q.v.). The two Ashvins caused Madri to give birth to twins, Nakula and Sahadeva. Pandu retired to the forests of the Himalayas accompanied by his two wives after their sons had been born. (See also *Pandavas*.)

Pani A pagan, a primitive race of cattle-thieves. Demonic Dwarfs who live on the other side of the River Rasa, which, like the Styx, separates this world from the Other World. The Panis stole the precious cows that belonged to Indra. So Indra created Sharama or Sarama, a bitch, to go in search of the holy cows. She crossed the wide waters of Rasa and met the Panis in their Twilight Land. They offered her brotherhood and a share of the cattle they stole. She refused but asked for the cows' milk. The Panis gave her some of the delicious milk. When she came back she lied to Indra, saying that she had not had any milk, so her master kicked her. Then Indra went himself along the path she had discovered, found the Panis, slew them and took his cows back.

Pansil, Panjasila (see also *Pancha-Sila*). The five rules of morality which are so widely accepted in South-East Asia that the Indonesian nation, though in majority Islamic, made this pentagram the basis of its national ethics. These five rules have never been a catechism nor the contents of a creed, but they are a simple and excellent formulation of a golden rule of conduct which every honest person can accept and follow. They are as follows:

1. Refrain from injury to all living beings.
2. Do not take that which has not been given to you.
3. Refrain from immorality (meant as sexual immorality).
4. Refrain from falsehood (i.e. speak the truth, deceive no one).
5. Refrain from substances which cause slothfulness (including alcohol, opium, etc.).

Papa-Purusha 'Evil Man'. Fortunately you do not often meet one of these, but if you do, remember that every part of him is vicious. Evil Man enjoys evil for the pleasure of seeing others suffer. An evil man is never without evil; everything he thinks of has the purpose of hatching harm for his fellow creatures, whose joy he envies.

Paradise See *Firdaus*; *Sukhavati*.

Paramatma Supreme soul, the immortal heart of the universe. (See *Brahma* (3).)

Paramatman Highest Spirit. The Supreme Soul of the Universe which pervades all space, unseen but conscious, knowing, understanding. In Hindu philosophy the Paramatman is often identified with Brahma as the creative principle but in Buddhist philosophy the Paramatman is a passive principle of enlightened thought. Here we see the two basic qualities of Spirit: creativeness and perception. Diffused throughout the universe there lives, according to some Hindu and Buddhist philosophers, the primal spirit out of which all spiritual beings, gods and men, have been developed and into which they will merge after their temporary separated existence on earth or some other planet or moon. This is the essence of all souls in that it contains and nurtures the nuclei of all human and divine souls and so, their ethical values which are the products of their refined sentiments concerning what must be done and what must be omitted, what must be avoided and what is worth striving for. In this way Paramatman imperceptibly directs the evolution of the human mind as new souls are born out of it and old ones merge back into it. It explains the development of humanity from animal barbarism to the intellectual heights that some scholars have already achieved and which, it is hoped, will one day be the normal spiritual standard for all people. By that time irrevocably the highest ethical values will be adhered to, since necessarily world peace will be maintained by all human beings when they realize that all their souls are one.

Paramita (1) One of 12 Buddhist goddesses of wisdom and correct behaviour, as follows: Dana 'charity', Shila 'good conduct', Kshanti 'patience', Prajna 'foresight', Ratna 'excellence', Virya 'strength of character', Dhyana 'reflection', Upaya 'learning', Pranidhana 'effort', Bala 'power', Vajrakarma 'perseverance', Jnana 'knowledge'.
  (2) The highest ideal, virtue, perfection.

Paranirvana The Buddha's willed transition from earthly life to Nirvana (q.v.).

Parashara A Brahmin, Rishi and poet of several hymns of the Rig-Veda. He taught Maitreya the Vishnu-Purana and composed a law-textbook, Dharmashastra. Parashara's mother was Adrisyanti; his father was King Kalmashapada, who was turned into a demon, Shaktar, by a Brahmin whom he had whipped. He at once devoured the Brahmin. He lived on an island in the River Yamuna. One day when Parashara was swimming across the River Yamuna he met Satyavati, daughter of the Apsaras Adrika, who had to live in the shape of a fish. They embraced and Satyavati became pregnant although she was still very young. She gave birth to Krishna Dvaipayana, better known as Vyasa, the poet of the Mahabharata or at least of some of its books, on an island in the river. Thus Parashara was the ancestor of the Pandavas as well as the Kauravas, all grandsons of Dvaipayana. Parashara performed a sacrifice which burnt part of the Himalayas.

Parashu-Rama 'Battle-axe Rama'. The sixth *avatara* of Vishnu, as son of Jamadagni and Renuka. In Parashu-Rama, Vishnu came to earth as a Brahmin for the specific purpose of defeating the Kshatriya or noble caste. He taught Arjuna the use of weapons and battled against Bhishma in the great war of the Mahabharata. Parashu-Rama had learned the handling of weapons from Shiva, who also gave him the *Parashu* or battle-axe. Around that time there lived a king, Kartavirya, who had a thousand arms. He once visited the hermitage of the sage Jamadagni, whose wife Renuka received him hospitably but, instead of showing gratitude for this, the king carried away one of his host's calves. Parashu-Rama, seeing how his father was robbed by a guest, rushed to attack the king and killed him. The king's sons then killed Jamadagni in revenge. Furious, Parashu-Rama swore that he would clear the earth of the Kshatriya caste and he did; he crossed the earth several times killing all the Kshatriyas he could find. Later, the Sea-god Varuna gave him a large tract of land in south-western India which was previously under the sea. Parashu-Rama called it the coast of Malabara and invited all the Brahmins to settle there.

Parijata A miracle tree 'perfuming the world with its blossoms' which stood in Indra's Heaven. It had emerged from the world ocean when the gods churned it. It was the favourite tree of Shachi, Indra's wife.

Parikshit Son of Abhimanyu, grandson of Arjuna. Ashvatthaman killed him treacherously, while he was still an embryo in his mother Uttara's womb, when the great war was already over, so he was born dead. However Krishna, the God, made him live again, so he could inherit the kingdom of Hastinapura. His son was called Janamejaya. Parikshit was a patron of poetry.

Parjanya (1) The Rain-god, one of the Adityas or weather-gods. Also called Parjanya-vata 'rain and wind'. There are three fine hymns in his honour in the Rig-Veda, as the bringer of clouds. Later he was identified with Indra.

(2) The Rain Cloud, the cloud bank heralding the rains, represented as a celestial cow. She had three voices: thunder, wind and rain. She rains her 'milk' as blessing for the earth.

Parsis The Parsis live mainly in Gujerat, in Bombay and Surate, as well as in Delhi. There are over 100,000 of them, whose ancestors fled from Iran to escape the onslaught of Islam. So far as we know all the Parsis who could not escape the persecutions in Iran have now been killed. Parsi is the Indian word for Persian. The Parsis are the only survivors of the once powerful religious community of the Zoroastrians who once dominated Iran and Iraq. The Parsis call themselves Zaradushti, after the founder of their religion, Zaradusht, in Greek Zoroaster and in Old Persian Zarathustra, one of the earliest prophets in human history. He preached the Word of Ahura Mazda (q.v.), the great god who created Man and enjoined him to remain pure by doing only good deeds. The evil spirit Angra Mainyu endeavours perpetually to lead Man astray from the straight path of physical and moral purity. In this way people can and must assist the good god Ahura Mazda in his eternal war against Angra Mainyu the spirit of darkness, ever since Bundahishn, Creation. One fortunate day, Ahura Mazda will vanquish his evil opponent and throw him out into utter darkness. Then the period of newness will begin, the Wizarishn, literally 'Separation', when Evil will have been sundered from this world and all people will be good, pure and joyful. Thus the Parsis have an optimistic outlook on life, since theirs is the religion of light, which Ahura Mazda created first. The fire is an emanation from this primeval light. Fire is the purifying element which plays a prominent part in Parsi ritual. The Parsis do not, however, worship the fire itself as the Muslims wrongly say. The Parsis worship only the One God whom they call Ahura Mazda, Lord of Wisdom, so they call themselves Mazda-yasni 'Worshippers of Mazda'. The Parsis have their Holy Book, the Avesta, and the Gathas, psalms or hymns composed by Zoroaster in old Persian. One day a Saviour, Soshyant, will be born from a virgin and restore righteousness. (See also *Zoroastrianism*.)

Parvati 'The mountain-goddess', 'daughter of the mountain'. A praise-name of Devi–Uma as the high goddess of the Himalayas, the same as Durga 'the impenetrable fortress' of the steep frozen summits. Thus she is also called Girija and Adrija, both meaning 'mountain-born'.

Parvati was a loving and devoted wife to Shiva, but one day, as he was explaining the Veda to her, she dozed off, so Shiva, indignant, told her to go and live among the fishermen. Parvati fell down to earth and was found by some poor fishermen on the seashore. She had assumed the shape of a human being, a little girl. She grew up and became so beautiful that all the young fishermen fell in love with her. Meanwhile Shiva had given his bull Nandi instructions to take the form of a shark and destroy the fishermen's nets. Therefore, Parvati's adopted father let it be known that the young man who could catch the shark would be allowed to marry his daughter. That was what Shiva had been waiting for. He took the shape of a handsome young fisherman, arrived in the village, went to the beach, called the shark and to the astonished eyes of the villagers, the shark came to the water's edge (his master was calling him after all) and let itself be tied. Thus Shiva had won the fisherman's daughter who was already his wife in heaven. He took her to Kailasa, the mountain where he lives. (See also *Chamunda*; *Devi*; *Devi Mahatmya*; *Shakti*.)

Pashupati Lord of Cattle. Epithet of Rudra. (See *Shiva*.)

Patala The region under the earth, inhabited by Daityas, Danavas, Yakshas and other beings. It is divided into a number of kingdoms, each with its own king and its own species of inhabitants. These include: Atala, ruled by Mahamaya; Vitala, ruled by Hatakeshvara; Sutala, ruled by Bali; Talatala, ruled by Maya; Mahatala, where monsters live; Rasatala, where the Daityas and Danavas live; and Patala or Nitala, ruled by Vasuki, the abode of the Nagas or Snake-gods. The sage Narada has said that Patala was a wonderful world, better than Heaven, a place of luxury and sensual delights. So, although Patala is thought to be beneath the earth we must not think of it as 'Hell' or 'Hades', or the Land of the Dead.

Pataliputra Capital city of the Nanda and Maurya dynasties near the confluence of the Ganges and Sone. Modern Patna is only a fraction the size of the ancient city.

Patanjali The creator of the philosophy called Yoga (q.v.). He lived *c*.200 BC. Also called Gonikaputra.

Patha, Path In Buddhism, the straight road to Nirvana. Only those who are indifferent to ambition, jealousy, fear or desire can tread this path. (See also *Way*.)

Patra Begging bowl for collecting alms, carried by mendicant monks. When Gautama had attained Buddhahood, he started out to preach his new doctrine. Two merchants in Orissa dreamed that they would meet the Buddha the next day, so they bought honeycakes and offered them to Buddha as soon as they recognized him from their dreams. Buddha did not yet have a begging-bowl and he could not receive food with his hands. At once a stone begging-bowl arrived from heaven, a present from the gods of the four quarters.

Pauravas Descendants of King Puru of the Moon-Lords. (See *Puru*.)

Pavaka 'The Purifier', a name of Agni as the fire purifies all unclean things.

Perfection In Buddhism, six qualities are needed for a perfect character: Generosity, Moral Conduct, Patience, Fortitude, Meditation and Wisdom.

Pinaka The name of Shiva's bow with which he can scatter the mountains.

Pinga 'Reddish-brown'. An epithet of Durga–Kali (q.v.).

Pir, Peer An Islamic saint of the highest order. Apart from teaching, the *pir* has two mystic functions. Firstly, he may intercede with God on behalf of the supplicant who comes to pray for children or any other boon. The *pir* may do so while he is alive and also after his death, when the supplicants will visit his grave to pray there or ask an officiant to address the saint's spirit on their behalf. Secondly, the mere presence of the *pir* will spread *barakat* 'blessing, good fortune' over his visitors whether he is alive or lying in his tomb. A man may become a *pir* by being the son of a *pir*, *pirizade*. The *barakat* will automatically adhere to the *pir*'s children. (In Islam there is no celibacy. Even a saint may have several wives. Indeed he is considered a desirable son-in-law by most people.) The highest class of *pirs* are therefore the *sharifs* and *sayids*, the descendants of the Prophet Muhammad via his grandsons Hasan and Husayn respectively, whose hands are still kissed by the believers in the hope of acquiring their *barakat*. Sainthood is thus a gift from God, *karamat*, a word which now means a miracle, since the *pirs* are believed to have worked wonders. They may, for example, effect miraculous healings of patients who are brought to them for the laying on of hands. They are especially expected to cast out evil spirits, in particular from rebellious women. Their deputies, who are appointed to cure people in their name, will beat these 'patients' with a stick in the expectation that the evil spirit (see *shetan*) will go away in awe of the *pir*'s proximity. Touching the *pir*, or his tomb, or any other object that once belonged to him, with one's hand, also gives *barakat*.

Pishacha (Also called Paisacha). A race of evil spirits, the most vicious creatures on earth. They embrace sleeping women. They have a language but they love human flesh.

Pishachi A vixen or shrew, a vicious female demon.

Pitamaha Grandfather. A name of Brahma the Creator.

Pitar, Pitri (1) Father. The soul of a dead man, an ancestor. The first Pitris were the sons of the gods who had to teach their fathers the rites of atonement, penance and humility. The spirit of a great ascetic is called Vairaja, the spirit of a Brahmin is called a Somapa and so every class of human being is transformed into a special class of Pitri after death. Yama, the God of the Dead, is the ruler over the Pitris and Svadha, sacrifice, is their mother.
  (2) Sometimes used for Prajapati (q.v.).

Pithasthana The goddess Sati, wife of Shiva in one of their early existences, ended her life in the sacrificial fire during Daksha's ceremony. Shiva arrived, lifted her body up and tore it to pieces in anger, in agony and aggrievement over the loss of his beloved goddess. Shiva was carrying her around during his mortuary dance, his unique funerary ritual, so the pieces fell across the face of India. At each place where a piece fell, Pithasthana, a shrine was erected by devotees. The best known of these sanctuaries, where a statue of Devi-Durga is worshipped, is Kalighat 'Sanctuary of Kali' (Kali being a later name of Sati).

Planets In Indian astronomy the planets' names are probably translations from Ancient Greek. They are: Budha, Mercury; Sukra, Venus; Mangala, Mars; Brihaspati, Jupiter; Shani, Saturn.

Pradhana Matter, as opposed to spirit; nature.

Pradyumna God of Love. (See also *Kama*, and *Rati* (his wife).) A son of Krishna and Rukmini. When he was a week old the demon Shambara came, took the baby and threw him into the sea, where a fish swallowed him. Later the fish was caught and bought by Mayadevi (see *Mayavati*), Shambara's housekeeper, who took it to her kitchen and cut it open. There she discovered the handsome baby, whom she adopted. The sage Narada, upon seeing the child, told Mayadevi that he was the son of a god. She fell in love with the young god when he was full-grown. When she told him his history he went up to Shambara, the owner of the house, and challenged him to a battle in which he slew the demon. He took his loving nurse Mayadevi and flew with her to his father's palace. Mayadevi became his wife as Rati, goddess of love, while Pradyumna is Kama the god of love reborn from the ashes. Rati is also the goddess of beauty who can make men feel any enjoyment they dream about. Pradyumna can change himself into a bee and visit a girl hidden in a bouquet of flowers given to her by her lover.

Prahlada Pious son of a wicked father, Hiranyakashipu, the sworn enemy of Vishnu. When Prahlada insisted on worshipping Vishnu, his father ordered his death but no weapon could harm him; nor could any snake bite him, since Vishnu protected him.

Prajapati 'Lord of Creation'. An epithet of Brahma, sometimes also of Indra. Later this title was also given to Manu, son of Brahma and to the seven (later ten) *rishis* or arch-priests whom he created: Angiras, Bhrigu, Daksha, Kasyapa, Narada, Vasishtha and Visvamitra. He is also the creator of the gods, so he is the first of the gods. They all emanated from him and so they owe both their essence and their existence to him. Prajapati has remained a god of the philosophers: he never acquired the colourful personality of Vishnu or Shiva. He is identified with Brahma.

Prajna Foresight, insight, wisdom. In Buddhism, transcendental insight.

Prakrit The language of northern India after Sanskrit had ceased to be a spoken language. It is used in some Buddhist texts.

Prakriti Nature, matter. The female principle. With two meanings: the living creation on earth, and the character of a person, which perceives nature in its own vision. Nature is a goddess who married Purusha in order to create the living world. (See also *Maya*; *Shakti*.)

Pralamba An Asura or evil demon who could assume the form of a huge elephant. One day he joined in the games of Krishna and his brother Balarama. The latter was carried away by Pralamba, who quickly assumed his elephant form, growing to colossal size. Frightened, Balarama called to Krishna: 'What shall I do?'
   Krishna replied: 'Forget that you are human!'
   Balarama laughed when he remembered that he was, of course, of divine nature and started beating Pralamba on the head until the elephant's skull burst.

Pramlocha A nymph from heaven, sent by Indra to the sage Kandu to distract him from his severe asceticism. She succeeded for a time until the old saint woke up to her delusory practices and dismissed her. By that time she was pregnant, for many ascetics are known to be healthy men. She gave birth to the beautiful, cool Marisha, goddess of the dew.

Prana Breath. The first thing a living being needs when it is born. Without it we all die. Thus Prana is personified as the goddess of life. The complete control over one's breath is the first course of *yoga*.

Prapti Adaptation, suitability; balance between the mind's extremes.

Pratyeka Buddha An individual Buddha as opposed to a universal Buddha.

Prayer (Puja, Prashansa, Prartha). Here are two short specimens of two Hindu prayers:

O Thou Ever-surviving, Never-ending Lord, the Source of Continuous Happiness, Lord of Light and Energy, May we attain Thy Blissful Peace.

O All-pervading mother sweet, divine!
Be pleased to bless the craving of my soul
To reach Thy bosom. May this world of mine
Be full of bliss and peace. May I be whole.
I make a vow before Thy sacred throne
To try and keep my heart away from sin
My hands, my eyes, my tongue, my head.
I give to Thee today to work for Thee.

Preta Spirit of a dead person, a departed soul.

Prithi, Prithu Son of Vena, grandson of Anga. The first king of righteousness. Vena was a wicked king and so the arch-priests beat him to death but, unfortunately, lawlessness soon became widespread and robbers proliferated. So, the priests then rubbed the dead king's thigh and there emerged a pitch-black dwarf with a flat face. His name was Nishada; he was the evil in the dead king and so there was now no wickedness left in Vena's flesh. The priests then rubbed the dead king's right arm and from there arose Prithu, resplendent like fire. All creatures rejoiced at the birth of the new king, the virtuous son of Vena.

Prithivi Vedic goddess, spouse of Dyaus, mother of Indra and Agni. She is the earth herself, comparable to the Greek goddess Gaia, the Roman Tellus. She is by some considered as the daughter of the sage Prithu, but according to others she was his wife. She is sometimes depicted as a cow, seeking the protection of Brahma, the Creator. Men have to work hard ploughing the earth before she will give them her treasures: grain and fruits. She symbolizes patience and endurance while suffering the plough, and also generosity, and hope, for Ushas, Dawn, is her daughter. She was regarded by some as the mother of all the gods, and she is also the mother of all people, indeed of the plants, trees, and animals too, so that the name Prithivi is sometimes used in the meaning of Nature, just as the Roman goddess Natura is the one who gives birth constantly.

Prithivi is the very model of kindness and gentleness, returning good for the evil that she receives, just as the earth gives the farmer grain after he has wounded her with his ploughshare.

Priya-Vrata One of the two sons of Brahma and Shatarupa. He owned a chariot with horses as fast as Surya's. With it he drove across the earth. His chariot was so big that its wheels cut the seven oceans dividing the seven continents. He married Kamya, 'lovable'; they had 12 children. Seven of their sons became kings of the seven continents.

Pulastya One of the *Prajapatis* and also one of the *Rishis* or arch-priests. He taught Parashara the *Vishnu-Purana* after he had learned it from Brahma, his father. Pulastya was father of Visravas, grandfather of Kubera and Ravana and an ancestor of the Rakshasas.

Pulinda One of a race of aborigines who live in the wooded hills of India.

Puloman Son of Danu, father-in-law of Indra, who killed him.

Punya-Sloka 'Sung by holy hymns', praise-name of Krishna.

Purana 'Old, old song, old book'. The Puranas are a distinct category of Sanskrit religious literature, describing the exploits of the gods in 36 volumes, including the Upa ('additional') Puranas. Each Purana has the name or praise-name of a god, or one of his incarnations, in its title. The main Puranas with the names of the gods in the title are: Brahma, Vishnu, Shiva, Garuda, Vayu, Agni, Skanda, Bhagavata (= Krishna). Several Puranas describe Vishnu's incarnations, namely Varaha, Vamana, Kurama, Matsya. Some Puranas describe the gods under different names, e.g. Linga (Shiva), Markandeya (Uma), Bhavishya (Shiva), Padma (Vishnu), Vaivarta (Brahma).

Purna Kalasha (Or Kalasa). A 'full vase'. River-goddesses like Ganga and Yamuna are often represented as beautiful women pouring out vases full of water symbolizing the rivers which give life and plants to India. This vase is sometimes represented more like a pot *Kumbha* with a spherical shape, which is compared to the body of a pregnant woman, in particular her womb, *yoni*, another 'container' from which life itself comes forth.

Purnavijaya Son of Indra who lived a sinful life with his girlfriends until Kunjarakarna was sent to him by Yama. Kunjarakarna had just been shown round in hell and told Purnavijaya of the tortures he had seen and that Yama had told him that he, Purnavijaya would be next to be so tortured. Thus, a short time before his death, Purnavijaya was converted to Buddhism, performed self-mortification and was saved, just in time.

Puru Sixth king of the Lunar Dynasty, son of Yayati. His descendants are called the Pauravas, the ancestors of the Kauravas and Pandavas.

Pururavas Originally the centre of the universe, where dawn was made every morning. As a king he was the son of Budha and Ila, the daughter of Manu. Pururavas fell in love with Urvasi, an Apsaras nymph who had descended from heaven. She, together with her female companion, had been caught by an Asura, a demon who had tied the ladies up in spite of their beauty. Pururavas rode out and slew the demon. He took the lovely ladies in his chariot and stopped where they had a rendezvous with their friends Menaka, Sahajanya and Rambha. When the chariot stopped, Urvasi, who was still in shock, fell over and woke up in the arms of the king. Quickly the five nymphs boarded their own celestial chariot and returned to heaven. However, the king could not forget Urvasi and was advised to go to sleep; perhaps she might come to him in a dream. She did not wait that long for she too loved Pururavas. She made herself invisible, travelled to his palace garden and there she revealed herself to him. She agreed to marry him on three conditions: she should be able to keep her two pet lambs, without whom she would be very unhappy, she must never see her husband naked and thirdly, her food must be nothing but ghee (clarified butter), to which Pururavas agreed. Though she was not allowed to go back to heaven because she married a mortal, they lived happily together, until the Gandharvas became jealous. One night they came and stole the lambs but because Pururavas was naked at that moment he could do nothing. However, when he heard Urvasi crying, he took his sword and pursued the thieves. That was just what the Gandharvas wanted. They produced a flash of lightning, which they had brought for the purpose, so Pururavas was exposed. Alas! Urvasi disappeared instantly. For a long time Pururavas wandered about in search of his beloved wife until he found her, bathing in the River Yamuna. She told him she was pregnant and asked him to come to her in a year's time for one night. He did and she showed him their son Ayu, who would succeed Pururavas as king of Pratisthana. A year later he came back and was given another son. This happened five times until the gods relented and granted Pururavas a boon. He said he had only one desire — to be permitted to live with his beloved wife in peace. The gods told him to perform the fire sacrifice, which he did. After that Pururavas and Urvasi lived in peace and had three more sons. The moral of this moving tale is that a man who wishes to marry a wife from heaven must expect to pay a high price for his love, but that marital fidelity will in the end be rewarded by the gods. The mythical interpretation of the tale is that Urvasi, whose name means 'dawn', is loved by the Sun before sunrise, but as soon as he becomes visible she must disappear, like the morning mist. The psychological interpretation is that this myth resembles that of Amor (Eros) and Psyche. As soon as the husband manifests himself, the nymph's soul vanishes, but she comes back to him as a wife, mature and conscious.

Purusha (1) Man. The original man, the first created body. A cosmic giant. The different parts of the universe are his limbs, his body is all matter, so that in his body Purusha unites all the heavenly bodies, the earth, the animals and plants, the trees and the mountains and all human bodies. Just as one atom in our body consumes another, so one fish eats another. Thus one part of Purusha is sacrificed to another and the body of Purusha becomes both sacrificer and victim so that consequently reality itself is *yajna*, the sacrifice. We are all *purushas*: creatures who are either victims or sacrificers and in whose bosoms one part is constantly sacrificed to another. Thus Purusha becomes one of the names of Brahma, the Creator, Purusha being the Creator's physical manifestation. In the Veda, Purusha is a cosmic giant with a thousand heads, primeval man whom the gods used as victim for their sacrifice. They carved him up into as many pieces as there are heads. From his feet they made the earth, his breath became Wind.

(2) The primeval male, the male principle of creation which conjoins with Prakriti, Nature, the female principle, to cause creation.

Pushan God of food and nourishment, of roads and journeys and of the charioteers. A cowherd-god whose chariot is drawn by male goats. He is a guide for travellers. He is the son of Aditi and the lover of Suryaa, the sister of the Sun. He is the guardian of the living creatures by keeping a watch on the regular succession of days and nights. He is toothless like a baby and so people make him offerings of gruel.

Pushpaka A celestial chariot or flying car, or as we would now say, an airbus or jumbo-jet. This spacious flying machine was constructed by Brahma for Kubera, but it was stolen by Ravana who flew it to Sri Lanka. When, at last, Rama had defeated Ravana, he transported all his family and friends in it back home to Ayodhya in the north.

Pushpa-Mitra 'Flower-friend'. The first of the Shunga kings who reigned at Pataliputra, after the Maurya dynasty.

Pustaka Book. For many centuries books in India were written on palm leaves, cut into long strips and affixed together along the long side, the line of writing following the line of the fibres, also along the long side. This tradition remained alive until well into the colonial period, long after paper had been introduced by the Muslims. In the Buddhist tradition, Buddha wrote down his philosophy in a book which he gave to the king of the Nagas. Long afterwards the sage Nagarjuna recovered it from the Nagas and based his teachings on it, which created the Mahayana school.

It contains the Prajnaparamita, the Highest Wisdom, which was made into a goddess who is shown in art with a book. Manjushri and Sarasvati, likewise, have books.

Putana 'Stinking'. Daughter of the demon king Bali. She wanted to kill the baby Krishna by offering him her poisonous breast, but he blew into it instead of sucking and so killed her.

R

Rama

Radha One of the *gopis* or cow-girls in the myth of Krishna. She is painted in numerous pictures of the finest art-work ever made in India; songs and poems are sung by devotees about her love affair with Krishna, that is, God. How she spends half the night patiently waiting for her lover, how she can hear him approaching, how they walk together in the flowering woods, she being too shy to look at his face, how they are sitting under a blossoming tree, she worshipping his feet. How they together, in a bedroom in the middle of the night, watch the rain-clouds approaching while lightning flashes and the cranes can be seen migrating, all symbols of new life on earth. Radha, like all the gods of India, is to the believers the fulfilment of their own *maya*. To the sensual-minded, Radha is the ravishingly beautiful girl bathing naked in the river, unsuspecting that Krishna is watching her, sitting in a tree above her. He has stolen her *sari* so that she has to stay when the other girls have gone, and beg him to give her it back. What price will she be prepared to pay for her clothes, her modesty? And what prize will she receive in return? The love of a god! The more traditional-minded identify Radha with Lakshmi, wife of Vishnu, who is none other than Krishna. When the goddess makes love with her god, they together, like Shiva and Uma, make the world. Krishna steals Radha's ornaments from her hair, in shining locks it falls loose around her shoulders, thus making her ever readier for love-making. They play together, she pouts about his late arrival, pretends she does not want him yet, while she is dying to feel his strong embrace. This traditional scene is called *lilia* 'play'. The gods are playing at creation. When they finally embrace each other in uncontrollable love-making, the world is coming into existence. Likewise every young married couple, when embracing, will make the future generation and so, the future. The union of man and wife is creation. Krishna is a million men, Radha a million women. They make the world. Afterwards she will ask her lover to comb her hair, plait it, pin it up and help her wrap herself in her *sari*. A period of withdrawal into herself, of slow gestation, of meditation begins. For the believers with a mystic inclination, Radha is the human soul, waiting, expecting everywhere to meet God in some human form, like the Christian soul expecting to meet Jesus at Easter. Rabindranath Tagore has given us his beautiful poems about this. Krishna, as a man loved by many fickle women, will always come back to the pure divine love of Radha who by worshipping him, makes him God.

Raga A melody, a musical mode, personified as a deity.

Raghu A king, son of Dilipa, descendant of Surya, great-grandfather of Rama.

Ragini 'Emotion'. One of 36 goddesses of music, a nymph belonging to a given melody, a Muse personifying one of the moods of music, which can also be painted as beautiful landscapes.

Rahu 'The Grasper'. The ascending node in astrology, personified as a deity, the cause of eclipses and ruler of the meteors. A Daitya by origin, he is depicted as a monster demon who, from time to time devours the Sun or the Moon. He has a tail like a comet and a dragon's head. He has a chariot drawn by eight black horses, the clouds of the night-sky. When the gods were drinking *soma*, Rahu, who was jealous, assumed the shape of a god and partook in the drinking session, guzzling the ambrosia like a river. The Sun and the Moon saw him, however, and reported it to Vishnu, for only the gods may drink the wine of immortality. Vishnu took his discus (see *Sudarshana*) and threw it skilfully at the demon. It neatly sliced through the monster's neck, so that Rahu's body fell down from heaven to earth, splitting it open, shaking it and uprooting the mountains and islands. The head of Rahu, however, stayed alive. It rose up into the sky and in revenge it devours the Moon every month, and, less frequently, the Sun too, thus causing eclipses.

Rajarshi A king, who by his saintly conduct and perseverance in purity from sin and desire, has earned the status of *rishi* or demigod.

Raja-Suya A royal sacrifice by which a king gained imperial status.

Raji A famous king, son of Ayus. He had 500 brave sons. In one of the wars between the gods and the Asuras, Brahma predicted that victory would go the party which had Raji as an ally. The gods sought his favour, agreeing to make him their king. After their victory all the gods, even Indra, paid him homage, so he ruled heaven; until he died that is, for he was, after all, a mortal man.

Rajneesh A re-inventor of transcendental meditation who taught, in Pune, that everything his followers wished was permitted. His full-time followers are called *sannyasis* and wear orange robes.

Rajnish From Rajan-Isha, 'King-god'. Title of a guru believed to be divine.

Rakshasa An evil spirit, a demon. A Rakshasa is a wicked creature belonging to a race of very diverse beings. Some are just spirits of nature like the Yakshas. Some Rakshasas are really vicious, others can be quite friendly at times. Some are colossal, dangerous giants who, like the Titans, have from time to time the evil courage to attack even the gods in heaven. A third type are malicious ghosts haunting cemeteries (see *Vetala*), devouring human beings and animating animal bodies. A female demon is called a Rakshasi. It is said the god Brahma created the Rakshasas out of his foot and made them guardians (*raksha*) of the precious primal waters on earth. The best-known Rakshasa was Ravana, who stole Sita from Rama and carried her through the air to Sri Lanka. When Hanuman entered Lanka disguised as a cat, he saw that the Rakshasas came in every conceivable shape, some being quite handsome while others had a revoltingly ugly appearance. Some had very long, grabbing arms. Some were as fat and heavy as elephants. Some were dwarfs and some were giants. Some females had hanging bellies and breasts. Some had two legs, some three and some four. Some had the heads of reptiles, donkeys, horses and elephants. Some had crooked legs, long protruding teeth and bulging eyes. Many Rakshasas wander about at night terrifying whoever is bold enough to be about then. They will rape women and drink their victims' blood.

These devils, servants of Kali, are called 'harmers, destroyers'. They come in all colours: yellow, blue, green. They have cats' eyes and deformed bodies. With their poisonous nails they kill and tear up people's bodies for they love human flesh. They roam free at night. Their king is Ravana (q.v.).

Rakta-Danti 'Bloody-toothed'. An epithet of Devi–Uma–Kali (q.v.).

Raktavira A vicious *asura* (demon) every drop of whose blood had the power to become numerous new *asuras*. So, when Kali was asked by the gods to kill him, she held him up in the air with two of her hands, pierced his heart with a spear in two of her other hands, then drank every drop of his blood. Thus Kali became the goddess of the murderous Thugs (from the Hindi *thugi*).

Rama See *Balarama*; *Parashu-Rama*; *Ramachandra*; *Ramayana*.

Ramachandra, Rama The seventh incarnation of Vishnu. Rama's life and heroism is the subject of the Ramayana (q.v.), the second great epic in Sanskrit literature. His father was King Dasharatha (q.v.), who performed the Ashvamedha sacrifice as a result of which he received four sons, all part-incarnations of Vishnu. Rama was the eldest, born for the specific purpose of defeating the demon-oppressor Ravana, for thus the gods had decreed. His mother was Kaushalya who received half of Vishnu's nectar. Rama grew up happily with his brothers, until the sage Vishvamitra arrived and requested Dasharatha to let him 'borrow' Rama for the sake of killing a certain Rakshasi, a female demon whose name was Taraka. Vishvamitra had no doubt perceived, in his wisdom, that Rama was an incarnation of Vishnu and thus possessed the superhuman powers needed to slay demons. Rama did, even though he objected to killing a female being. Later, Vishvamitra took Rama to the court of King Janaka where he met Sita. At the archery contest, which normally preceded the choice of a husband by a princess, Rama was the only prince who could bend the royal bow which had once belonged to Shiva. So, Rama married Sita and they were very happy. At the instigation of his stepmother Kaikeyi, Rama was sent into exile in the forest. He was accompanied by two loving friends who would stay loyal to him for life: his brother Lakshmana and his wife Sita. Dasharatha ordered Rama to stay away for 14 years but he died soon after this decree, leaving the kingship to Bharata, the second prince. On his father's death, Bharata at once entered the forest in search of his brother and, when he had found him he offered him the throne as he was the eldest brother. Rama, however, wished to obey his father's command and remained in the forest for 14 years. So Bharata went back to Ayodhya and ruled in his brother's name. Rama, Sita and Lakshmana wandered in the forest until, near the River Godavari, Rama was seen by a Rakshasi named Surpa-nakha. She fell in love with him but he rejected her; she then attacked Sita in a rage, but Lakshmana came to her defence and wounded the Rakshashi. Surpa-nakha then called on two of her brothers with an army of Rakshasas, but they were all destroyed. Surpa-nakha then appealed to her biggest brother Ravana, the most vicious and dangerous demon alive on earth at that time. One of the Rakshasas assumed the form of a splendid deer, thus arousing the princes' weakness for hunting. While they were away at the chase, Ravana quickly swooped down, captured Sita and took her to Sri Lanka, where he imprisoned her in his palace. Rama, upon coming back and finding no trace of his wife, at first despaired, but then went in search of her, accompanied by the faithful Lakshmana. On the way they killed Kabandha, a spirit in the body of a demon. When Rama had liberated the spirit by killing the body, the grateful Kabandha told him: 'Go and seek the help of King Sugriva.'

Rama at once went in search of Sugriva, who turned out to be a monkey whose kingdom had been usurped by his half-brother, Balin. Rama defeated Balin and restored Sugriva to his throne. Sugriva agreed to help Rama by putting at his disposal his best general, Hanuman, a famous monkey who could fly like a bird. Hanuman discovered the whereabouts of Sita and suggested that a bridge should be built to allow his army of brave monkeys to march on Sri Lanka. After incredible feats of valiance, Rama and his friends entered Ravana's castle and slew the villain with all his fellow demons. Sita was liberated and brought before Rama who, however, received her coolly because he was afraid that she had been robbed of her honour by Ravana and the other demons. Anxious to prove her purity, Sita agreed to pass the fire-test. The fire, however, could not even be lit because Agni knew she was innocent and carried her gently into her husband's arms. Rama, Sita, Lakshmana and all their suite went back to Ayodhya by air, carried on a magically flying vehicle named Pushpaka. In the seventh book of the Ramayana, perhaps a later addition, the people of Ayodhya begin to murmur that Rama had brought an impure wife back home with him. Instead of silencing those evil tongues and stupid minds, Rama became suspicious again, in spite of the fact that even the gods had told him that his queen was pure. He sent her away into exile where she gave birth to twins. Many years later he saw them by accident, and recognized them as his sons. He took them and their mother back into his palace, but the damage was done. Sadly, Sita called the earth, her mother, to testify once again to her purity. The earth opened in the form of a long furrow and into it Sita sank down, never to appear again. Rama, now disconsolate for missing that which he could have had all his life, decided to follow her. He walked into the River Sarayu and disappeared. Brahma himself welcomed him to Heaven. In the Uttara-Rama-Charita a different version of the seventh book of the Ramayana is presented; after Sita has gone into exile, Rama, full of remorse, goes in search of her and, when reunited with her, lives happily ever after with Sita and his two sons Kusha and Lava.

Rama is still worshipped in many provinces of India, from Gujerat to Bihar. Rama is the symbol of the husband of one wife who never indulged in licence with other women like Krishna or Shiva. It is true that he is excessively jealous by nature but that is quite natural for a man in India and, I daresay, elsewhere. It is his tragedy. As an incarnation of Vishnu, Rama is worshipped in many parts of India as a statue with bow and arrows, accompanied by Lakshmana and Sita. Rama or Ram is in many Hindu communities the word for 'God'.

Rama-Setu Rama's Bridge. A line of rocks between Sri Lanka and the coast of south India. Nala, son of Vishva-Karma, commander-in-chief of Rama's army, built it so that the army could invade Sri Lanka, as described in the Sundara-Kanda (chapter 5) of the Ramayana.

Ramayana Great epic poem of 50,000 lines, composed by the famous Valmiki probably in the third century. (For the later, medieval Ramayana, see Tulsi Das.) Diverse versions have come to light in different parts of India, in the north, east, south and west, giving rise to divergent traditions of Rama-worship. This epic celebrates the exploits of Rama, or Ramachandra, the seventh incarnation of Vishnu. The Ramayana is divided into seven books, each book (*kanda*) dealing with an episode in the life of Rama, son of Dasharatha, his brothers Lakshmana, Bharata and Shatrughna. Even reading the Ramayana will remove all the reader's sins, for the epic text itself is believed to be charismatic. (See also *Rama*.)

Rambha An Apsaras or water-nymph of unsurpassed beauty. She rose from the waters of the ocean when it was being churned by the gods. She failed to seduce the ascetic Visvamitra. She was the wife of the god Kubera but was raped by his brother Ravana (q.v.).

Rasa Sap of a tree, essence, distilled liquor (*sura*), also a symbolism for honey, mead (*madhu*), *soma*, *amrita*, milk, rain and even sperm. It is the liquid which contains the vital energy, the essence of life by which all creatures are born and grow up.

Rasa-Lila Dance of creation danced by Krishna with each of the Gopis, shepherdesses, at one and the same time, after he had multiplied himself. This love-dance creates as many bodies for the Ananga (*kama*) as there are couples.

Ratha Wheel, chariot. Every god has a chariot, like the kings on earth.

Rati 'Love'. Rati was the daughter of the sage Daksha. She is the goddess of sexual passion and is therefore identified as the Aphrodite–Venus of India. The Indian god of love, her male partner, had been consumed by Shiva's third eye, but Rati, desirous to marry the god of love, implored Parvati to intercede on her behalf with Shiva that he might bring the Love-god back to life. Finally Shiva agreed and Kama was reborn as Pradyumna, the first baby born to Krishna and Rukmini. However, the sage Narada predicted to the demon Shambhara that he, Shambhara would be killed by the boy Pradyumna. Quickly, Shambhara flew to Rukmini's house and snatched the child Pradyumna from her bosom. Then he flew out over the ocean and dropped the baby in the waves, where a big fish opened its mouth and snapped the child up. A fisherman caught the fish, sailed to the shore and sold the fish to a woman called Mayavati who was the cook of the demon Shambhara. Mayavati 'the deceitful one' was none other than Rati in disguise,

determined to rescue the boy who was destined to become her
husband. She cut the fish open and out came Pradyumna, still alive,
for who can kill a god? Rati looked after the boy in secret while
hiding him in the very house of the demon he was destined to kill.
She made him invisible, though invisibility has always been a
characteristic of the god of love: Love approaches unnoticed. One
day, Shambhara, displeased with Rati's cooking, beat her.
Pradyumna who by that time was a grown man, rushed at
Shambhara and killed him, after resuming his visible form. Rati,
upon seeing this handsome youth, and knowing that he was her
predestined husband, fell in love with him, and told him of her
love. At first he hesitated, thinking she was his mother, but when
she told him it was the gods' will that he should become her
husband, and resumed her divine form, standing before him in all
her splendour as the goddess of love, he fell in love with her and
they were married. Rati soon became pregnant; they went and
settled in Dwarka.

Ratna 'Jewel'. When the gods churned the ocean many jewels, i.e.
precious objects appeared, especially Kamadhenu, the wish-cow,
which could make anything for its owner; Lakshmi, who became
Vishnu's faithful wife, and the Amrita-Kumbha, the vial of the
Water of Immortality, which the gods keep jealously to themselves.

Ratnasambhava This is the third of the Dhyani-Buddhas or
Buddhas of Meditation. He represents the spiritual element of
vedana, sensation, feeling, the gateway of knowledge. He therefore
presides over the spring season when new life begins. His colour is
yellow and he is represented in art with a *ratna*, a jewel called a
cintamani, 'a thought-magnet', an instrument for learning the art of
concentration, keeping one's thoughts on one point without being
distracted by anything whatsoever.

Ravana The evil King of Lanka, the island south of India, in the
days when Dasharatha was King of Ayodhya. Ravana was a son of
Visravas, son of Pulastya, and ruler of all the Rakshasas, the evil
demons of India. Ravana was invulnerable, which meant that
neither god nor man could kill him. He could fly through the air and
assume any shape he wanted. He is described as Dashanana, having
10 heads, 20 arms, burning eyes and sabre teeth. However,
sometimes he had the appearance of a pall of smoke, or a rock, or
of the god of death, looking like a huge corpse. He could break
mountains in two and cause storms on the ocean. He could stop the
sun and the moon with his hands and block the course of the wind
with his body like a rock wall. Indra had already hit him with his
vajra and Vishnu with his discus, but though Ravana still bore the
scars of those divine weapons, his abilities were not diminished by
them. Finally the gods requested Vishnu to destroy this dangerous
monster, so he decided to become incarnated in the four sons of

King Dasharatha. The eldest, Rama, was destined to become the hero of the epic Ramayana (q.v.). The gods also created hundreds of monkeys and bears with the specific purpose of fighting the Rakshasas. Ravana's special pastime was raping the wives of princes, including the wife of his own brother, Kubera. While flying over a forest he saw Sita, Prince Rama's wife, and decided to take her. He waited till Rama was lured away by a golden hind during a hunt, then approached Sita, having cleverly taken the shape of a begging saint. He suddenly seized her and flew off with her to Lanka. Rama organized the siege of Lanka with his regiments of bears and monkeys. After a long battle Rama and Ravana finally faced one another. As soon as Rama cut off one of Ravana's heads, another one grew up in its place. Finally Rama shot an arrow which had been specially created by Brahma. It hit Ravana in the chest, came out at the back, cleaned itself in the ocean, then returned to Rama's quiver. At last the Creator's own arrow killed the most evil demon who ever lived and the gods rejoiced in heaven.

Ravi The Sun. Another name for Surya, the Sun-god. Ravivara, Sunday, is named after him. Every morning the priests pray to the Sun-god, thus: 'Divine Sun who art approaching in Thy golden chariot, rousing mortal and immortal beings, removing the shadows of night and surveying the worlds. May this oblation to Thee have the desired effect.' In astrology, Ravi is an inauspicious heavenly body, foreboding disease, exile, captivity, the loss of wife, children and property, physical and mental suffering and anxiety. Symbol: a golden disk. (See also *Surya*.)

Revanta The second Manu, son of Vivasvat, the sun, and Sanjana (Sanjna). He practised asceticism on Mount Malaya for a million years so Brahma granted him a boon. Revanta wished: 'To be able to protect all living beings.'

Revati Daughter of King Raivata who thought her so beautiful that no man was good enough to be her husband. So he went in search of a god and found Balarama, an incarnation of Vishnu.

Riddhi 'Prosperity', Queen of Kubera, ruler of the North, god of wealth.

Rishi Priest, poet and sage. The original 14 Rishis were born from the brain of Brahma. Portions of the Vedic hymns were revealed to them. They were Gorama, Bharadwaja, Jamadagni, Vasishtha, Kasyapa, Atri, Visvamitra, Marichi, Angiras, Pulaha, Kratu, Pulastya, Bhrigu and Daksha. They were the first men who had the power to perform valid sacrifices for the gods. (See also *Prajapati*.)

Rishya-Shringa 'The one with deer horns'. The hermit Vibhandaka lived in the forest for so long that he became a friend of the deer and married a doe. She gave birth to a human boy whose only cervine feature was a pair of tiny antlers on his head. One day there was a severe drought in the kingdom of Anga so the king, Lomapada, consulted his Brahmins, who advised him to send a search-party to the forest for Rishya-Shringa, the young forest-dweller, who must marry the king's daughter Shanta. The king's messengers found Rishya-Shringa and brought him to court where he was married to Shanta. On the night after the wedding the rains fell in abundance. Shanta was in reality Lomapada's adopted daughter, her real father was King Dasharatha, who later invited Rishya-Shringa to perform the great sacrifice which caused Vishnu to appear.

Rita (Rta) The Cosmic Order, the regular course of the world. Consequently, all people must live according to the rules of Rita. Rita, or Arta was a goddess who supervised the seasons and so she was worshipped by farmers. She in turn was ruled by Varuna.

Rituparna Son of Sarvakama, King of Ayodhya, who employed Nala (q.v.) the exiled king and taught him to play dice.

River-goddess See *Ganga*; *Sarasvati*; *Yamuna*.

Rohini 'Red'. (1) Daughter of Daksha and wife of the Moon-god.
   (2) Wife of Vasudeva, mother of Balarama.
   (3) Wife of Krishna.
   (4) Daughter of Kasyapa, mother of the wish-cow Kamadhenu.

Rohita 'Red'. One of the fiery horses of the Sun-god.

Rudra 'The howling, roaring one'. The God of Storms, the Lord of Time and Death. The year is his bow, his shadow is its string, that is the night of Doomsday. He is the dark smoke of the funerary pyres. Rudra is the father of the Rudras and Maruts. He is, like Bacchus, the sanguinary god of furious, inebriated behaviour and of sudden hurricanes. He also sends attacks of fever and sickness; in this way he is like Apollo, the god of medicine, and the archer who never misses. Sometimes he was identified with Agni, but later always treated as another shape of Shiva, often invoked jointly as Rudra-Shiva. Shiva, a name which originally meant 'friendly', restores the divine balance which is disturbed by the terrible Rudra, god of disease, of the horrible Maruts, of death and destruction. Thus of the two gods one is represented as white and gentle, the other as black and furious. In paintings of a much later date, Shiva is represented as dark blue like Krishna. He is one of the oldest gods.

Rudrani 'The wife of Rudra'. An epithet of Devi–Uma–Kali (q.v.).

Rukmini An incarnation of Lakshmi (Devi Shri), on earth a daughter of Bhishmaka, King of Vidarbha. Krishna came to ask for her hand in marriage and she fell in love with him. Alas! Her brother Rukmin was a friend of the tyrant Kansa, who was killed by Krishna, so Rukmin arranged for his sister to marry Shishupala,

King of Chedi. Just before the wedding Rukmini, while on her way to the temple, was suddenly seized by the hand. It was Krishna, who placed her in his chariot and drove away, pursued by the brother and the bridegroom. Krishna defeated them both and brought Rukmini to his home in Dvaraka. They had 10 sons, the eldest of whom was Pradyumna, and a daughter, Charumati.

Ruma Queen of the Apes, wife of King Sugriva.

Rupa Form, outward shape. The image of a Buddha. The Buddha, or any other god, is a spiritual substance who may appear to some seers in a particular shape, called a manifestation. These seers may instruct sculptors and painters wishing to depict the god, in the details of what they have seen. It is therefore only from these artworks that we obtain a vague notion of what the deity looks like. In any case, the philosophers know that the *rupa* is not the true appearance of any deity, since the divine spirit can not be seen, and that is the essence of the gods.

Rupastra 'The weapon of beauty'. Epithet of Kama (q.v.).

S

Shiva Nataraja

Sachi Son of Bahu, King of Ayodhya, descendant of the Sun-god. Sachi was driven into exile by his enemies the Haihayas and died in the jungle before his son Sagara was born, who had survived for seven years in his mother's womb. When Sagara came of age, the sage Aurva gave him the Agneyastra, a new fire weapon, by means of which Sagara nearly exterminated the Haihayas, which enabled him to ascend his father's throne. His wife Sumati gave birth to 60,000 sons as a result of Aurva's magical powers. They were not good sons though. They let their father's favourite horse escape. Or was it stolen? Their father told them not to come back until they had found it. They were told the horse was in the nether-world, in Patala, so they dug an enormous pit until they opened up Patala, and there was the horse. There was also a holy man, the sage Kapila whom they accused of horse-stealing. In his anger the sage burnt them all to ashes with his eye-rays. Now King Sagara had one grandson, Anshumat who, when in search of his 60,000 uncles found Kapila and the horse in the deep pit. He showed profound reverence for Kapila, who told him that the sons of Sagara could only be purified by the river from heaven that flows from the feet of Vishnu. Anshumat was allowed to take the horse back to King Sagara, after whom the big hole in the earth was called (Sagara meaning 'ocean'), where the ashes of his sons lay. It was left to

Anshumat's grandson to dig the bed for the River of Heaven which would one day flow across India. His name was Bhagiratha; he was so devout that Shiva finally agreed to let the River of Heaven flow through his hair before allowing it to descend onto the earth, otherwise it would have washed India away. The river came down and flowed through Bhagiratha's canal into the deep pit which it filled, becoming the ocean Sagara. That was how the Ganges came to earth: to purify the ashes of all sinners.

Sacrifice, Yajna Sacrifice was the centre of the Aryan (proto-Hindu) religion. In every house, sacrifices ought to be made daily. The oldest texts, the Rig-veda, however, are concerned mainly with the great sacrifices paid for by clan heads. The purpose of the sacrifice is to obtain boons from the gods. Animals of all kinds were sacrificed and portions were burnt in the sacrificial fire. The proper sacrifices could only be performed by the professional Brahmins, who knew the correct formulas by means of which the gods were induced to descend from the heavens and partake in the festive meal. The royal patrons who drank *soma* must have had visions of the gods descending. The Brahmin priests, masters of ceremony, became gods themselves, since they possessed the magic power to induce the gods to be present. Those deities who appeared in the first place were Agni, the sacrificial fire himself, the stern Varuna, god of water and libations, and the greatly feared and unpredictable Rudra. The most mysterious presence was Brahman, the magic power of the sacred formula itself, the potent energy of the gods together. The priests who could evoke Brahman were called Brahmins for that reason.

Sadhu A saint, a person who has succeeded in suppressing his desires, so that he has acquired true insight into the essence of reality, which is that all people and all creatures are one.

Sagara See *Sachi*.

Sahadeva Youngest son of King Pandu, whose mythical father was Dasra, one of the Ashvins. His wife was Vijaya.

Saka, Shaka A central Asian people of Iranian descent who ruled northern India in the first two centuries AD.

Sakra A name for India. (See *Bharata* (4).)

Samadhi Complete concentration of the mind, deep meditation. Collection of all thoughts, conscious or subconscious, on one object. The state of mental elevation which precedes *dhyana*. Silence.

Samana A (Buddhist) ascetic.

Samantaka 'The destroyer of peace'. Kama (q.v.) or Cupido.

Sama-Veda The third book of the great Veda.

Sambhogakaya 'Enjoyment Body', one of the three aspects of the Buddha as the ultimate living reality of the universe, in which wisdom and compassion have become one spirit.

Sampati An eagle, a huge speaking bird, son of Garuda and helper of Rama. When Hanuman and his fellow monkeys were searching for Sita, they met Sampati and asked him if he had seen her. He soared up into the sky and flew all the way to the south, to Sri Lanka, where he saw how Sita was being threatened by the tyrant Ravana. He told Hanuman this, thus avenging his brother Jatayu who had been killed by Ravana in a sky-battle.

Samsara, Sansara A chain. The chain of existences in Buddhism. Every person is dragged from one life to the next until he has liberated himself from all greed, fear and anger. Then he has broken the chain, and may enter *nirvana*. Thus, *samsara* now means 'fate, destiny, misery'.

Samsara-Guru 'Teacher of the world'. Kama the god of love.

Samvara In Jainism, the prevention of *karma* adhering to one's soul, *jiva*.

Samvarta The gigantic mare, with fire inside her, that lives in the sea but will emerge on doomsday and release all the fire so that all living beings will perish. According to some sources there are seven doomsday horses, or clouds of smoke burning and suffocating earthlings.

Sandhya 'Twilight'. A shy goddess like a hind in the forest, Brahma's daughter.

Sangha 'Society', a congregation. The order of Buddhist monks founded by Buddha himself.

Sanghata-Parvata One of two mountains in Yama's Hell, between which there is only a narrow gorge. The dead sinners are chased through this canyon, which will suddenly disappear as the two mountains collide, crushing the bodies between them. The Indian Scylla and Charybdis, in Hell.

Sani, Shani The planet Saturn, in Urdu, Zohal. Sanivara is Saturday. Sani is the son of Surya and Chhaya. Sani is represented as a black man riding on a vulture. (The vulture was venerated as a goddess in ancient Egypt.) Being born on a Saturday forbodes bad luck and disaster, poverty, defamation and loss of loved ones. Even the gods fear an ominous conjunction, which only Dasaratha can avert.

Sanjna 'Conscience'. Wife of the Sun-god Surya, by whom she bore three children, Vaivasvata, Yama and Yami, or the River Yamuna. To seek shade for a while from such a fiery husband, Sanjna entered the forest disguised as a mare. The Sun-god followed her in the shape of a stallion. From this jungle tryst were born the two Ashvins, the Indian Gemini.

Sankhya A philosophical system. (See *Yoga.*)

Sannyasin One day the king of a certain kingdom had died. It was the custom in that country when the old king had died to send the king's white elephant out into the country to select the new ruler. Elephants are wise animals because they are guided by Indra. This time when the elephant was released it walked into the forest where it found a sannyasin (a sage of true renunciation who has realized God in his innermost soul) meditating, having all his desires under control. It picked up this saintly scholar with its strong trunk, put him on its back and carried him to the palace. There he was received with great honour and hailed as the new king. The sannyasin protested that he preferred a free life without having to worry about regal status and power, but the old *mantri* (prime minister), delighted that at last a true philosopher would mount the throne, persuaded him to accept, saying that it was Indra's decree that he, the sannyasin, should be king.

Thus the sannyasin sat on the throne and held court daily receiving a stream of supplicants and petitioners seeking justice. The poor received alms, the flatterers received nothing, while those who had been wronged received justice and those who had enriched themselves at the expense of the weak had their possessions taken from them. Those who threatened the king or promised him treasures if he would bend the law were executed. Soon no one in the land raised his hand wrongfully against his neighbour. Peace reigned. But this very peacefulness attracted the greed and ambition of a neighbouring king, who raised an army and marched across the frontier. The sannyasin waited quietly until the enemy king marched into his palace and demanded the throne. Then the sannyasin rose quietly, descended from the throne, and invited his enemy to take it, saying: 'If you covet my golden throne, take it. I do not want to keep what others wish to own. I did not ask to be king. Take what you desire. Leave me my forest.'

The enemy king was so impressed by the sannyasin's spiritual superiority that he bowed down and not only declined to take the sannyasin's kingdom but offered him his own as being worthier of it than he himself. Thus peace reigned once again without blood being shed.

Santa A saint, probably a Portuguese word. (See *Dharmaatma; Sadhu; Sannyasin.*)

Santi Peace of mind, intrepidity. (See *Abhaya; Shanti.*)

Santosha Contentment, awareness of peace and serene happiness.

Sanyasa, Sannyasa Abandonment, renunciation of the world, abstinence.

Saptarshi The seven great Rishis. (See *Rishi*.)

Sapta-Shati 'Seven hundred'. A poem of 700 couplets celebrating the victories of Devi–Uma over the demons. (See *Devi-Mahatmya*.)

Sara Essence, essential part of a person, his soul, strength, worth.

Sarama 'Quick', the female dog belonging to Indra, who explores the path to the land of the dwarfs (see *Pani*). She is the mother of the two four-eyed, striped dogs which guard the Land of Yama, the City of Death. Cf. the Greek Cerberus.

Saranyu, Sharanyu Daughter of Tvashtri (Twashtar), wife of Vivasvat, mother of the Ashvins, the twins. She fled from her husband in the shape of a mare, but he took the shape of a stallion and followed her. After a long while he finally caught up with her and from their union the Ashvins 'horse-twins' were born. Also: Sanjna or Sanjana.

Saraswati, Sarasvati The goddess of the arts. Originally Saraswati was the holy river flowing from the Himalayas past what is now Patiala, along the frontier between the northern states of Panjab and Haryana, to pour her sweet waters into the Indian Ocean where there is now the Salty Rann of Cutch; since then this once great river has completely disappeared. Her green banks have become the vast Tharr or Indian Desert, stretching to near the Indus. This river, over which the Vedic poets exult in their hymns, is a sign on the wall of what may become of the other famous rivers of India if deforestation continues at the present rate. Once the banks of the Saraswati were densely populated. There it was that the poets recited their verse and so the elegant Saraswati became the goddess of literature, of poetry, song, music and *belles lettres*. So we see Saraswati in colourful paintings smiling happily, dressed in her gold-embroidered sari, holding a book, symbol of scholarship and writing, in one hand, and the *vina*, a stringed instrument in the other. She is riding a swan, symbolizing that she is in control of her passions, which is a condition for the success of any artistic or literary endeavour. She is often identified with Vak or Vach, the goddess of speech and eloquence. She is the inventress of Sanskrit, the 'polished' language. Saraswati is also often shown sitting on a lotus to signify meditation, lucidity of mind and clarity of expression. Her spouse is Brahma the Creator, the most revered of the gods. For the Buddhists she is the spouse of Manjushri, the Bodhisattva of Wisdom. She is also seen in the company of the peacock, the Indian royal bird so admired for its beauty. Her swan floats on a pond as smooth as a mirror, reflecting the goddess faithfully, signifying the serenity of mind necessary for clarity of language. In her temple soft music is heard and devout hymns are sung. Her image has four hands, two carrying vina and hymnbook, two others rosary and lotus. Sometimes she carries the *vidya*, emblem of knowledge, and a vessel of ambrosia. As goddess of eloquence (Vak) she masters the rivers of speech, and as inventress of the Devanagari, the letters of the Sanskrit syllabary, she collects these waters of words as the ocean receives the rivers.

This important goddess survived the transition from Hinduism to Buddhism in many communities and neighbouring countries. In Buddhism, she was associated with Manjushri the god of learning, and became his *shakti* (spouse), as goddess of poetry and music. As Vajravina she holds the *vina* in her right hand in medieval sculpture. She has even replaced (or 'merged with') Prajnaparamitaa as the goddess of the Highest Wisdom. She has three eyes, a book and a white lotus. She has the moon in her crown. She gives her worshippers *buddhi* (intelligence), *medha* (memory) and *prajna* (wisdom). Arya Sarasvati is worshipped in a tantric form in Tibet, depicted with three faces, six arms, bright red and belligerent. In Japan she is called Benten.

Satarupa, Shata-Rupa 'She of a thousand shapes'. Brahma made her out of himself just as Eve was formed out of Adam. She was the first woman. Brahma fell in love with her, but she hid at his left elbow so he quickly created a head on his left shoulder looking left to admire her beauty. Shatarupa then hid behind him, but he grew a third head looking backwards. She then hid on his right side so he grew a fourth head looking right. Satarupa then flew up to heaven but Brahma formed a fifth head looking upwards. Finally she agreed to be his wife. Their son was Manu the First.

Sati 'The true woman', 'the virtuous, faithful wife'. An epithet of Devi–Uma–Kali. A wife who proves her total faithfulness to her husband by willingly following him into death and into the Other World, whence the two souls may be reborn into two new lives and hopefully marry again. This first happened to the goddess Sati, who, when her husband Shiva was burnt, entered the fire and abandoned her body. She was reborn as Uma and married Bhawa (Shiva). English spelling: Suttee.

Satori (Japanese). A state of temporary elatedness, of superior perception.

Satyavan 'Possessing Truth', Savitri's husband whose death-hour was known.

Satyavati 'Truthful'. Daughter of the King of Chedi. Her mother was an Apsaras or water-nymph called Adrika, who had the shape of a mermaid. Satyavati met the guru Parashara while swimming in the river as a very young girl. After that meeting (old gurus can be quite virile) she gave birth to Krishna-of-the-Island (see *Vyasa*) and later married King Shantanu, becoming the grandmother of the Pandavas.

Satyavrata, Vedhas One of the Sun-kings descended from

Ikshvaku. He is also known as Trishanku 'triple sinner'. He hoped all his life to be admitted to Indra's heaven as an immortal and so he performed penance giving much charity to the Brahmins. Finally Visvamitra helped him to gain salvation.

Saubha A beautiful city built on a large platform suspended in mid-air between Heaven and Earth. Its king was Harischandra (q.v.). Another city of that name (or Tranga or Dhapura) apparently floated on the ocean near the west coast of India and was owned by the Daityas.

Saubhari A wise hermit who had acquired magical powers through his many years of asceticism which had left him old and shrivelled. In his old age — this happens to some men — he suddenly wished to marry and have sons. So he went to King Mandhatar and demanded one of that king's 50 daughters. The king dared not refuse, knowing how irascible old sages can be. So he agreed in principle on condition that the princess whom the old man chose would consent. The king thought that none of his daughters would wish to marry such an old wrinkled man. How wrong he was for the old wizard possessed the magic secret of rejuvenation. When he appeared to the 50 princesses he looked young and irresistibly handsome, so all 50 of the girls suddenly decided they wanted very much to marry old Saubhari. The king could not refuse, for how can a father stand between a determined daughter and a dangerous bridegroom? The 50 girls had 150 sons between them.

Savarna 'Of the same colour'. Daughter of the Ocean and wife of Vivasvat the Sun-god, identical with Sanjna or Sharanyu (q.v.).

Savitar, Savitr, Savitri 'The one who brings forth'. The Sun-god, to whom many Vedic hymns are sung. (See *Aditya*; *Surya*; *Vivasvat*.)

Savitri (1) Daughter of King Ashvapati. She fell in love with a simple man called Satyavan and wanted to marry him. The sages at her father's court warned her that it was Satyavan's fate to die in exactly one year. However, Savitri insisted that she wanted to marry no one else and so they were married. After exactly one year, Satyavan went out in the morning to cut firewood, but Savitri followed him. In the middle of the forest he fell down into her arms, dying. While she held him, she saw the shadow of the God of Death (see *Yama*), who took her husband from her and went away with him to the Land of the Dead. She followed him through the depths of darkness for countless hours. At last Death turned to her and said: 'Go back to your country. I am Death. Your husband belongs to me now.'

But Savitri replied: 'He is my husband for ever. I must follow him. I will never leave him alone.'

Death went on with her husband through the lightless landscape of the world between life and death. After innumerable hours of walking on her bleeding feet, Savitri saw the God of Death turning to her again. He spoke: 'Very well, you have braved Death to follow your husband. I will grant you a boon, but not your husband.'

Savitri knelt and prayed: 'Oh God! I beg you for a dozen children from my husband.'

So, Death had to restore her husband to her, so that she could have children by him, for even the God of Death keeps his word.

The name Savitri suggests that she is a sun-goddess and her husband the dying sun.

(2) Daughter of the sun, wife of Brahma.

Self-confidence for a Buddhist is based on the knowledge that:

1. All that we believe to be real is illusion, e.g. great dangers are imaginary.
2. He knows which obstacles (q.v.) he has to overcome before he is free.
3. He knows the means that will cause the extinction of sorrow and suffering.
4. He has overcome his desires so that he suffers no more fear, anxiety, disappointment, jealousy, ambition or any other impediment to happiness.

Setu-Bandha 'Causeway, link'. Rama's bridge, a line of rocks built by Hanuman's monkeys across the strait from India to Lanka.

Sevenfold Buddha A combination of Akshobhya, Amitabha, Amoghasiddhi, Lokeshvara, Ratnasambhava, Vairochana and Vajrapani. The first five are Dhyani-Buddhas (q.v.); Vajrapani is a Bodhisattva (q.v.).

Shaibya A pious woman who worshipped Vishnu and remained faithful to her husband during many incarnations. As he often lapsed into sin he was reincarnated as a dog, a jackal, a wolf, a crow and a peacock before he became a man again. In each new incarnation she recognized him and reminded him of the sins of his previous life so that he died of shame. When he finally came back as a man, she married him again and they lived happily until they both died and together rose to Indra's Heaven.

Shaitan, Shetan Satan, an evil spirit in Islamic belief. Evil spirits will often possess people, especially women, who will then have to be beaten in order to expel the evil spirit which is tempting the woman to disobey her good husband. Often a *shetan* takes the shape of a serpent, a long snake, which lives in a woman's (less frequently in a man's) body and makes her act sinfully against her will. (Disobeying her husband is already sinful for a woman in Islam.) The spirit's name has to be known before he can be expelled. (See also *vagina dentata*.)

Shakini One of a bevy of demonesses who serve the goddess Durga.

Shakra The owl, 'powerful', a symbol of Indra.

Shakrani Another name of Indrani or Shachi.

Shakta A worshipper of Shakti. 'Possessed by Shakti', i.e. the goddess Kali. One of a growing sect of worshippers of Shiva and Parvati, divided into two groups, the right hand and the left hand. The latter sect worship Shiva and his *shakti* by imitating their conjugal union. Their ceremonies are closely guarded secret sessions. (See also *Shaktism*; *Tamas*; *Tantrism*.)

Shaktar A hermit who cursed King Kalmashapada. The king became a cannibal and devoured the hermit.

Shakti 'The power'. Another name for Uma, Parvati or Kali. (See also *Chamunda*; *Shiva*; *Tantra*.)

Shaktism This is one of the many branches of *Kali-puja*, the worship of Kali–Durga–Shakti, popular in eastern and southern India. The principles of Shaktism are as follows: Kali, also invoked as Prakriti (q.v.), is the highest deity. The occult purpose of this religion seems to be to accumulate magic energy and potency. In this doctrine Brahma and Shiva are inactive, but Kali is the Shakti — the fountain of energy. If a man feels unbearable passion, it can be purified by means of more passion. To this end there exists the institution of ritual women, intercourse with whom is the source of mystic pansexuality. By so doing, said Shiva, a man will become Me, he will be identical with all living beings. Kali demands human sacrifices, accompanied by naked dancing and communal orgies. The human victim becomes God and is worshipped before the ritual slaughter takes place.

Shakuni A vulture, a greedy, wicked character.

Shakuntalaa Daughter of the nymph Manaka and the sage Visvamitra. She grew up alone in the forest where the birds brought her food. The hermit Kanwa found her as a little girl and brought her up as his own daughter. One day when she had just come into womanhood, a king arrived whose name was Dushyanta. As soon as the king and the nymph saw each other they both fell in love at first sight. They married there and then according to the custom which is called the Gandharva rite, which means that there is no rite at all and no witnesses, but two persons indulge in the act of procreation by mutual consent. The king left her then, but gave her a ring as a royal token. Alas! Shakuntalaa, coming home to the hermitage, did not notice the presence of the Brahmin Durvasas, feared for his power, absorbed as she was in her love affair. Durvasas, filled with his own importance, cursed her for forgetting to greet him with the obsequiousness he demanded of ordinary people.

'For your negligence I will punish you. Your royal lover will not know you when you arrive at his palace, unless he sees the ring.' So, when Shakuntalaa arrived at the royal palace to tell the king that he had made her pregnant, he did not recognize her and she was unable to show him the ring for she had lost it in a river while bathing. So, she had to go back to the forest where she gave birth to a son, Bharata, with the help of her mother Menaka. The ring meanwhile was swallowed by a fish which was caught by a fisherman who brought it to King Dushyanta. The king immediately recognized his ring and suddenly remembered his brief affair with the nymph in the forest. He sent messengers to search for her and finally there was a reunion and a happy ending. This tale was made into a famous drama by the poet Kalidasa.

Shalwa Ancient name for modern Rajasthan.

Shalya King of the Madra people, a traitor who sided with the Kauravas until he was killed by Yudhisthira in battle.

Shamba Son of Krishna who was captured by Duryodhana. His uncle Balarama liberated him by threatening to level the city of Hastinapura with his enormous plough. Later, Shamba displeased Durvasas, who cursed him so that he became a leper. Shamba did penance and built a temple for Surya who cured him.

Shambhara Also called Dasyu, the demon of drought, sometimes compared to Vritra. He was defeated by Indra. (See *Rati*, who was his cook.)

Shambhu See *Rudra*; *Shiva*.

Shami, Shamidevi A tree, *Acacia suma*, whose wood burns well. Firesticks have been made of it since the oldest times, so she is called the Mother of Agni, the Fire-god. Shami is personified and worshipped as a mother-goddess.

Shani The planet Saturn, in Urdu, Zohal. Shanivara is Saturday. Shani is the son of Surya and Chhaya. Shani is represented as a black man riding on a vulture. (The vulture was venerated as a goddess in ancient Egypt.) Being born on a Saturday forebodes bad luck and disasters, poverty, defamation and loss of loved ones.

Shankara (1) 'Auspicious', 'propitious'. Shiva in his aspect as Creator.

(2) Religious philosopher who lived c.700. He revived Hinduism, which in his time was almost swamped by Buddhism.

(3) 'Peace', Shiva who gives peace to his worshippers through his yoga.

(4) An aspect of Bhairava, himself a form of Rudra–Shiva. Shankara is sometimes shown as a separate image, looking fierce and naked. There are 64 types of Bhairavas.

Shankha The conch, a type of seashell used for blowing. Attribute of Vishnu.

Shanta Daughter of King Dasharatha, wife of Rishya-Shringa.

Shantanu Son of Pratipa, father of Bhishma. His praise-name was Satyavach 'speaker of truth'; whichever old person he touched with his hand became young again.

Shanti Peace, tranquillity, peace of mind, lasting happiness, which is the result of overcoming one's desires, one's fears and one's ambitions. The goddess of peace.

Shanti-Niketa The Abode of Peace, life-goal of the Krishna-worshippers.

Shapa An oath, a curse. Curses pronounced by enraged Brahmins were inescapable and terribly effective. Even the slightest unintentional neglect of the elaborate ceremonial greeting which the Brahmins felt was their right as priests and elders of the highest caste, would hurt their pride to the extent that they would ruin a person's life and often the lives of his unborn descendants as well, simply to inculcate their social and sacred status.

Sharabha A form of Shiva, a black monster over a hundred miles long, with eight legs and tusks, long claws, nose and ears, who lives in the Himalayas.

Sharabhanga A pious hermit who yearned to see the god Vishnu. One day as he was meditating in the forest of Dandaka, there appeared before him Rama and Sita. Overjoyed, the hermit proclaimed that his life's wish had been fulfilled so his life had no more purpose. He lit a fire and entered it. His body was burnt to ashes but his spirit emerged in the shape of a handsome young man and flew to heaven.

Sharada A lute, symbol of Sarasvati as goddess of the arts.

Sharama The dog of dawn who brought back the cows of the Sun-god Surya. She had two sons, the Sharameyas, who became the four-eyed watchdogs of the nether-world, serving Yama the God of Death.

Sharanyu 'Quick'. The Sun-goddess, queen of the Sun-god Vivasvat. She bore her husband the twins Yama and Yami, or Death and River. She then changed into a mare, fled into the terrestrial forest where she was again united with the Sun-god disguised as a stallion, after which she gave birth to the equine twins Dasra and Nasatya called the Ashvins. (See also *Sanjna*.)

Shashi, Shashin The Moon, from *shasha*, a hare. It is believed that a hare can be seen sitting on the face of the moon. Some say that the Moon-goddess is a hare. The king of the hares sought her protection against the elephants in the famous fable, showing that we need outside powers to survive.

Shashthi A mother-goddess who protects children, who is worshipped on the sixth day after birth. It is believed that if the child has survived this long it will continue to do so. Shashthi is a form of Uma.

Shasti A Bengali goddess who protects women in childbirth. She is depicted as riding a cat.

Shata-Rupa See *Satarupa*.

Shatpura The Kingdom of the Six Cities, given by Brahma to the Asura king, Nikumbha, and later conquered by Krishna.

Shatrughna 'Destroyer of Enemies'. Twin-brother of Lakshmana, the sons of King Dasharatha and brothers of Rama. The twins had half as much of the essence of Vishnu in them as Rama had on his own. Shatrughna married Shrutakirti, a cousin of Sita's. He fought bravely in the siege of Lanka and killed Ravana, one of the demon generals.

Shaumya Shiva in his pacific aspect, the opposite of *raudra* 'horrific'. Shiva can be a peaceful yoga teacher or a terrifying god. (See also *Bhairava*.)

Shaykh, Sheikh In Islam, the leader of a Sufi brotherhood in a town or other locality, the Shaykh was thought to be capable of punishing evildoers by sending his slipper through the air to hit the offenders on the head. The Shaykhs are said to visit Heaven and talk to the angels.

Shesha King of all the serpents or Nagas. Ruler of the Lower Region called Patala. Shesha lives in the primeval World Ocean serving Vishnu, who reposes in the Ocean resting his head on the broad chest of the monster. In the traditional paintings, Shesha can be seen shading the god's head with a canopy formed by its hundreds of heads. Shesha is clothed in royal purple with a necklace of white pearls. Also called Ananta 'the Endless One' as he is wrapped around the world. Shesha is usually identified with Vasuki. He is represented as holding in one hand a pestle, symbol of making bread by crushing grain and in the other a plough, symbol of preparing new land for crops by cutting the earth open. The plough symbol links him to Balarama who is an incarnation of Shesha. He lives in Mani-Mandapa 'jewel-palace'. When the gods decided to churn the Ocean, they took Shesha, using him as a rope to turn the churning vessel. When one of Shesha's 1,000 mouths yawns, there is an earthquake somewhere. At the end of our time (see *Kalpa*), when the gods decide the earth must be destroyed, Shesha's mouth will leak an inflammable poison which will burn the whole of creation.

Shikhara A tower composed of several storeys built over or near a temple.

Shiksha Study, teaching, science, modesty. Reciting the Veda.

Shishumara 'Porpoise'. The ecliptic. Ancient Indian astronomers described the movement of the planets as a huge porpoise in whose heart Vishnu resided whilst Dhruva the pole-star ruled its tail. Shishumara rolls around all the time like a real porpoise in the sea. As Dhruva revolves, so the sun, the moon and the planets have to move round as well, since they are tied to the pole-star with silver-shining threads.

Shishu-Pala Son of Dama-ghosha, King of Chedi, and Shruta-Deva, sister of Vasudeva, father of Krishna. Shishu-Pala was in a previous existence the valiant king of the Daityas, Hiranya-Kashipu by name, who was unjust and so was killed for his tyranny by Vishnu in his *avatara* as man-lion (see *Narasimha*). Krishna and Vishnu are names for the same god. Next, Shishu-Pala was born as Ravana, the demon-tyrant who abducted Sita and was vanquished by her husband Rama, another incarnation of Vishnu. Having slain his cousin Shishu-Pala, his own dark aspect who had aroused his displeasure, Krishna–Vishnu permitted him to reunite with his divine self. This epilogue of the epic myth by the philosophers transfigures their thesis that the essence of the Divine Being is the identity of opposing forces.

Shitala Goddess of smallpox, which she causes, and so, she is invoked by the people to protect them against the dreaded disease. She is depicted as riding an ass. She is sometimes identified with Devi. She wears red robes and carries reeds with which she chastises her victims.

Shiva Shiva is the Moon-god of the mountains. He has the moon in his hair, through which flows Ganga, the River Ganges. As it poured down from the heavens, Shiva thus protected the earth against the mighty goddess Ganga, who could certainly have flooded all India. Shiva forced her to stream through his *jata*, his matted hair, a sign of his asceticism, until, after a long time, the waters reached the earth. That is why we see many small streams converging in the lower Himalayas to form the one great divine river, Ganges. Her beneficient power is so strong that all people will be purified by her holy waters, the living as well as the dead.

As Lord of the mountains, Shiva is seated on Mount Kailasa, facing south, towards India, while he is teaching the Rishis, the Brahmin priests. Thus Shiva is seen as the master of the mountains where the sages go to meditate, the master who teaches them the exalted wisdom of his cool abode, for Hima-alaya means 'the abode of snow'. Whoever has seen the immense landscape of snowy peaks reaching from horizon to horizon, where at night the moon shines almost as brightly as the sun by day, will perceive the link between Shiva and the starlit skies. This is how we know Shiva and how his devotees love him and worship him: seated on the tigerskin to demonstrate he has subdued greed and aggression, as white as the snow in which he resides, as white as the bright moon of wisdom in his hair. His whiteness is a sign of his asceticism, for Shiva is the god of the Yogis, the father of Brahmins who knows and recites the Veda, the sacred hymns of the ancient Aryans, composed in a language that is even older than Sanskrit. This is how Shiva appears in sculpture and painting. Accompanied by the white bull, Nandi, his faithful animal; with strings of prayer beads around his neck and the god Ganesha, his son with the elephant's head, at his feet.

The elephant occurs in many folk-tales in India, as a character of great wisdom and knowledge, of immense strength and power, who knows the paths of the jungle and the hidden waterwells. Wisdom and knowledge are the chief objects of the Shaivas, the worshippers of Shiva.

Round his neck he has the long writhing body of Vasuki, the cobra, symbol of sudden anger which Shiva keeps under control near his throat. His throat is blue since he once took Vasuki's poison in his own mouth for, otherwise, it would have destroyed all humanity. Shiva cannot swalow it for it would destroy him too, so he has to keep it in his throat, which is blue as a result. In this way Shiva has saved the world, and at the same time, he keeps the virulent poison under control, like the seasnake, Vasuki, itself.

On his forehead, Shiva has the three horizontal golden stripes that mark the Shaiva devotee, on either side of his third eye. The myth of this third eye is as follows.

Once Uma, Shiva's consort, playfully held her hands over his eyes, which are normally open. At once darkness spread across the universe, no sun, no stars, not even the moon could be seen. Quickly, Shiva had to open a third eye in the centre of his forehead, so that light would return to the cosmos and with it, order and justice. For Shiva is also the god of Dharma, the rights and duties of men and women, symbolized in Nandi, his loyal animal. Shiva is also, we should remember, Pashupati the Lord Protector of the animals.

It has been argued that Vishnu, not Shiva, is the protector of the cosmos, but that is quarrelling over names. Vishnu and Shiva are essentially identical, as both are in essence indistinguishable from Brahma = Prajapati, the Creator. The difference between the gods is not in their function, but in their character, their qualities. Each god, by his special nature, teaches us something about the universe that we had not seen before, because each god highlights a unique aspect of creation and with that, of our own world of dreams, our own deepest souls.

Shiva has three essential qualities (*guna*); *Sattva*, *Rajas* and *Tamas*, i.e. Truth, Energy and Darkness. With these three words, Indian philosophy has revealed three major basic principles of creation, i.e. of our own world, the world that exists, because we can see it and conceive it. Truth and energy together create light, which permits us to see the truth and to do justice, for justice requires the light of day. Energy plus darkness will cause crime, the inhuman activities that thrive in darkness and grow big in dark minds. Solely among the Indian deities, Shiva embodies the contradictions of the universe and of human thinking. Contradictions are resolved in music, so Shiva is also the god of music, always accompanied by his drum, and often by the *vina*, the beautiful stringed instrument of early India. Music, like justice, is the harmonious result of the careful balancing of two extremes into unison.

So far, we have spoken only of Shiva as the god of truth, Yoga, asceticism, self-control and justice. The second aspect (*guna*) of Shiva is his energy, his *shakti* or creative power, for Shiva was and is also the Creator, like Brahma, but with his own unique nature. In order to explain this we have to go back to the earliest times of religion in India. In the oldest effigies we see Shiva represented with weapons. He is always accompanied by his trident, perhaps the oldest instrument for fishing. As god of the rivers, fishing would be the art he taught his followers first. Further, Shiva is seen holding a bow and arrow, a javelin for throwing at wild boars and a noose to catch animals with, even elephants. He carries a deer in his hand, sometimes even a lion or elephant's skin. As god of the forest he is the god of the hunters in the forest, for the ancient peoples knew that the forest soaks up the rain and releases it gradually, preventing floods. In the oldest days of humanity, Man was a hunter, wandering through the woods in search of game, praying to the Lord of the Animals to send game in his direction. In ancient Europe the same customs were found, and still in some regions of Africa, the Forest-god has to be placated before the hunters dare to enter the jungle, which is everywhere full of mysterious creatures, spirits, demons and dwarfs. All these are ruled by Shiva, the Ganesha (Lord of Dwarfs), the Elephant-god, who controls tigers, lions and snakes. All hunters have to be masters of magic, the *tantra*, which is also taught by Shiva as his secret lore. For the primitive hunter, big game was not just something you could shoot for fun with high-powered rifles; animals were part of the mysterious magic world of the jungle. Game is elusive. It remains invisible if the Forest-Lord has cast a spell on the hunters' eyes. Suddenly the elephant or the tiger will stand there, huge and fearsome, facing the hunter, who needs the courage of despair. He also needs his *shakti*, his spear. *Shakti* has become the word for energy, strength, power. An elephant cannot be killed with arrows or javelins. A solid spear is needed, to be thrust in its side. What made the hunters hunt? Hunger! An elephant meant food for a week for a whole village. The more food, the more energy, the more life. Shiva's energy is represented as the fire, Agni, which he holds in one of his hands.

A god is only *sattva*, essence. In order to create he needs matter which is also energy. This is also called *shakti* in Sanskrit, and represented as a goddess, the god's other half. The divine powers that needed each other in such an intimate way were believed to be related to each other, like man and wife. The source of a man's energy is his wife, for she gives him a reason to live, to work and fight. In order to understand this we must again go back to the oldest myths, in the Veda itself. There Shiva ('kind') was still called Rudra 'roaring', like a fire or a storm. He was created by the first god, Brahma, in order to create the world. When there was nothing, there was total silence, so the first creation was like a storm or a raging fire, like the very first manifestation of energy itself. Rudra said: 'In order to create I need a wife.'

Brahma knew that he was right, so he created a wife for him, whose name was Gauri 'wild cow', the daughter of the Himalaya, hence her name Parvati, 'she of the mountains', by which she is best known. Rudra then plunged into the water to begin Creation. The land rose up.

We must leave aside here the complex myth of the churning of the Ocean of Milk by the gods, their joint act of creation. They were in search of Amrita, the elixir of eternal life, but they found it only after Shiva had taken the *visha*, the poison that came out first and had to be safely deposited out of harm's way. Only Shiva was strong enough to take it and hold it, in his throat.

We also have to omit the myth of the first quarrel among the gods, who did not invite Rudra to the first sacrifice because they thought him uncivilized. Gauri, feeling aggrieved because her husband was insulted in his absence, mounted the sacrificial fire, and burnt herself, thus becoming Sati, the first suttee. When Rudra returned, he collected her charred remains and carried them around, singing the famous litany of the first widower:

> Arise O my beloved wife
> I am thy husband Shiva-ji
> Open thy eyes and look at me!
> With thee I can create all things
> Without thee I am powerless
> I am a corpse, I cannot act
> Forsake me not, come back to me!
> O let me see thy smile again
> Say something sweet into my ear
> Dost thou not see me weeping here?
> Thy words will be unto my heart
> Like summer rain on thirsting land

You used to greet me when we met
With joy and with a happy face
Why art thou still and without voice?
Canst thou not hear how I lament?
O Mother of the Universe,
O Mistress of my soul, arise!
My beautiful and loving wife,
My faithful spouse, come back to me!

Going round and round in circles, while singing his lament, Rudra–Shiva began to dance, whirling round in ever wider circles, accompanying himself on his drum, the first dance and the first funeral rite. The entire creation began to shake in the rhythm of his grief, as he danced round the world seven times. Finally the gods agreed to restore his spouse to life, fearing that his violent sorrow would destroy the world. Thus Shiva became Nataraja, the king of the dance. Filled with sadness he went up into his mountains to spend many days in meditation, until his revived queen found him there. Her new name was Uma, mother.

Shiva's dance marks the transition from one stage to another. It is a rite of passage. Gauri was his bride; as a virgin she had to die, then she was reborn as his wife, Uma, the mother, a new name. Something has to die before we can be created; without sacrifice we cannot be born.

Now there is a long episode in which Rudra–Shiva, wandering in the forest deep in mourning, with dishevelled hair and naked, because the bridegroom who has lost his bride has lost all that matters, meets the six wives of six Brahmins who are performing *tapas*, asceticism. The women are bathing in the stream; perhaps they feel neglected by their ascetic husbands. There appears to them a tall god, whose appearance is both friendly (*shiva*) and terrifying (*rudra*) and so he has everything that makes a man irresistibly attractive: they fall in love with him and he, the bridegroom without a wife, spills the seed from his *linga* on the bank of the river. It looks like fire, for *agni* is only an emanation of Shiva, the Fire-god. It looks like golden grains of wheat: the germs of nature. (See *Hiranya-garbha*.)

Linga or *lingam* is the Sanskrit word for 'phallus' and though there have been long arguments as to whether it really means that, there can be no doubt that if a god is represented in the shape of a man, he must be a real man and not a eunuch. No god can create if he is not a man, and no goddess can create who is not a woman, because gender is the essence of generative power. The *linga* is found in many places in India, represented as a cylindrical stone, standing up in a circular basin, the *yoni*, symbol of female pudenda. In a country where children are the dearest wish of every couple, it should not be surprising that their worship concentrates on the organs of reproductive power, in a symbolic manner. The *linga* is regularly washed with milk by some women in some regions of India, as a form of worship, hoping for children.

Shiva has phases, regularly recurrent cycles, like seasons of rain and drought. Shiva alternates between meditation and creativity, the one is necessary in order that the other take place. When Shiva resides in a state of meditation he will abstain from procreation, so that Parvati his spouse, also has to perform asceticism hoping to regain his love. This is because, during these periods of suspended activity, the world does not exist bodily, only in essence. Only the Spirit continues its burning existence, like the sun in the desert, like fire in a forest. Both the fire and the forest are manifestations of Shiva; the fire is symbolized by the lion, the voracious beast of prey, often seen in his presence. The forest is an alternative interpretation of the *trisula*, the trident in his left hand, which is often depicted as a lotus-stem, with roots and a flower with three petals, or branches.

When Shiva had meditated for a very long time, the gods began to worry that the world might never be created, so they sent Kama, the god of love, who was formed for the purpose. He is identical to the Greek Eros, the Roman Cupido, for all those names mean desire. Shiva opened his third eye, the eye that sees the hidden truth, and its beam burnt the god of love. Kama was consumed to ashes, for love cannot survive the glare of intellectual analysis, of scepticism. From then on the god of love was called Ananga, 'he without body'. The spirit of immortal love is condemned to wander around in the world and wherever a man and wife embrace in true love, in that moment when two bodies unite, the god of love, Kama, has a body; which other faith expresses love so beautifully?

Finally, Shiva is persuaded to create the world, that is, to marry. There are numerous paintings in India where the god and his goddess can be seen sitting together in love. Often the goddess Parvati is seen sitting on her husband's knee, gazing up at him in rapture, in complete concentration upon his radiant face, while he holds his beloved wife lightly around the waist. In many religions God is depicted as a man, in some as a woman, but Hindu artists represent God complete, as man and wife, for it is only in holy matrimony that divine love between equals is present and is working, functioning for the future — because creation belongs to the future. Everything that we make, we plan for the future. That which contains the entire universe is as big as a man and a woman embracing each other. Thus complete love fills the cosmos, like the divine spirit.

Shiva and Parvati are often represented together in sculpture as a married couple in the act of physical love. Books have been filled with attempts to defend this seeming sacrilege: to represent God the Creator in an act of sex. I think it needs no defence. The male and the female principles of the cosmos have to be united in order for creation to be possible and complete. The Indians do not see creation in the way it was painted by William Blake, who showed us the Creator as an artist, busy designing the world with rulers and compasses. For the Hindu, as for the scientist, the genesis of the universe is a natural process that takes light-years to fulfil itself. Of all the numerous natural processes on earth, the one that is dearest to the Hindu is the creation of his children. It is thus a matter of course that Indians should represent the creation of the universe as the moment of conception by a mother in the full embrace of her loving husband.

When he meditates, Shiva thinks the world; when he creates, Shiva loves the world in the same way as the instrument-maker loves the tender wood out of which he will make a thing of beauty. Like his *linga*, the plants rise up at the moment of creation, raising their tender stalks out of the earth. However, to that end the existing vegetation has to be destroyed, as one can see happening in a tropical forest. The Indian concept of this process is that the appearance dies, but that the spirit assumes new forms to return in. Western theology teaches that the spirit created matter but remained aloof from it. In Hinduism, the spirit is the inside, the matter is the outside; the two are inseparable like the two sides of this page. When the spirit withdraws, there is no existence for a time. Therefore, destruction is not ruin but only a change of shape. These days, science has come to the same conclusion: molecules shift, like clouds in the sky, changing form and colour all the time.

Shiva, the master of creation, is also the God of Death. He has to be. Shiva the hunter-god dances the dance of death. He is himself the god of desire, of longing. The hunter longs to kill and to give life, to bring dead animals to his people so that they shall live. Shiva, the god of marriage and meditation, how can he be the ugly face of death? Because a god must be complete to be really universal. Death is part of life just as much as birth, love, marriage and children. Death is inescapably part of our gruesome real world. On paintings, the style and subject of which were adopted by the Buddhists, we see Shiva dancing, surrounded by corpses, on an immense cemetery. Shiva has changed now. Or was the way we first saw him an illusion? Yes, all visual images are illusions, but without images we cannot reflect. The beads of his necklace suddenly appear to be skulls; his drinking-cup is also a skull. Garlands of skulls hang round his waist. This is no longer the benign Shiva, it is again the terrifying Rudra, who has the character of the voracious lion, the symbol of time devouring everything, Kala, the god of decay. The royal cobra now appears the cause of a sudden death, while the poison that Shiva swallowed would suffice to kill humanity. Every sign and symbol can have more than one meaning, every coded message can be read in more than one way. We are staring at a mystery. Shiva is as complex as Man himself — and infinitely more so.

Shivaratri The feast of the wedding of Lord Shiva and Parvati, celebrated in the dark fortnight of the moon-month Phalaguna, when the sun enters Pisces. That night the Linga is worshipped from dusk to dawn by washing it every three hours with milk, curds, honey and rose-water, while the mantra *Om Namah Shivaya* is recited. Hymns glorifying Shiva are sung, notably the Shiva Mahima Stotra by Pushpadanta, and the Shiva Tandava Stotra by Ravana. Whoever repeats the name of Shiva during Shivaratri with perfect concentration and devotion in his heart is freed from all sins. He will live happily free from rebirth.

Shivi King of Ushinara, famous for his virtue and honesty. One day the gods decided to test the king's righteousness. Agni took the form of a dove and perched on the king's shoulder speaking: 'Oh Lord of Justice, a hawk is pursuing me, wishing to kill me. Please grant me refuge, hide me in your robe.'

The king could not refuse to protect those who sought shelter with him. Seconds later a hawk arrived who was Indra in disguise, and claimed the dove as his food by right. The king's honesty did not permit him to deny that he was hiding the dove, nor would it permit him to deliver the dove to the hawk since he had promised the dove his protection. The hawk, however, claimed that the dove belonged to him as his food by right since it is a law of nature that hawks must eat doves. The king offered to slaughter a cock or a sheep for the hawk's satisfaction but the hawk was unmoved. It demanded nothing less than a piece of the king's own body equal in weight to that of the dove. The king, who had given his word to protect this dove, and had thereby deprived the hawk of his daily food, ordered a pair of scales to be brought and cut off his leg to be eaten by the hawk. However, the king's leg was lighter than the little dove. So, the king had to place himself on the scales. He weighed as much as the dove, no more! At that moment the two gods revealed themselves and restored the king's leg. Satisfied, they flew away. Shivi had earned his reputation. In a later version of this tale the dove is Dharma the god of justice. The moral of the story is that a clean conscience is worth one's life. Only total self-sacrifice buys total justice.

Shraddha Faith. Wife of Dharma the God of Justice and mother of Kamadeva, the God of Love.

Shramana Literally 'one who makes an effort'. An ascetic; in China, a Buddhist missionary. It is the origin of the word *shaman*, a seer.

Shri Prosperity, wealth, majesty, splendour, fortune, intellect. (See *Devi Shri*; *Lakshmi*.)

Shudra The lowest of the four Hindu castes, actually the 'casteless' caste. It is a myth that the Shudras are descendants of the aboriginal Indians.

Shuka-Saptati 'The Parrot Seventy'. A famous story-book containing 70 tales told by an intelligent parrot to a young woman who wants to run off to her lover, at night while her husband is away on a business trip. The wise parrot tells (at least one) story every night, until dawn prevents the woman from going out unnoticed. The parrot is more faithful to its master than his own wife. It tells these entertaining stories to instruct the woman in prudence and skill in handling people in tricky situations. The Persian translation, the Tuti-Nameh, is famous in the Middle East.

Shukra, Sukra 'Bright'. The planet Venus, also called Ushanas. Sukravara is the word for Friday (the Old Saxons identified their goddess Freia with Venus).

The Urdu name for Venus is Zuhra 'the beautiful, flowering one'. Sukra is the most auspicious of all the planets. A person born as Venus is appearing in the sky will have the knowledge of the past, the present and future. He will rise to high office and be honoured by the highest in the land. He will be loved by many women. His symbol is a silver square.

In Indian lore Sukra, 'the seer', is a god and the son of Bhrigu. Sukra is the guru of the Asuras and knows the incantation which brings the dead back to life. He had to teach this knowledge to his pupil Kacha, because the latter was in his (Sukra's) stomach and could only come out by killing the old guru. So, Kacha broke out of his teacher's side, then revived him by using his own magic formula. He is blind in one eye, like Wodan.

Shumbha and Nishumbha Two evil demons, brothers whose power, as a result of 6,000 years of performing asceticism, was so enormous that the gods feared they might have to relinquish their thrones. Only Durga, Shiva's queen in her powerful aspect, was strong enough to defeat and slay them.

Shvetaketu A saintly king, the first man to protest against the Brahmins' habit of demanding intercourse with other men's wives, which the latter did not dare to refuse for fear of the Brahmins' magically powerful curses.

Siddha One of a class of men whose saintly lives have made them demigods.

Siddhartha 'He who has achieved his purpose'. Father of Mahavira. Praise-name for both Gautama Buddha and Vardhamana Jina (q.v.) as well as other saints. The purpose of such men is total enlightenment and self-control.

Siddha-Sila According to some sources, the bright region in the zenith of the universe, above the Kalpas, according to Jain cosmology. There live the Siddhas, liberated souls, in eternal bliss.

Siddhi The divine ability to make one's body infinitely small, or big, or light, etc.

Sikhism The religion founded by the Guru Nanak, 1469–1539, in Panjab. He taught the Unity of God and the unreality of the caste system as well as the futility of all forms of worship. Some of his very beautiful hymns to God have been preserved. The Sikh doctrine was laid down by the fifth guru Arjun, in 1604. The sanctuary of Amritsar was opened by permission of the emperor Akbar in 1577. The Sikhs call themselves *khalsa* 'pure', which word now means 'the nation'. The men are characterized by wearing five things: long hair, short trousers, an iron discus (usually on a bracelet), a small steel dagger and a comb. They call themselves *Singhs* 'Lions'. The word *Sikh* means 'disciple'.

Simha Leo, a sign of the Zodiac (q.v.).

Simha-Rathi 'Riding a lion'. A praise-name for Devi–Durga.

Simha-Vahini 'Riding a lion'. An epithet of Devi–Kali–Durga–Uma (q.v.).

Sin Ajamila was one of the most famous sinners. He lived in open sin with a Shudra (Untouchable) Harlot (this abomination is mentioned first!) He never read the Vedas though he was a Brahmin by birth, and he never performed a sacrifice. He left his aged parents to their fate though he was rich as a result of thieving, lying and embezzlement. When the moment of death approached he saw dimly Yama and his torturers waiting for him with their chains and ropes with which to truss him up. In his despair, Ajamila called Narayana, his son. He went on calling Narayana until Vishnu, who is also called Narayana, sent his messengers to Yama telling him to return to Deathland, because Yama has no power over whomever repeats Vishnu's holy names.

Sindhu The great river which the Persians called Hindu (now Hind) and the Greeks: Indus. The region around its mouth is still called Sindh and the great plains of central India are named after it: Hindu-staan. The name India was formed from Indus. Originally the Indus valley (now Pakistan) was the central kingdom of the Aryans.

Sishana The male organ, worshipped by a certain sect as a god. (See *Linga*.)

Sita Originally the goddess of agricultural land, the soil and the crops. Her name means 'furrow', the scar in the earth left by the ploughshare. In it the farmer sows his crops and for the mentality of antiquity the identity of Sita the furrow and Sita the wife was evident. In the oldest times of the Indo-European farming culture, the farmer and his wife had to lie together in the furrow after sowing, on the eve of the sun's entry into the sign of Aries, otherwise the crops would fail.

One day, in ancient times when the kings still ploughed their own lands, King Janaka suddenly saw a beautiful girl spring up from his furrow; she was his daughter Sita, an incarnation of the goddess Lakshmi, who knew that the evil tyrant Ravana would be killed for a woman and Lakshmi had decided to be that woman. When Sita had come of age, King Janaka organized a *svayamvara*, a festive competition for princes whereby the winner would receive the princess' hand in marriage. Shiva himself lent his bow to the king for the occasion. The princes had to string it and hit the target using it. Only Rama, son of King Dasharatha, succeeded in stringing the celestial bow. This was because he was an incarnation of Vishnu, so Sita was predestined for him. Sita is the model for all Indian women: pure, affectionate, faithful. She followed her husband when he was sent into exile in the forest. One day Rama went off in pursuit of a beautiful doe he had seen and which, unbeknownst to him, had been sent by his enemies to lead him astray. While he was away the demon Ravana swooped down and carried Sita off to his palace in Sri Lanka. There he did his best to seduce her but she rejected all his advances with firmness and courage. At last her husband won the war which had started for her sake and killed Ravana. But Sita was not received back graciously by her husband, he had a nagging suspicion that the demon, who was able to disguise himself as the most attractive of young men, had succeeded in seducing her. So, Sita vowed that she would enter the fire in the presence of men and gods, to prove her purity. Thus it happened; she mounted the pyre, but the Fire-god Agni refused to hurt her because he knew that she was pure. He took her from the woodpile and placed her in Rama's arms. Together they went home to Ayodhya. However the slanderous citizens murmured that their king had brought home a queen who had been ravished by an evil demon. Rama, overcome by doubts, sent her into exile even though she was pregnant by him. She went to live in the forest with the sage Valmika and there, in due course, she gave birth to twin sons, Kusha and Lava. They stayed there until they were about 15 when one day, Rama saw them and recognized them. He recalled Sita, but her heart had been hurt too much. She died by sinking back into the earth from whence she had come.

Skambha 'Support, fulcrum'. The god who carries the heavens and the earth, Atlas. Sometimes identified with Brahma.

Skanda Skanda is the god of war. He is the son of Agni the god of fire (q.v.), who was at that time identified with Shiva, the god of death. Skanda has six heads because he was the son of Daksha, who had observed that Agni had fallen in love with the wives of six Brahmins. These women who were neglected by their husbands had taken a bath in the river, while Agni was watching them. Daksha quickly took the form of these six women and seduced Agni, whom she loved passionately. The result was the birth of Skanda. A variant of this myth relates that it was Uma who seduced her own husband Shiva when she saw him watching the six women.

Smara 'Memory'. The god of love, Kama, since we love what we remember.

Smarta, Smriti 'What is remembered'. The Indian oral tradition.

Smashana The cemetery where the dead bodies are burnt to purify them. It is the place where Shiva dances his funerary dance with garlands of skulls. It is the place where Vetalas clutch the visitors and never let go. Smashana also means lying down on the floor and relaxing every muscle of the body, the first exercise in the book of yoga. For Buddhist monks, paintings of cemeteries full of corpses serve as visual aids to learn the futility of this earthly life.

Soma Another name for Chandra, the Moon-god. Somavara, Monday, is named after him. His symbol is a silver crescent. It is very auspicious to be born at full moon. Such a person will have many friends, will be rich and powerful, have a fine house, good food, ride horses, travel much and be honoured. The priests will pray: 'Oh Moon which hast no enemy! Son of the Sun-disk! Thou who advancest knowledge among men, who givest us protection from danger, who givest us power to overcome our enemies. May this prayer be efficacious!'

According to some scholars the moon is a female deity called Somavati. As a god, Soma was married to Rohini and had a son called Budha.

In the original texts of the oldest period, Soma is the mysterious beverage which makes the gods immortal. For that reason, Soma is the most precious liquid in the universe; it is the water of life. Gradually, Soma became a god, the god of the intoxicating beverage, Soma, comparable to the Greek Dionysos or Bacchus. Soma is also called Oshadhi-pati 'Supervisor of Herbs'. The identity of the plant or tree from which the hallucinogen Soma was distilled, is uncertain. It may have been figs from the *Ficus religiosa*, the tree which is still worshipped (see *Fig-tree)*. Wine can be made from figs.

Soma, as the Moon-god, was said to be the son of the Rishi Atri and his wife Anasuya. Apart from Rohini, Soma married the 27 daughters of the Rishi Daksha, no doubt symbolizing the 27 days of the sidereal circumambulation of the moon. His preference for Rohini made the other wives jealous, so they complained to their father Daksha, who cursed Soma so that he became afflicted with leprosy. However, the wives then took pity on Soma and told their father this disease was too severe a punishment for their husband. Daksha could not lift his own curse but he could mitigate it so that now the moon gradually becomes 'grey-skinned' and finally disappears within one fortnight, but then gradually recovers its original fine silvery colour again within the next fortnight. Soma then wanted to be recognized as king of the sky and invited the planet gods with their wives to a *raja-suya* ceremony, i.e. the installation of a king. Soma fell in love with Tara, wife of Brihaspati (the planet Jupiter) and eloped with her. The result was terrifying; two parties formed, in which the gods sided with the indignant Brihaspati, the aggrieved husband. A war ensued which shook the foundations of the universe until the Supreme God, Brahma, intervened and ordered Soma to return Tara to her lawful husband. He did so but she was found to be pregnant and in due course gave birth to a son who was called Budha, the planet Mercury. Brahma compelled her to speak the truth so she had to confess that Soma was the father of Budha. However, Soma was sufficiently punished since Shiva had slashed Soma's face in half with his trident during the battle. Budha became the father of the Lunar Race. Soma rides through the sky in a chariot with three wheels, drawn by ten horses as white as jasmine flowers. The moon is also called Shasha, 'hare', since it is believed that 'the man in the moon' is a hare, in Indian folklore. Thus the hare is regarded by some as a moon-deity. (See *Hare*.)

Soshyant, Saoshyant   The World Saviour, who, predicted Zarathustra, will be the Living One, the Embodiment of Truth, son of a virgin mother, Vispa-Taurvairi. He will come to earth to expel Drug (deceit) from the Realm of Asha (truth), and make the earth pure, according to the Zoroastrians.

Soul   According to some Buddhist sources there are five Atmans: Atman 'sight', Niratman 'hearing', Antaratman 'breath', Paratman 'voice' and Chetanatman 'consciousness', which gives unity to the whole. (See *Atman*.)

Spenta   In the Zoroastrian or Parsi religion, the word for Holy. Spenta Mainyu (or Menog) is the Holy Spirit, with whose help Ahura Mazda created the world, yet the two are essentially identical. Amesha Spenta, 'Immortal Holy', is one of six divinities who assisted Ahura Mazda when He created the worlds, after which each of them guarded one of the seven celestial spheres by residing in it, as immanent gods.

Spirits   Invisible beings that can make themselves visible at any time in any form they wish, and of any size. Some are weak and appear only as whispering voices or as vague shades in daytime, white vapours at night. Some are more powerful so they can lift objects or persons up and fly away with them. A spirit has intelligence and will-power; it acts powerfully and knows both the future and the past, this human world, the gods' world and the underworld. A spirit can reside in an animal, a tree, a river, a mountain or in the sea. Many human beings are possessed by spirits, which make them act against their will. For example, Nala abandoned his beloved wife Damayanti because he was possessed by the evil spirit Kali because he had made a mistake in his prayers. (For evil spirits see *Demons*.) The good spirits are often worshipped.

They may be the ancestral spirits or the gods. (See *Gods*; *Deva*.) Some scholars maintain that the Yakshas and Nagas were the gods of prehistoric India, being respectively tree-spirits and snake spirits. Tree-worship can still be observed in India, while vestiges of snake-worship have been discovered in many countries' religions including ancient Egypt and Israel. Yakshas or Yakhas (feminine Yakshinis, Yakshis or Yakhis) are sometimes naughty but never vicious. There are numerous Yakshas known by name: Supavasu, Virudhako, Gangita, Suchiloma, Kupiro, Sirima, Chada, etc. The Ramayana distinguishes three classes of people worshipping three types of deities: the upper-class people called *Sattvika* 'pure' worship a god, *deva*; the *Rajashika* 'emotional' people will worship Yakshas and Rakshasas, while the *Tamasika* 'dark' people worship Pretas and Bhutas, or goblins, ghosts and spirits of the dead. Vaisrava is Lord of the Yakshas, while Shiva is Bhuta-Natha, Lord of the Bhutas, and Yama is Preta-Raja, King of the Ghosts. Kubera is Master of the Rakshasas; the Guhyas are his servants. Naras are winged horses who carry Kubera through the skies. Guhyakis are the females of the Guhyas. A Yakshagraha is a demon that possesses people, making them rave like madmen. Evil spirits for example were Sitala the goddess of smallpox and the goddess of cholera, Olabibi. A Dakini is described as a female imp.

Statue See *Murti*, *Rupa*.

Sthanu 'The Pillar', Shiva as an ascetic, standing motionless, meditating.

Sthaviravada 'Teaching of the Elders'. (See *Therevada*.)

Subhadra 'Well-omened'. Daughter of Vasudeva, sister of Krishna, wife of Arjuna who carried her off from Dwarka and had to save her from his cousin and arch-enemy Duryodhana. Abhimanyu was her son. She accompanies Krishna as Jagannatha (q.v.) on his enormous, heavy vehicle when it is pulled through the city. She is said to have had a relationship with Krishna. In modern Hinduism, Subhadra appears in religious art side by side with Krishna as Jagannatha, with Balarama in third place.

Subrahmanya War-god. Other names: Skanda, Kumara, Karttikeya. Son of Agni the Fire-god and his wife Svaha (oblation), although she is also said to have been an incarnation of Parvati, while Agni is identified with Rudra. Subrahmanya–Skanda is also associated with Surya. He is famous for his bravery when leading the gods in their numerous wars against the demons Taraka, Kraunch and others. His symbols are the cock, the banner, bow, *dhanu*, shield and spear, *shula*. His vehicle is the peacock.

Sudarshana 'Beautiful to see', name of Vishnu's weapon the discus. This discus lives in the sky and has the form of a wheel which by its rotation comes back to Vishnu's hand. It has a very sharp edge which can slice off the heads of demons as big as mountains, but it also sprays fire in sparks, blasts, beams and lightnings, so that it can burn down entire cities. With his arm like an elephant trunk, Vishnu aims it repeatedly at enemy armies. It fells demons in battle order by the thousand at a throw, cutting and burning at the same time.

Sudyumna Son of Vaivasvata. He changed sex several times in his life.

Sufiya Sufism, Sufiism, the collective term for the Sufi communities, of which there are at least four major orders, *tarika*, plural *turuk*, in India. All Sufis claim that the Prophet Muhammad himself founded their order. The Prophet, they say, made Ali his successor (*khalifa, caliph*) as leader of the faithful, *imam*. Present leaders may be taught by Masters who have already died. The disciple (*murid*) first has to learn the ordinary ritual prayers of Islam. After that he may rise through many stages until he perceives the Divine Light. A master may become a *wali* 'saint'.

Sugata 'Going well', a name for the Buddha, walking the correct path.

Sugriva Sugriva was the son of Surya and king of the monkeys in Kishkinda. When Rama, wandering in the forest in search of Sita, had killed Kabandha, a giant demon who was condemned to wander around for his sins as an evil monster until Rama would destroy his body, Kabandha, grateful for his liberation, advised Rama to make an alliance with the king of the monkeys who was then living in exile, like Rama himself (see *Bali*). Sugriva was described as Lord of the Vanavasas (forest-dwellers) and a just and truthful ruler. Intelligent, resourceful, brave, kindhearted, he would be a good friend for Rama. Thus counselled the dying Kabandha, and then his spirit flew away. Rama found the exiled King Sugriva together with Hanuman, his commander-in-chief, on a hill in the forest. They made an alliance promising each other that they would help one another to regain their thrones. Rama, guided by Sugriva, found Bali the usurper on the throne of the monkey kingdom, and killed him. Thus, Sugriva was again king of Monkeyland. Now it was his turn to help Rama, but he forgot his promise. Rama had to send his brother Lakshman to remind him of it. Finally, Sugriva agreed to send his monkeys in search of Sita. In the end he proved himself a valiant warrior in the battle for Sri Lanka. He jumped upon Ravana's head and dashed Ravana's crown to the ground, but he lost the first round of serious fighting against that terrible demon. Surgiva then tackled the giant Kumbhakarna. The latter uprooted a mountain and threw it at Sugriva who just escaped. Sugriva killed many other enemy generals. When the battle was over and Sita was freed, Sugriva and Hanuman accompanied the happy couple to their home city of

Ayodhya (now called Oudh) where they celebrated for a month.

Suicide *Atmahatya*, 'killing self', is recommended only by the Jains, as their founder, Mahavira, fasted until death ensued. Some Buddhist leaders have also practised it, by fasting.

Sukha Happiness, an easy life, absence of suffering, pleasure.

Sukhavati The Buddhist Paradise (although this translation is somewhat misleading). It is often called the land of Amitabha (q.v.), the Bodhisattva of Compassion. Sukhavati means 'Happy Earth'. In that world-system there is no hell. Hell, in Buddhist thought, is to go back to earth for another life of pain. Sukhavati is the fragrant garden with the most abundant variety of flowers in all colours. Birds are singing numerous songs with harmonious voices. The trees are covered with glittering jewels of all colours, gold and silver, beryl, crystal, coral, pearls, emeralds and more. Bananas are the only real fruit mentioned. There are lakes on which lotus flowers float which are as large as three miles across. These giant flowers emit a light in which Buddha can be seen. There are wide rivers full of crystal-clear water that are as deep as one wishes: the body goes in as far as the bather desires and no more. It will also change its temperature to please the blessed bathers. The bottom is of golden sand and no one can drown in them. The blessed will smell the odours they enjoy and find the food they like to eat and hear the music they love most. They will find the clothes they wish and they only have to think of a palace and it will exist. There, they will be surrounded by beautiful *apsarases*, nymphs who will attend to their smallest wishes.

Sumantra 'Good Justice'. Name of Indra's palace in heaven.

Sumitra 'Good friend'. Wife of King Dasharatha.

Sun See *Surya*.

Sunnata See *Emptiness*.

Sura A god, a benign spiritual being of great power, but not as great as a *deva*. The *suras* live in Swarga, heaven. (See *Gods*.)

Suradevi The goddess of wine and spirits. The Greek Hebe.

Surapat From Suryapatya, a sun-worshipper, one of a small sect of devotees of the god Surya.

Surya The same word as the Greek Helios, the Latin and Norwegian Sol, the sun-god, son of Aditi the Sky-goddess and Dyaus, the god of the light in the sky, the Greek Zeus. Surya, like Helios-Apollo, rides through the sky in a chariot, which is drawn by seven red mares. He is also called Savitar 'the stimulator', Pushan 'benefactor', Bhaga 'distributor of wealth', Vivasvat 'the father of humanity', Mitra 'the friend'. Ushas is his wife, or his daughter, she is Aurora the goddess of dawn. His twin sons, the Ashvins, precede him in their own golden chariot, as the sun-rays precede the rising sun. In other texts the Sun-god's wife Sanjna, who was overcome by her husband's heat, created a twin-sister goddess who looked exactly like her and whose name was Chhaya 'shade'. Chhaya had to stay between her sister and the Sun-god, while Sanjna escaped into the forest disguised as a mare. Soon, however, Surya discovered that Chhaya was not his real wife and pursued the mare, disguised as a stallion. The resultant children are the Ashvin twins. Surya's son Vaivasvat had a son, Ikshvaku, who was the ancestor of the Sun-kings. Thus the sun-cult is closely associated with the horse-cult. Surya as a king has his own capital, Vivasvati, the Sun-city, from Vivasvat 'owner of rays' a praise-name of Surya. He is also called Dina-kara, 'day-maker' and Karma-sakshi, 'witness of the deeds'. As a god, Surya, was widely worshipped in the Vedic and Puranic periods. Statues of the Sun-god were made according to detailed instructions and widely distributed across India.

Suryaa Daughter of the sun, who married the Moon-god Soma (q.v.).

Sushena A wonder doctor who could bring the dead back to life.

Sutra Literally a piece of string, used as a 'rule of thumb', a 'yardstick'. It is also a book of rules for a religious community. The Kalpasutras are textbooks for ritual formalities, the Grihyasutras regulate domestic life (from *grihya* 'house'). For Buddhist students, Sutras have been composed mainly on philosophical subjects, but also to regulate monastic life. A sermon by the Buddha.

Svaha Wife of Agni who is instrumental in the birth of Skanda.

Svarga, Swarga The heaven of Indra on Mount Meru.

Svayambhu 'Self-existent', 'created by himself, from himself'. Praise-name of Brahma as Creator.

Svayamvara, Swayamwara Grand ceremony during which a princess chooses her husband from among the invited kings and princes. Sometimes the ceremony was preceded by competitions in archery and other martial arts, and the winners were then candidates for the final selection. (See also *Nala.*)

Swanaya A generous king who married his daughters to a great sage.

Swastika Sign of the Sun-god Surya, as a symbol of his generosity.

Syama 'Black'. A name given to Shiva (see *Kala*).

Syamantakara The Sunstone, a priceless jewel which brought eight loads of gold a day to its wearer and protected him against fire, famine, thieves and wild animals. It brought nothing but good if its wearer was virtuous, but if it was owned by a wicked man it would destroy him. The result of this property was that most of the men who somehow got hold of Syamantakara, the gem that shone in the dark, died miserably.

T

Trimurti

Takshaka 'The carpenter'. A name for Vishvakarman as the Creator. (See *Twashtar*.)

Tamas The principle of darkness as one of the original elements of the genesis of the universe, according to the Sankhya philosophy. At first there was nothing but *tamas*, until *rajas* (passionate desire) caused matter to exist. This is the element of Shiva's other side which he shares with Kali, the Black Goddess who merges with him in erotic union. Both are depicted as grinning blood-stained monsters, carrying skulls. They are the deities who sow fever, plague and death. The patrons of the sorcerers and of the ascetics who torture themselves with knives and nails, with ashes rubbed into their bodies, waiting to be consumed by the death-ray from Shiva's third eye, that which destroyed the god of love. (See *Shiva*.)

Tamraparni Greek Taprobane, the old name for Sri Lanka.

Tandu The god of dancing at the court of Shiva.

Tanha (Pali; Sanskrit *Trishna*). Craving, desire, the cause of unhappiness and rebirth, according to Buddha. (See also *Devi Shri*; *Lakshmi*.)

Tantra 'Ritual, Rule'. Also: the *shastras*, religious scriptures, textbooks of rules for rituals, originally designed for performing the correct ceremonies for the gods, which were revealed by Shiva to the Rishis. Later they became magic rituals intended to force the gods, by their own rules, to grant boons. The Puranas are the *shastras* for the *dvapara-yuga*, the age that is now past. The Tantras are the *shastras* for the *kali-yuga*, the present age in which there is only a quarter of the world's original virtue left, and depravity reigns, because people are no longer intelligent. The Tantra literature has been misinterpreted as a result of the fragmentary character of the available manuscripts, the obscurity of the technical terminology and the metaphysical doctrines it contains. In Mahayana Buddhism, certain groups began to worship the goddesses who had been assigned as 'potency', i.e. as spouses (see *shakti*) to the Bodhisattvas and Dhyani-Buddhas. These multiplied Buddha-gods, originally purely philosophical concepts, became saviours as well as frightening deities who had to be propitiated. Gradually, magical methods were introduced by means of which, it was believed, the deity could be induced to grant boons to their worshippers. These methods were described in magical text-books — the Tantras.

The great majority of these rites centre around Devi, wife of Shiva, in her manifestation as Shakti, 'procreative power', both 'white', i.e. gentle and Kali 'black', i.e. ferocious. Shakti is the special energy needed for sexual intercourse and magical spells. Five *makaras* (m's or 'monsters', i.e. magically charged things) are needed for the success of a *tantra* ritual: *madya* — wine, *mansa* — flesh, *matsya* — fish, *mudra* — mystic gestures and *maithuna* — sexual intercourse. These rituals are performed by the Shaktas, the worshippers of Shakti. The right-handed Shaktas worship Shakti in her gentle aspects as Uma and Gauri, while the left-handed Shaktas worship Shakti in her wild aspects as Durga and Kali, and promiscuous sex is part of their orgiastic rites. This cult is practised mainly in eastern India.

There is one branch of worshippers of Shiva and Kali, who keep their rituals secret. We know little about these rituals or their mysteries, which are laid down in the *tantras*. A *tantra* originally meant a loom, (connected with *tantu* 'thread'), then any structure, then a systematic textbook, finally a sorcery book of magic formulas. By pronouncing the right formula (*mantra*) in the correct manner, or by drawing the appropriate magical symbol (*yantra*), the magician might force the gods to bestow magical power on the worshipper and lead him to the highest bliss.

Among the many formulas of Tantric Buddhism, one is especially famous, the six syllables *Om mani padme hum*, which originally meant: 'Bliss, the jewel is inside the lotus.' Clearly, this formula belongs to the Shakta religion, where it can only have meant: 'the Linga is in the Yoni', indicating the climax of the mystic wedding.

These magic Shaktas or 'left-hand' Shaktas, as the Tantric Hindus were called, have had an unexpected influence on Buddhism, as exemplified by the formula cited above. During some of the rituals, Tantric weddings are celebrated, known as Shiva marriages. The details of these rites are little known.

The advocacy of fish in the diet of a follower of Shiva and Kali should not surprise us. In art, both Shiva and Kali are distinguished by a trident, which Kali used in her battles. The trident is a tool for fishermen. (See *Shiva*.)

Tantrism A curious system of esoteric rituals which has influenced both Hinduism and Buddhism in the Middle Ages. Its first doctrine is the belief in a coherent world order in which both macrocosmos and microcosmos have a place. All visible objects in the universe have issued from Brahma's potency. Rites of Sacral magic have been instituted to enable a man:

1. To acquire the highest insight.
2. To control transcendental powers.
3. To obtain *moksha*, salvation.

Tantrism is based on a series of texts, the *tantras* which contain details of:

1. *Jnana*, the cosmology which leads to salvation.
2. *Yoga* (q.v.).
3. *Kriya*, prescriptions for the correct execution of rituals.
4. *Charya*, instructions for festivities, customs and the Dharma.

It is believed by the Tantrists that their *tantras* have made the Vedic rituals unnecessary. This *tantra*, the collection of religious treatises teaching magical and mystical formulas for the worship of the deities and the attainment of esoteric power, promises to fulfil all wishes, avert danger and give salvation. These formulas, the *mantras*, must be memorized, after which the believer will feel healthy and happy. Each *mantra* contains refined magic energy since it is concentrated divine truth: the power of the word. In spite of the fact that the *diksha* is esoteric lore, women and even Shudras can be initiated. *Diksha* is the 'teaching', i.e. the whispering of the relevant *mantras* into the ears of the initiands, accompanied by symbolically branding the sect signs on the initiands' bodies. The *guru* promises salvation to his followers by means of his transcendental knowledge and his divine power.

There are 10 sacraments, *sanskaras*: conception, pregnancy, birth, name-giving, parting of the hair, seeing the sun for the first time, eating for the first time, being shaved, becoming a disciple and marriage. *Yantras*, diagrams with magic power, especially *mandalas*, magic circles, and *mudras*, ritual finger gestures, have great mystic significance.

Tapas 'Heat'. Austerities, self-mortification for long periods of time, by fasting and suppression of all one's desires. This acquisition of merit results in the accumulation of spiritual energy which the gods experience as heat, *tapas*, so that they, or one of them, will appear before the ascetic and grant him a boon. Even wicked demons may perform successful asceticism and accumulate so much *tapas* that the gods may have to give away their own kingdoms.

Tapati 'Heat', 'the Hot One', a daughter of the Sun-god.

Tara Tara is in Hinduism the wife of Brihaspati (Jupiter) or Soma. Her son is Budha (Mercury). She has been identified with Juno, but as goddess of the sea she is more closely related to Venus (Stella Maris), who is called Tara (star) in some languages.

There is a Hindu tale which relates that Soma the Moon-god, fell in love with the lotus-white Tara and carried her off to ravish her. This misdeed sparked off a war called Tarakamaya in which the gods sided with Brihaspati against Soma. Finally Brahma the creator stepped in and restored Tara to her lawful husband. When Budha was born Brahma commanded Tara to tell him who the father was and she confessed that it was Soma.

In Buddhism, the name Tara is derived from the word for 'to cross' (the sea), so, to help us cross safely from birth to death is the function of Tara. The worshippers pray to her specially as the Shakti ('spouse') of Avalokiteshvara. This is the White Tara, Shveta Tara, or Tara of the White Lotus (*Nymphaea lotus*, also the favourite flower of ancient Egypt), the goddess of daytime, depicted with a wheel on her chest, playing the lute. She is seen among the gods at Ellora as a great, very beautiful woman with children. At nightfall the lotus flower closes and so, shows the green outside of its sepals. This is the Green Tara, Tara Utpala, the goddess who helps us at night. She is shown with a rosary and a book, leading us across the dark Ocean of Existence, as the Saviouress, Tara-Dharani, soothing our sorrow. As Tara-Amba, Tara the mother, she enjoys great popularity. Captains at sea worshipped her and she was well known in Java. Since there is also a blue lotus (*Nelumbo*), so there is a Blue Tara, Nila Tara, who is regarded as the Shakti of Akshobhya, the second Dhyani Buddha, venerated especially in Nepal; he represents the virtue of Vijnana or 'consciousness', specially the faculty of hearing any sound.

Taraka A demoness who lived in a forest near the Ganges where she devoured all travellers. Rama and Lakshmana finally killed her.

Tathagata 'The One who walks exactly the right path'. The Buddha.

Temple The original Buddhists had no temples, only monasteries where the community, *sangha*, could stay, study and meditate. The *vihara*, the first such building, where Buddha preached, stood at Bodhigaya. Of a much later date are the actual temples, i.e. the buildings where images of the Buddha and his incarnations (see *Bodhisattva*) were placed, which are actually worshipped. (See also *Mandira*.)

Theravada This is the Pali form of Sthaviravada, the Lore of the Elders. According to its adherents this is the original purest form of Buddhism; it forms the major section of the Hinayana and differs fundamentally from the Mahayana (q.v.) form of Buddhism. It spread from western India by sea to Sri Lanka in the days of King Ashoka. It still flourishes there. It is also the dominant form of Buddhism in South-East Asia: Burma, Thailand, Cambodia, Laos and parts of Assam in India. In recent years Buddhism is reviving in India, after 900 years. The Theravada is based on the Pali Canon, i.e. the books composed in Pali, a form of the Magadhi language which Ashoka spoke. Whether Buddha himself spoke Pali or a language closer to Sanskrit is still a debated question. The Pali Canon was written down probably around 20 BC in the Tipitaka or Tripithaka, the 'Three Books (literally "baskets") of the Law', i.e. the Dharma, in Sri Lanka, from the extensive oral traditions which had been faithfully handed down by the generations of *bhikkhus* from Buddha's time 500 years before. These books contain all the known sermons and lessons of the Buddha, although it is not always certain whether a given sentence is part of the commentaries or the Buddha's own words. Almost the entire Pali Canon has been published in English: 136 volumes. The Theravada is a reasonable moral philosophy, making no appeal to dogmatic assumption; it is objective and logical. It is self-reliant, claiming assistance from neither God nor gods, saviours nor priests. It is the most tolerant and least militant creed on earth. It expresses compassion for all people and animals. It does not assume the existence of an immortal soul nor God. It is a religion without passion and without violence. Anyone can become a Buddha by overcoming emotion and illusion. Nothing stays the same, all things follow the Wheel of the Law (*dharma*) with four spokes: birth, growth, decay, death. Every living being suffers until it dies. Happiness is temporary and is marred by the sight of others suffering. Deliverance, *moksha*, is possible through *bodhi*, enlightenment, the insight that we are *anatta*, selfless.

Time For Christians and Muslims, time moves forward in a straight line from Creation till Doomsday, when time will end. For Hindu philosophers, time begins when Brahma emerges from his period of dormition in the bosom of the world ocean and begins to breathe out. All things take shape and this world is created. When Brahma breathes in, all material things disintegrate and their essences are reabsorbed by Brahma's spirit, so that none of the physical world is left. Time stops. When it pleases Brahma to awake again and breathe out, an entirely new world begins and with it, a new time. Only some great saints will remember their lives in previous worlds. For the Buddhists, time is both a friend and an enemy since time causes both the beginning and the end of suffering. In general though, time is an enemy because it accompanies the chain of rebirths into ever new lives of new pain and grief. Time itself is often regarded as the chain and the wheel (see *Chakra*) from which every person has to liberate himself by ceasing to look forward to the future or regretting the past. Those who have achieved *moksha*, liberation, are absolved from time. They are in a state of not-being (and not-not-being as well) where time has no more power over them. For other people time will go on until all souls have liberated themselves from it.

For the ordinary Hindu people in India, time is personified as Kala, an aspect of Shiva as the terrifying Bhairava, husband of the ferocious Kali. Holding a skull in his hand, with garlands of skulls round his neck, the snake of eternity on his shoulder, the crescent by which time is measured in his hair, he appears to a man *when his time is up*.

The Jain philosophers teach that time is a moving point on the circumference of a revolving wheel. The point of time moves up and down in eternal succession. Under the influence of an evil serpent it moves downward so that on earth a time of *avasarpini*, deterioration, begins. Under the influence of a good serpent, the time-point moves up, initiating a period of *utsarpini*, amelioration. The first period of history was the best; it was called Susama Susama 'Great Happiness'. People were very tall and healthy then. All mothers gave birth to twins who could look after themselves after four days. Seven weeks later the parents died without suffering old age. This kept the population stable. There were 10 trees on earth of the species *vrikshakalpa*, Wishtree, which grew not only fruits in abundance but every object people could possibly need. No one had to kill, no one even had to cook. People ate only once in four days. There was as yet no sin, no religion, no misery, no pain. At present, six epochs later, we live in the Age of Unhappiness called Dusama. Dusama will be followed by a yet worse period called Dusama Dusama (double misery), in which men follow only their base instincts without any virtue. Famine and plague will alternate with howling storms. Few people will be left, hiding in caves. Then, a new Utsarpini will begin. (See also *Creation*; *Kala*; *Kalpa*; *Samsara*; *Yuga*.)

Tirthamkara A pioneer, precursor, literally: one who makes a ford in the river. One of 23 ascetics who, according to the Jains, preceded Mahavira Vardhamana as promulgators of the true lore of Jainism. They taught that a man is like one drowning in a torrent who is carried away and will ultimately suffer death. The adherence to the principles and practices of Jainism will liberate the man who is dragged forth by the strong current of life, by creating a ford where he can regain his footing and walk out of the stream. The last

Tirthamkara, Parshva or Parsvanatha, probably lived c.750 BC.

Tortoise See *Kurma*; *Vishnu*.

Trayatimsa Indra's Heaven (Jaka) above the four kings. Here live the 33 gods of Hinduism; hence the name.

Trikuta Triple Peak, Ravana's hill fortress on Lanka Island before Rama came.

Tri-Lochana 'Having three eyes', i.e. Shiva. One day when Uma, Shiva's wife, playfully laid her hands on Shiva's eyes after he had been meditating with complete concentration for a long time, a third eye suddenly burst open like a flower in the middle of his forehead, surrounded by a circle of flames and emitting intense heat. With this third eye Shiva can kill at a distance for if he opens it, a ray of light beams onto whomever displeases him and that person is reduced to ashes in the blinking of an eye. It happened to Kama (q.v.), Shiva's own son.

Trimurti 'Triple Form'. Brahma, Shiva and Vishnu, sculpted as three heads on one body, but the body is often omitted by the sculptor. Brahma represents Rajoguna, the wish to create, which called the universe into being. Shiva's essence is the Tamoguna, the wish to cover all things under the darkness (*tamas*) of non-existence. Shiva also represents the fire of the funeral pyre which consumes the earthly bodies to ashes, as well as the divine wrath caused by the evil on earth which has to be destroyed. Finally, Vishnu represents the Satva-guna or the quality of goodness which preserves the earth. The Trimurti is called *guhya* 'secret' because it is difficult to understand for non-philosophers. It is also called Parama 'The Supreme Being' because the three gods, merged into one being are supreme, the creator and master of the universe. Finally the Trimurti is Sarvatma, 'The Total Soul', the unified spiritual force in the world. In general Christians can understand the doctrine which holds that, with reference to the divine, 'three-ness' does not exclude 'one-ness'. The texts indicate that the Trimurti was the result of an original division of the Creator by himself. All three gods are creators and all three are likewise destroyers. Thirdly they all work together to preserve this universe until its time has come to an end. Then it will fall to pieces due to its own decadence. Likewise the gods will work together when the time has come for a new world to arise. They agree without words and they work without action. The world grows out of their beings the way a pine-tree grows out of its seed, using the earth as food. Just as out of the earth sprout a million forms, so the three-one creator makes the world happen by simply willing it, and when its autumn has come it will disappear because the gods have ceased willing it to be. In Hindu thought, the form (*rupa*) is an illusion, a superficial way of thinking. The philosopher penetrates into the essence where neither numbers nor shapes matter. (See also *Dattatreya*.)

Tripada The god of fever, usually malaria, causing the body to suffer heat, cold and sweat.

Triratna The Three Jewels. In Buddhism, the three fountains of morality: Buddha, Sangha, Dharma, which together teach the devotee his duties.

Trishanku See *Satyavrata*.

Trishiras 'Three-headed'. (See *Trimurti*.)

Trishula or Trisula The trident. One of the objects with which Shiva is recognizable. Originally it is the symbol of fishermen for whom trident and net were the oldest utensils. Later the trident sprouts leaves in Indian sculpture, signifying Shiva as the god of the forest and its hunters. For the philosophers it represents the three major functions of the god: creation, preservation, destruction. It also signifies the three virtues or qualities (*guna*) of Shiva: *sattva*, truth, *rajas*, will-power and *tamas*, quietude, tranquillity.

Trisna, Trishna 'Thirst, desire'. Sister of Kama, daughter of Lakshmi. (See *Devi Shri*; *Tanha*.)

Trivikrama 'Taking Three Steps'. An epithet of Vishnu. (See *Vamana*.)

Tula Libra, a sign of the zodiac (q.v.).

Tulsi The flower basil *Ocimum sanctum* or *basilicum*. Tulasi or Tulsi is the feminine of Tulas or Tulasa, the name for the basil plant of the herb *ocimum*, of the *Labiatae* family. It is known as the 'royal herb' in European languages (Greek: *Okimon basilikon*) and is highly prized in Islamic countries (Arabic: *rihan*). This plant was well known in ancient Egypt but originates no doubt from tropical India. It is used for many purposes. In medicine the leaves are used as a tonic, antiseptic and digestive which also relieves nausea. Basil oil rubbed on the temples relieves headaches. It was used to ease childbirth and it is also said to be an aphrodisiac. The flowers keep away the flies with their scent and are made into garlands. This flower is identified with Lakshmi, and the plant with her husband Vishnu. Tulsi was the wife of Jalandhar, a demon born from the ocean. He obtained from Brahma the favour that he would be invincible as long as his wife Tulsi would be faithful to him. Knowing that Tulsi was the most faithful of all wives on earth, Jalandhar forgot his place and claimed from Indra the Ocean Jewels which Indra had taken from the treasures that were discovered when the ocean was churned by the gods (see *Vishnu*). Indra, knowing that Jalandhar was invincible, asked Shiva for help. Shiva took the form of a handsome young man and went to Tulsi, hoping to seduce her but was rejected. Vishnu, however, took the shape of Jalandhar and succeeded in misleading Tulsi who succumbed to his caresses. Jalandhar could now be defeated and so, Tulsi discovered that she had been deceived. She cursed Vishnu so he became the stone Salagrama (Ammonite or riverstone) and he cursed Tulsi, so she became the basil flower. It is probable that Jalandhar was an emanation of Vishnu, who himself rested in the ocean before creation. Tulsi, i.e. Lakshmi, is Vishnu's wife in all their incarnations and metamorphoses, since they are destined for each other.

Tulsi Das (Tulasi Dasa, 'servant of Lakshmi'), celebrated poet of the great epic of the Ramayana in late medieval Hindi. He lived 1541–1605. This beautiful poem is still recited by professional singers at religious gatherings.

Tushita One of the 24 heavens of Buddhism. Maitreya resides here.

Twashtar, Twashtri, Tvashtr, Tvashtri The Artisan-god, comparable to Hephaistos in Ancient Greece. With his great metal tool he forges the thunderbolts for Indra (see *Vajra*). He loves beauty and artistic workmanship. He even forms the man and wife who are destined for one another, whilst they are still in their mothers' wombs. He even created the water and the fire, Agni. He protects the performer of the sacrifice and gives him food and wealth. He had a son called Vishva-rupa, whom Indra killed, and a daughter called Sharanyu who married Vivasvat. He is identified with Vishvakarman and also with Prajapati.

U

Uma

Ugra A name for Rudra-Shiva.

Ugrasena King of Mathura who had a beautiful wife with whom a demon fell in love. The demon took the king's form and one night, when the king was away, the demon slipped into her bed. In due course she gave birth to the cruellest of all people, Kansa, who fought Ugrasena, threw him in prison and sat on his throne. Even a king should never be away, and women should always be wary. Ugrasena was finally released by Krishna after he had killed Kansa.

Ujjayani A city, the modern Ujjain. In antiquity it was King Vikramaditya's capital. It is one of the seven holy cities of India.

Uma 'The bright one'. Light. The goddess Devi, consort of Shiva, who performed austerity standing in water until the gods granted her a boon. Another name for Parvati, Durgaa, Sati, Gauri, Chamunda and Kali. When Sati, 'the Faithful One', Parvati, had burnt herself in the sacrificial fire for the sake of her husband's honour, she was reborn as Uma. She wanted to marry Shiva again, but he was meditating profoundly so she could not 'catch' his attention until she had practised asceticism for several centuries by standing in a river up to her middle. When this had no effect, she asked Kama the god of love to come and make her husband love her, but when he in turn tried to catch Shiva's attention, Shiva opened his third eye, the radiation from which burnt the body of Kama to ashes. (See also *Kama*.)

Upanishad One of about 150 highly philosophical works, some in prose, some in verse and some in both, composed between *c*.600 BC and *c*.200 BC. They mark the beginning of mysticism and Hindu philosophy. Some are called Aranyakas 'forest treatises', as the ascetics taught in the forest. They teach the essential identity of the Atman, the individual soul, with the Paramatman, the highest, universal, all-embracing world-soul, the positive nucleus of peace, light and understanding. The philosopher must recognize this essence in the nucleus of all beings, just as the future oak is already in the acorn. Brahma, God, is one and lives in the human heart, his fortress. This Atman remains a pure and sinless soul which reverts to Paramatman at death.

Upashruti A mysterious voice which some perceptive people can hear in the middle of the night announcing future disasters.

Upavasatha, Uporatha Confession by a Buddhist monk of any breach he has committed against the monastic rules, *pratimoksha*, of the order, in the monks' gathering.

Uruvela A town in Bihar. Near here, the Buddha received enlightenment.

Urvasi Born from *Uru*, the thigh. The ascetic Naranarayana was performing austerity until the gods, alarmed at seeing his power, sent a beautiful nymph from heaven to disturb his meditation. Upon seeing her, the sage, unperturbed, placed a flower on his thigh. Out came Urvasi, who was yet more beautiful than the heavenly nymph. Her father sent both to heaven where Urvasi created havoc, for all the gods wanted to marry her.

Usha Daughter of King Bana, who had a dream in which she saw a handsome prince. She asked the artist Chitralekha, a friend, if such a man existed. Chitralekha commenced to paint the portraits of all the gods and princes then living on earth. Usha chose Aniruddha, son of the Love-god Pradyumna. Chitralekha, who was a sorceress, transported Aniruddha by magic into the arms of Usha. King Bana discovered him and kept him prisoner, but Pradyumna and his father Krishna arrived to liberate him taking the two lovers with them to Dwaraka.

Ushas Dawn, the goddess Aurora, the ancient Saxon Easter (Osra in Germanic), daughter of heaven and sister of the sun. She is also a goddess of poetry, a smiling muse who befriends people by bringing light into the humblest hovel every morning. She is called Dyotana, the 'light-bearer', daughter of the Sky-god Dyaus who wakes people for another day of living.

Ushnisha The raised dome on top of the Buddha's head, as seen on all sculptures and paintings. It contains his superior knowledge and understanding. It also implies that he was predestined for enlightenment.

Utathya A sage who married Bhadra (Prosperity), daughter of the moon (Soma), a princess so famous for her beauty that the Sea-god Varuna coveted her and carried her off, promising her palaces on the seashore, rather than her husband's hermitage. However, when he would not surrender her at Utathya's request, the latter addressed a prayer to the River-goddess Sarasvati, begging her to withhold the water of all the rivers. She did, and so, the ocean dried up and Varuna had to give Bhadra back to her husband. Fresh river-water filled the ocean soon enough, but the River Sarasvati never came back and where she once flowed there is still a desert, the Tharr.

Uttanapad The position of a woman while giving birth with her legs spread wide, and so, the Goddess (Aditi) while creating the physical world, is pictured as crouching (rather than lying down).

V

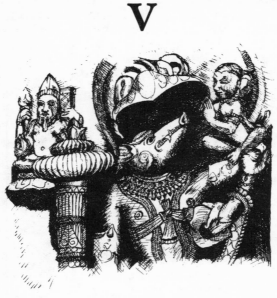

Vishnu as Varaha

Va 'Wind'. One of the names of the god Vayu (q.v.).

Vach, Vac 'Speech'. The goddess of the word, eloquence, and of language, human and divine. When she 'enters into' a man, he will speak words that will alarm even the gods. If she loves a man, she will make him whatever he wishes to be, a great priest, a powerful king or a rich merchant. She is the 'Queen of the Gods', and associated by some with Prajapati the Creator when he is pronouncing the terrifyingly powerful words which create the earth, the ocean, thunder and lightning. She is herself those words and thus it is her magic power which makes the world. Prajapati marries and embraces her while he is creating his universe. She brought forth the waters as the first creation, then all the other created beings. She is considered the daughter of Kama, the god of love and desire, for it is desire for a thing that makes a man eloquent, and it is love that makes a man a poet, a master of words. Vach is also identified by some with Sarasvati, goddess of the waters, queen of Brahma and goddess of wisdom. Vach is comparable to the Greek Logos (which however is a masculine concept), the biblical *Chochma* 'wisdom' (see Proverbs, 8) and the Egyptian Apis, the divine word.

Vagina Dentata Some peoples in India and the Middle East believe that this is caused by a demon snake who lives in a woman's belly and bites off whatever enters it.

Vahana A vehicle, animal, bird, fish or chariot. Most of the Indian gods may ride on something if they wish. Brahma has his Hansa, a swan; Vishnu has his Garuda, an eagle, later represented as a peacock; Shiva has his Nandi, a bull; Yama has a buffalo; Indra an elephant; Agni a ram; Shani a vulture; Durga a tiger; Vayu an antelope; Kamadeva has Makara, a sea-serpent, or a parrot.

Vahuka A charioteer. (See *Arjuna*; *Krishna*; *Nala*.)

Vairocana The fourth of the Buddhas of meditation or Dhyani-Buddhas. In Nepal, however, Vairocana ranks first and resides in the inner sanctum of the *stupa*. His colour is white. He presides over the autumn season, *hemanta*. He represents the philosophical concept of *rupa* 'form', which Plato defined as the limitation of space. Without form there is no individual existence. Autumn is the season of disintegration of forms which teaches us that we must distinguish form from essence.

Vairochana A name of Bali.

Vaishravana A name for Kubera, the master of Ravana.

Vaishya (Vaisya). The third caste or hereditary class of Indians, after the Brahmins and Kshatryas. Traditionally, the Vaisyas are farmers, traders, shopkeepers and craftsmen, so they consider themselves to be the backbone of society because they create the economy.

Vaivasvata Son of Vivasvat (Surya) the Sun and father of Ikshvaku, ancestor of the Sun-kings. Vaivasvata is the seventh incarnation of Manu, the Indian Noah, and he is himself referred to confusingly as Manu. He is devoted to the service of Vishnu. One day Manu who as a sage, *guru* and *rishi* was served by his disciples, found a fish in his washing water, which his assistants had brought in from the river as usual. The fish began to speak — of course the saints understand the languages of the animals — and said: 'Look after me with care and I will save your life.'

Manu asked: 'From what will you save me?'

The fish answered: 'A great flood will drown all living beings. I will save you from it.'

Manu placed the fish in a large water-jar and fed it from his own bread every day. Soon the fish grew too large for the jar so Manu put it in a pond formed by a weir, but soon the fish, fed faithfully by the kind sage, grew too large for its pond, so Manu opened the lock and let it swim towards the ocean. Before disappearing, the fish foretold Manu the exact date on which the flood would take place.

'Before that day,' it said. 'You must build a large ship, then pray to me and I will come to save you.'

When the day of the deluge approached, Manu built a seaworthy vessel and prayed to the fish who, he already knew, was an incarnation of Vishnu. Soon the fish appeared. It was huge! It opened its mouth and told Manu to fasten the ship's cable to its horn (perhaps a dorsal spine or nasal crest is meant). Manu did as he was told and the fish pulled the vessel out into the ocean. Soon the heavens opened and the waters flooded the earth until even the Himalayas were submerged. Finally the ocean level began to descend again until they saw a small island with a living tree on it. The fish told Manu to fasten his ship to the tree. As more and more of the earth became dry land, Manu saw no trace of life anywhere. Soon grass sprouted and trees grew up but Manu was alone. He prayed for company and one fine morning a woman appeared who said she was his daughter. Manu lived with her and they had many children. (It was quite normal for early man to live with his daughter.) Other sources mention that the fish called itself a manifestation of Brahma. Others again relate that right from the beginning of the voyage Manu was accompanied by his wife, and that after the deluge they had many children.

Vajra The thunderbolt of Indra, comparable to Jupiter's *fulgur* and Thor's *hamar* (hammer), the object which the Thunder-god throws (we have to think of a disk-like object rather than a hammer with a handle which it is held by and by which it is struck) at his enemies or at sinners who must be punished. The disk has a hole in the middle and rotates when launched; lightnings shoot from it all the time so that we may imagine it like a catherine-wheel spraying fireworks. It is represented in Indian sculpture with lightnings pointing outwards in four directions like stylized wings. Sometimes the disk is omitted, so there is only a cross of four tridents each one ending in three flame-blades.

Vajrapani One of the eight principal Bodhisattvas, Vajrapani is the spiritual son of the Dhyani-Buddha Akshobhya and his *shakti* Mamaki. His mantra is: *Om Vajrapani Hum*. He can be recognized by his *vajra* and his lotus flower, His colour is white, and in the mixed Hindu-Buddhist tradition he is equated with Indra.

Vak Speech, language; also Vach. The origin of speech (who is a goddess) is sung in the tenth book of the Rig-veda, in hymn 71. Here are some quotes from this philosophical hymn. 'When they (the first poets and seers, see *Kavi*) set speech in motion, giving names (to all things), their most pure and perfectly guarded secret was revealed through love. When the wise ones had fashioned speech with their thought, sifting it as grain is sifted, (at once) friends could recognize their friendship ... The path of speech began inside the sages ... who apportioned it to the people ... the singers praised it.'

Vaka (1) A crane, considered a holy bird by some Buddhists. The cranes are migrating waders.

(2) A demon who lived near a city from which he demanded enormous portions of food which he devoured together with the servants who brought it. Finally, the great hero Bhima was invited to fight the demon. A terrible battle ensued in which both champions tore out trees to hit each other with. Finally Bhima got hold of the demon's feet and tore the monster asunder.

Valmiki One of the greatest poets of India, who wrote the Sanskrit (as opposed to the Hindi) Ramayana, after having had a vision of this great poem in heaven. He is said to have taught the princes Kusa and Lava, sons of Sita, and to have lived in Banda in Bundelkand. His great epic has had a lasting influence on the many literatures of South-East Asia, especially Thai, Malay and Javanese. Valmiki lived in the second century BC.

Vamana Vishnu's fifth *avatara* or descent to earth, in which he appeared, at the gods' request, in the shape of a dwarf, Vamana, begging King Bali for 'a little land, as much as I can cover in three steps'. The king agreed, whereupon Vishnu resumed his true form of omnipresent god, stepped over the earth in his first stride, across the firmament in his second but then stopped, leaving King Bali one kingdom in the lower world, Patala.

Vamsa, Vansa A race, tribe, clan or dynasty.

Vana-Prastha 'Sojourn in the forest'. The third stage in the life of a Brahmin. When he is past 40 a Brahmin will hand over all his work to his eldest son and withdraw to the forest where he will study with very old and learned Brahmin scholars.

Var Enclosed garden, refuge. In Parsi lore, the kingdom of Yima.

Vara Choice, wish, boon which a god may grant to a mortal.

Varaha The third *avatara* of Vishnu in which the god appeared on earth as a wild boar, symbolic for the Creator who raised the earth up from the sea like a hog pushing up the mud. The demon Hiranyaksha 'gold-eye' had pushed the earth down into the sea.

Varanasi Also called Benares or Kashi, the holy city of India where the faithful go to bathe in the river Ganges to be purified.

Vardhamana Founder of Jainism. (See *Mahavira*.)

Varna Caste, literally 'colour', although it cannot be concluded that originally caste was a distinction between the black southerners and the white northerners. The four main castes are as follows: Brahmin, Kshatriya, Vaishya and Shudra or caste-less. In modern India there are numerous castes, which are by no means divided into inferior versus superior, but are religious groups claiming equality one to the other. These groups are divided not only by ethnic distinction, such as the 'tribes', nor only by profession such as the farmers or merchants, but by religion first and foremost, so that the Sikhs, Sunnis, Khojas, Vaishnavas, Shaivas, Parsis and all the separate Christian groups as well, form as many castes, whether they want to or not. Every caste is endogamous, since no father wants his daughter to marry a man of another religion or social class. Thus there is not really any change possible in the caste system.

Varsha Climate, 'clime', region, continent. In Indian cosmology, India, Bharat (or in full: Bharata-varsha) is, of course, the centre of the universe.

Varuna Son of Aditi 'infinity'. One of the great gods of the Vedic period, whose name (equated with the Greek Ouranus, Latin Uranus) dates back to Indo-European times. He is the god of the Ocean, and is thus compared to the Greek Okeanos and identified with Poseidon, the great Lord of the surface of sea and land. He is the element water, *vari*. In the oldest Vedic times, Varuna was king of the universe and of the starry sky, the bringer of rain, until Indra, the Thunder-god, took that boon-giving function away from him. Varuna dug the river-beds and the oceans. Out of the ocean arose Brahma, ready to create the worlds. 'Varuna fixed the stars in the night-sky and makes them vanish at dawn. Varuna makes the moon walk in brightness, the blowing winds are his cool breath travelling far from the sea, he knows the flight of birds, the path of ships at sea, he knows the secret things that have been and shall be, he knows truth and untruth'.

Later, like Poseidon's, Varuna's territory and function was restricted to the oceans, the western ocean from where the rains are blown to India, and the rivers. Varuna rides on the Makara, an aquatic monster often sculptured on buildings with its large mouth gaping at the observer. It was originally a fish, later a sea-serpent or a crocodile, it may well have been a dolphin, like Poseidon's 'horses'. Varuna rules the west, the quarter from whence the Aryans originally entered India. Varuna was described as a Creator god in the oldest hymns. Varuna possesses the secrets of the creation which he taught his son, the sage Vasishtha born from Urvasi's soul. It was Varuna who assigned to every planet its path and taught the birds to fly and the winds to blow. He knows the secrets of health, possessing a hundred thousand medicines, and he can foresee the destinies of all men and women. Varuna is also a moral god who punishes the evil-doers and liars, but he may also forgive sinners in his wisdom and graciousness. Varuna is the keeper of heaven and earth who ties the guilty in his noose, called Nagapasa, originally a symbol of the river fishermen. Varuna's own capital (since all the gods are kings ruling their own kingdoms) is Sukha, 'happiness', on Pushpa-giri, 'flower-mountain'. His praise-names are Jalapati 'Lord of the Waters' and Yadahpati 'Lord of the Living Beings in the Water'.

Varunani, Varuni   Queen of Varuna and goddess of wine. She rose up from the ocean when the gods were churning it.

Vasanta   Spring; the deity presiding over the season of flowers.

Vasanta-Bandhu   'Friend of Spring', the god of love. (See *Kama*.)

Vasantaduta   'Herald of Spring', the Indian cuckoo.

Vasava   A name of Indra while he is Vritra who rules the earth.

Vashat   Ceremonial exclamation by the Hotri, the sacrificer, at the end of the Yajya, whereupon the oblation is cast into the fire by the Adhvaryu, another indispensable officiant at the Brahmanic sacrifice, who in turn exclaims '*kri*', symbolizing the burning.

Vashita   In Buddhism, the goddess of discipline and self-control, who helps the disciple on his way to self-liberation.

Vasistha   'Most wealthy'. A sage, one of the seven Rishis and one of the 10 Prajapatis, owner of Nandini the cow that fulfils all wishes, hence his unlimited wealth. Son of Varuna, father of a hundred sons, the eldest of which was Shaktar. When a Rakshasa had devoured all his sons, Vasistha endeavoured to commit suicide. He jumped from a high mountain but the rocks he fell on suddenly became soft like cotton wool. He walked into a burning forest but the fire would not even scorch him. He jumped from a ship in the middle of the ocean, but it washed him safely ashore. He tied his hands and jumped into a river, but it untied his ropes and led him safely to its bank. This river, the Byas in the Panjab, is still called 'the Untier'.

One day King Visvamitra attempted to steal Nandini, but in his defence Vasistha simply blew at the hundred sons of Visvamitra who accompanied their father. Vasistha's breath was so hot that all the young men were burnt to ashes. Visvamitra changed Vasistha into a crane, whereupon the latter reciprocated and the two great magicians fought a fierce war causing the death of numerous creatures. Vasistha married Urja, a daughter of Daksha, who bore him seven sons.

Vasu   'Wealth'. One of eight demigods, servants of Indra. The others are: Apa, water; Anala, fire; Anila, wind; Dhara, earth; Dhruva, the pole-star; Prabhasa, dawn; Pratyusha, light; Soma, moon.

Vasudeva   Brother to Kunti, scion of Yadu, father of Krishna who is himself also called Vasudeva 'God of Wealth'.

Vasuki   King of the Nagas or serpents who live in Patala. He was used as a rope for the churning of the Ocean by the gods. See *Shesha*.

Vata (1) Fig-tree, the sacred tree of India. Also *anjira*, or *vatavriksha*, the 'Banian' tree, a well known symbol of India. Even today some fig-trees are still worshipped by women wanting babies.

(2) The gale, a strong wind, riding through the sky on a red chariot. (See *Vayu*.)

Vatsalya Love, affection, as expressed by the myths of Krishna.

Vattagamani King of Sri Lanka, 89–77 BC. He ordered the great canon of the Theravada school of Buddhism to be committed to writing.

Vayu Vayu is the god of the winds, like the Greek Aiolos. He is depicted as riding through the sky in a chariot drawn by deer. Sometimes he functions as a charioteer of Indra the Storm-god, in a golden chariot as high as the sky, drawn by a thousand red horses. Vayu is also the god of the soft breeze and even of the breath, that which gives life to all people and animals. Indeed he is Breath himself and as such the God of Life, since the first thing every child needs when it is born is Breath. Vayu is a Vedic deity which means that he belongs to the oldest-known gods of India. He is the father of the Monkey-god Hanuman and of the Pandava prince Bhima. Vayu's mount is a deer; he is seen with a wheel in his hand as a symbol of speed. He has a goad to urge the horses on. He rules the North-West, the region from which the cool mountain wind blows down to India. Vayu is also a god of violent character, restlessly travelling all over the earth. One day when he felt offended by Indra, he broke off the top of Mount Meru and hurled it into the ocean; it is now known as Sri Lanka.

Veda Knowledge. The word comes from the same source as the Icelandic *Edda*. Like the Edda, the Veda is a collection of poems containing the mythology of the people who used to recite them. The Veda is a collection of hymns composed in pre-classical Sanskrit during the second millennium BC. The hymns are divided into four books: Rig-Veda, Yajur-Veda, Sama-Veda and Atharva-Veda, the latter being of a later date, *c*.1000 BC. The Rig-Veda is the original Veda, as it contains the largest number by far of original hymns (1,018). Each original hymn is a *mantra* (q.v.), a ceremonial recitation, to which in later centuries a Brahmana was added, a prose-work, containing commentaries and, still later, reflections on the Veda hymns. The Vedic hymns created the first stage of Hindu mythology as we know it. They were addressed to the Vedic gods: Agni — fire, Indra — thunder, Surya — sun, Vayu — wind, Aditi — firmament, Varuna — rain and sea, Ushas — dawn, Prithivi — earth, the Ashvins (Castor and Pollux), Dyaus-piter — father of light. The feared gods were Yama — death, Vritra —

drought, Rudra — storm and the Maruts — whirlwinds. In later centuries the pantheon changed as some gods were no longer heard of whereas others were absorbed by new gods, e.g. Rudra = Shiva.

Vedanta This is a philosophical school whose teaching is summarized in a famous treatise, the first Brahmasutra. It became popular after the Vedic period, but the Vedic rituals are accepted by the Vedantists. It taught that man must distrust much of what he knows, and replace it by real knowledge. The Vedantists are indifferent to this world so they withdraw from it, preferring non-activity. They teach a form of monism: all matter is an appearance of the spirit, i.e. of Brahma, the Universal Soul; our sensual impressions are all *maya*, illusion. The distinction between Brahma and the worm is only one of gradation. People who believe in the physical reality live in a dream. Brahma, who is identical with Vishnu and Shiva, is the ultimate reality out of which all things issue forth. Realizing this brings us back to our source.

Vedavati 'Possessing knowledge' (i.e. foreknowledge). Daughter of Kusha-dhvaja, a son of Brihaspati. She was a lady of great beauty but very devout. She lived the life of an ascetic in the forest. One day, as Ravana the evil demon was flying over the forest, he saw Vedavati and fell in love with her. He came down and asked for her hand in marriage. Vedavati told him that gods and Gandharvas had already wooed her, but she would marry only Vishnu; thus her father had told her. So she had begun practising austerities hoping thereby to win Vishnu's favour. Ravana boasted that he was superior to Vishnu, he even boldly touched her hair with his fingertips; this rightly incensed the lady as it was a grave insult.

'Now I shall have to burn this hair that vile fingers have touched,' she complained. 'I will die but I will be reborn as the woman for whose sake you will be destroyed!'

She made a huge fire and, entering it, burnt to ashes while flowers fell from heaven all around her. She was reborn as Sita, Rama's wife. (See also *Rama*.)

Vedavyasa Satyavati was crossing the Yamuna when, on an island in the river she met the priest Parashara, who made her pregnant. She gave birth to her son, Vedavyasa, on that island. Satyavati later married King Santanu, or Shantanu, by whom she had two sons who both died childless. Satyavati then persuaded her own *kanina* (illegitimate son) to marry both widows and beget sons with them, which he did. One woman's son was Dhritarashtra and the other one's was Pandu. Vedavyasa was the poet or compiler of the Vedas. (See *Vyasa*.)

Vema Goddess of sexual love. See *Parvati*; *Shakti*; *Yoni*; *Tantra*.

Vena (1) A king who wanted to abolish the sacrifical rites, so the Brahmin priests assassinated him ritually with blades of holy grass.

After that they caused Agni to create a new king from his arm, called Prithu.

(2) 'Longing', the sun-bird that wins the *soma*.

Vendidad Collection of prose texts in Persian written before about AD 225. They contain explanations of the laws of purity for the Parsis. Purity of mind and body combats the forces of evil.

Venus (1) Goddess. (See *Rati.*)
(2) Planet. (See *Shukra.*)

Vetala A terrible spirit which creeps into dead bodies and makes them behave as if they were alive, committing atrocious crimes, like zombies.

Vibishana 'Terrifying'. A demon, younger brother to Ravana. He was by nature of good character and refused to obey Ravana who wanted him to behave like a Rakshasa. Ravana exiled him, so Vibhishana visited Shiva to seek his advice. Shiva suggested that he join Rama, which he did. Rama welcomed him and made him viceroy of Lanka.

Vidyadhara A race of demigods who inhabit the regions between earth and sky where they have their own kingdoms. They are described as *kamarupin*; i.e. they can assume any form they wish. They often take on human shapes and human spouses.

Vidyadhari (Bijadari, Wijadari) One of a race of nymphs who live in woods, ponds and on riverbanks where they charm travellers.

Vihara Originally a field for sport. Now a Buddhist monastery.

Vijaya 'The victorious'. An epithet of Devi–Uma–Kali (q.v.).

Vikramaditya (1) 'Shining Hero', an adventurer-king, famous for his knowledge, wisdom and wit. Son of Gardabhila, King of Ujayyini. He lived around 2,000 years ago and patronized at his court the *navaratna* or nine precious scholars of learning and literature. Many sagas are told about his conquest of countries by force of arms, and of princesses by his ability to answer all questions and solve all riddles.

(2) **(or Vikrama)** A famous king of Ujjain who ruled in about AD300, and who knew the answers to all the questions. In a neighbouring country there lived a queen of famed beauty called the Pomegranate Princess. She slept every night in a pomegranate which grew on a tree with two others, in which her two ladies-in-waiting slept. Every morning the tree bent the three branches on which the three pomegranates hung, to the ground, opened the fruits and the princess with her two maids jumped out to begin the day.

One night King Vikrama had a dream in which his father told him to go to the priest in the temple and study there. The king followed his father's spirit's advice and learned everything that could be learned from the priest, who was Vishnu in disguise. At the end of the course Vishnu granted the king a boon and Vikrama asked for the power to change bodies. So, Vishnu taught him the secret formula for transporting his soul into any dead body. Unfortunately all this was overheard by the carpenter's son who was spying on the king at night. Now the king took the shape of a night owl, and flew to the palace of the Pomegranate Princess, which was magically impenetrable to normal human beings. The owl-king picked the three pomegranates and flew back with them to his palace, where, the next morning when the princess appeared from the fruit, he married her. After living with her very happily for six months, he had to go into exile for half a year owing to a favour which Kali had granted him. So, he took the body of a parrot and flew away. The carpenter's son, who was spying again, saw this, and quickly moved into the king's body. However, the king's wise minister perceived that he could not be the true king. He ordered the cook to prepare workmen's food for the king, which the carpenter's son in the body of the king gobbled up. The king would not have touched such coarse food. So, Bhatti, the prime minister knew that he was an imposter and locked him up in gaol. After many adventures the king, still disguised as a parrot, lived in a temple where he made the statue of the god speak. There, Bhatti recognized him while he was in search of his king, whose time had come to reascend the throne, six months having elapsed. He took the parrot to Ujjain, where he opened the prison and said to the carpenter's son: 'You and the king's soul will have to decide in a fight who is the true king. His ram and your ram will fight and whoever's ram wins will be king.'

The carpenter's son in the king's body agreed and went to fetch his ram. Of course the ram was underfed since its master had been in prison, so it was weak, and after a long fight the true king's ram killed it. In order to continue the contest, the carpenter's son relinquished the king's body and entered his dead ram's body. That was the moment the king's soul had been waiting for. He left the parrot's body and entered his own, drew his sword and killed the ram again. Its body was burned so that the carpenter's son could not get back into it. His own body, alas, had rotted in those six months while he was in the king's body.

Vimalanatha 'Master of Insight', the thirteenth Tirthamkara of the Jain hierarchy of Jina's precursors. Once upon a time a man went to the temple with his wife. In that temple there lived a demoness who fell in love with the man and took the shape of his wife. Thus the man could no longer know who his real wife was. Vimalanatha solved the problem by telling the two women to stand at a distance of four steps from their husband on either side of him.

Then he told them to stretch out their arms and touch the man's shoulder. The human wife could not reach him but the demoness could extend her arms by magic and so touched him.

Vina A famous Indian stringed instrument carried by Sarasvati.

Vinata Wife of Kasyapa, daughter of Daksha, mother of Garuda.

Vinaya-Pitaka 'The Book of Sermons', the rules of the Buddhist order, as recited by a monk at Rajagriha, the basis of all Buddhists' lives.

Virabhadra Virabhadra is an emanation of Shiva. Shiva's father-in-law was Daksha Prajapati, second only to Brahma in seniority among the gods. He was very critical of his son-in-law Shiva, all the more so since his daughter Uma-Sati defended her husband Shiva, as a faithful wife should. One day in the Hall of the Gods, when Daksha entered he paid his respects to Brahma, after which all the other gods paid their respects to him, except Shiva, who still felt offended by Daksha vilifying him in the presence of his wife. Daksha was so incensed that he organized a hecatomb, a grand ceremony of sacrifices for all the gods except Shiva. Out of his wrath upon seeing this insult, Shiva created Virabhadra, the Monster of Destruction, with a thousand arms, a thousand feet, a thousand eyes, flaming brightly like the fire of Armageddon, that will consume all living things on Doomsday. It had enormous tusks sticking out of its sides and it was so big that it crushed the Moon-god with one of its toes. It plucked out the eyes of Surya the Sun-god, it cut off the hands of the Fire-god Agni, it chased away Garuda, Vishnu's bird-mount, and it even made Indra's arm stiff. Daksha declared himself vanquished and ready to apologize. Shiva forgave him.

Viradha One of the most terrifying Rakshasas, son of Kala and Shatahrada. He was invulnerable, as tall as a mountain, clad in tigerskins, his voice resounding over the hills like thunder. He had enormous hollow eyes and a cavernous mouth dripping blood as he was always devouring people. He carried an iron pike with dead animals and people impaled on it. Rama, Sita and Lakshmana met him in the forest one day. Viradha abused them, then picked up Sita and threw the brothers over his shoulders. The two brothers rained arrows on him but could not kill him. With their maces they broke his arms and threw him to the ground but they still could not kill him, so they dug a deep pit and buried him alive. Out of the earth there appeared a handsome young man, a Gandharva named Tumburu (= Viradha) who thanked the two brothers for liberating him from the curse which Kubera had imposed on him.

Viraj The Creator, Brahma, divided his own body into two parts, one male and one female. He married this goddess who was his sister because she was of the same flesh and blood and married his daughter, also, because she was born from him. Their first son was Manu-Purusha, the first man, the first creature. Viraj was the male aspect of Brahma, the female aspect was called Shata-rupa, later identified with Sarasvatí.

Virata A city now called Bairat, 168 kilometres south of Delhi. The King of Virata employed the Pandavas after they spent 12 years in the forest and when they had beaten off an attack by the Kauravas on Virata, he joined them in their war to destroy the Kauravas.

Virochana A demon, son of Prahlada, father of Bali.

Visha Poison. When the gods were churning the ocean, a wave of poison came suddenly to the surface which had to be taken out and put in a safe place so that it would not destroy creation. Shiva agreed to keep it in his throat. He must not swallow it for it could destroy even the great Shiva. He was henceforth called Nila-kantha 'blue-throat'. The peacock *mayura* is dedicated to him because it has the same colour in its feathers.

Vishnu In origin probably a Sun-god, Vishnu is praised in the oldest texts as the one who strides through the universe in three giant's steps. This can be interpreted as the three phases of the sun: at sunrise, at noon and at sunset. Furthermore, Vishnu's incarnations seem to be an indication that he is a Sun-god, reborn each morning in order to sustain the cosmos. Like Apollo the Greek Sun-god Vishnu rises from the sea where he sleeps during Brahma's night, i.e. during a period of cosmic history when there is no creation, because, like day and night, creation and non-creation are cyclical. Creation of new worlds follows the twilight of the gods when Vishnu and Brahma enter in a state of meditative suspension. The Indian gods do not create the worlds in the way Jehova and Allah do. Hindu philosophy (no less Platonic than Greek philosophy) regards creation as a formation of the worlds and their inhabitants out of the gods' own bodies, because the gods' bodies, *that* is the substance of the world as it appears to us. This world is illusion, Maya (q.v.) as the philosophers teach, and this Maya is a special aspect of Vishnu himself. According to this philosophy, the gods create illusions which we see as matter, but in reality even the gods themselves are illusions, a beautiful world of light playing with sound which we take for real. The true reality is the concentrated unity of divine will unencumbered by matter or other sensory impressions, which are no more than the playing of wind and sunshine on the waves and rushes along the river. Here, the Hindu philosophers anticipated centuries ago Kant's concept of the real thing which we can never know. Once, Vishnu showed himself to Arjuna in his 'real' form, as hundreds of bodies, heads and arms — a terrifying sight. (See under *Bhagavadgita.*) This is one of the reasons for the confusing variety of names for what appears to be the same deity. Precisely that is the essence of Hinduism: the creation of a beautiful mythology to describe the undescribable. In the *avataras* or appearances (the term 'incarnation' has to be used with circumspection. It is not a translation of *avatara*, which literally means 'descent'), Vishnu proves this point by unexpectedly assuming a certain shape, then changing it, demonstrating his divine nature to those present.

For the ten *avataras*, see under *Matsya* (fish), *Kurma* (tortoise), *Varaha* (hog), *Nara-simha* (man-lion), *Vamana* (dwarf), *Parashu-Rama*, *Rama-chandra*, *Krishna*, *Buddha*, *Kalki*, and see below.

Vishnu's 'normal' appearance, i.e. the position in which he is most frequently depicted in Hindu art, is reclining on Shesha, the hooded sea-serpent with a thousand cobra heads, a lotus flower rising up from his navel which is partly submerged by the world-ocean. On the lotus Brahma is seated, both gods are absorbed in profound meditation. If the reader is wondering whether from this description one might conclude that Vishnu created Brahma, whereas one is usually led to believe that Brahma created everything including the gods, the answer is that there is no contradiction since Vishnu and Brahma are only different names for the one divine essence, *Sat* 'that which is', the opposite of Maya.

With respect to what distinguishes Vishnu from the other gods, it is his *sattvaguna*, his virtuous character, i.e. the kindness and mercy for human beings. This quality is sometimes described as *narayana* 'moving the waters', i.e., granting rain on the desert of human needs.

As preserver, as keeper of life, Vishnu is one of the three great gods placed together in the Trimurti (q.v.). Whenever humanity is threatened by a powerful enemy such as Ravana or Kansa or Hiranya-Kashipu, Vishnu is entreated by the other gods to descend upon earth and put things right by slaying the evil demon and by so doing, delivering humanity of a scourge. In this aspect of divinity Vishnu has been compared to Jesus Christ, who was also born in human form to 'take on' evil. Yet one must be careful not to compare the dogma of one religion to the mythology of another. Vishnu should rather be compared to Hermes the Greek god, who is constantly travelling from the gods' world to the human world with messages, and intending to help human beings in distress.

One of the endearing characteristics of Vishnu's myths is that whenever he descends to earth as a human baby, his wife Lakshmi will also arrive on earth in human form, to grow up, to meet him, destined to be his wife on earth as well as in heaven. Thus the immortality of marital love is repeatedly reaffirmed in India, leading to the ideal of married life as the perfect and divine status of two human beings together. More than that, a man and his wife once married, will forever stay together, since there is no reversal of divine preordination.

Thus, when Vishnu is born as Rama, Lakshmi will soon be born as Sita, to become his wife; when Vishnu is born as Krishna, Lakshmi is born as Rukmini, with the same purpose. It may objected that Krishna made love to the Gopis, including Radha and was that not polygamy? One must not forget that gods, even in human shape, are not men, and that what men do 'at the same time', a god can do in a period of centuries, for the gods are endlessly immortal. In space and time the non-humanness of the gods becomes acutely obvious, as when Vishnu and Lakshmi are comfortably seated on a lotus flower which is as large as the surface of the earth and of heaven as well. They may also sit together on Garuda's neck, flying to Vaikuntha, Vishnu's own heaven where they enjoy love and mutual respect.

In Hindu art, Vishnu is recognizable by his four hands, holding his Shankha or conch; his Sudarshana, a disc; his Kaumodaki, a mace and his Padma or lotus. He also owns a bow, a sword called Nandaka and a famous jewel called Kaustubha.

Vishnu — Avataras An *avatara* is not the same as an incarnation. The word *avatara* means 'descending', so the god descends to earth and assumes a visible form since earth is a place where only our sensory impressions give us information. The souls in Heaven can communicate directly by spiritual vibrations. A god may choose any visible form or just an audible form such as thunder or a speaking voice. However, that is just a manifestation. An *avatara* walks about on earth and works for the good of humanity by defeating the forces of evil and helping the good. An incarnation occurs when the spirit of a god, or his essence, actually enters a woman's womb, after which the woman gestates as if she had been fertilized by a man. Subsequently the god is born as a baby, but of course he has only the appearance of a baby and does not have a baby's mind. The baby thinks and speaks like an adult and performs miracles, like Hercules strangling two snakes in his cradle. In India it is Krishna who performs miracles while still a toddler. Hindu theologians maintain that Krishna is different from other manifestations of Vishnu because Krishna is Vishnu, whereas Rama was only an *avatara*. (See under *Rama* and *Dasharatha*.) We do not here have to digress on the question of whether the *avataras* of Vishnu are a method for Hindu theologians to identify a number of primal Indian deities with the Aryan gods and to absorb 'native' Indian deities into the Hindu pantheon.

1. In any case the Fish, Matsya, Vishnu's first *avatara*, seems to link the Sun-god to the Sea-god. The myth relates that Vaivasvata, the seventh Manu, and himself a Sun-figure, was in danger of being submerged in the Flood, the Great Deluge. When Manu asked for a bowl of water for his religious ablution, he found a tiny fish in it which spoke to him: 'I will save you from the flood which is imminent if you will look after me.'

The fish began to grow to such enormous size that Manu thought it could only be happy in the Ocean, so he carried it there. Having regained its natural element, the fish began to instruct Manu to build a ship. When the deluge began the ship came afloat and Manu boarded it. Soon the fish emerged. It had grown a horn to which it said Manu should fasten his ship. The fish then towed the ark to safety. On it were the seeds of all the plants which humanity would need after the flood. Manu recognized the fish as an incarnation of Vishnu, perhaps when Matsya offered him Shesha as the rope with which he could fasten the ship to the horn.

Another myth relates that the demon Hayagriva stole the Veda and Vishnu assumed the shape of the fish in order to keep a watch during the period when there was no earthly life. In Indian cosmology a deluge, like every other cosmic event, is cyclical. The beginning and the end of the world will take place at least four times and a flood is one way of ending it. Only Vishnu was watchful, Brahma and Shiva were both deep in thought. When Brahma emerged and the world began again, Vishnu slew Hayagriva and returned the Veda to Brahma. The Veda is such a sacred text that only gods and priests may hear it; it is not for profane ears. Yet, how the text could be stolen if it was not written in a book is not clear. Can words be stolen from a god's mind?

2. The tortoise Kurma. Perhaps it was a turtle because it lives in the sea, but it is always translated as 'tortoise'. Kurma could also mean 'deed, act', i.e. the act of creation. Vishnu assumed the shape of a tortoise in the Satyayuga, the first cosmic epoch, in order to recover certain treasures which had been lost in the deluge. In this way the best things of previous worlds can be preserved in the present period of history. In those days the Ocean was made of milk. Vishnu as the tortoise placed himself at the bottom; the gods placed a mountain, Mandara, on his back, twisted the long snake Vasuki round it, divided themselves into two teams and started churning. This myth demonstrates how butter was held in such high esteem by the ancient Indians, that they regarded making it as a supreme act of creation. The first thing of value that emerged from the sea of milk was *amrita*, ambrosia, i.e. the beverage of immortality which is reserved for the gods. It is in the hands of Dhanwantari the gods' doctor who emerged also from the sea of milk. Indeed a good doctor is the second most precious thing in life, after immortality. Third, there arose Lakshmi, goddess of beauty and good fortune who was to become Vishnu's wife for eternity. Fourth was Sura, goddess of wine, indeed a priceless substance. Fifth was Chandra the Moon. Sixth was the nymph Rambha, the most beautiful Apsaras. Seventh was the first and finest horse. Eighth was Kaustubha, Vishnu's breast-jewel, i.e. a sort of brooch; in India it is worn by men as an amulet which originally had the magic powers of healing and protecting its wearer. Ninth was the miraculous tree, Parijata, which grows up in heaven. Tenth was the cow Surabhi which could feed multitudes with her milk. Eleventh was Airavata the splendid elephant, Indra's mount. Twelfth was Shankha, a large shell. The

warrior who could blow it during a battle was certain of victory, rather like the horns of Jericho. Thirteenth was Dhanus, a bow that never missed, i.e. an arrow shot from it would always strike its target and kill it. The fourteenth object to arise from the ocean, the last one, was Visha, a word that means 'poison' but also 'power' and 'medicine'. Thus the fourteen treasures which rose to the surface of the Ocean of milk, when the gods churned it, were all very special things; some of them caused wars between the gods and the demons who coveted their possessions; others saved the lives of whole nations in times of crisis.

3. Varaha, the wild boar. The hog or bush pig is an earth symbol or rather an earth deity. Vishnu as the creator makes the land mass of the Indian continent by shoving mud out of the sea, much as a pig might do. The reason for this work having to be done was that the evil demon Hiranyaksha had dragged the earth down under the water. Vishnu first had to slay the demon after a battle lasting a thousand years. Thus Vishnu watches constantly over the safety of the earth so that we earthlings may live in peace. The question of whether Vishnu has been identified with the earth-god of a more primitive aboriginal people is resolved by the Indian philosophers in the sense that all the gods are emanations of manifestations of the one Divine Principle. (See *Bhu*.)

4. Vishnu's fourth manifestation, as Narasimha, was the last one to take place in the Satya-yuga or first epoch of world history (see *Yuga*). Thus the series of Vishnu's *avataras* goes right through the history of humanity, demonstrating the god's constant care for humanity. A Daitya, a demon-tyrant called Hiranya-Kashipu, who was invulnerable, oppressed the world with terror and wickedness. He could not be wounded by men, animals or even gods. One day, blinded by his own hubris, Hiranya-Kashipu hit a stone pillar in his own palace, wondering mockingly whether the omnipresent Vishnu was inside the stone. He was. Vishnu suddenly emerged from the stone in the shape of Narasimha, man-lion, neither man nor animal and tore the proud demon-king to pieces.

5. Vamana, the dwarf. Another Daitya or ruler of the beings of the lower world, called Bali, had become ruler of the three worlds so that he had more power than the gods. They begged Vishnu to terminate this tyranny. Vishnu agreed to 'descend' to earth, where he was born as Vamana, the stunted child of Kasyapa and Aditi. When he had become of age, Vamana approached King Bali, pretending to be a peasant in need of land. He begged the king to give him as much land as he could cover in three steps. The king agreed and Vamana chose his site. There he suddenly grew to cosmic size. His first step covered the entire earth. His second step took him to the outer edge of the heavens and his third step would easily have reached to the bottom of the worlds below the earth. However, since Bali was not really a vicious king, Vishnu left him the kingdom of Patala (q.v.).

6. Parashu-Rama. 'Rama with the axe'. Vishnu was born as a Brahmin who was at the same time a warrior. In those days, the Epoch of Treta, the Kshatriya caste of professional soldiers had become dominant in the world. The gods decided that it would be better for the world if the priests dominated it. Neither the merchants (Vaishya) nor the military (Kshatriya) but the scholars should rule this world to make it just and peaceful. Vishnu carried out the gods' decree.

7. Rama or Rama-Chandra 'Moon-Rama' or 'Gentle Rama', in contrast to the warlike Parashu-Rama. This Rama was the son of King Dasharatha of Ayodhya, of the Sun-clan, born for the purpose of slaying the demon Ravana and his fellow monsters, who would abduct Rama's wife Sita. Rama's brothers shared parts of Vishnu's spirit: Lakshmana and Bharata. (See *Dasharatha*.)

8. Krishna (the name means 'black', though Krishna is always painted blue). Krishna is the most popular of all the Indian gods. It is agreed by some of his followers that he is not an incarnation of Vishnu, he *is* Vishnu. However, since he was born from a human mother he was by definition an incarnation, i.e. a person with the appearance of a human being, with a body of flesh and blood, but with a divine spirit. (See *avatara*. See further under *Krishna*; *Balarama*; *Nanda*; *Devaki*; *Kansa*; *Radha*; *Rukmini*.)

9. Buddha. The greatest religious teacher of India was also an incarnation of Vishnu: he was born of Queen Maya. (See under *Buddha*; *Gautama*; *Shakyamuni*; *Bodhisattva*; *Jataka*.)

10. Kalki or Kalkin, literally 'white horse'. At the end of the Kali-yuga or iron age, when this world-history will come to an end, Vishnu will come back to this world riding a white horse and with his flaming sword. Then he will, like the Messiah and the Islamic Mahdi, destroy the last demons and all the wicked people, before the world can be renewed. In Buddhism, Kalki has been compared to Maitreya.

Many other characters in Indian mythology are, we have been told, incarnations of Vishnu or are imbued by the god's spirit. They include: Purusha, the first man, Nara, Narada and Narayana, Dattatreya and Rishabha, Vyasa (Veda-vyasa or Krishna-Dvaipayana) and the Law-giver Manu. All these names belong to famous sages and gurus.

Vishravas Son of Pulastya. By his first wife Ilavida he had a son, Kubera (q.v.) the god of wealth and Lord of the Rakshasas. By his second wife, a Rakshasi, he had three sons, Ravana (q.v.), Kumbhakarna and Vibhishana (q.v.).

Vishvakarma, Viswakarman Maker of the Universe. One of the names of the Creator, sometimes identified with Indra. Vishvakarma is described as the great architect of the universe, the all-seeing god who possesses arms, faces and eyes on all sides. He creates by blowing the creatures into existence, fanning them with his wings. He knows all the worlds and has given them names. He was the son of Bhuvana, 'existence, becoming'. He instituted the sacrifice known as the Sarva-medha 'total sacrifice', offering the worlds to himself and ending by sacrificing himself, then starting the creation again. He is sometimes identified with Tvashtri, and also with Brahma himself. He forged the weapons for the other gods and revealed the science of *sthapatya*, engineering, carpentry, etc. He was also the first wainwright. He built the city of Lanka on Sri Lanka, then he created Nala the able ape who constructed the bridge from India to Sri Lanka. His mother was Yoga-siddha, 'she who achieved union' and his daughter was Sanjna whom he married to Surya the Sun-god. When Sanjna could not endure the heat of the sun, her father filed off some chips, from which he created Shiva's trident and Skanda's spear.

Vishvamitra, Visvamitra (1) A sage, son of King Kushika. He was a lifelong rival of Vasishtha, an enmity which reflects the animosity of the Brahmins against the Kshatriyas in old India. Both sages were employed as priests at the court of King Sudasa. Both had a hundred sons. Vasishtha burnt the sons of Vishvamitra with his fiery breath, when his own sons had been devoured by a king, Kalmasha-Pada, who was possessed by a ferocious Rakshasa. The boys were born again as degraded casteless babies, who would have to live their lives in poverty and be born again 700 times before they were back at the same level of Brahmin nobility as their father.

Another tale relates that Vishvamitra tried to steal Kamadhenu, a miraculous cow owned by Vasishtha. This 'wish-cow' could provide a complete banquet when asked. However, the cow could also call up hundreds of soldiers to defend her, which she did on this occasion and they defeated Vishvamitra and his sons. Later Vishvamitra decided to perform austerities until Indra, worried over his perfection, sent a nymph to him, an Apsaras of extraordinary beauty called Menaka. She succeeded in seducing the ascetic and became pregnant, giving birth in due course to a daughter, Shakuntala. He also had an affair with the nymph Rambha, but later he became ashamed of his loss of concentration, so he settled on a rock in the Himalayas and performed austerities for a hundred years. At last the gods granted him the status of a Brahmin and he was reconciled with his rival Vasishtha. For Vishvamitra's testing of the noble King Harischandra, see under that name. It was also Vishvamitra who persuaded King Dasharatha to send his son, Rama, into the forest to fight the savage Rakshasas who were threatening the ascetic Brahmins in their hermitages.

In another incarnation, Vishvamitra and Vasishtha bewitched each other into becoming birds of prey and fought in the sky until Brahma stopped their fighting, turning them back into men and telling them to be friends; they were his sons after all. Vishvamitra is one of those semi-divine men who accompany the kings and heroes of history, generation after generation. They influence the course of world affairs by their eloquence, their mastery of magic and their aplomb. They are often incarnations of gods; Vishvamitra was an incarnation of Dharma.

(2) 'Friend of all', a Brahmin of great wisdom.

Vishvanatha 'Lord of All', a name of Shiva, especially at his shrine in Varanasi.

Vishvantara Vessantara, a prince who was so generous that he even gave away his four children to a mendicant ascetic who needed children to beg alms for him. The ascetic appeared to be the god Dharma who had decided to test the prince's true unselfishness.

Vivasvat 'The Bright One'. The Sun (see *Surya*). Father of Yama (q.v.).

Viveka Wisdom, insight, literally — discernment. The goal of Buddhists in particular.

Vivekananda, Swami Indian philosopher, 1863–1902, who visited Europe and America. He had a lasting influence on both East and West. He sought to revive the study of the Sanskrit classics, in particular the Vedas, and also to make them accessible to the West. He is credited by his followers to have formulated the very essence of Hinduism. First he underlined the essential unity of all religions; the Veda says it already: *Ekam sat*, *vipra bahudha vadanti*, 'One is the Truth, widely various is speech'. There should thus be no bigotry, no hatred or persecution. The spirit of religion is peace. Religion teaches the unity of all people in their divinity. Hence Vivekananda's second doctrine: all people are of divine nature, *amritasya putrah*, 'children of immortality'. The purpose of a person's life is to manifest this divinity from within by psychic control so that the human soul becomes entirely free. From this follows the third point of his creed: the dignity of the individual, even if he is miserable, hungry, poor and suffering. These suffering millions must be helped, so the fourth doctrine is: 'you may renounce the world but you still have to work for it', and 'you can work for your own salvation (*moksha*) and for people's welfare as well'.

Vraja The area around Mathura where Krishna lived as a child.

Vratya A priest of a non-Vedic fertility cult which involved ritual dancing and flagellation. He travelled in a cart with a woman for his satisfaction and a musician to perform at the dances.

Vrihaspati Jupiter (the planet). (See *Brihaspati*.)

Vrindavana A wood in Vraja where Krishna was born. At present there is a town there, Brindaban, where he is still celebrated.

Vrishabha Taurus, a sign of the zodiac (q.v.).

Vrishchika Scorpio, a sign of the zodiac (q.v.).

Vrishni 'Manly', one of the clan of Yadavas from whom Krishna sprang.

Vritra, Vritrasura The demon of drought who is constantly at war against the Rain-god Indra. Drought causes death and misery.

Vyaghra, Baghira, Babur The tiger, symbol of greed. Riding a tiger, as Kali does, signifies controlling one's desires.

Vyakti Manifestation (of a spirit), personality, individual.

Vyantara One of a race of demons who, in Jain cosmology, inhabit Patala, the spirit world. They are the Pishachas, Bhutas, Gandharvas and Mahorgas, each demon haunting a particular species of tree. A Vana-vyantara is an even more dangerous evil spirit.

Vyasa (1) 'The Compiler'. The poet of the great epic of Mahabharata, according to the poem itself. (See also *Vedavyasa*.)

(2) A demigod. Son of the sage Parashara and the water-nymph Satyavati, 'the Truthful One'. Also called Krishna Dwaipayana because he was black (*krishna*) and was born on an island (*dwipa*). He was a hermit who lived in the forest. Vyasa was asked to 'raise seed' on behalf of his half-brothers by the same mother Satyavati, who were the sons of Shantanu, King of Hastinapura. Both brothers had died childless, so their widows had to suffer Vyasa's embraces. One shut her eyes so that her son was born blind: Dhritarashtra was his name. The other woman turned pale with fright when she saw Vyasa approach her, so her son was born pale and called Pandu. These stories throw into sharp relief the ancient custom of 'raising seed' by which a brother of the deceased had to fertilize the widow who had to undergo this in order to bear a child which would legally be considered the child of her dead husband. The custom was widespread in antiquity. See the biblical story of Tamar (Genesis 38:8).

W

Wheel of the Law

Wali, Vali Short for Waliu-Allah, a Friend of God, an Islamic Saint. Walis can fly through the air, discover stolen goods as well as the thieves, they have knowledge of people's minds, of the future and of all diseases. They also expel evil spirits, like Jesus.

Water See *Varuna*.

Way The Way, *marga* or *patha*, the Path. In Buddhism this means the way out of this life of suffering towards the Nirvana. In Zen Buddhism the 'way' acquires the meaning of the perfect life itself which is *Akama*: wishlessness.

Wheel See *chakra*, the cycle of Brahma's creations by breathing; see *dharmachakra*, the wheel of Buddha's law, allegory of the endless return of painful lives of Desire's slaves. See also the Zodiac, often depicted as a wheel-of-seasons, *Kalachakra*.

Wind See *Vayu*.

Wisdom See *Viveka*.

Y

Yaksha, the forest god

Yadava One of the clan of descendants of King Yadu, into which Krishna was born, in Vrindavana, in the Vraja region of the kingdom of Mathura in the days when Krishna lived there. Their first king was Ugrasena. Krishna led many Yadavas to Gujerat where he founded a kingdom. Many who were there when he died were drowned in the floods, but some survived to become the ancestors of kings.

Yadu Son of King Yayati of the Lunar Race, ancestor of Krishna. His devotion gave him prosperity in spite of adversity.

Yajna 'Sacrifice'. A demigod with a deer's head, named Yajna, son of Ruchi, husband of Dakshina. He was killed by Virabhadra while Daksha performed the first sacrifice. The constellation Mriga-shiras 'deer's head' was created out of him by Brahma.

Yajnesha, Yajneshvara 'Lord of Sacrifices'. Praise-name of Vishnu.

Yajur Veda One of the four books of the Veda, dealing especially with sacrifices.

Yaksha, Yaksa, Yakkha, Yakho A forest deity. The female Yaksha is called a Yakshini. The Yakshas are minor gods who represent the

forces of nature like the fauns, satyrs and imps of Greek antiquity.
They are usually good gods but sometimes wicked. They usually
appear in human form, even as handsome men, but sometimes they
are ugly black dwarfs with pot-bellies. The king of the Yakshas is
Kubera (q.v.). His chief attendant is Manibhadra or Manivara.
Yakshas are protectors of the good, and fierce guardians of the gates
of the palaces of their masters. They can assume any shape they like
and even look like ordinary trees in the forest, or peep at you from
between the thick foliage. They are called Punyajana 'friendly folk'.
They are bearers, carrying their master through the sky if he wishes
to travel. They are called the 'Supporters of the Houses'.

Yakshini Female deity who lives in the forest. The unwary
traveller may meet one at any time while, unknown to himself, he
is losing his way. She will look like a very seductive buxom woman
smiling invitingly at him. A Yakshini is often found sculpted on
pillars of temples and gateways as a voluptuous woman with a
sensual smile. Some Yakshinis are half-horse, half-woman. These
are called Ashvamukhi ('Horse-face') so presumably they are the
opposite of Centaurs, who have human faces but equine abdomens.
A prince called Vijaya once entered a forest with his men. They saw
a big bitch who was a Yakshini. She led the men astray and
bewitched them so they could not move but she could not devour
them for they were protected by special charms. Vijaya followed her
deep into the forest, where she suddenly turned round and became
a beautiful girl called Kuvanna. Kuvanna offered to release Vijaya's
men on condition that he would marry her. They had two children,
Pulinda and Pulindi. Vijaya slew many invisible demons and
became king.

Yama The God of Death. Yama was the first man to be born on
earth and so he was the first one to die for no man can escape that
fate. Yama was the son of the Sun who has to die every evening.
Yama's sister was Yamuna the holy river which flows south, the
Yamuna or Jumna. Yama had to travel south to the Land of the
Dead, where he became king over the ever-increasing multitudes of
souls, like Pluto. Yama married a wife Yami, who said to her
husband: 'Please embrace me, for we two are the only human
beings and if we have no children, there will be no one left when we
die.'

    She sang this to her husband and her song is preserved in the
Veda. When he died, Yama, or his soul, was the first to find the path
to the other world, which in Hindu cosmology is in the south. Since
then all men and women who died have followed that path. Yama
owns two ferocious dogs with four eyes each and big snouts. The
poor traveller on his way to the homeland of the dead has to hurry
past them. When someone is about to die, Yama will send to him his
Bird of Doom. When the soul of the dead man arrives in Yama's
abode he will meet Chitragupta the Registrar of the Dead, who will

read out the Agrasandhani, the register of all his deeds. After the reading Yama will give judgement, always a fair one. The souls will then travel to one of the 21 hells (*Naraka*) for the wicked in the Underworld, or they will go to Swarga, Heaven, if they have been good, or they will be told that they must be reborn on earth for a try-again life. Yama's vehicle is a buffalo, which he rides dressed in red and green, armed with a heavy mace and a noose to snare his victims with. Yama is king in his city, Yamapura, where he resides in his palace called Kalichi, attended by trusted servants, known by name. His messenger is Yamaduta, who guides the souls from the human world to the home of the dead in the extreme south of the Earth. The journey to Deathland takes 4 hours and 40 minutes. The body of the deceased may not be cremated before that time is past.

Yamapura The city of the dead, where all the souls live. Yama reigns supreme in this kingdom, the green god in red apparel, as Pitripati, the Lord of the Ancestors, as Samavurti, the impartial judge and Dandadhara who carries out punishment. In this city finally friend will find friend, mother and child will meet, brother and sister, husband and wife, parted by death, after many years of waiting on earth, will embrace here.

Yami Twin-sister of the Death-god, Yama, both children of the Sun-god Vivasvat, 'the radiant one'. She is also identified with Yamuna, the river now called Jumna. Yami is not only Yama's twin sister but his wife as well, for since they were the first people on earth there was no one else there to marry. (See also *Yamuna*.)

Yamuna The sacred river now called Jumna which flows past such famous buildings as the Red Castle in Delhi, Shahjahan's palace at Agra, and the Taj Mahal, finally joining the Ganges at Prayaga, now called Allahabad. It is 1400 kilometres long. Yamuna was the daughter of the Sun-god and a sister of Yama, the Death-god. Balarama used his gigantic plough to divert her waters for the purpose of irrigation, or so we may conclude from the myth in which it says: 'He forced her to follow him wherever he went with his plough.'

Yasapani King of Varanasi at the time when the Bodhisattva walked upon earth. When the king saw him he appointed him judge at his court. However, when the Bodhisattva sentenced some court officials for corruption, the prime minister, Kalaka, was angered for he too was corrupt and the officials had been his accomplices. Kalaka then suggested to the king that such a competent judge might be able to construct a pleasure garden for the king in a single night. The king agreed and gave the Bodhisattva orders accordingly. The latter spent a sleepless night knowing that he would be put to death if he did not comply. Suddenly the god Indra appeared to him assuring him that the garden would be ready in the morning. It was, and the king was much impressed but Kalaka was not. He suggested that the king should ask for a lake next to his garden, then for a palace next to the lake. When each of these miraculously appeared the next morning, the king was convinced that the Bodhisattva was a friend of the gods. He dismissed Kalaka and made the Bodhisattva his prime minister.

Yasht One of the holy hymns which the Parsi priests sing while worshipping the lesser divinities of *Zoroastrianism*. The great Yashts are the longest hymns, at the same time the oldest and most beautiful.

Yasna The act of worship in the Parsi religion, solemnized daily. These rites were accompanied by the singing of prescribed portions of the book of Gathas. They included the traditional offerings to Fire and Water. Thus the Yasna is the central ritual of *Zoroastrianism*, with sacred power.

Yasoda Wife of Nanda the kind herdsmen, and foster-mother of Krishna. She agreed to nourish baby Krishna when Kansa threatened to kill him.

Yatu One of a race of demons having the shapes of dogs or vultures.

Yayati Son of Nahusha, a king of the Moon-dynasty, scions of Soma. He married Devayani, by whom he had two sons, Yadu, the ancestor of the Yadavas being the elder. Yayati had found Devayani in a deep well and only with great difficulty and risk to his own life had he succeeded in rescuing her. She had fallen in love with this noble king, so she begged her father, Shukra, a Brahmin, to marry her to Yayati, 'the king who has taken my right hand and lifted me up out of Death's mouth'.

Normally a marriage of a Brahmin's daughter with a Kshatriya, even a king, was not permitted. However, Shukra consented and Devayani entered Yayati's palace together with Sarmishtha, her bondsmaid, who had been a princess, the daughter of Vrishaparva. Shukra spoke to Yayati: 'Devayani will be your wife. Do not call Sarmishtha to your bed.'

However, when Devayani had a son and another, Sarmishtha called out to the king while he was on one of his walks saying: 'I am a woman too, and I am wasting away. I too want to give you sons.'

The king objected: 'If I do this all my subjects will do similar things.'

She replied: 'You are the husband of my *sakhi* (best friend), so you are my husband too.'

Yayati was seduced by Sarmishtha for she was still a very beautiful girl. She bore him Puru, who was to become the ancestor of the Pauravas, and two other sons, Turvasu and Anu. Puru was the most devoted son to his father, for he agreed to take over his father's affliction of infertility. One day Devayani saw Sarmishtha with the

three boys and asked her who the father was. Sarmishtha lied: 'I
saw a dazzling figure in the forest. I dared not ask his name. He was
a sage of great spiritual power.'

Devayani believed her, until the boys were big enough to tell her
who their father was. Devayani was deeply hurt and left the court
of King Yayati forever.

Yayati was one day invited to heaven by Indra and when he came
back to earth he had become so pious that his subjects, by their
virtue, became free of human passions. As a result they ceased to
decay physically, so that none of them died. The god of death,
Yama, complained to Indra that his Nether-World became ever
emptier, so Indra sent Kamadeva the Love-god to earth to rekindle
people's passions. Gods do not want all people to be saints.

Yima First man and first king of the world, according to
Zarathustra, to whom Ahura Mazda gave a golden whip and goad.
Yima went to live on earth where his herds prospered, as did his
children until the earth was full of men, dogs, birds and flocks.
'Then Yima, son of Vivahvant (the Sun) went forth to the south
along the path of the sun, and made a home there with his people;
because of the bad winter he left his land.' This may refer to the
migration of the Iranians from South Russia to Iran not later than
the second millennium BC. God (Ahura Mazda) told Yima to build
the Var, as an enclosed territory for the best people with their cattle
and sheep. Was this Iran?

Yoga 'Zeal, hard work'. Religious meditation, while standing or
sitting in a particular position (*asana*) for prolonged periods.
Westerners regard yoga as a type of gymnastics, but that is only the
Hatha-yoga. What few people realize is that yoga is entirely based
on some fundamental theses of Hindu philosophy. The first is that
there is a distinction between mind and matter, and the second that
mind must control matter otherwise matter, i.e. the body, will run
wild like a naughty child. The third thesis is that the mind can
acquire power over the body by concentration. Thus the body can
and must be habituated to hunger and thirst, cold and sexual
abstention. Fear, too, can be overcome so that yoga is
recommended for soldiers. Nor is yoga something that takes place
only when seated in concentration or in the gym room. Yoga
becomes part of a person's nature. The body becomes a useful tool
for the owner's purpose, but the mind too, must be disciplined: all
imaginary thought and reveries must be stopped so that there will
be no more useless desires or fears. Basic axioms are, further, that
the spirit will outlive the body just as the body will live longer than
its clothes. After the body's death the spirit will migrate to a more
exalted form of existence if and only if, this spirit has ennobled
itself by many years of yoga.

The physical side of yoga can be briefly classified as follows:

1. *Niyama* — purity of the body, both the outside by frequent bathing, and the inside by eating only simple, healthy food — no meat, but milk and butter are recommended.

2. *Yama* — purity of one's way of life is also necessary: refrain from lying, from adultery, from greed for possessions, from anger and envy.

3. *Asana* — one has to sit in a position which is agreeable, dignified and durable.

4. *Pranayama* — deep, controlled and regular breathing has to be practised. This reduces the effects of pneumonia and will control hiccoughs.

5. The student has to learn *pratyahara*, i.e. to withdraw his senses from the world. No mental concentration is possible as long as the mind is constantly distracted by what it hears, sees, smells, etc. In the end the *yogi* will no longer react to sudden flashes of light or peals of thunder. Nothing will terrify him, not even seeing a murderer. He has learned to think only what he wants to think and when he wants to think. He is not disturbed by someone calling him, shaking him or even kicking him.

6. *Dharana* — this is the concentration of the attention, first on one visible point, e.g. a disk painted on the wall, then on one's own soul, then on God.

7. *Dhyana* — the 'stream of thinking', the flow of one's thoughts must be homogeneous, completely subject to one's will, with the thinker's always conscious mind constantly lucid, without interruption or distraction, without the fantasies or random images most people see in their minds.

8. *Samadhi* — finally, is the achievement of *shunyata*, emptiness. This means that all ego-centrism has disappeared, the *yogi* has no more of his own thoughts, day-dreams or fantasies intruding in his concentrated consciousness, so that his mind is entirely opened to God as the total object of his thinking. The result is that the limits between subject and object will disappear, since the subject no longer thinks of himself but only of God. As a result, the *yogi* is never insulted or offended, since he is no longer there. He suffers no pain because he has learned to concentrate his mind away from pain. A *yogi* never lies because he fears nobody and has no purpose for lies. He can be trusted because he does not covet anything, certainly not money.

A *yogi* is advised never to fill his stomach but to eat half a stomach full, drink a quarter and leave a quarter of his stomach empty. The physical exercises are intended to teach complete control of the body and with it, hard concentration of will-power, the power of mind over body.

The practice of yoga is based on the philosophy called Sankhya 'synthesis', designed by the philosopher Kapila in the seventh century BC. It is a rationalistic system based on the irreconcilable dualism of mind and matter. Matter is the principle of darkness, *tamas*, whereas the mind possesses *sattva*, truth. With this it can acquire consciousness of the law of *karma*, and so overcome the inertia which makes us relapse into desire and so, close the cycle of rebirths and suffering. The mind of the *yogi* is free and will be at peace for ever.

Yogi (Yogin). From Sanskrit *Yoga*, a person who performs *yoga*, asceticism, for a long time.

Yogini One of eight demonesses, servants of Durga. They have beautiful names like Marjani, Matali, Nayaki, Jaya, Sunanda and Malaya.

Yoni The vagina and vulva, usually including the womb, symbolized as a round jar in which the women used to pickle vegetables. The Yoni is dedicated to the goddess Devi-Durga in her aspect of Shakti (the power and potency of God) and is worshipped by the Shaktas or Yonijas.

When Devi, before her cremation as Sati, was carved into many pieces by Vishnu (who was afraid that Shiva's funerary dance would destroy the world), the piece that contained her *yoni* fell down in Assam and from there her worship spread to all parts of India. We are told that once upon a time Shiva, to prove that the worship of his *linga* (the phallus worship, also found in the ancient Near East) was good for people, created a human race which worshipped it alone. At once, Devi Parvati created a human race which worshipped her *yoni* and this latter tribe was much stronger, healthier, handsomer and more virile.

The oldest localities of *yoni* worship were probably the sources of rivers, the caves where water comes rushing forth from the rocks. In ancient Gaul, too, such places were dedicated to the blue goddess of water, fertility and prosperity of the Celts. If a man had travelled away from India to foreign parts and was thus polluted, when he came back (all foreign countries were considered suspect then), he had to undergo the ceremony of rebirth in order to be purified and re-Hinduized. To this end he had to go through the *yoni* in the shape of a ring, made from metal, and so come out as new.

The Lingayats or Linga worshippers may worship together with the Yonijas; to this end they have a combined statue around which they congregate; sometimes it is just a pillar placed in a pond, or an egg-shaped stone placed inside a stone ring, its *argha* 'vessel'. This combined sex-symbol indicated the union of the two principles, for we must remember that for gods coitus is not what it is for men and women; it is the union of principles, the ones that are known as Yin and Yang in Chinese.

Yudhisthira King of Hastinapura. One of the leading characters of the epic Mahabharata, but no hero. Yudhisthira was the son of Kunti by the god of justice, Dharma. He was the eldest son of his

earthly father Pandu and therefore the leader of the Pandavas. King
Pandu seems to have been sterile, since his five sons were not his
but the sons of gods. His wife, Kunti, had a charm by means of
which she attracted the god of her preference so that he would
descend and make her pregnant. In this manner she attracted
Dharma, the god of justice, who became the father of Yudhisthira,
one of the most varied characters of the Mahabharata and certainly
the ideal of an elder brother in early India. He was described by his
admirers as a man of humble righteousness and law-abiding life.
The maharaja of Hastinapura, Dhritarashtra, appointed the just
Yudhisthira *yuvaraja*, crown prince, over the head of his own eldest
son, Duryodhana who was a dishonest cynic. Till the hour of his
death, Duryodhana persecuted the Pandavas, his own full cousins,
out of jealousy and hatred. He burnt the house, in which they lived
in exile, hoping to be safe from his revenge, but to no avail.
Fortunately Yudhisthira foresaw the wicked plan so the Pandavas
had time to escape. Later the Pandavas decided to try their luck at
the *svayamvara* of Draupadi at Panchala. Arjuna won all the archery
prizes, so Yudhisthira thought it fair that Arjuna should marry
Draupadi. However, Kunti and the sage Vyasa (Krishna) agreed
that such a formidable woman as Draupadi could be shared by the
five brothers on equal terms. Each of the five brothers had a house
in which Draupadi should spend two nights in succession, then
move on to the next brother. She bore a son to each of them. To
Yudhisthira she bore Prativindhya. Dhritarashtra, wishing to
reconcile the Pandavas, his dead brother's sons, after the fire,
installed Yudhisthira as a minor king or viceroy in Indraprastha
(now part of greater Delhi). Yudhisthira was liked by his subjects
because he was honest, fair, just, modest, humble and capable of
persuading others to refrain from injustice and violence. As a result
peace reigned in the kingdom and robbery was absent, so many
merchants settled in Indraprastha, making it a rich city. This in turn
made Yudhisthira rich so that the neighbouring rajas knew that
they could never win a war against him since he could buy more
elephants, horses and chariots than any other king. Only one raja
dared to oppose him, Jarasandha of Magadha, and he was defeated
and killed. Yudhisthira had a queen all to himself (as opposed to the
shared Draupadi, whom he probably did not approach after the
birth of Prativindhya), Devika, who bore him Yaudheya. The
Pandavas' prosperity rekindled the Kauravas' envy so the latter
persuaded their father to invite the Pandavas for a dice match.
Yudhisthira felt he could not decline his uncle's invitation, so he
went. Shakuni, Duryodhana's uncle, invited Yudhisthira to a game
of dice. Again the latter thought he could not decline and playing,
lost his kingdom, his freedom and that of his brothers and their
wife. It was his darkest hour. It was for him a matter of honour to
accept slavery as a result of the unlucky falling of the dice. Old,
blind Dhritarashtra, having been told what had happened, berated

his sons for their dishonesty and decreed that the Pandavas should go into exile.

While living in the forest, Yudhisthira heard that a gang of robbers had captured Duryodhana, and went to rescue his wicked cousin because one should always help a kinsman. That was Yudhisthira's rectitudinous conviction which caused endless trouble to himself, his brothers and their wife, but it was his conviction that all the rules of justice must be observed. In spite of the great injustice done to him and his brothers, he refused to punish the perpetrators because 'punishment will come to them by the universal law of Karma, setting them back on the road to salvation'. Jayadratha kidnapped Draupadi but Arjuna and Bhima caught up with him. Yudhisthira told his brothers to set the criminal free. At the court of Virata again pretty Draupadi was insulted and again Yudhisthira told his brothers to abstain from seeking redress. Yet Yudhisthira is neither a weakling nor a coward in battle. After 13 years of exile, Yudhisthira hoped to regain his kingdom of Prativindhya but Duryodhana refused. So, war was necessary, said cousin Krishna, and so it broke out.

Yudhisthira fought in the war but without any distinction. He declined to fight Karna even though he did not know that they were both sons of Kunti. When all the Kauravas had died in the battle, Krishna saluted Yudhisthira as king, but the latter hesitated, reflecting on the immense price of suffering that had been paid for his kingship. He went out of his way to console his uncle Dhritarashtra, and Queen Gandhari, for the loss of all their sons. Yudhisthira felt much regret for the past and so he should for he knew that he could not play dice, and yet had gone ahead and done so. He decided to go on a lifelong pilgrimage to the Himalayas in search of Indra's Heaven on Mount Meru where he begged Indra to grant him admission to his Heaven, but only if his brothers would receive the same favour. He thereby remained their faithful elder brother. He made Arjuna's grandson, Parikshit, King of Hastinapura.

Yuga An epoch, a period of world history, lasting at least 400,000 years, beginning with a long time of dawn, Sandhya, and ending with the twilight of the gods, because even the gods will disappear with it.

Four major periods are distinguished in the history of gods and men: Krita-yuga, the Age of Benefit, Treta-yuga, the Age of the Sacred Fires, Dvapara-yuga and Kali-yuga, the Iron Age.

The first epoch, called the Golden Age in classical mythology, was marked by an absence of sin, when all people did their duty and were honest. No one lied or cheated. There was no envy or hatred, no fear nor cruelty. They all worshipped one god and obeyed one law.

In the second age, there was a beginning of decay because people began to desire rewards for what they did; instead of simply acting out of a sense of duty they had ulterior motives. Thus, there was a beginning of dishonesty, of hypocrisy; people still pretended to be good but their intentions were egotistic.

In the Dvapara 'half' period, every person was half-good, so his deeds were likewise half-good. Only half the people studied holy scripture, the others were not interested in devotion. People spoke the truth only half of the time. Because people were only half wise, there was much ageing, decay and disease for they were leading healthy lives only half of the time.

Finally the present age of history is called Kali-yuga, the iron age, because iron is the least valuable of the four metals: gold, silver, copper and iron. People neglect their duties and their religion, they become weak in mind and body, they are no longer motivated nor have they any morality left, so there is anger, frustration, laziness, hunger, distress, disease, fatigue, fear and decadence.

Yuva-Raja Crown prince, heir apparent.

Z

Wheel of the Zodiac

Zand, Zend 'Interpretation', the exegesis of the Avestan texts of the Zoroastrians in the form of glosses to the text accumulated over the centuries. The last of these are composed in the Pahlawi or Middle Persian language of the Sassanian period, in about AD400.

Zarathustra 'The religious concepts in the message of Zarathustra are completely universal, and the ethical imperative of good thoughts, good words and good deeds is utterly timeless. Seeing this world and human life therein in radically moral terms, and giving significance to human life in the moral endeavour to perfect this world, is as relevant and meaningful today as it was when Zarathustra preached it.' This testimony from a Parsi in 1980 shows how the religion that Zarathustra founded is as alive today as it was at the beginning of its long history, and that in spite of many centuries of persecution by Muslim rulers up to the present time. It is a peaceful religion, like Christianity or Buddhism, and its philosophy is worthy of equal recognition with those great religions. Mary Boyce, retired professor of Iranian studies at the School of Oriental and African Studies in London, has given a fascinating survey of the long history of the *Zoroastrian* religion by means of the texts composed by its own adherents, and written down mainly during the Sassanian period before AD640. Many priceless manuscripts have been lost, but an incredibly rich heritage remains of the Persians who were already a highly civilized nation in the early Middle Ages, when Arabs and Englishmen were still uncivilized. There is fierce controversy over the dating of Zarathustra, which was customarily placed at *c*.600 BC, but which Mary Boyce places in the fourteenth century BC, supporting this on recent discoveries of Bronze Age material in western Asia and southern Russia where the Iranians then lived, as well as a comparison of the Old Persian texts with the early Vedas of the Aryan tradition.

Zen The Japanese form of the Sanskrit word *dhyana* (q.v.) 'insight'. (See also *Yoga*.)

Ziyarat Pilgrimage to a shrine, and the shrine itself. In Islam all the holy places are associated with a dead saint, whose spirit still lingers near his tomb, where he is invoked to bestow good health and children.

Zodiac Astrology being a highly developed and ramified science in India, the signs of the solar zodiac are well known. These are based on the ancient Greek names which arrived perhaps via the Persian language. The majority of the Hindu astrologers, certainly those of the Shaiva sect, work with the lunar signs which are of pure Indian origin. Here are the solar signs with their meanings and Latin equivalents:

Sanskrit	Meaning	Arabic	Latin	Entered by the Sun in:
Kumbha	Water-jar	Dalu	Aquarius	January
Mina	Fish	Hut	Pisces	February
Mesha	Ram	Hamal	Aries	March
Vrishabha	Bull	Thaur	Taurus	April
Mithuna	Twins	Jauz	Gemini	May
Karkata, Kirka	Crab, lobster	Sartan	Cancer	June
Simha	Lion	Asad	Leo	July
Kanya	Girl	Sunbula	Virgo	August
Tula	Scales	Mizan	Libra	September
Vrischika	Scorpion	Aqrab	Scorpio	October
Dhanu	Bow	Qaus	Sagittarius	November
Makara	Monster	Jady	Capricornis	December

The Islamic scholars work on the basis of the Arabic names of the signs. They have their own books on astrology and divining in Arabic, Persian, etc.

Zoroaster Prophet of the Ancient Iranians, in about the fourteenth century BC. (See *Zarathustra*.)

Zoroastrianism The religion of the Parsis in India, refugees from Iran in the seventh century, with later arrivals. The task of the Zoroastrian is to meditate upon the attributes of the seven Amesha Spentas (see *Spenta*) in order that one may consciously integrate into one's life each quality of Ahura Mazda as represented through each of His seven Bounteous Immortals. Every man requires the Wisdom and the Spirit of God, *Spenta Mainyu*, in order to be aware of the Mind of God, *Vohu Manah*. The Good Mind is God's greatest gift to a man, for it is from the Good Mind that a man learns to develop a perception of the Best Truth, *Asha Vashishta*. A combination of these gives him spiritual strength, i.e. the Sovereign Kingdom, *Khshathra Vairya*, to carry out God's will in this world and represent His Goodness here below. Man must learn to accept His will through Piety and Devotion, *Armaiti*, in order that he may experience cosmic harmony, if only for one moment. Whatever he is doing, Man should work for the Perfection, *Haurvatat*, of the experience of this Harmony. Every thought, word and deed must be purified so as to assist in the attainment of the purpose of Creation: the defeat of Evil, which will give Man immortality, *Ameretat*. Man has the constant duty to actualize the nature of these seven abstract principles, the Heptad, and so he will himself become a guardian of God's Good Creation. The realization that everything good in this world is a sign of God's Goodness is the essence of Zoroastrianism.

God, Ahura Mazda, has an adversary, called Dregvant or Ahriman, the Trickster, the God of Lying (*drug*). Liars among men are his followers, since their words and thoughts are impure, untrue. The two gods are in constant conflict. Each person has to decide on whose side he is, for the God of Life, or for the Evil One of Non-Life. Those who opt for Impurity shall be punished after this life in Worst Existence (which translates as Hell), because they chose Worst Purpose. For the just souls there will be the Best Existence, i.e. Heaven, Peace. The liars will ultimately become the slaves of Aeshma, the Devil of Wrath and Fury. 'In the end, retribution will come and the Lie will be delivered into the hands of the Truth. May Man then be with those who will make this a Good World. May Ahura Mazda be constantly present to support Man with His Truth (*asha*), so he may learn understanding and concentration of good thoughts.'

By the same author . . .

AFRICAN MYTHOLOGY
An Encylopedia of Myth and Legend

Africa: the most distinctive land mass on the surface of the earth. Yet for all its majesty it is a country whose historical and religious wealth remains a mystery to all but a very few of Western observers. How many people know anything at all about pre-Colonial Africa?

African Mythology is the first comprehensive overview of the beliefs, myths and cosmology of African peoples. It deals not only with traditional stories woven around a pantheon of gods and mythical figures but also with legends, fables and more general subjects that played a part in African mythology and African life. The wide range of entries include religious concepts, prophets, the best-known tribes, mystical phenomena, spirits and demons, and the many animals that played such a large part in African mythology.

Dr Jan Knappert's alphabetical guide is founded on his many years of personal experience in Africa. Its very accessible style makes it ideal not only as a reference work for students of anthropology but as a sample for general readers wishing to dip in and be informed on any subject that appeals to them. The book is fully cross-referenced and is illustrated with examples of African art. Wherever the reader opens it, he or she will be informed, stimulated to further thought and study, and entertained.